STOP!

This is the back of the book.
You wouldn't want to spoil a great ending!

This book is printed "manga-style," in the authentic Japanese right-to-left format. Since none of the artwork has been flipped or altered, readers get to experience the story just as the creator intended. You've been asking for it, so TOKYOPOP® delivered: authentic, hot-off-the-press, and far more fun!

DIRECTIONS

If this is your first time reading manga-style, here's a quick guide to help you understand how it works.

It's easy... just start in the top right panel and follow the numbers. Have fun, and look for more 100% authentic manga from TOKYOPOP®!

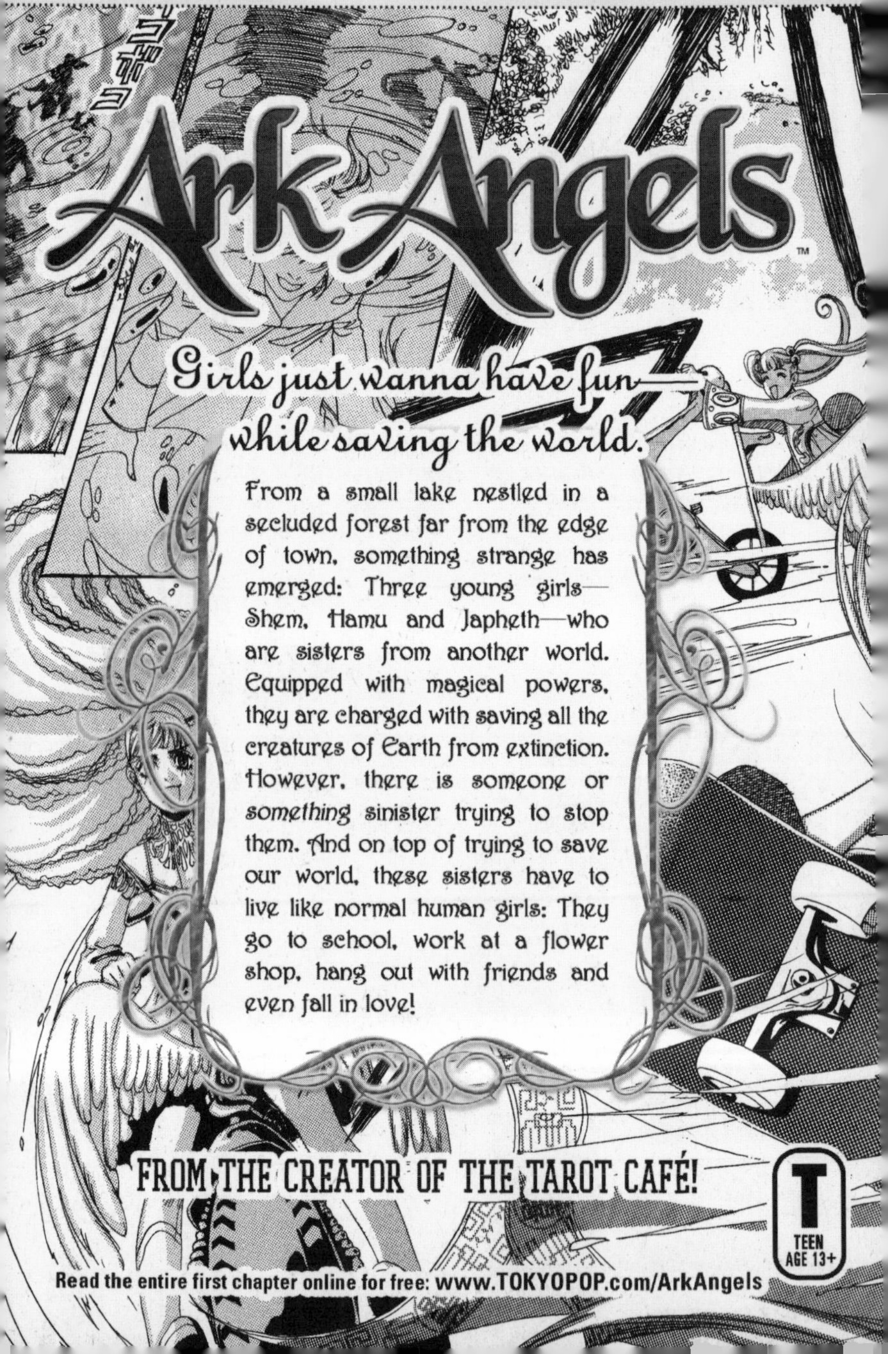
Ark Angels™
Girls just wanna have fun— while saving the world.
From a small lake nestled in a secluded forest far from the edge of town, something strange has emerged: Three young girls—Shem, Hamu and Japheth—who are sisters from another world. Equipped with magical powers, they are charged with saving all the creatures of Earth from extinction. However, there is someone or *something* sinister trying to stop them. And on top of trying to save our world, these sisters have to live like normal human girls: They go to school, work at a flower shop, hang out with friends and even fall in love!
FROM THE CREATOR OF THE TAROT CAFÉ!
T TEEN AGE 13+
Read the entire first chapter online for free: www.TOKYOPOP.com/ArkAngels

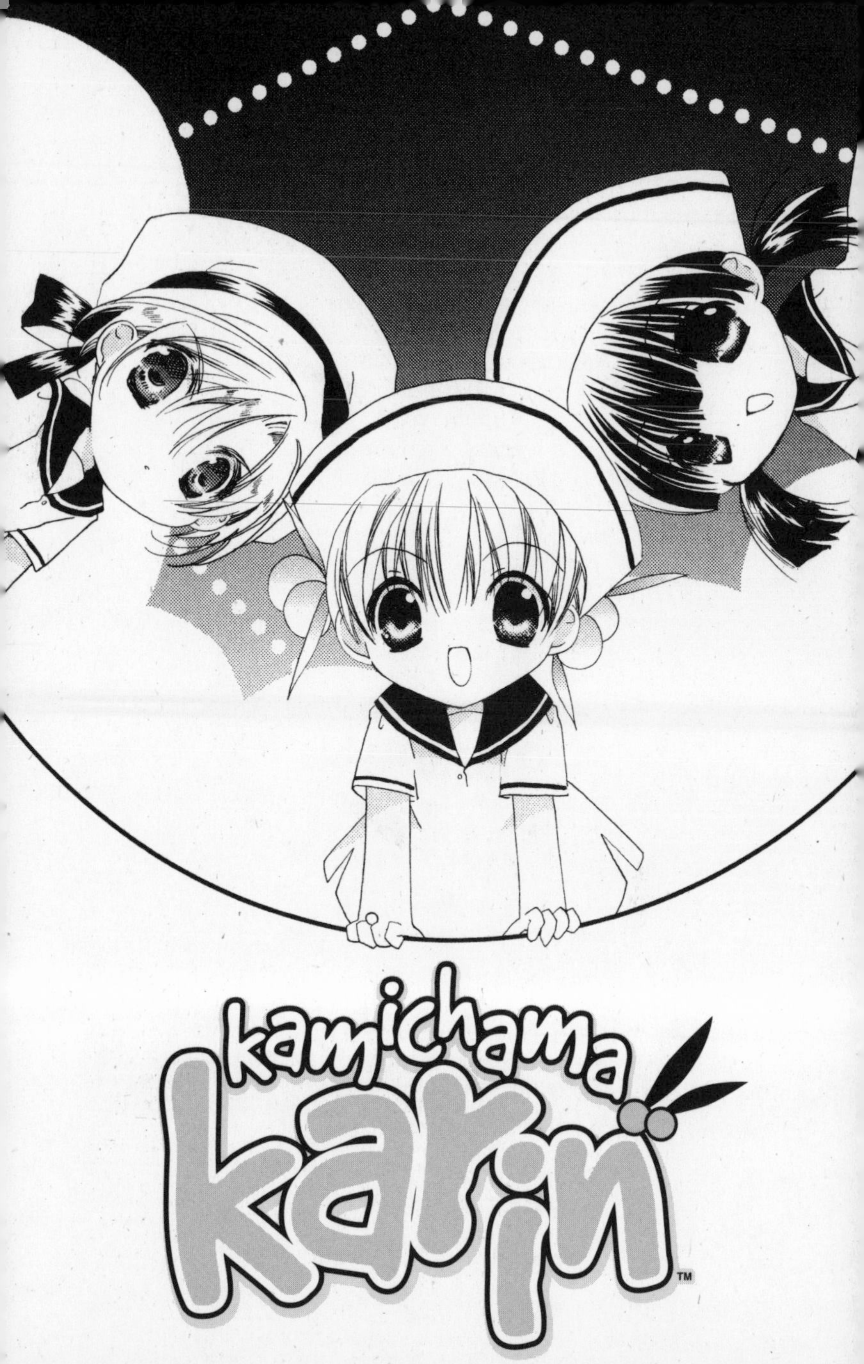

kamichama karin™

Kamichama Karin Vol. 2
created by Koge-Donbo

Translation - Nan Rymer
English Adaptation - Lianne Sentar
Retouch and Lettering - Creative Circle
Production Artist - Jason Milligan
Cover Design - Thea Willis

Editor - Carol Fox
Digital Imaging Manager - Chris Buford
Production Managers - Jennifer Miller and Mutsumi Miyazaki
Managing Editor - Lindsey Johnston
VP of Production - Ron Klamert
Publisher and E.I.C. - Mike Kiley
President and C.O.O. - John Parker
C.E.O. - Stuart Levy

A **TOKYOPOP** Manga

TOKYOPOP Inc.
5900 Wilshire Blvd. Suite 2000
Los Angeles, CA 90036

E-mail: info@TOKYOPOP.com
Come visit us online at www.TOKYOPOP.com

ISBN: 1-59532-848-3

First TOKYOPOP printing: December 2005
10 9 8 7 6 5 4 3
Printed in the USA

kamichama karin™

Volume 2

Created by
Koge-Donbo

TOKYOPOP®

HAMBURG // LONDON // LOS ANGELES // TOKYO

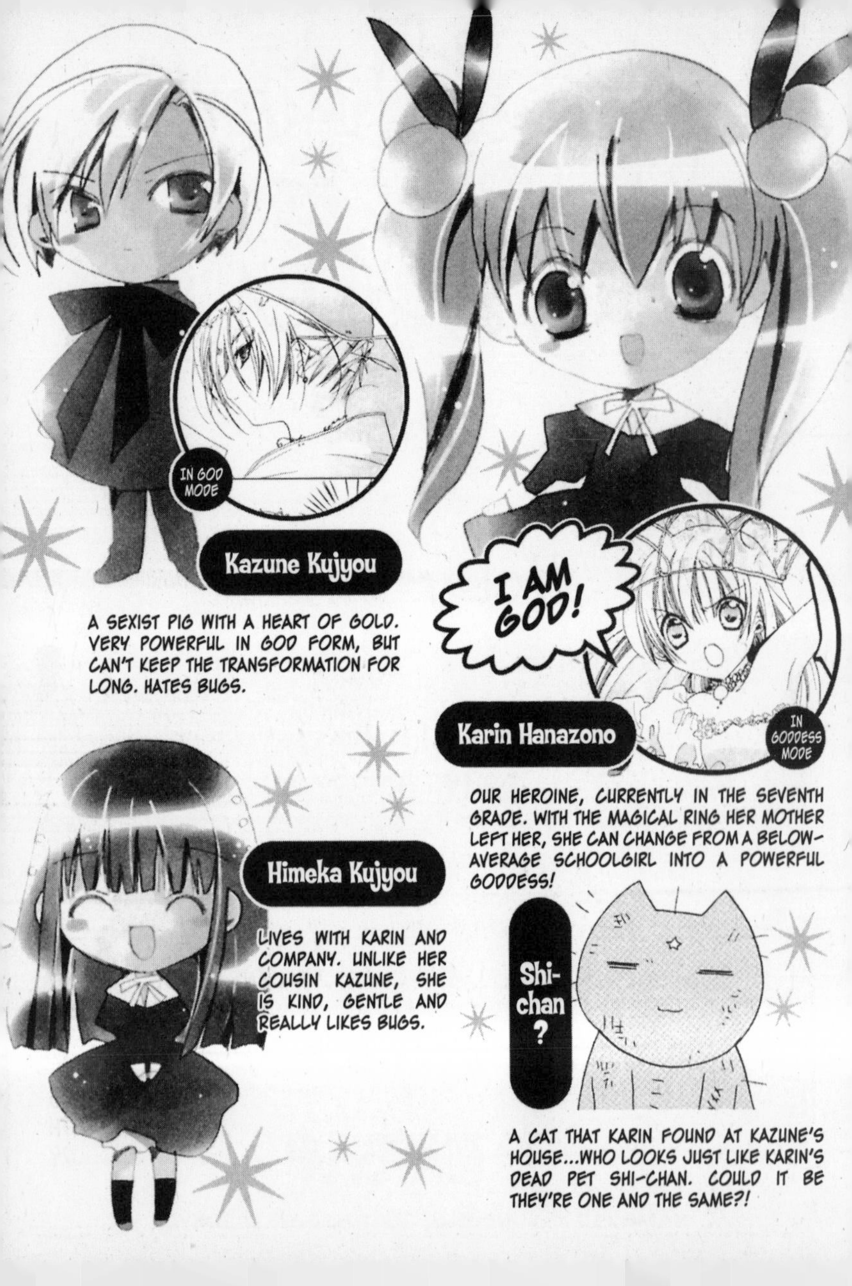
I AM GOD!
IN GODDESS MODE
Karin Hanazono
OUR HEROINE, CURRENTLY IN THE SEVENTH GRADE. WITH THE MAGICAL RING HER MOTHER LEFT HER, SHE CAN CHANGE FROM A BELOW-AVERAGE SCHOOLGIRL INTO A POWERFUL GODDESS!
IN GOD MODE
Kazune Kujyou
A SEXIST PIG WITH A HEART OF GOLD. VERY POWERFUL IN GOD FORM, BUT CAN'T KEEP THE TRANSFORMATION FOR LONG. HATES BUGS.
Shi-chan ?
A CAT THAT KARIN FOUND AT KAZUNE'S HOUSE...WHO LOOKS JUST LIKE KARIN'S DEAD PET SHI-CHAN. COULD IT BE THEY'RE ONE AND THE SAME?!
Himeka Kujyou
LIVES WITH KARIN AND COMPANY. UNLIKE HER COUSIN KAZUNE, SHE IS KIND, GENTLE AND REALLY LIKES BUGS.

Characters and

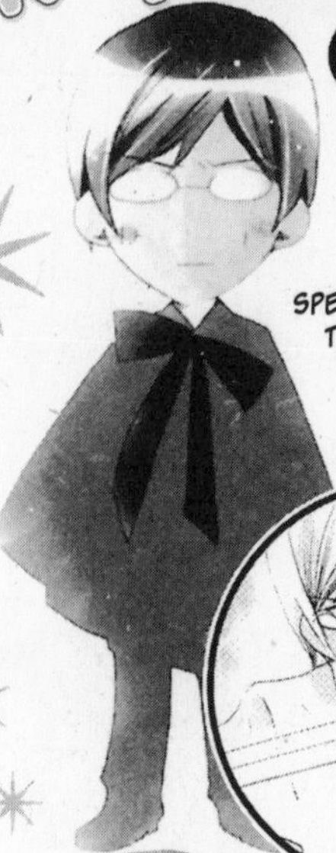

Kirio Karasuma

STUDENT COUNCIL PRESIDENT AND VILLAIN EXTRAORDINAIRE. SPENDS ALL HIS FREE TIME TRACKING AND ATTACKING KARIN.

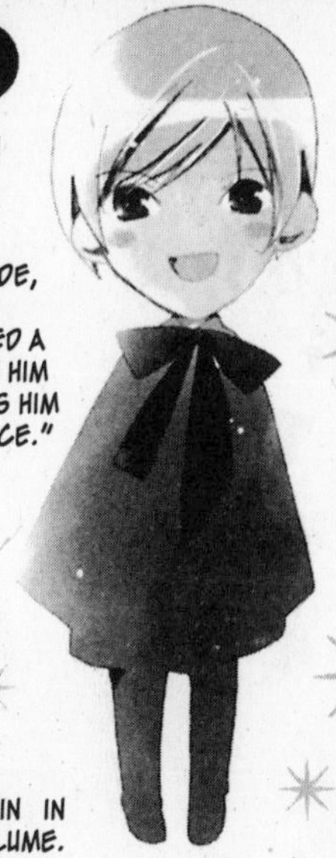

Kirika

ALTHOUGH KIRIKA IS OFTEN SEEN BY KIRIO'S SIDE, KARIN HAS DEVELOPED A CRUSH ON HIM AND CALLS HIM HER "PRINCE."

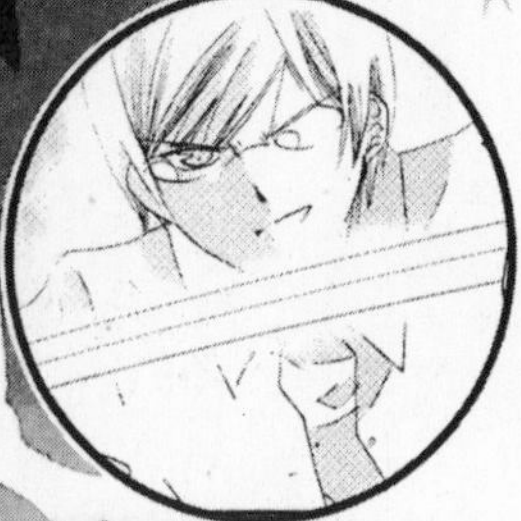

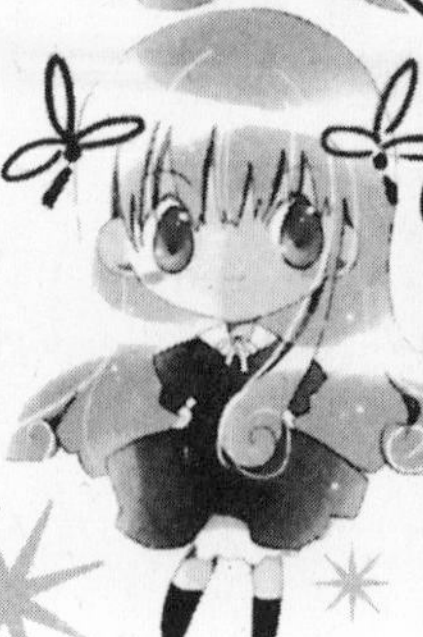

Miyon

HIMEKA'S FRIEND FROM ELEMENTARY SCHOOL. THEY'RE STILL VERY CLOSE.

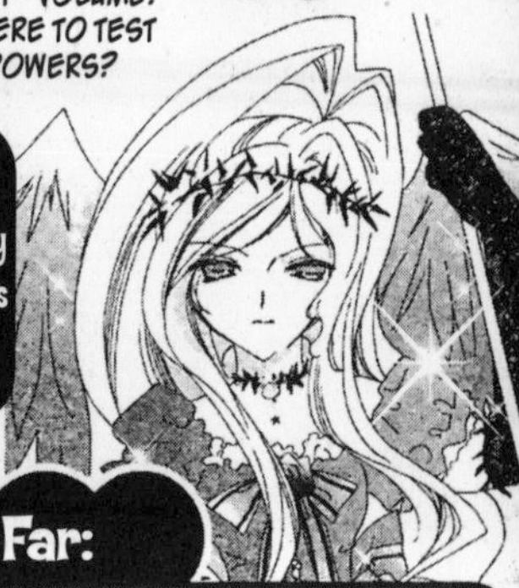

Mystery Goddess

ATTACKED KARIN IN THE LAST VOLUME. IS SHE HERE TO TEST KARIN'S POWERS?

The Story Thus Far:

KARIN WAS A NORMAL GIRL WHO LACKED TALENT IN SCHOOL AND SPORTS...UNTIL ONE DAY, WHILE MOURNING HER DEARLY DEPARTED CAT SHI-CHAN, SHE MET A MYSTERIOUS BOY NAMED KAZUNE. AFTER THAT ENCOUNTER (AND WITH THE HELP OF A MAGIC RING), KARIN DISCOVERED THE GODDESS INSIDE HER! NOW KARIN HAS BEGUN A NEW CHAPTER IN HER LIFE, LIVING AND STUDYING WITH KAZUNE AND HIMEKA. BUT AT HER NEW SCHOOL, SHE'S ALREADY MET THOSE WHO WOULD WISH HER GREAT HARM!

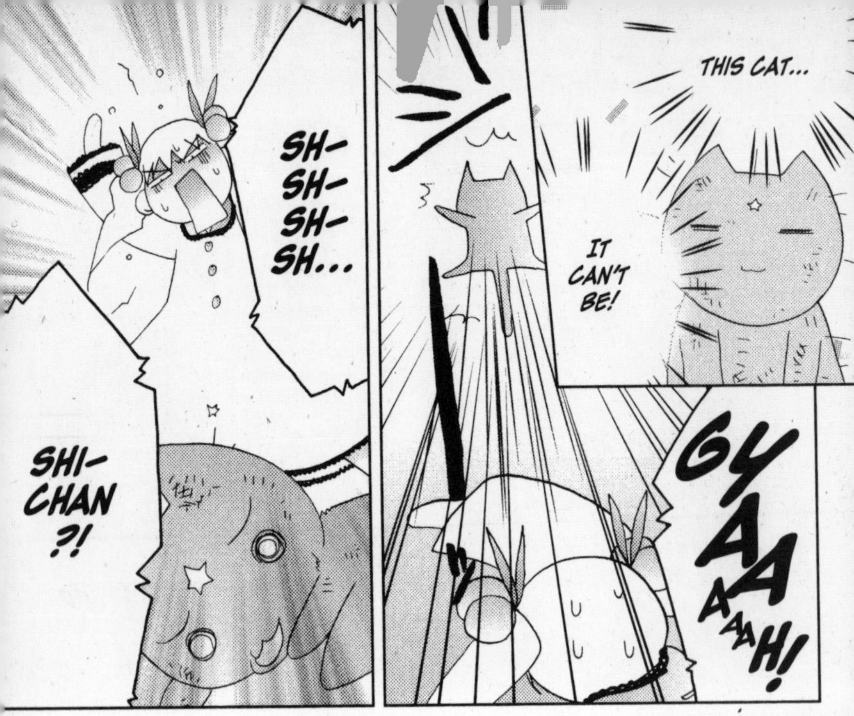
THIS CAT...
IT CAN'T BE!
GYAAAAAH!
SH-SH-SH-SH...
SHI-CHAN ?!

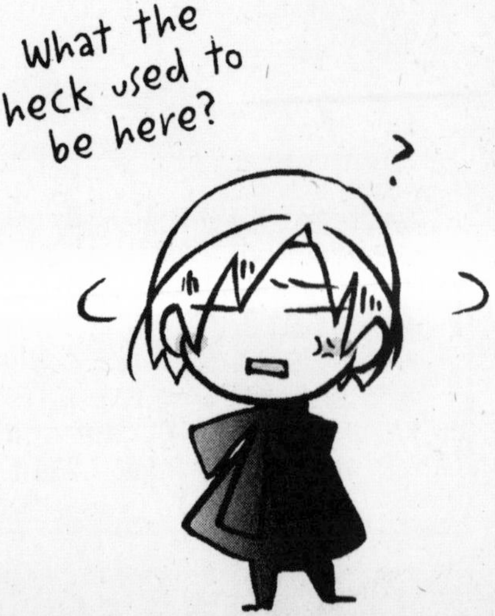
What the heck used to be here?

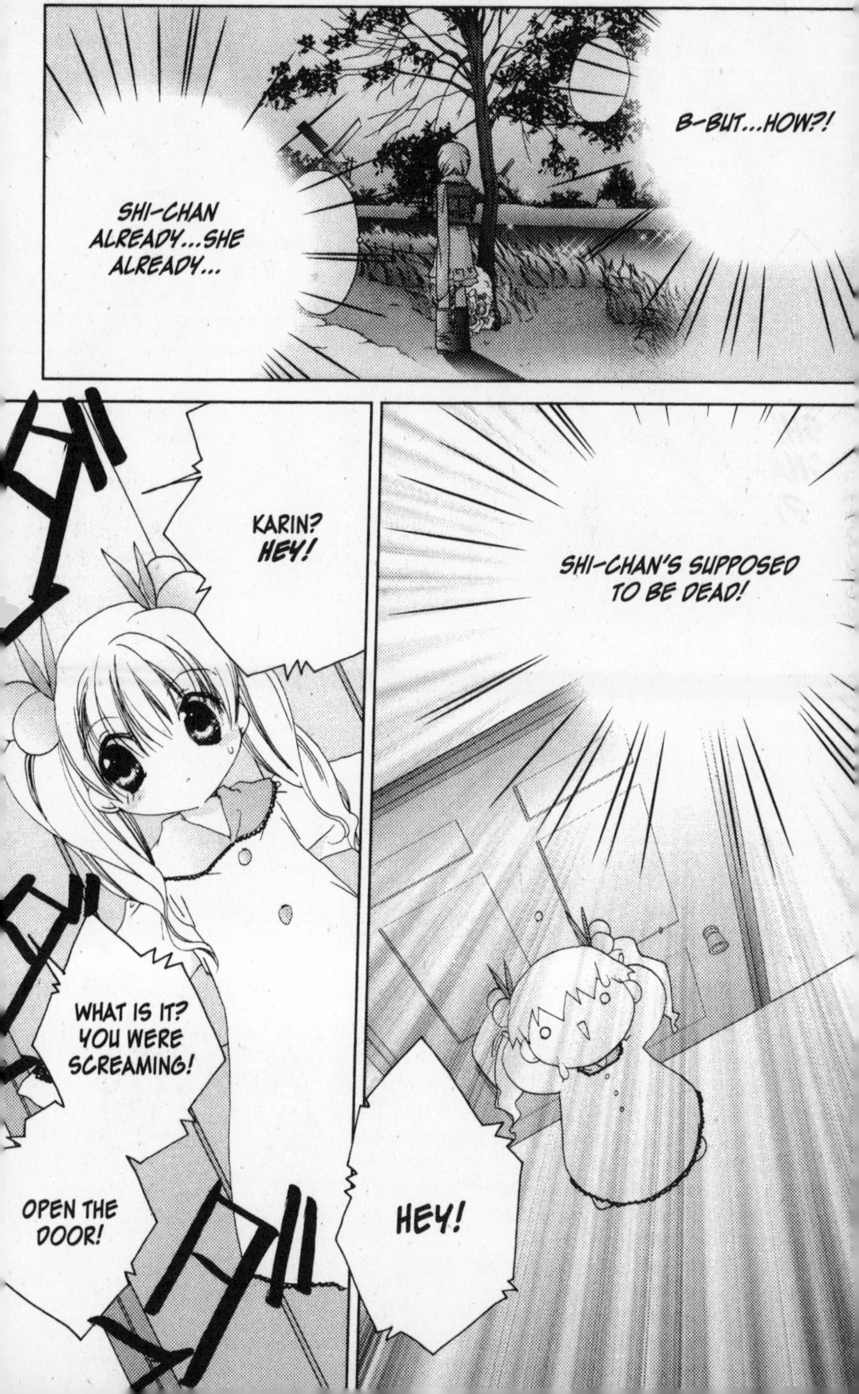
B-BUT...HOW?!
SHI-CHAN ALREADY...SHE ALREADY...
SHI-CHAN'S SUPPOSED TO BE DEAD!
HEY!
KARIN? HEY!
WHAT IS IT? YOU WERE SCREAMING!
OPEN THE DOOR!

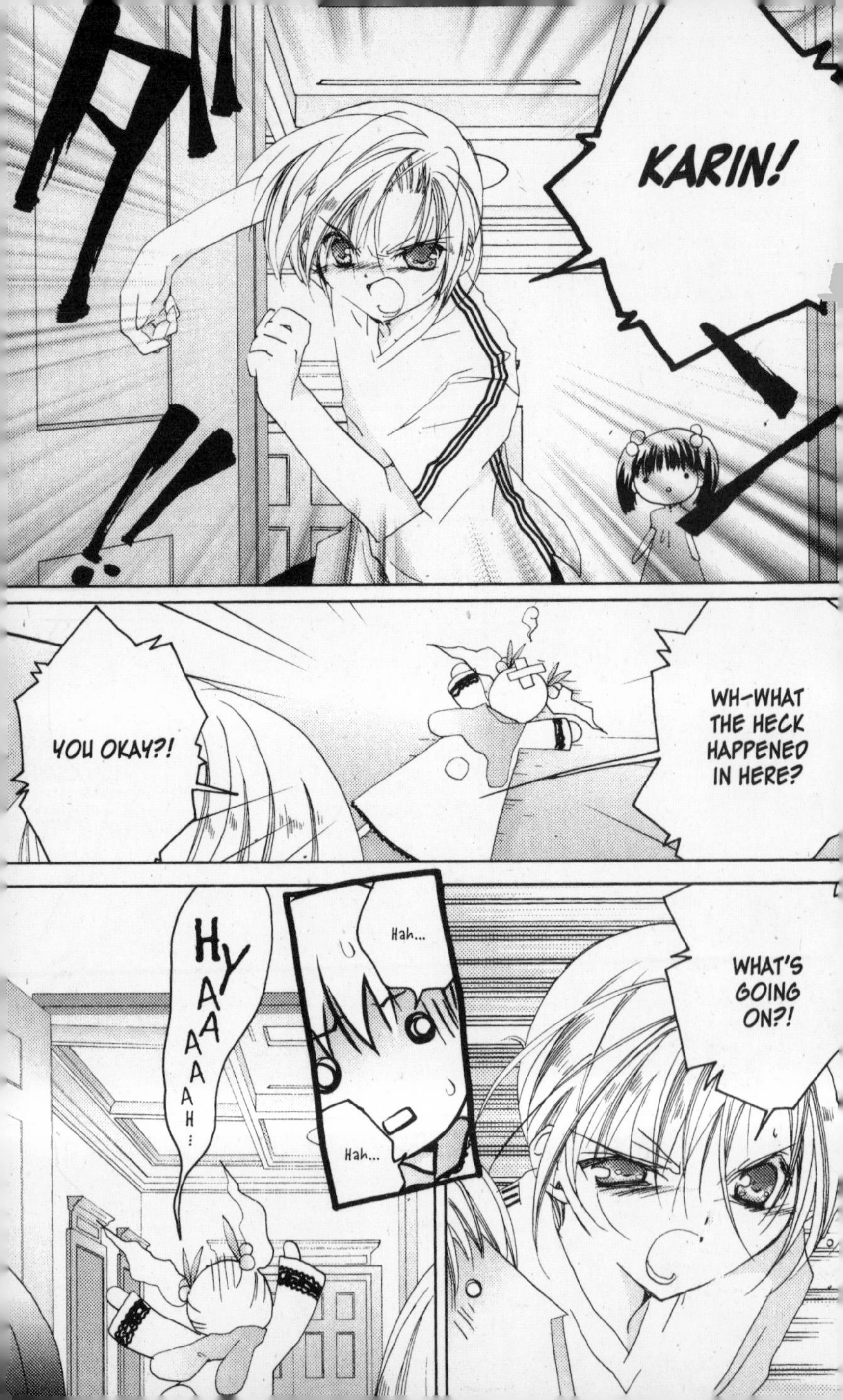
KARIN!
WH-WHAT THE HECK HAPPENED IN HERE?
YOU OKAY?!
WHAT'S GOING ON?!
Hah...
Hah...
HyAAAAAH...

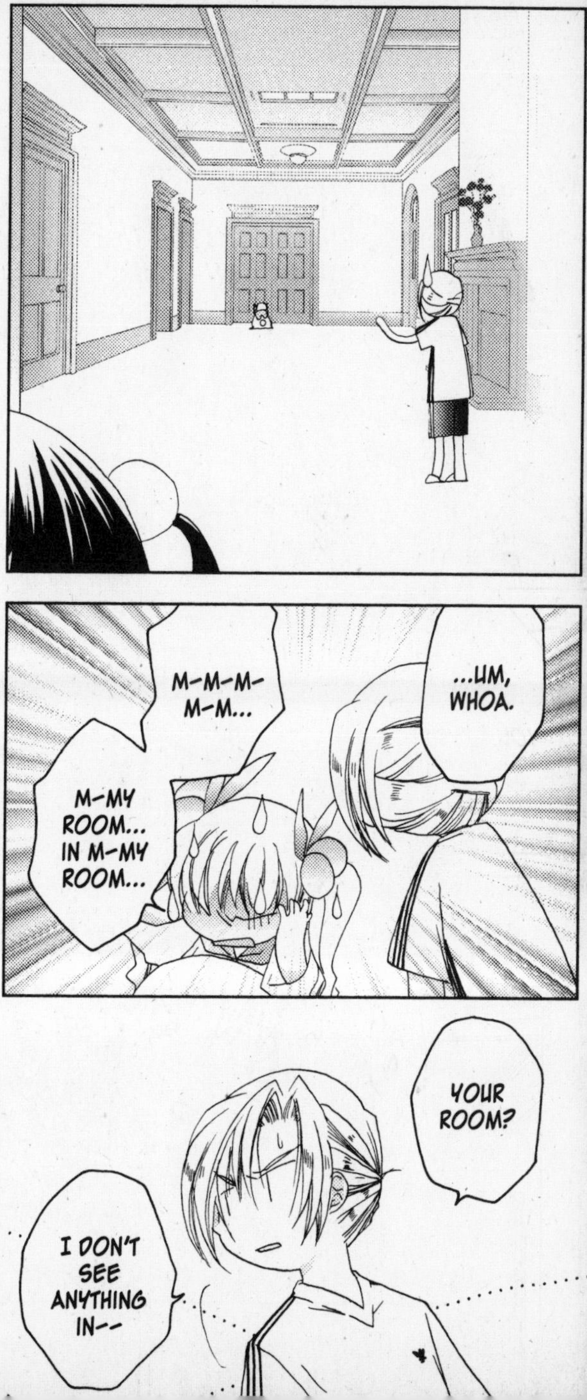
...UM, WHOA.
M-M-M-M-M...
M-MY ROOM... IN M-MY ROOM...
YOUR ROOM?
I DON'T SEE ANYTHING IN--

Today's lunch includes generous helpings of rice, natto, eggs and milk. Indeed.

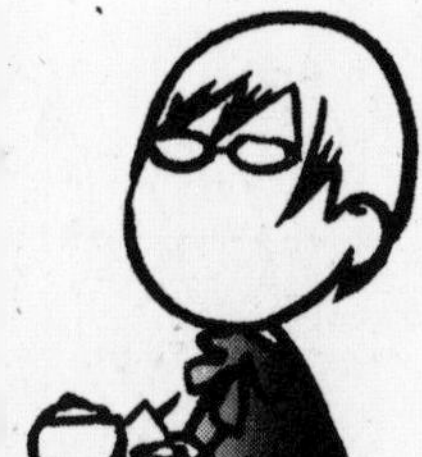

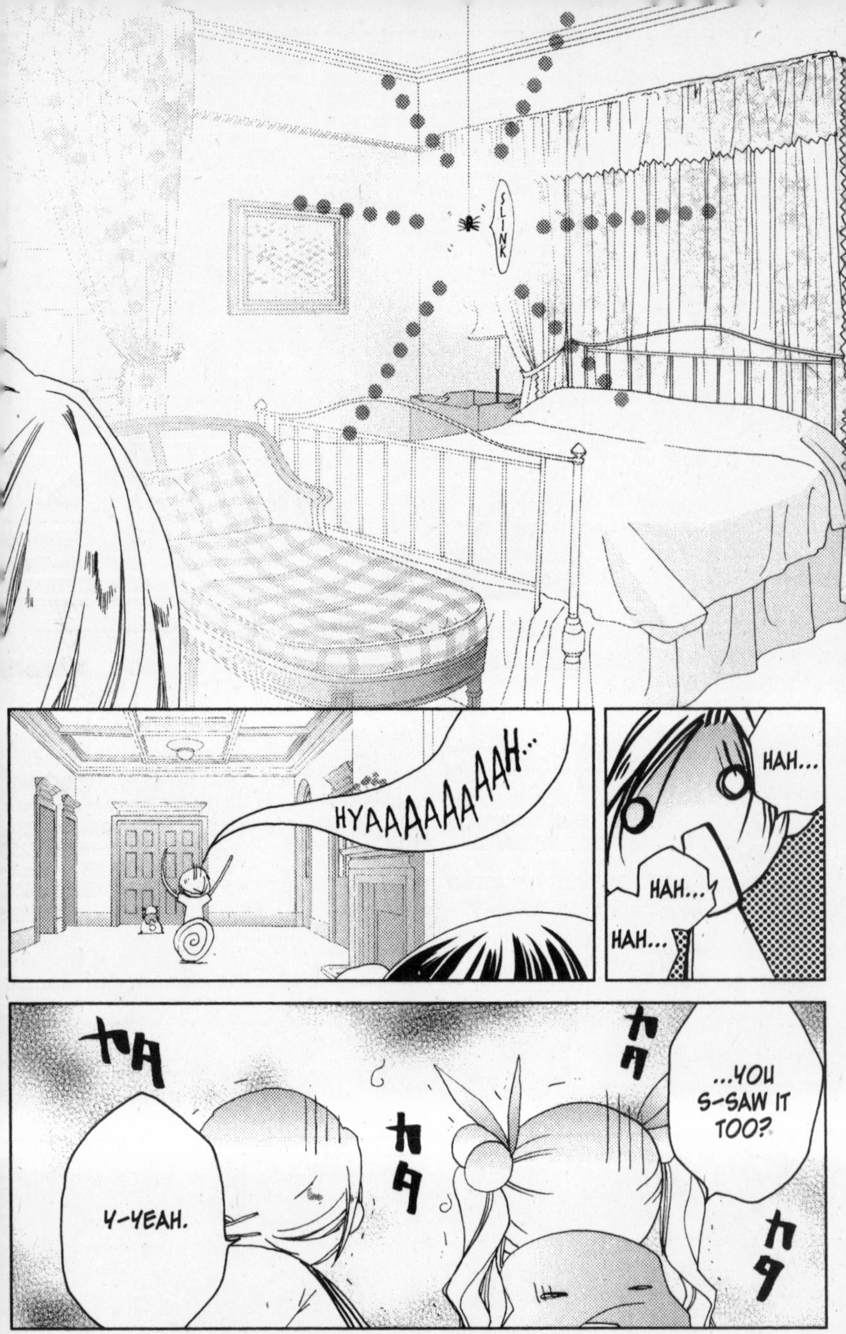
SLINK
HAH...
HAH...
HAH...
HYAAAAAAAAH...
カタ
...YOU S-SAW IT TOO?
カタ
カタ
Y-YEAH.

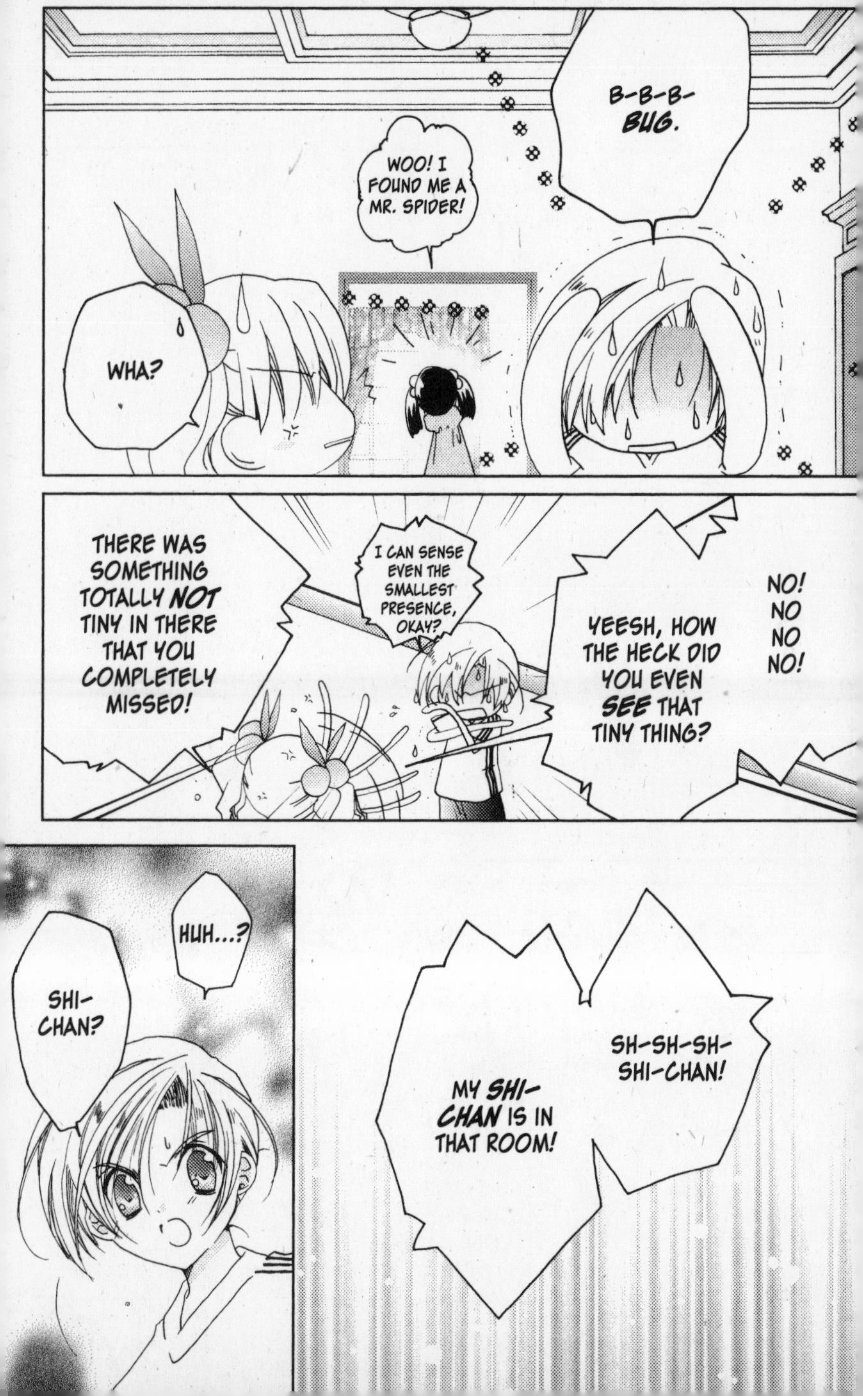
B-B-B-BUG.
WOO! I FOUND ME A MR. SPIDER!
WHA?
NO! NO NO NO!
YEESH, HOW THE HECK DID YOU EVEN SEE THAT TINY THING?
I CAN SENSE EVEN THE SMALLEST PRESENCE, OKAY?
THERE WAS SOMETHING TOTALLY NOT TINY IN THERE THAT YOU COMPLETELY MISSED!
SH-SH-SH-SHI-CHAN!
MY SHI-CHAN IS IN THAT ROOM!
HUH...?
SHI-CHAN?

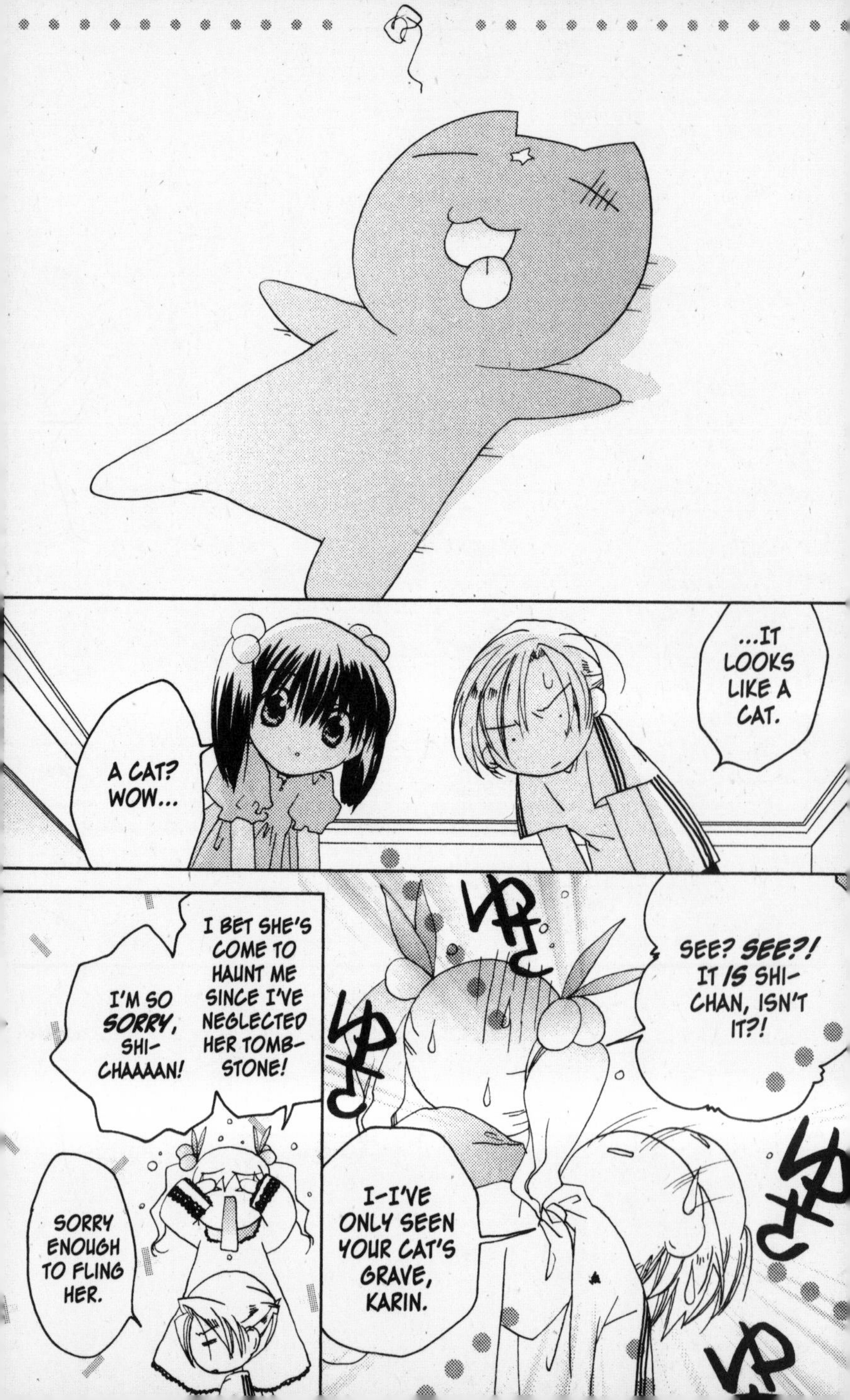
...IT LOOKS LIKE A CAT.
A CAT? WOW...
SEE? *SEE?!* IT *IS* SHI-CHAN, ISN'T IT?!
I-I'VE ONLY SEEN YOUR CAT'S GRAVE, KARIN.
I BET SHE'S COME TO HAUNT ME SINCE I'VE NEGLECTED HER TOMBSTONE!
I'M SO *SORRY*, SHI-CHAAAAN!
SORRY ENOUGH TO FLING HER.

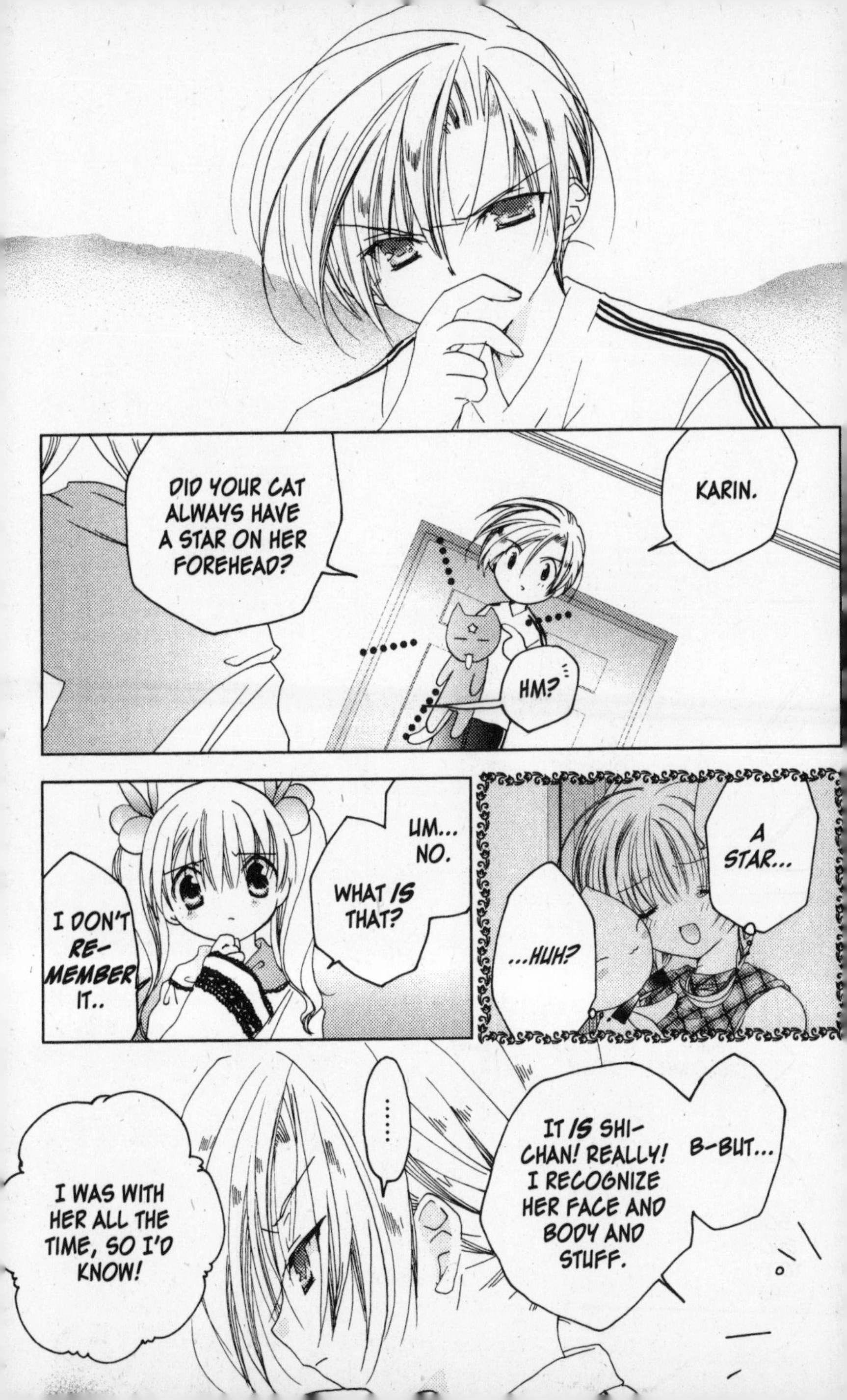
KARIN.
DID YOUR CAT ALWAYS HAVE A STAR ON HER FOREHEAD?
HM?
A STAR...
...HUH?
UM... NO.
WHAT *IS* THAT?
I DON'T RE-MEMBER IT..
B-BUT...
IT *IS* SHI-CHAN! REALLY! I RECOGNIZE HER FACE AND BODY AND STUFF.
......
I WAS WITH HER ALL THE TIME, SO I'D KNOW!

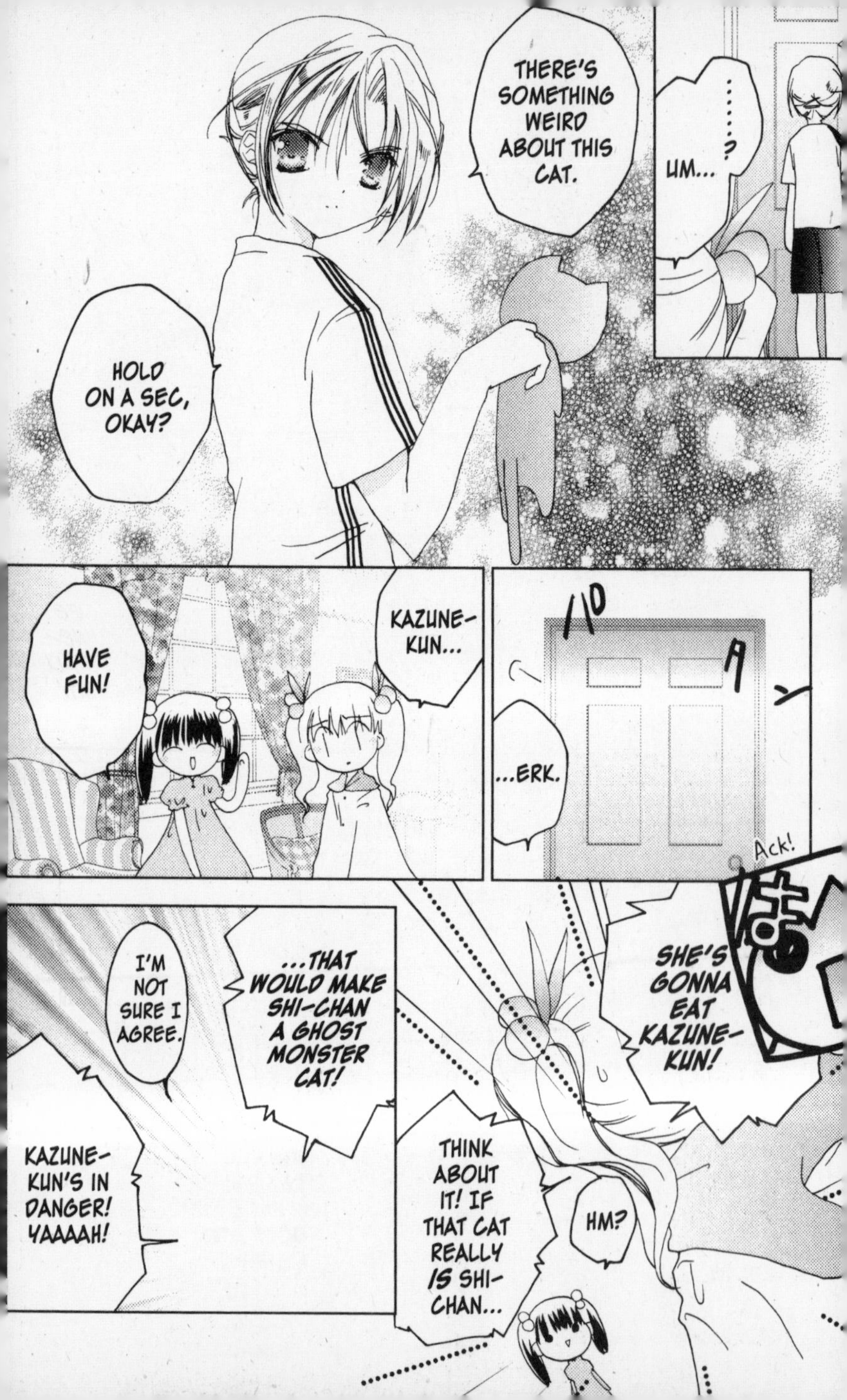

......
UM...?
THERE'S SOMETHING WEIRD ABOUT THIS CAT.
HOLD ON A SEC, OKAY?
...ERK.
KAZUNE-KUN...
HAVE FUN!
Ack!
SHE'S GONNA EAT KAZUNE-KUN!
HM?
THINK ABOUT IT! IF THAT CAT REALLY IS SHI-CHAN...
...THAT WOULD MAKE SHI-CHAN A GHOST MONSTER CAT!
I'M NOT SURE I AGREE.
KAZUNE-KUN'S IN DANGER! YAAAAH!

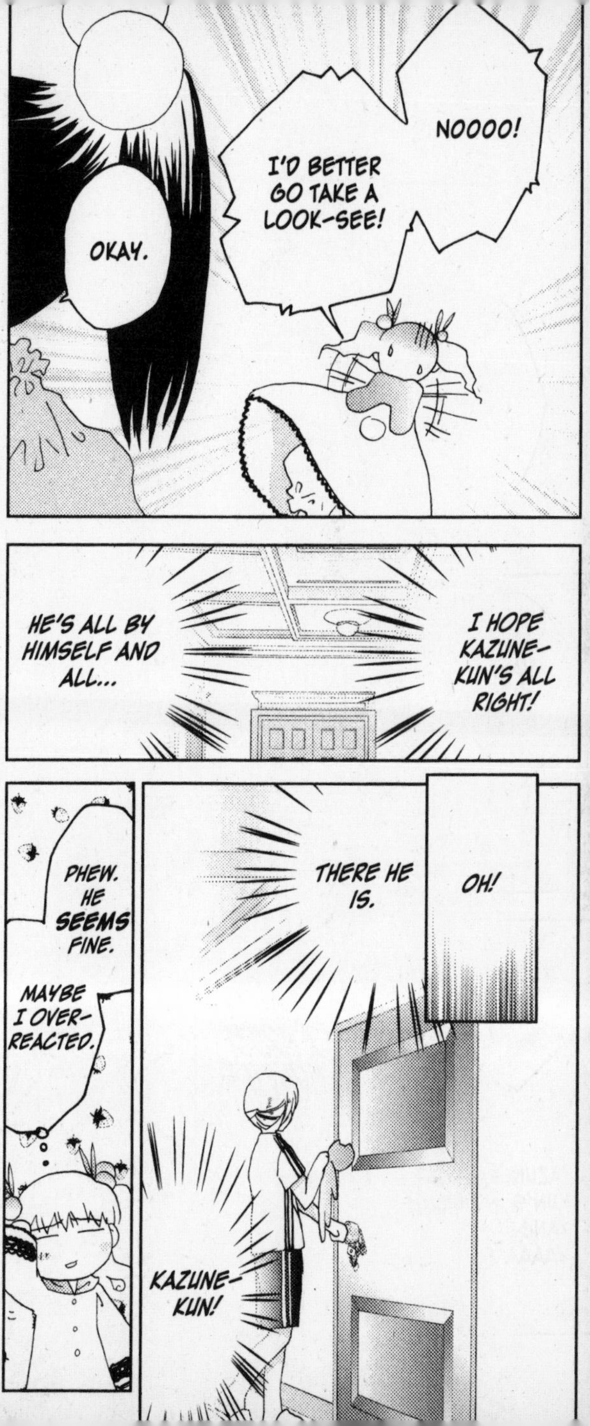
NOOOO!
I'D BETTER GO TAKE A LOOK-SEE!
OKAY.
I HOPE KAZUNE-KUN'S ALL RIGHT!
HE'S ALL BY HIMSELF AND ALL...
OH!
THERE HE IS.
KAZUNE-KUN!
PHEW. HE SEEMS FINE.
MAYBE I OVER-REACTED.

Ooh, I'm left-handed.

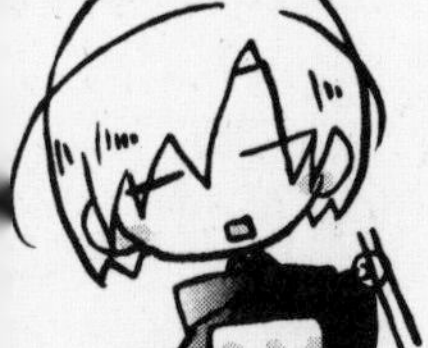

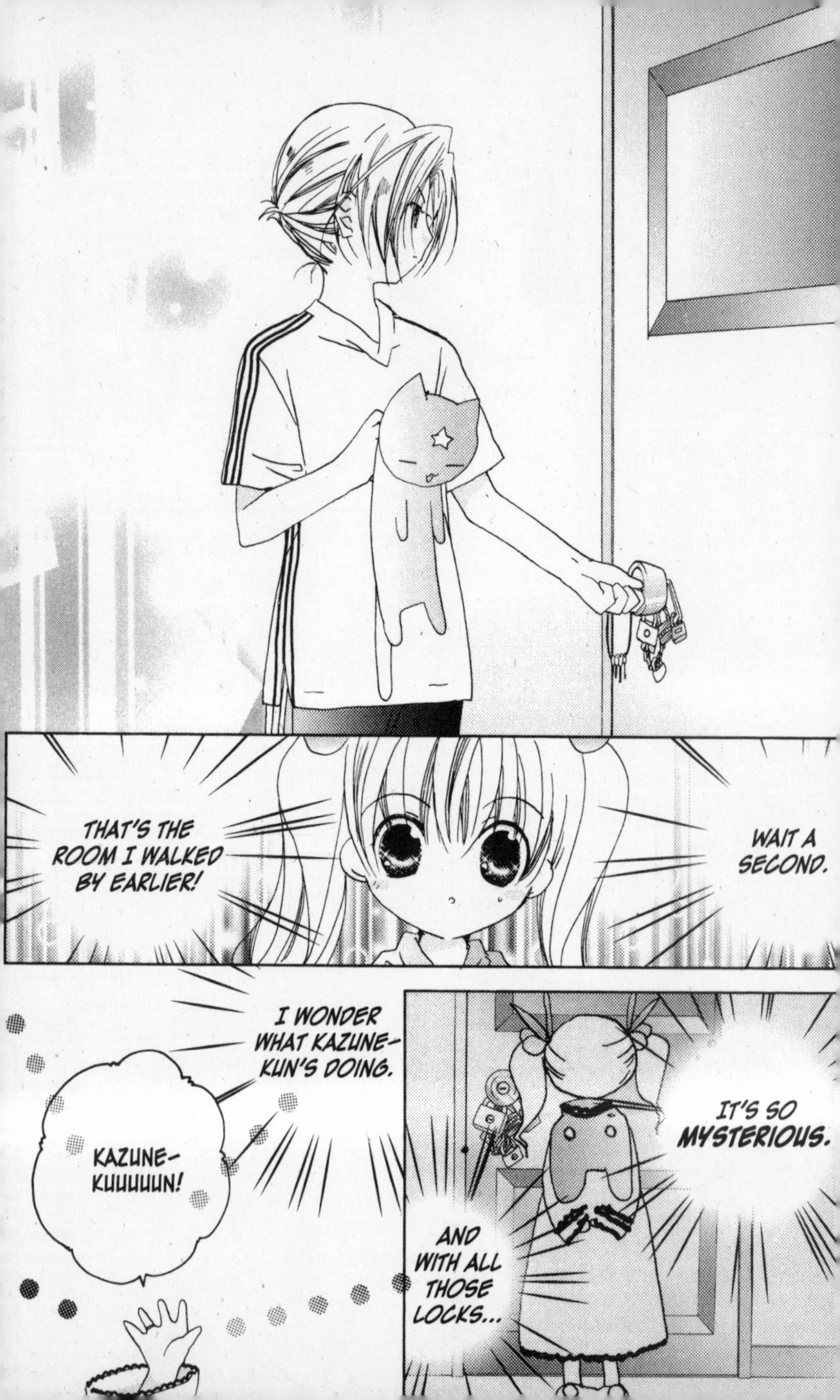
WAIT A SECOND.
THAT'S THE ROOM I WALKED BY EARLIER!
IT'S SO MYSTERIOUS.
AND WITH ALL THOSE LOCKS...
I WONDER WHAT KAZUNE-KUN'S DOING.
KAZUNE-KUUUUUN!

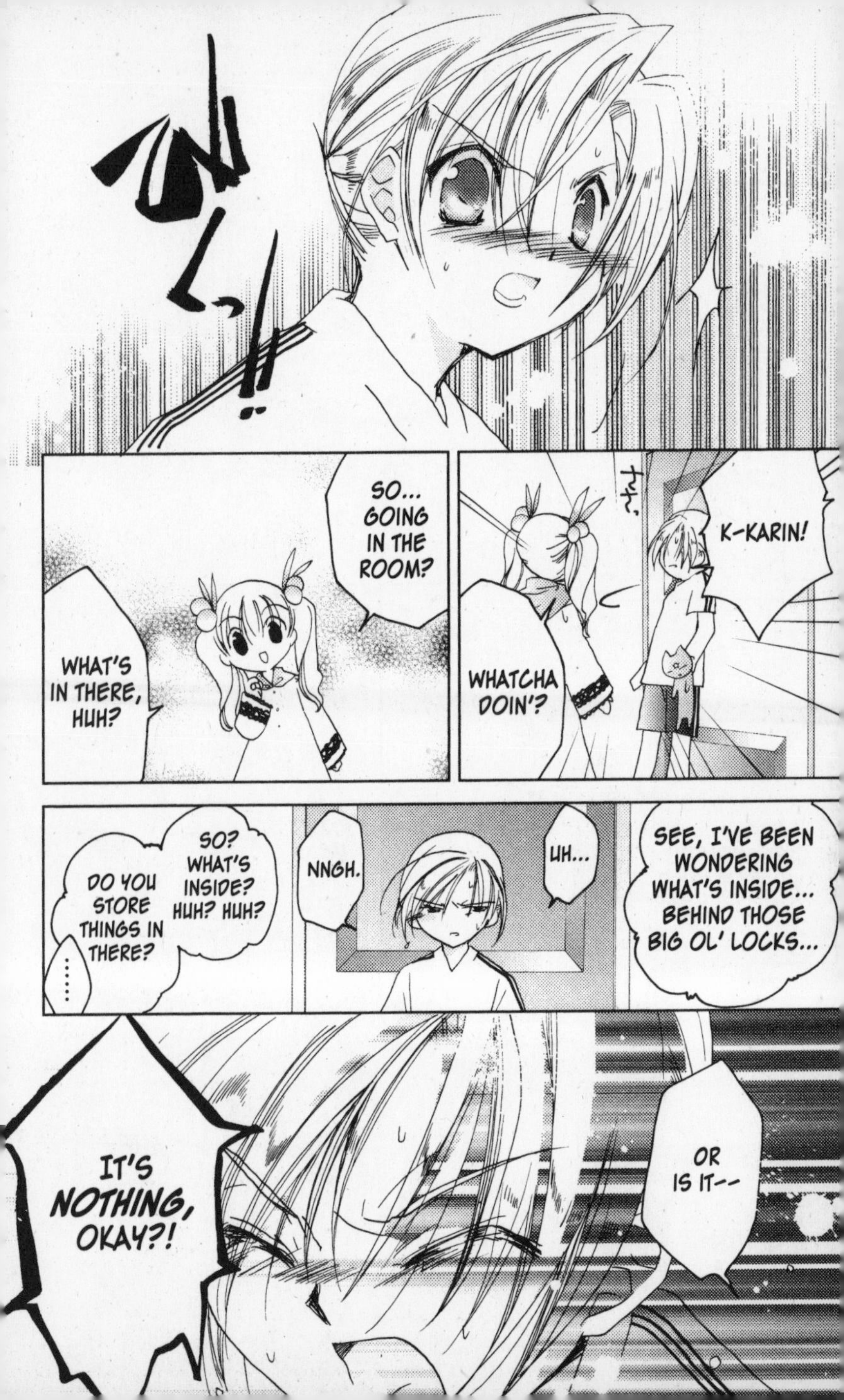
K-KARIN!
WHATCHA DOIN'?
SO... GOING IN THE ROOM?
WHAT'S IN THERE, HUH?
SEE, I'VE BEEN WONDERING WHAT'S INSIDE... BEHIND THOSE BIG OL' LOCKS...
UH...
NNGH.
SO? WHAT'S INSIDE? HUH? HUH?
DO YOU STORE THINGS IN THERE?
......
OR IS IT--
IT'S *NOTHING*, OKAY?!

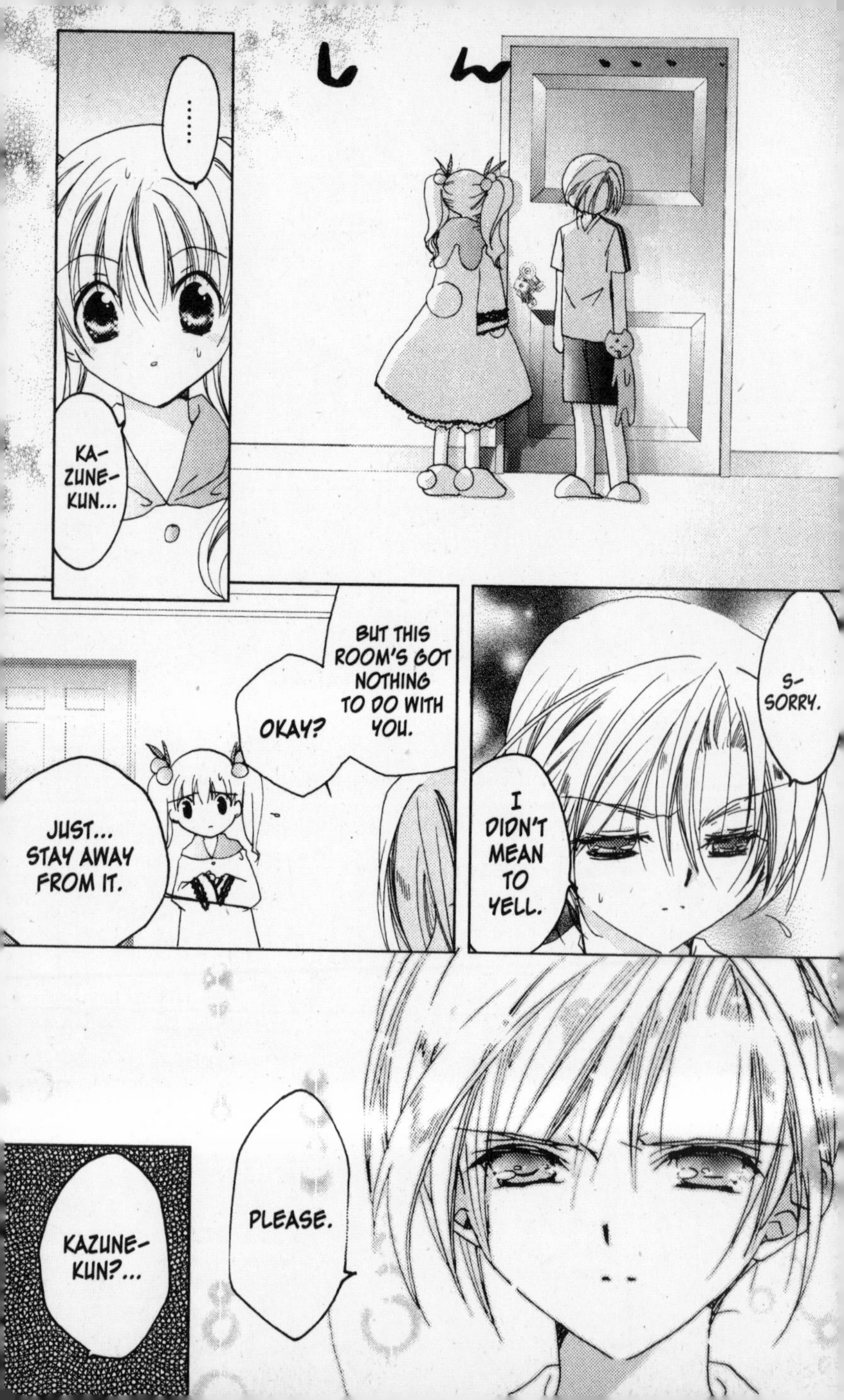

しん…
......
KA-ZUNE-KUN...
S-SORRY.
I DIDN'T MEAN TO YELL.
BUT THIS ROOM'S GOT NOTHING TO DO WITH YOU.
OKAY?
JUST... STAY AWAY FROM IT.
PLEASE.
KAZUNE-KUN?...

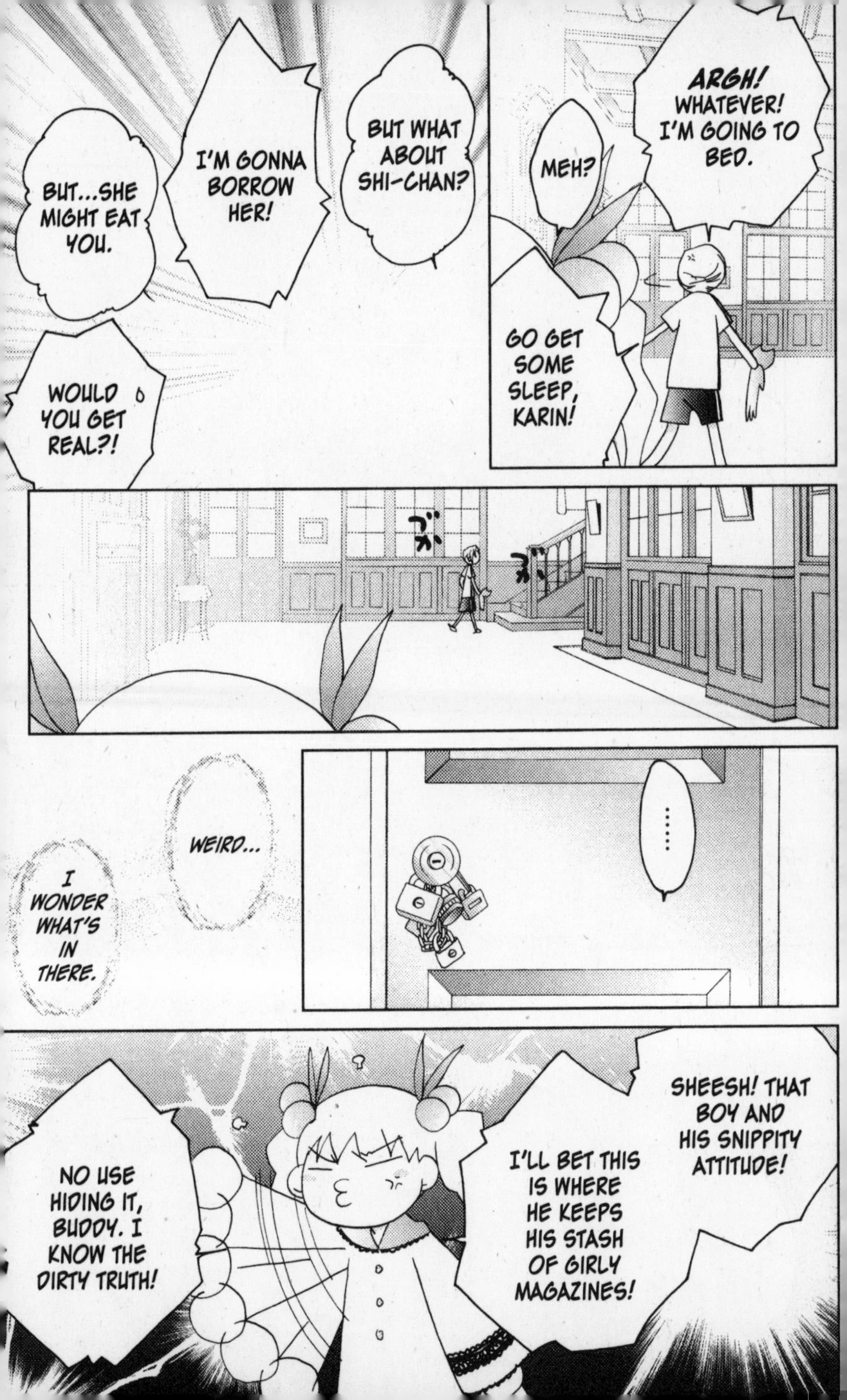
ARGH! WHATEVER! I'M GOING TO BED.
MEH?
GO GET SOME SLEEP, KARIN!
BUT WHAT ABOUT SHI-CHAN?
I'M GONNA BORROW HER!
BUT...SHE MIGHT EAT YOU.
WOULD YOU GET REAL?!
......
WEIRD...
I WONDER WHAT'S IN THERE.
SHEESH! THAT BOY AND HIS SNIPPITY ATTITUDE!
I'LL BET THIS IS WHERE HE KEEPS HIS STASH OF GIRLY MAGAZINES!
NO USE HIDING IT, BUDDY. I KNOW THE DIRTY TRUTH!

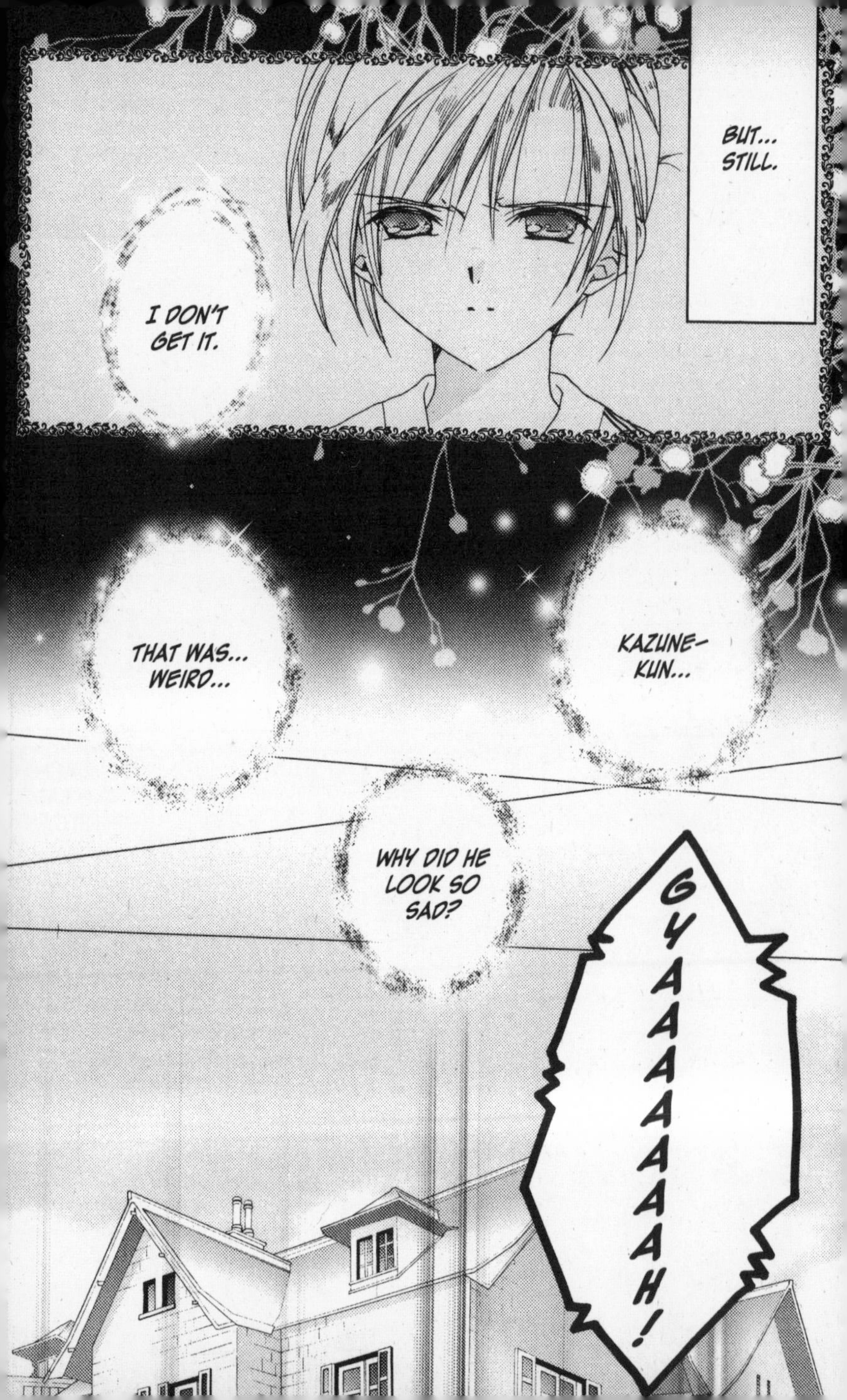
BUT... STILL.
I DON'T GET IT.
KAZUNE-KUN...
THAT WAS... WEIRD...
WHY DID HE LOOK SO SAD?
GYAAAAAAAAAAH!

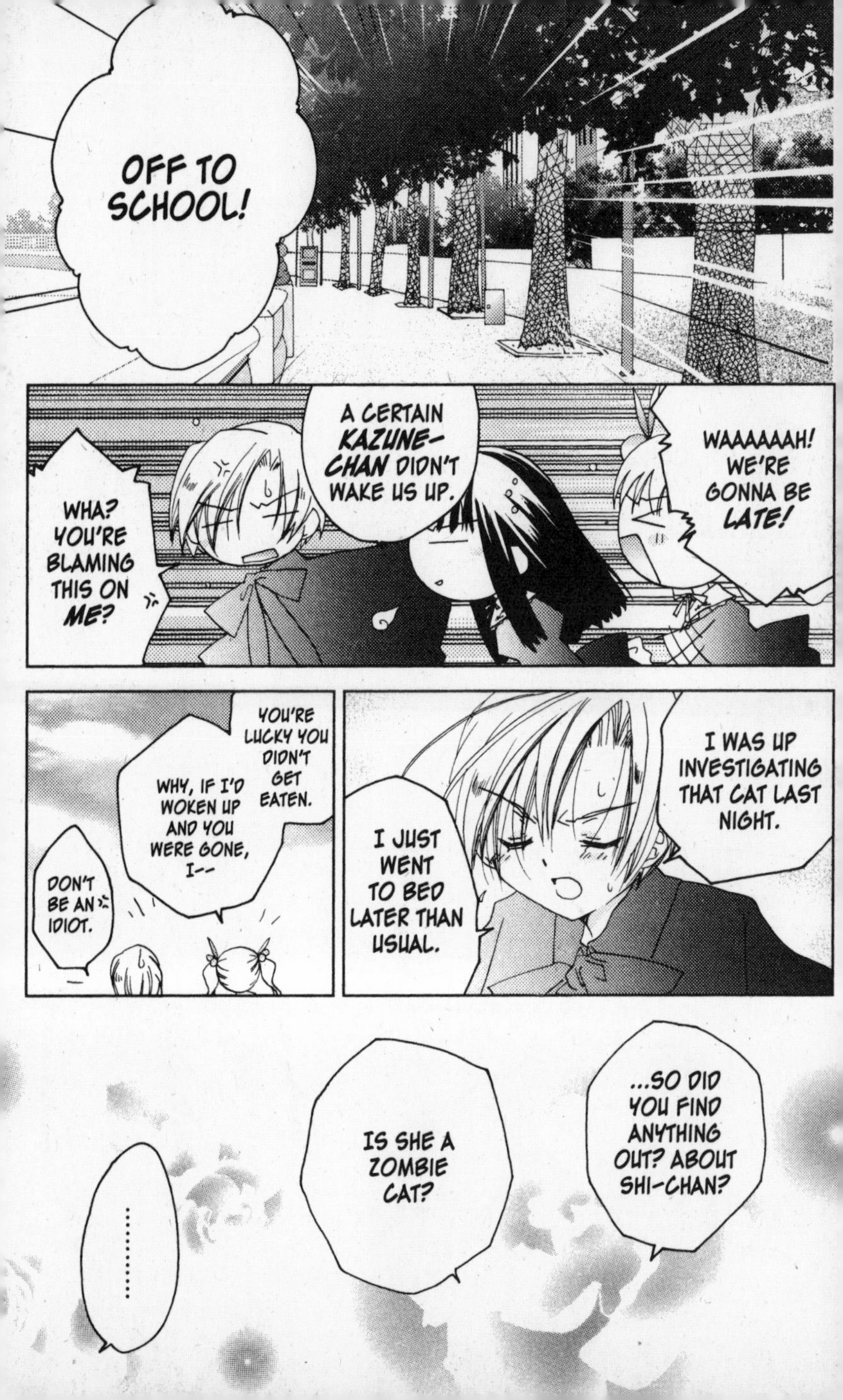
OFF TO SCHOOL!
WAAAAAAH! WE'RE GONNA BE LATE!
A CERTAIN KAZUNE-CHAN DIDN'T WAKE US UP.
WHA? YOU'RE BLAMING THIS ON ME?
I WAS UP INVESTIGATING THAT CAT LAST NIGHT.
I JUST WENT TO BED LATER THAN USUAL.
YOU'RE LUCKY YOU DIDN'T GET EATEN.
WHY, IF I'D WOKEN UP AND YOU WERE GONE, I--
DON'T BE AN IDIOT.
...SO DID YOU FIND ANYTHING OUT? ABOUT SHI-CHAN?
IS SHE A ZOMBIE CAT?
....

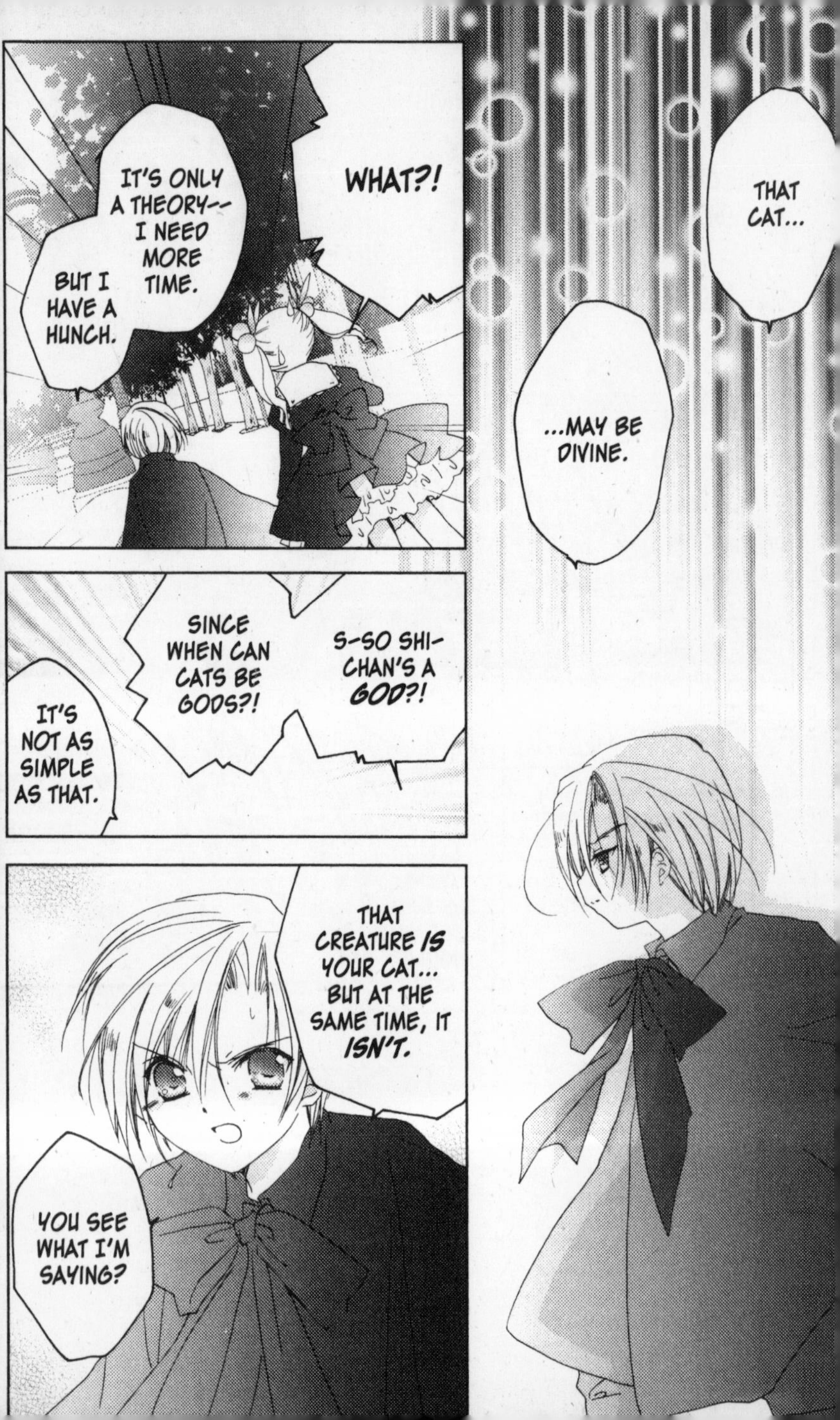
THAT CAT...
...MAY BE DIVINE.
WHAT?!
IT'S ONLY A THEORY-- I NEED MORE TIME.
BUT I HAVE A HUNCH.
S-SO SHI-CHAN'S A GOD?!
SINCE WHEN CAN CATS BE GODS?!
IT'S NOT AS SIMPLE AS THAT.
THAT CREATURE IS YOUR CAT... BUT AT THE SAME TIME, IT ISN'T.
YOU SEE WHAT I'M SAYING?

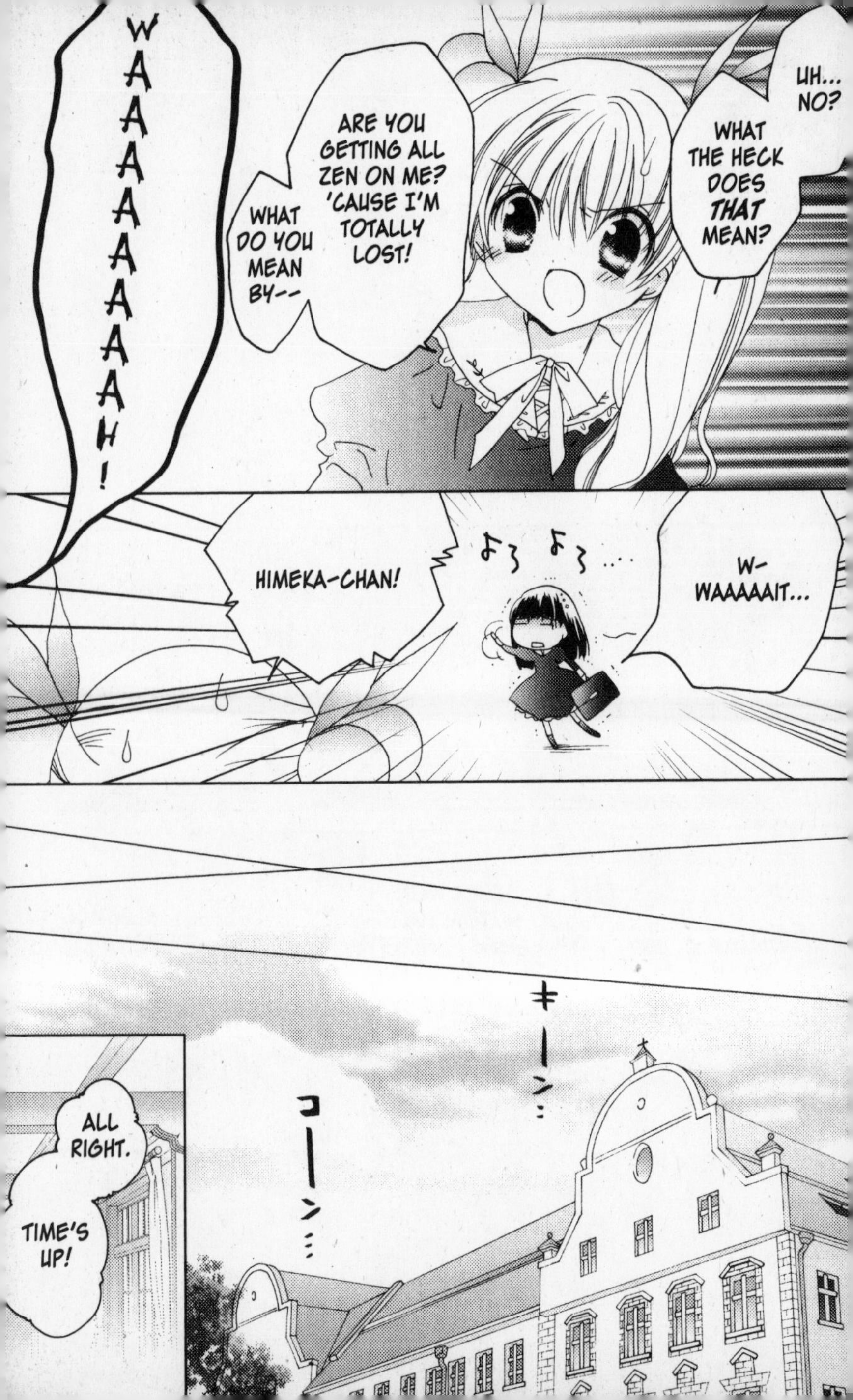
UH... NO?
WHAT THE HECK DOES *THAT* MEAN?
ARE YOU GETTING ALL ZEN ON ME? 'CAUSE I'M TOTALLY LOST!
WHAT DO YOU MEAN BY--
WAAAAAAAAAAH!
W-WAAAAAIT...
よろよろ...
HIMEKA-CHAN!
キーン
コーン
ALL RIGHT.
TIME'S UP!

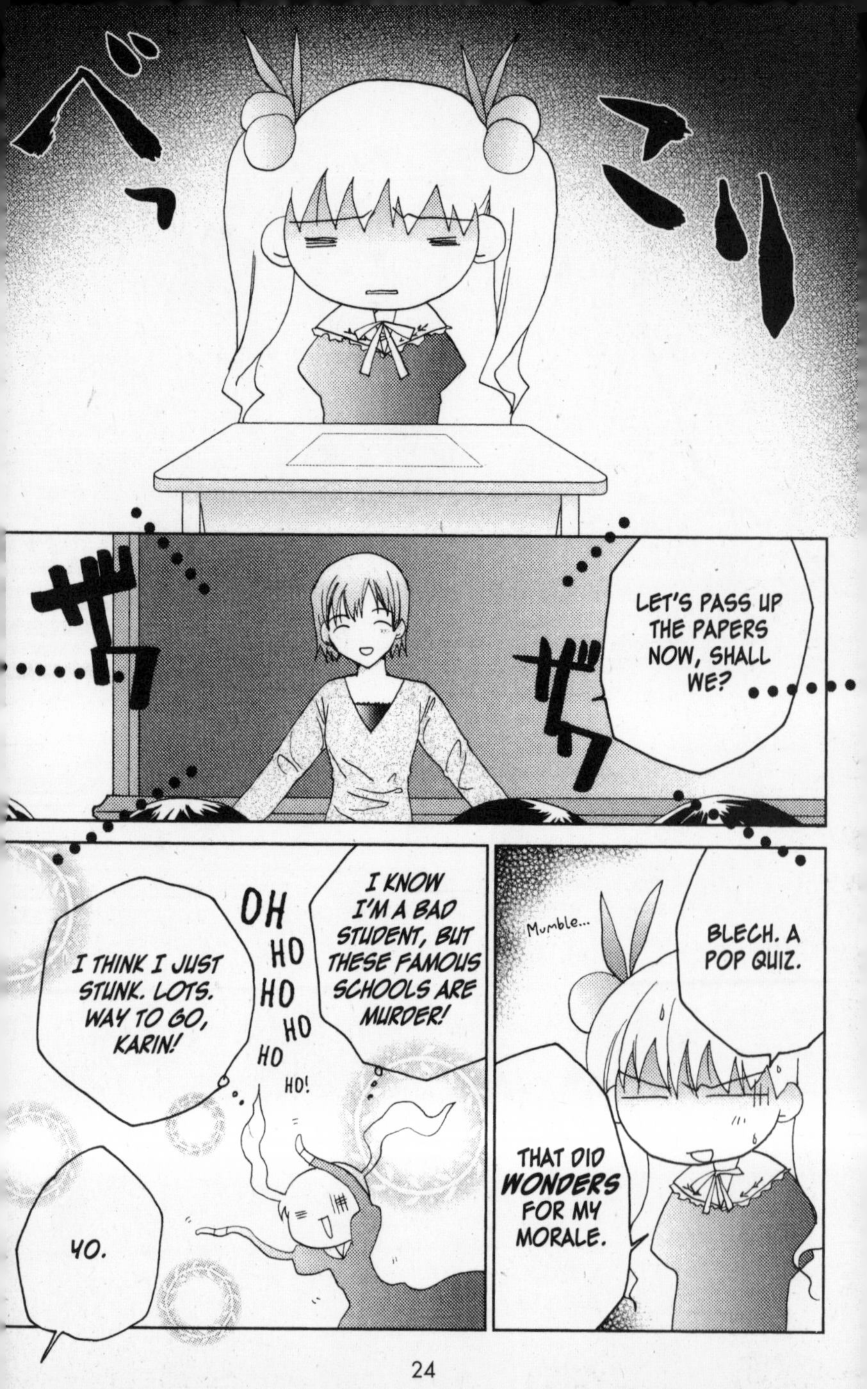
ザワ
ザワ
LET'S PASS UP THE PAPERS NOW, SHALL WE?
BLECH. A POP QUIZ.
Mumble...
THAT DID WONDERS FOR MY MORALE.
I KNOW I'M A BAD STUDENT, BUT THESE FAMOUS SCHOOLS ARE MURDER!
OH HO HO HO HO HO!
I THINK I JUST STUNK. LOTS. WAY TO GO, KARIN!
YO.

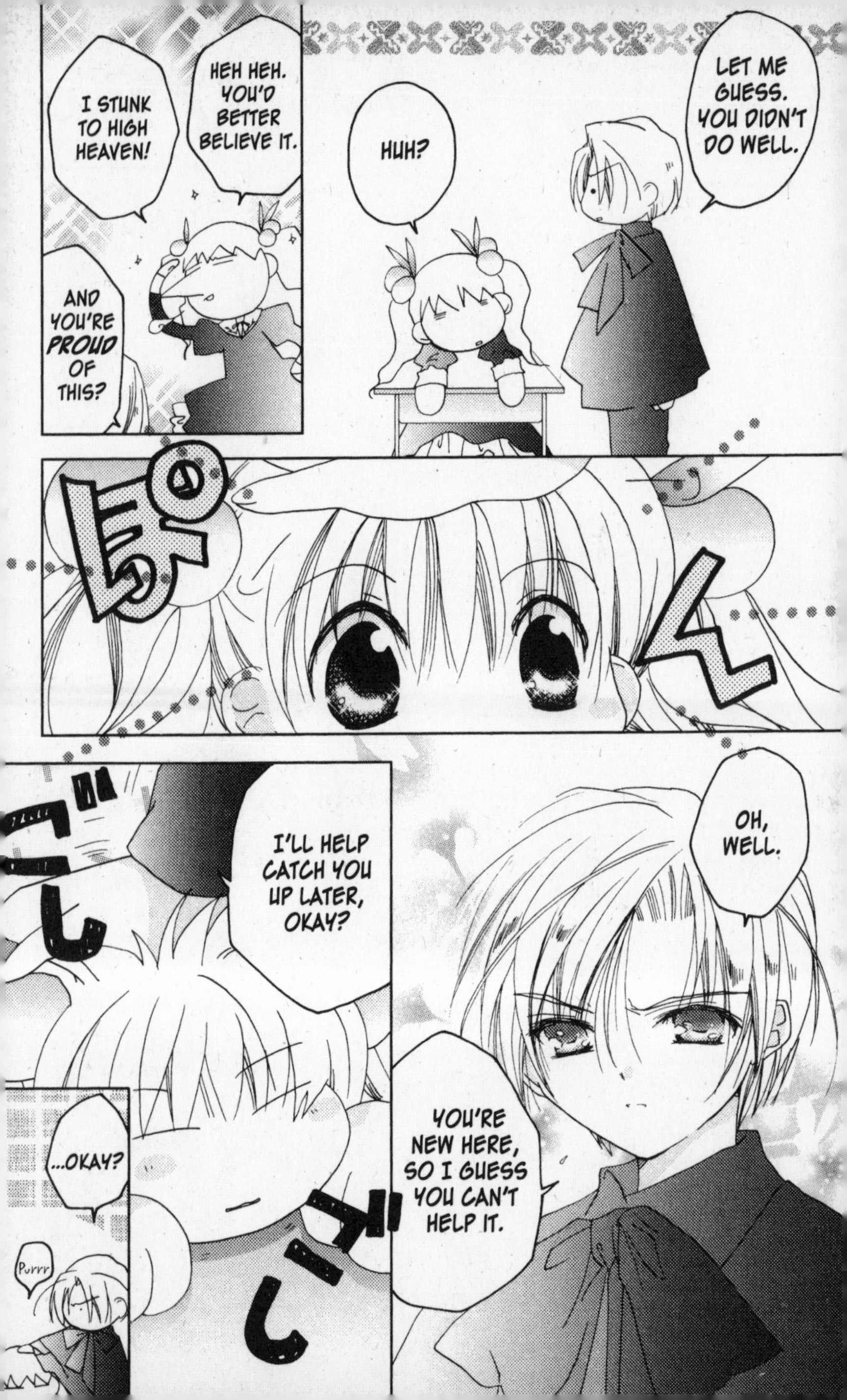
LET ME GUESS. YOU DIDN'T DO WELL.
HUH?
HEH HEH. YOU'D BETTER BELIEVE IT.
I STUNK TO HIGH HEAVEN!
AND YOU'RE *PROUD* OF THIS?
ぽん
OH, WELL.
YOU'RE NEW HERE, SO I GUESS YOU CAN'T HELP IT.
I'LL HELP CATCH YOU UP LATER, OKAY?
ごし
ごし
...OKAY?
Purrr

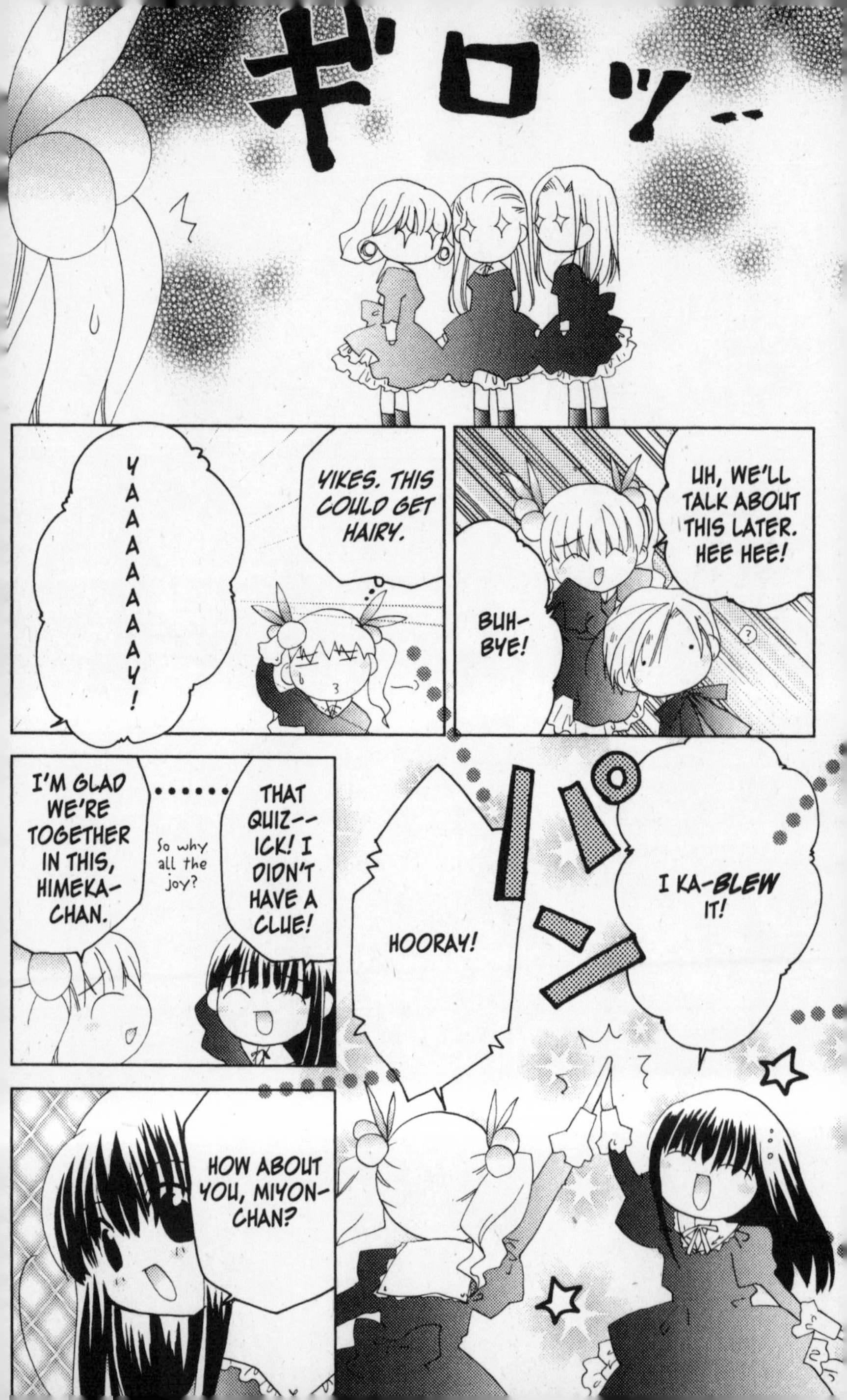
ギロッ
UH, WE'LL TALK ABOUT THIS LATER. HEE HEE!
BUH-BYE!
YIKES. THIS COULD GET HAIRY.
YAAAAAAAAAY!
パン
I KA-BLEW IT!
HOORAY!
THAT QUIZ--ICK! I DIDN'T HAVE A CLUE!
......
So why all the joy?
I'M GLAD WE'RE TOGETHER IN THIS, HIMEKA-CHAN.
HOW ABOUT YOU, MIYON-CHAN?

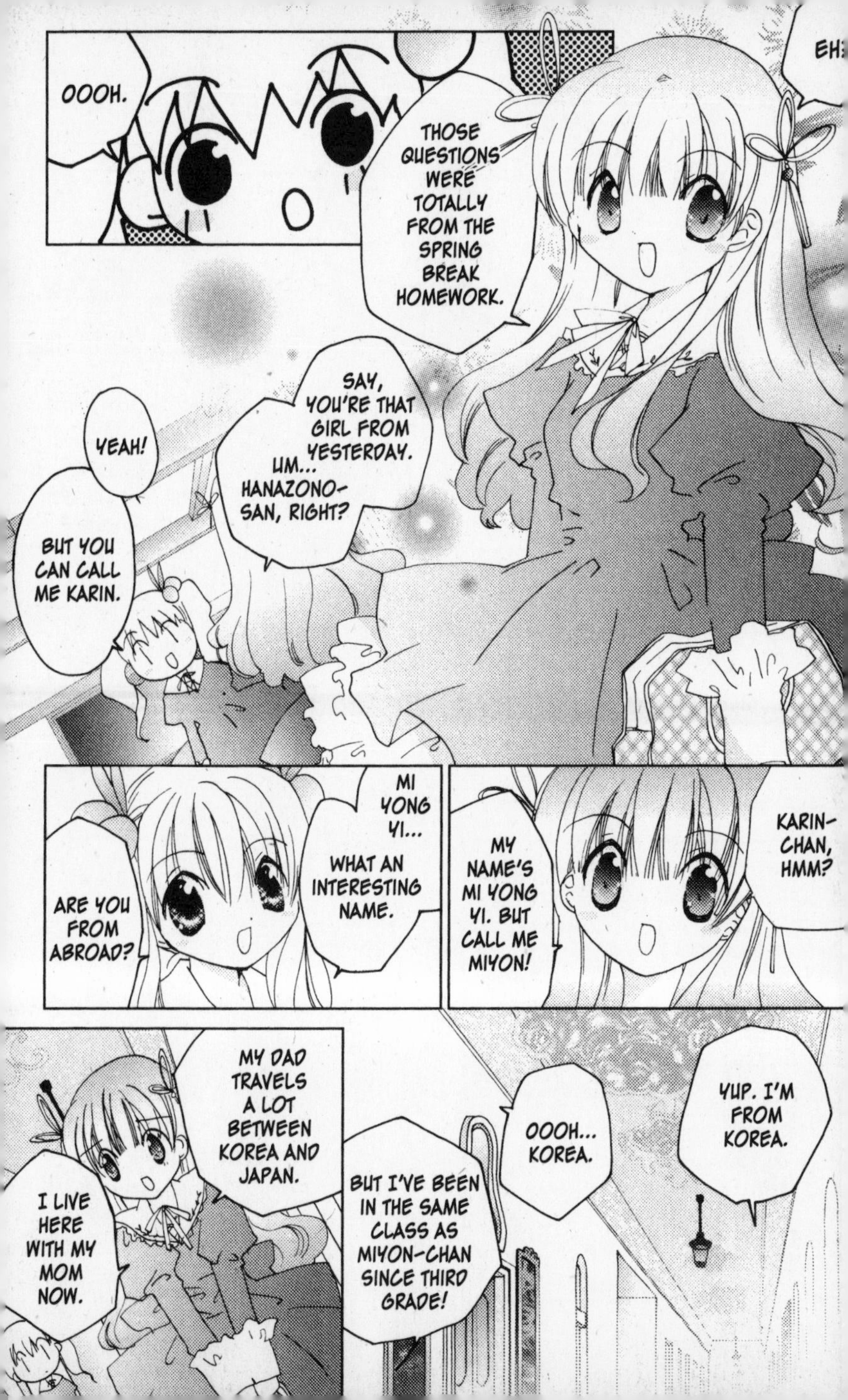
EH
THOSE QUESTIONS WERE TOTALLY FROM THE SPRING BREAK HOMEWORK.
OOOH.
SAY, YOU'RE THAT GIRL FROM YESTERDAY.
UM... HANAZONO-SAN, RIGHT?
YEAH!
BUT YOU CAN CALL ME KARIN.
KARIN-CHAN, HMM?
MY NAME'S MI YONG YI. BUT CALL ME MIYON!
MI YONG YI...
WHAT AN INTERESTING NAME.
ARE YOU FROM ABROAD?
YUP. I'M FROM KOREA.
OOOH... KOREA.
BUT I'VE BEEN IN THE SAME CLASS AS MIYON-CHAN SINCE THIRD GRADE!
MY DAD TRAVELS A LOT BETWEEN KOREA AND JAPAN.
I LIVE HERE WITH MY MOM NOW.

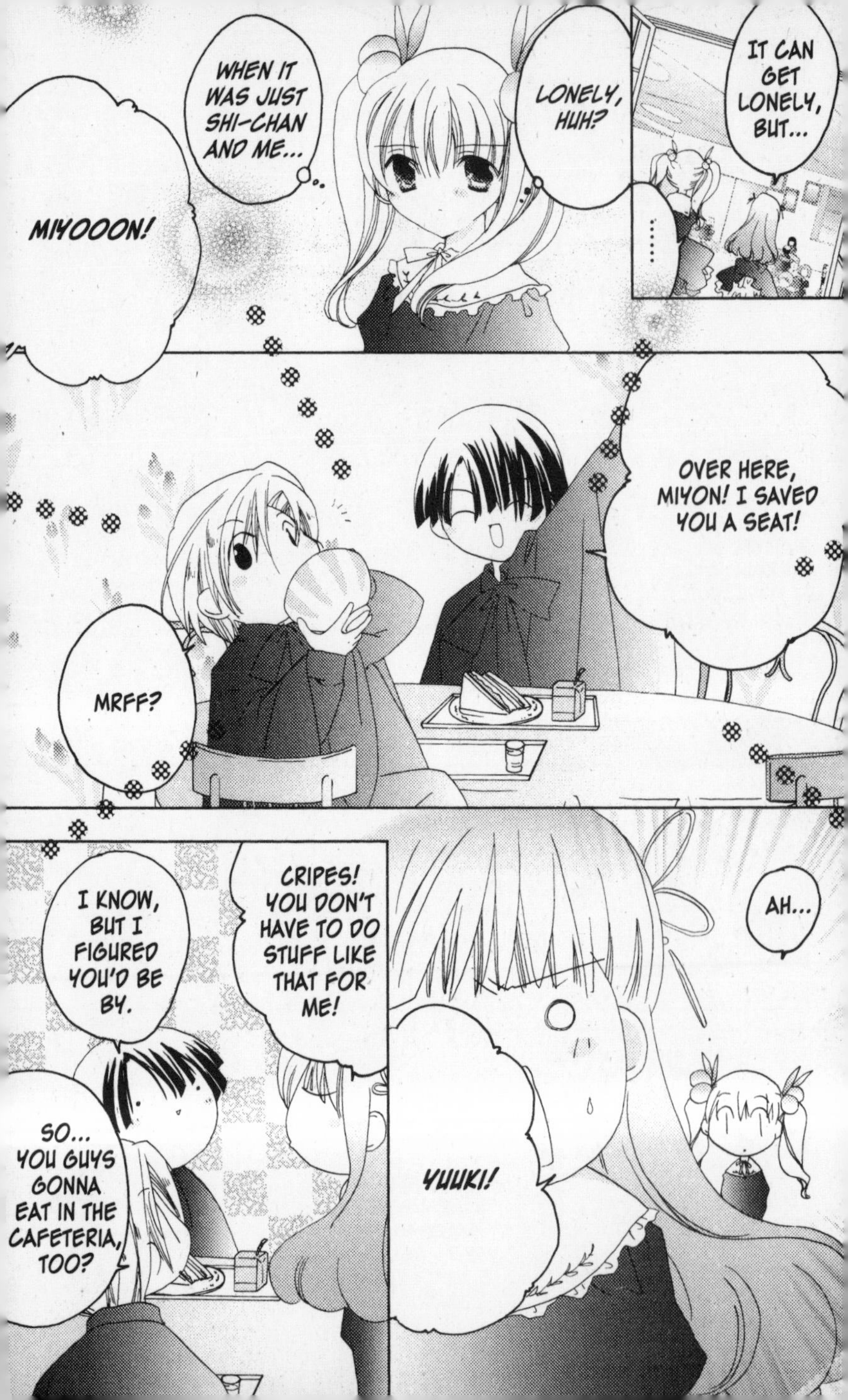
IT CAN GET LONELY, BUT...
......
LONELY, HUH?
WHEN IT WAS JUST SHI-CHAN AND ME...
MIYOOON!
OVER HERE, MIYON! I SAVED YOU A SEAT!
MRFF?
AH...
YUUKI!
CRIPES! YOU DON'T HAVE TO DO STUFF LIKE THAT FOR ME!
I KNOW, BUT I FIGURED YOU'D BE BY.
SO... YOU GUYS GONNA EAT IN THE CAFETERIA, TOO?

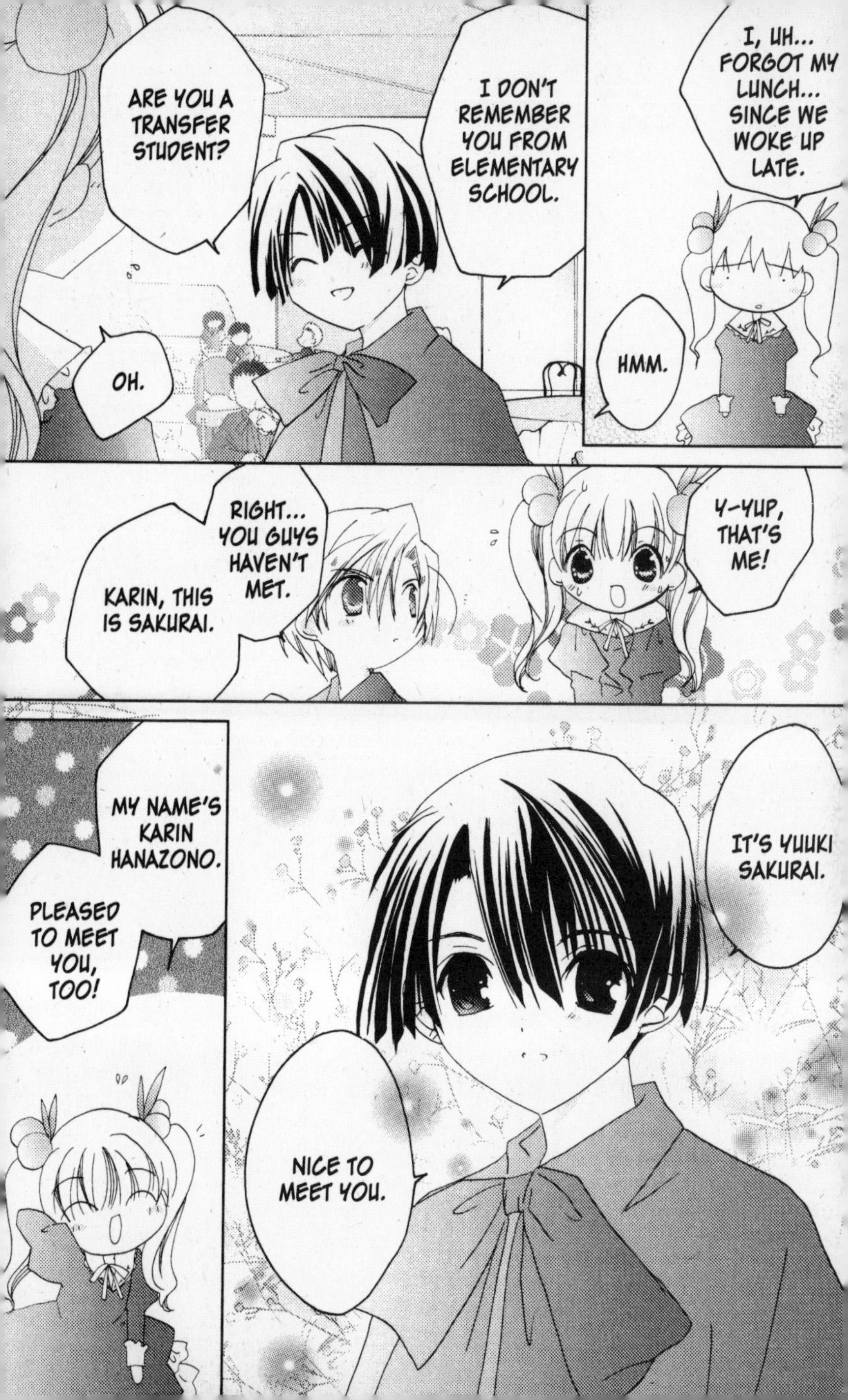
I, UH... FORGOT MY LUNCH... SINCE WE WOKE UP LATE.
HMM.
I DON'T REMEMBER YOU FROM ELEMENTARY SCHOOL.
ARE YOU A TRANSFER STUDENT?
OH.
Y-YUP, THAT'S ME!
RIGHT... YOU GUYS HAVEN'T MET.
KARIN, THIS IS SAKURAI.
IT'S YUUKI SAKURAI.
NICE TO MEET YOU.
MY NAME'S KARIN HANAZONO.
PLEASED TO MEET YOU, TOO!

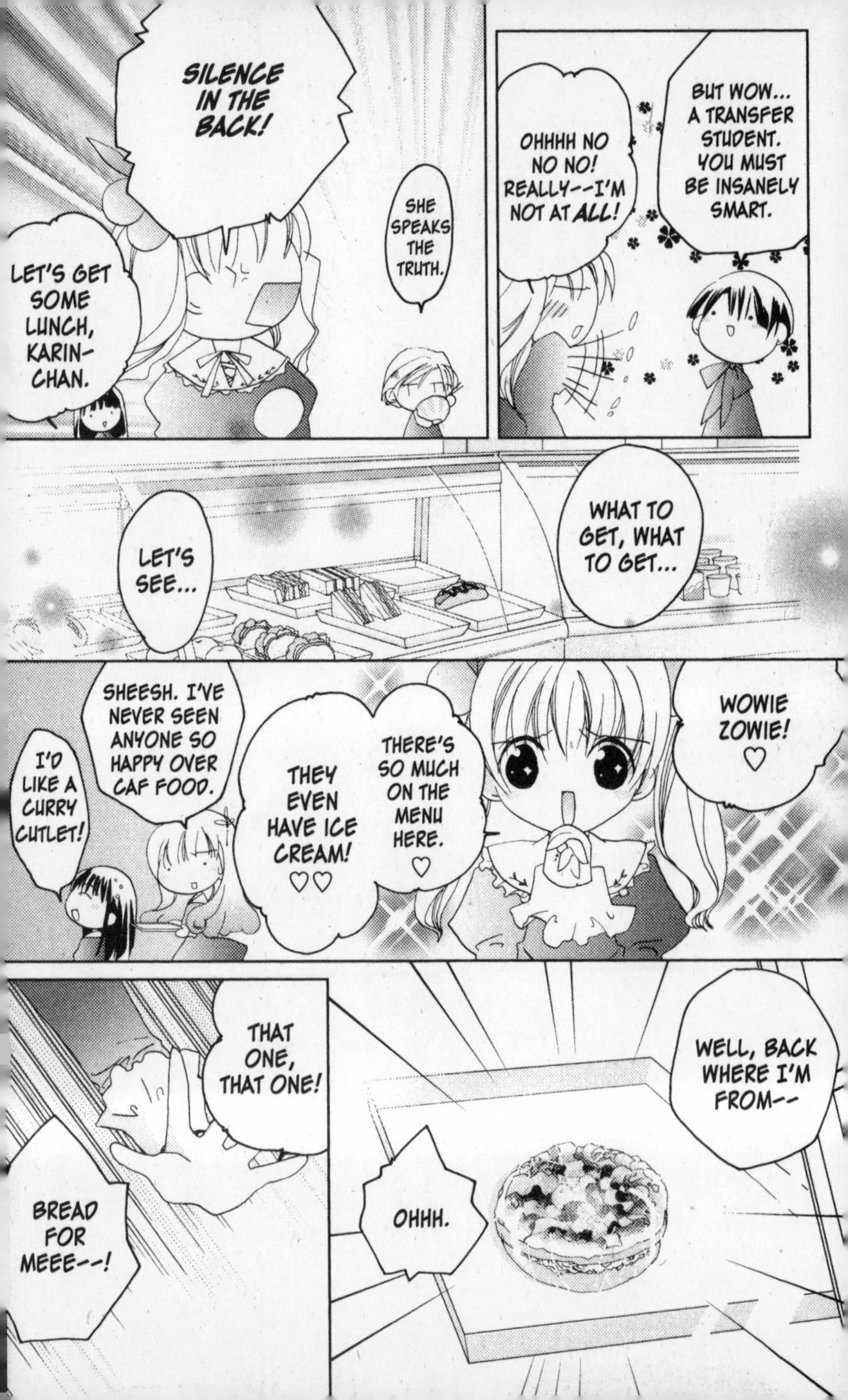
BUT WOW... A TRANSFER STUDENT. YOU MUST BE INSANELY SMART.
OHHHH NO NO NO! REALLY--I'M NOT AT ALL!
SHE SPEAKS THE TRUTH.
SILENCE IN THE BACK!
LET'S GET SOME LUNCH, KARIN-CHAN.
WHAT TO GET, WHAT TO GET...
LET'S SEE...
WOWIE ZOWIE! ♡
THERE'S SO MUCH ON THE MENU HERE. ♡
THEY EVEN HAVE ICE CREAM! ♡♡
SHEESH. I'VE NEVER SEEN ANYONE SO HAPPY OVER CAF FOOD.
I'D LIKE A CURRY CUTLET!
WELL, BACK WHERE I'M FROM--
OHHH.
THAT ONE, THAT ONE!
BREAD FOR MEEE--!

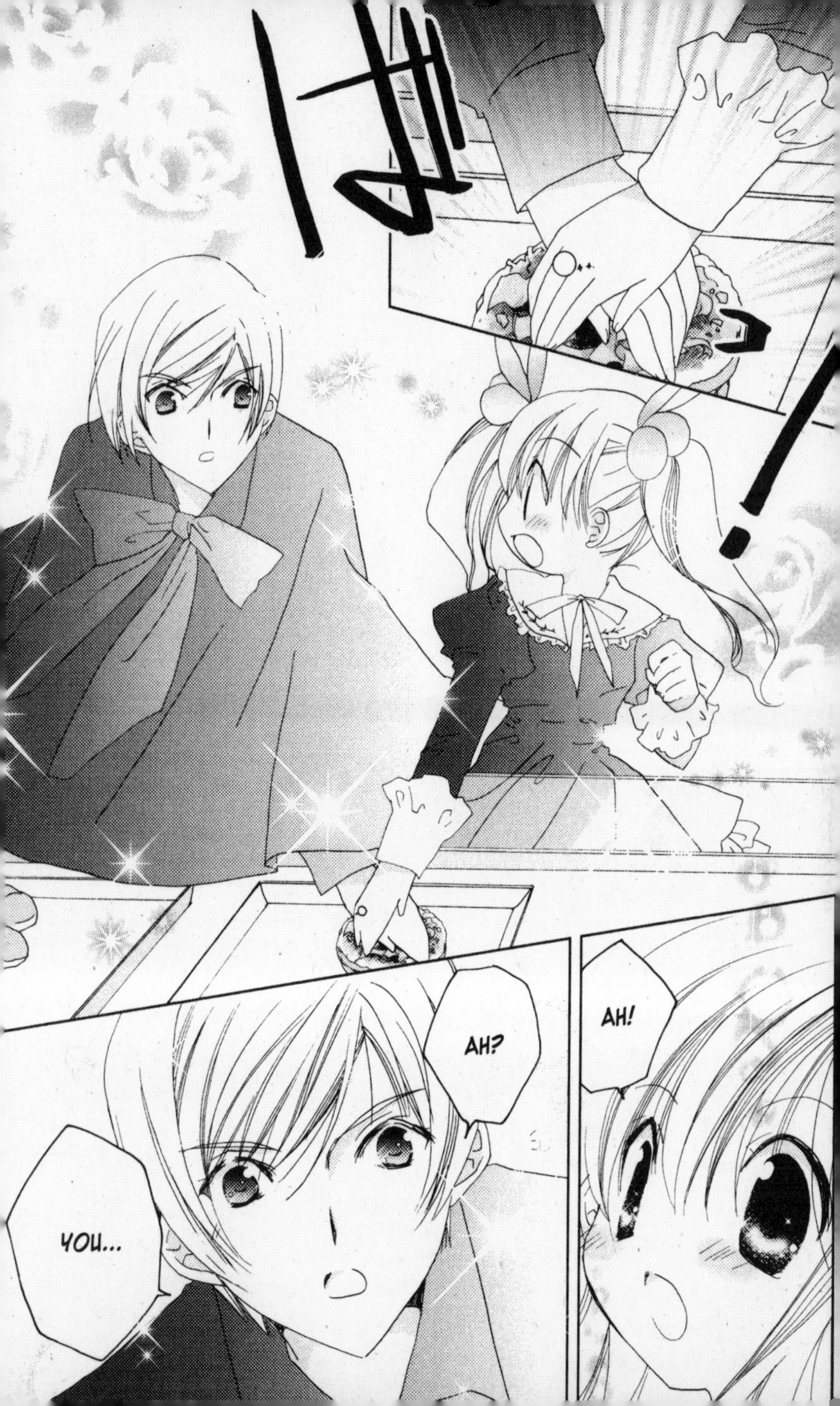
AH!
AH?
YOU...

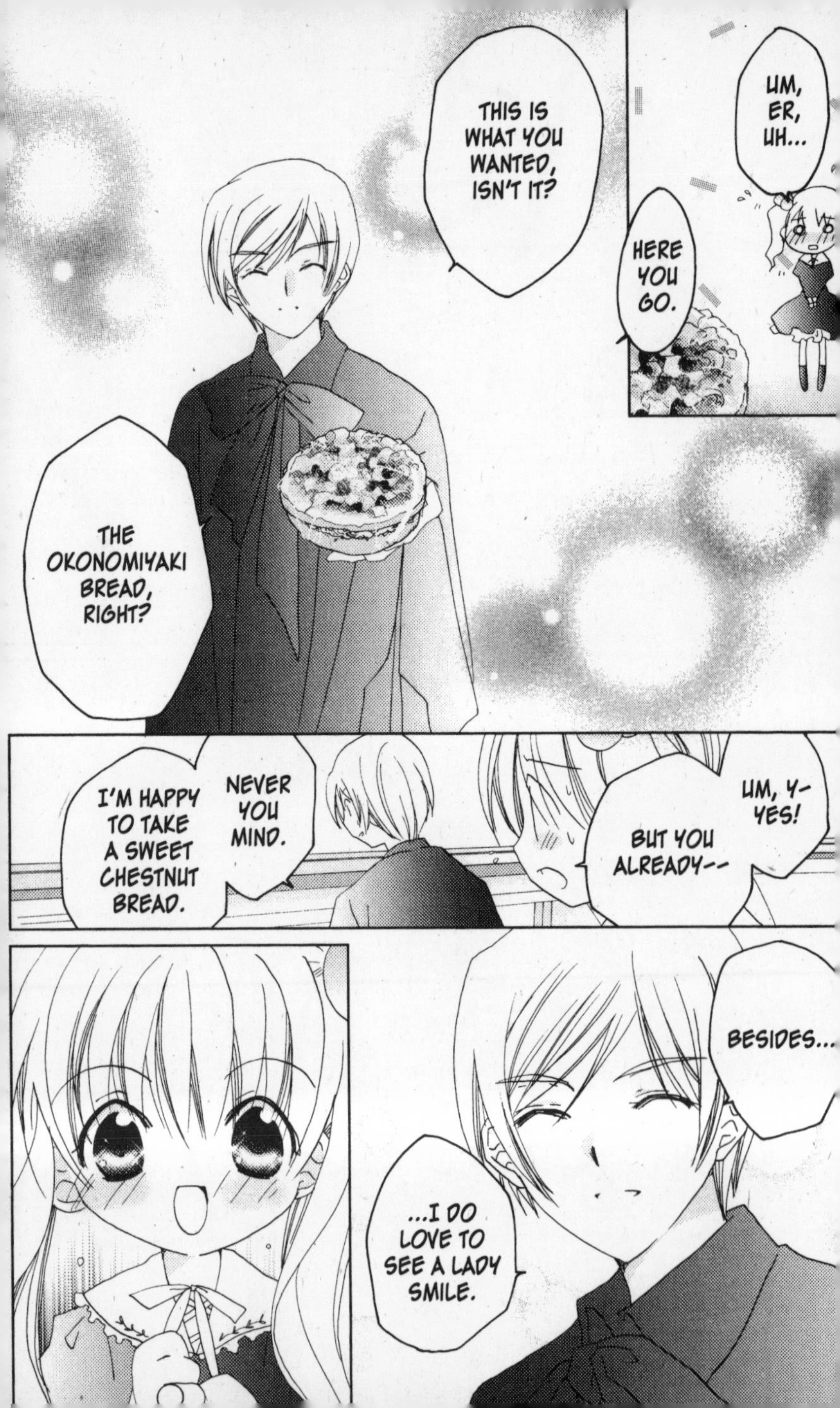
UM, ER, UH...
HERE YOU GO.
THIS IS WHAT YOU WANTED, ISN'T IT?
THE OKONOMIYAKI BREAD, RIGHT?
UM, Y-YES!
BUT YOU ALREADY--
NEVER YOU MIND.
I'M HAPPY TO TAKE A SWEET CHESTNUT BREAD.
BESIDES...
...I DO LOVE TO SEE A LADY SMILE.

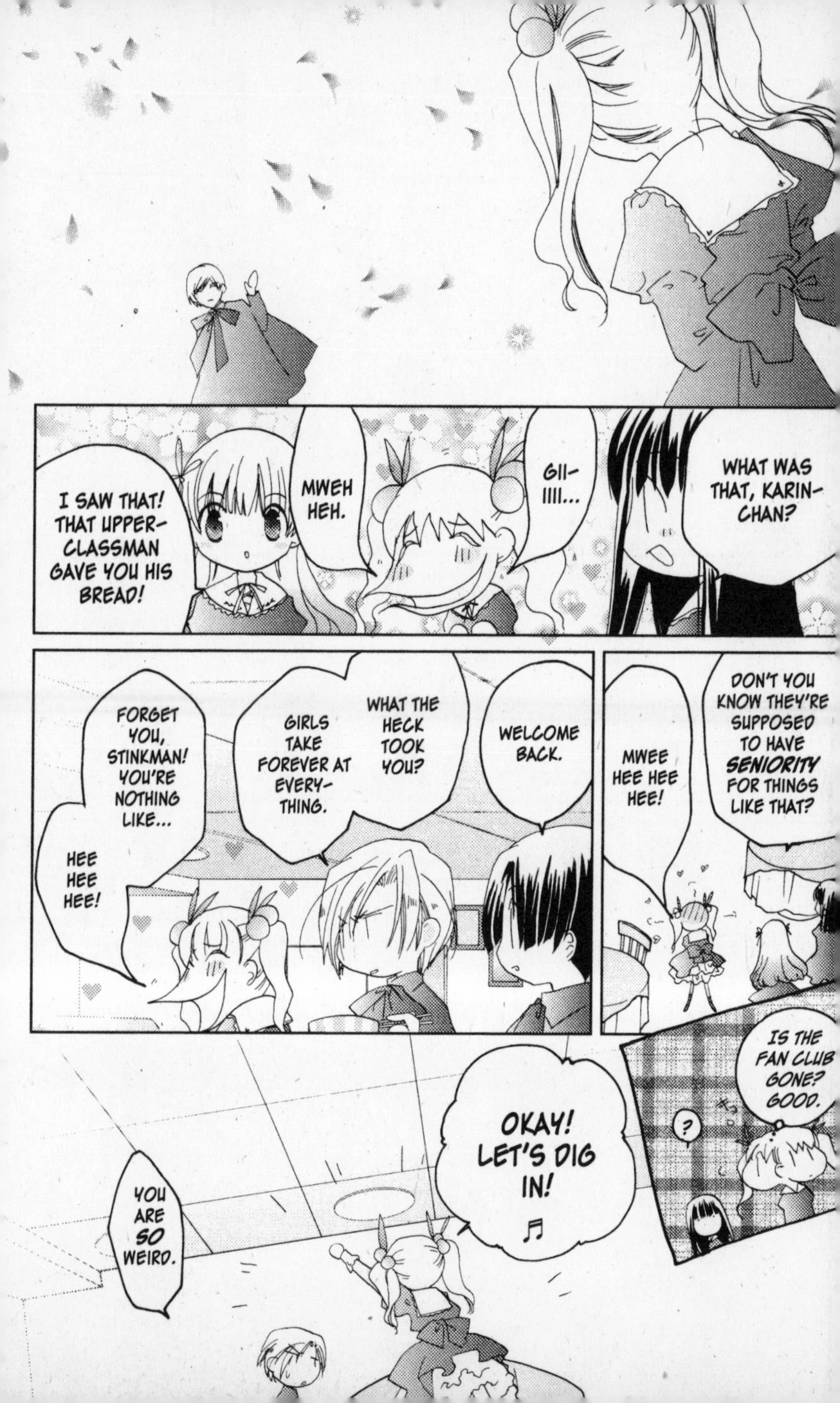
WHAT WAS THAT, KARIN-CHAN?
GII-IIII...
MWEH HEH.
I SAW THAT! THAT UPPER-CLASSMAN GAVE YOU HIS BREAD!
DON'T YOU KNOW THEY'RE SUPPOSED TO HAVE SENIORITY FOR THINGS LIKE THAT?
MWEE HEE HEE HEE!
WELCOME BACK.
WHAT THE HECK TOOK YOU?
GIRLS TAKE FOREVER AT EVERY-THING.
FORGET YOU, STINKMAN! YOU'RE NOTHING LIKE...
HEE HEE HEE!
IS THE FAN CLUB GONE? GOOD.
?
OKAY! LET'S DIG IN! ♫
YOU ARE SO WEIRD.

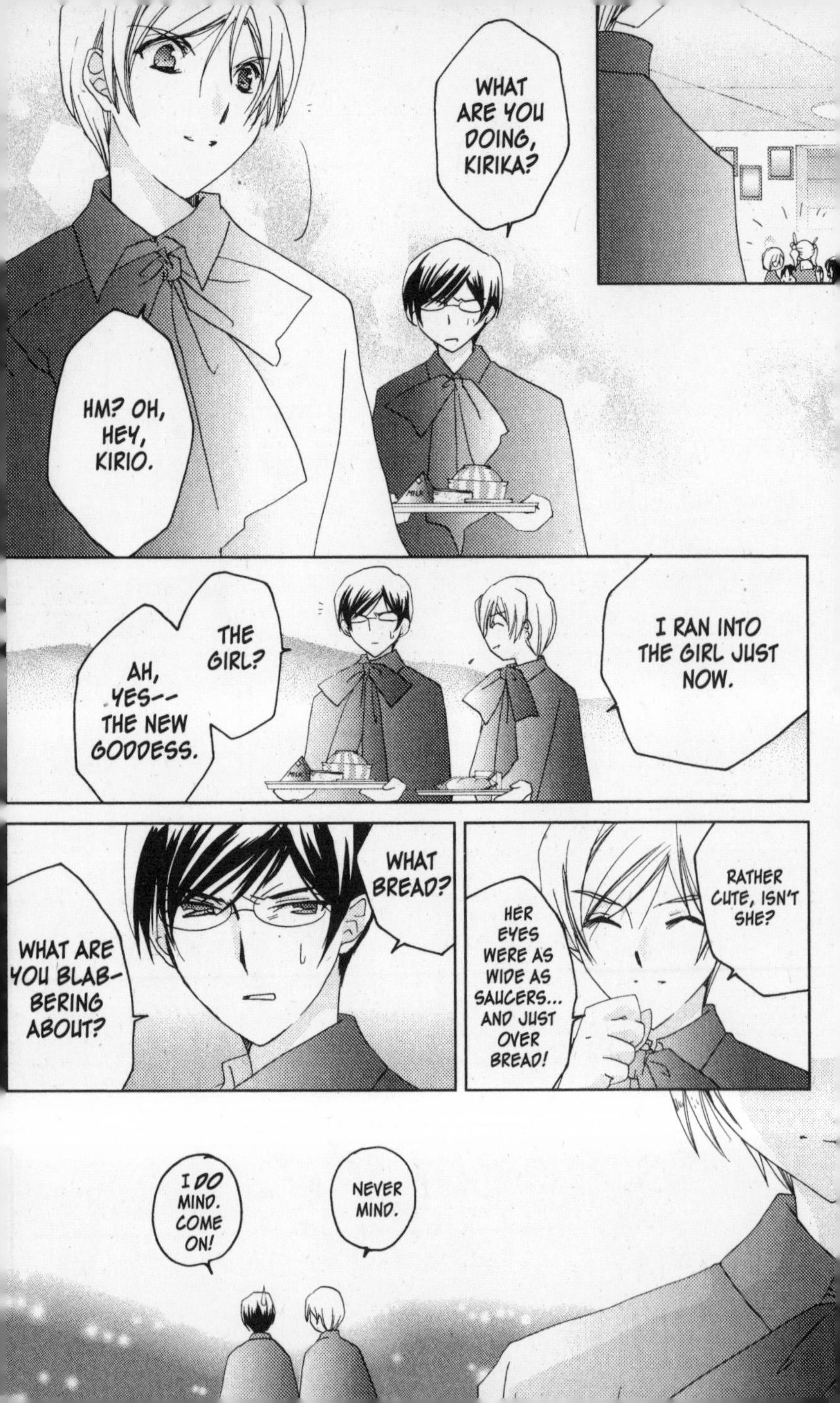
WHAT ARE YOU DOING, KIRIKA?
HM? OH, HEY, KIRIO.
I RAN INTO THE GIRL JUST NOW.
THE GIRL?
AH, YES-- THE NEW GODDESS.
RATHER CUTE, ISN'T SHE?
HER EYES WERE AS WIDE AS SAUCERS... AND JUST OVER BREAD!
WHAT BREAD?
WHAT ARE YOU BLAB-BERING ABOUT?
NEVER MIND.
I DO MIND. COME ON!

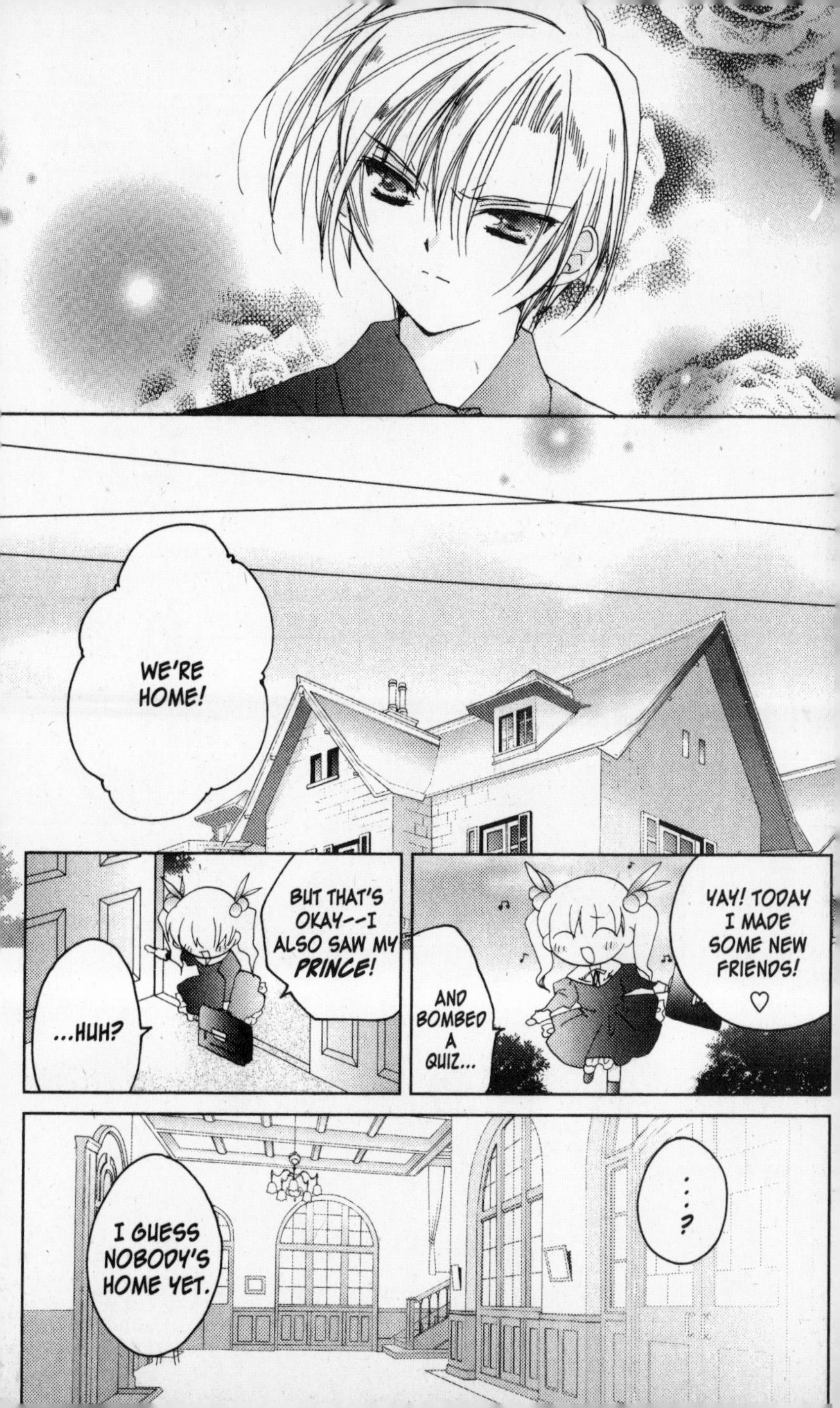
WE'RE HOME!
YAY! TODAY I MADE SOME NEW FRIENDS! ♡
AND BOMBED A QUIZ...
BUT THAT'S OKAY--I ALSO SAW MY *PRINCE*!
...HUH?
...?
I GUESS NOBODY'S HOME YET.

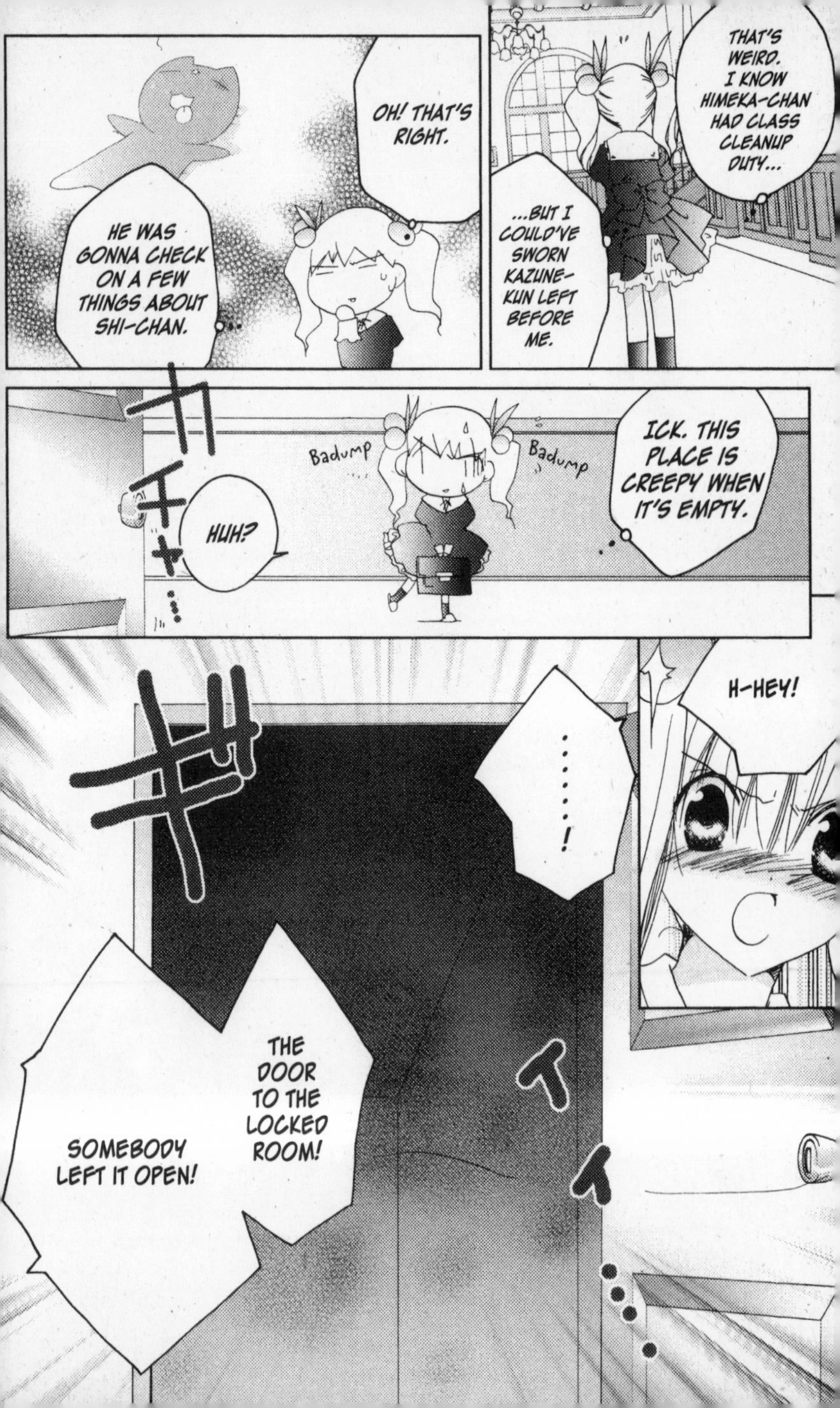
THAT'S WEIRD. I KNOW HIMEKA-CHAN HAD CLASS CLEANUP DUTY...
...BUT I COULD'VE SWORN KAZUNE-KUN LEFT BEFORE ME.
OH! THAT'S RIGHT.
HE WAS GONNA CHECK ON A FEW THINGS ABOUT SHI-CHAN.
ICK. THIS PLACE IS CREEPY WHEN IT'S EMPTY.
Badump
Badump
HUH?
H-HEY!
......!
THE DOOR TO THE LOCKED ROOM!
SOMEBODY LEFT IT OPEN!

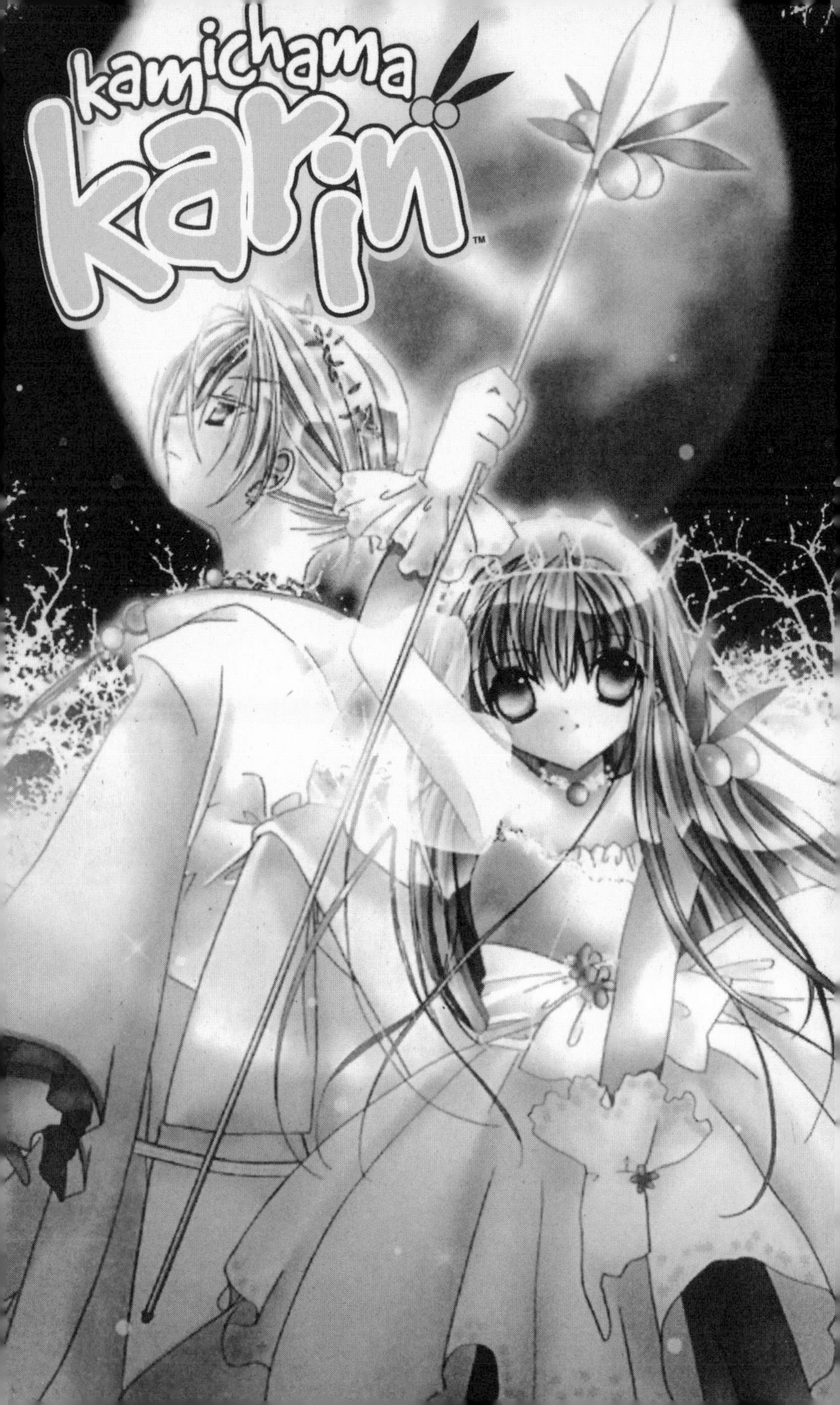
kamichama karin™

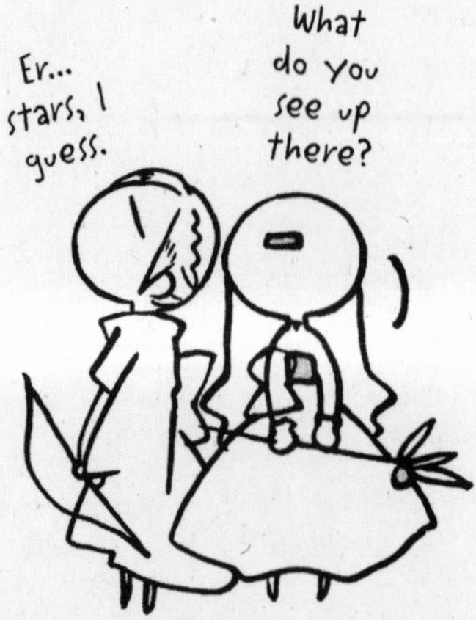
What do you see up there?
Er... stars, I guess.

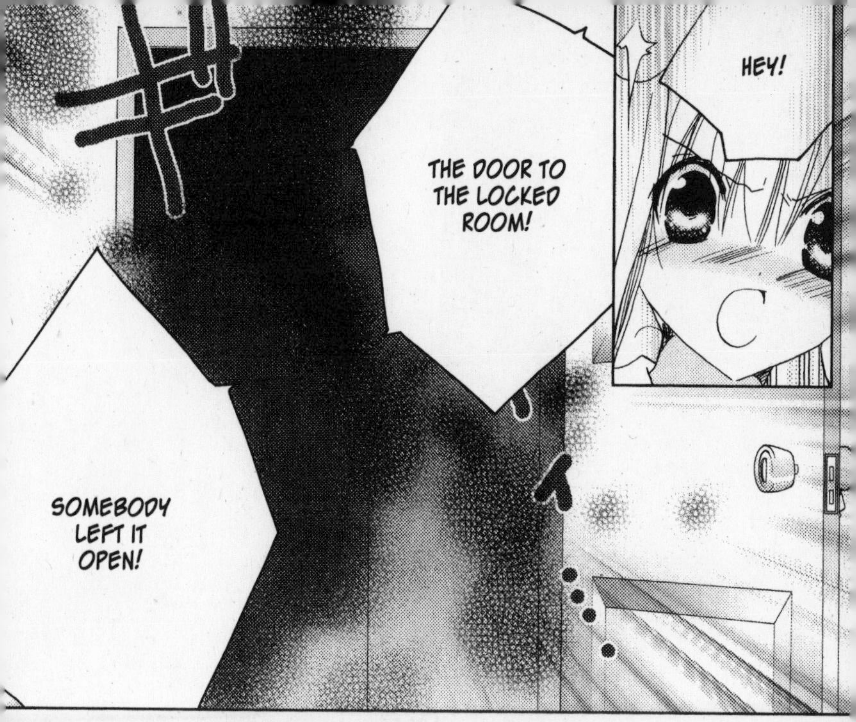
HEY!
THE DOOR TO THE LOCKED ROOM!
SOMEBODY LEFT IT OPEN!

I can't shake the feeling that some-thing used to be here!

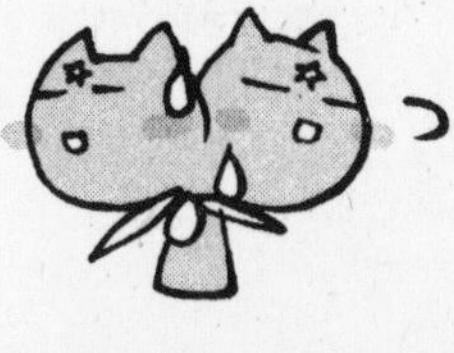

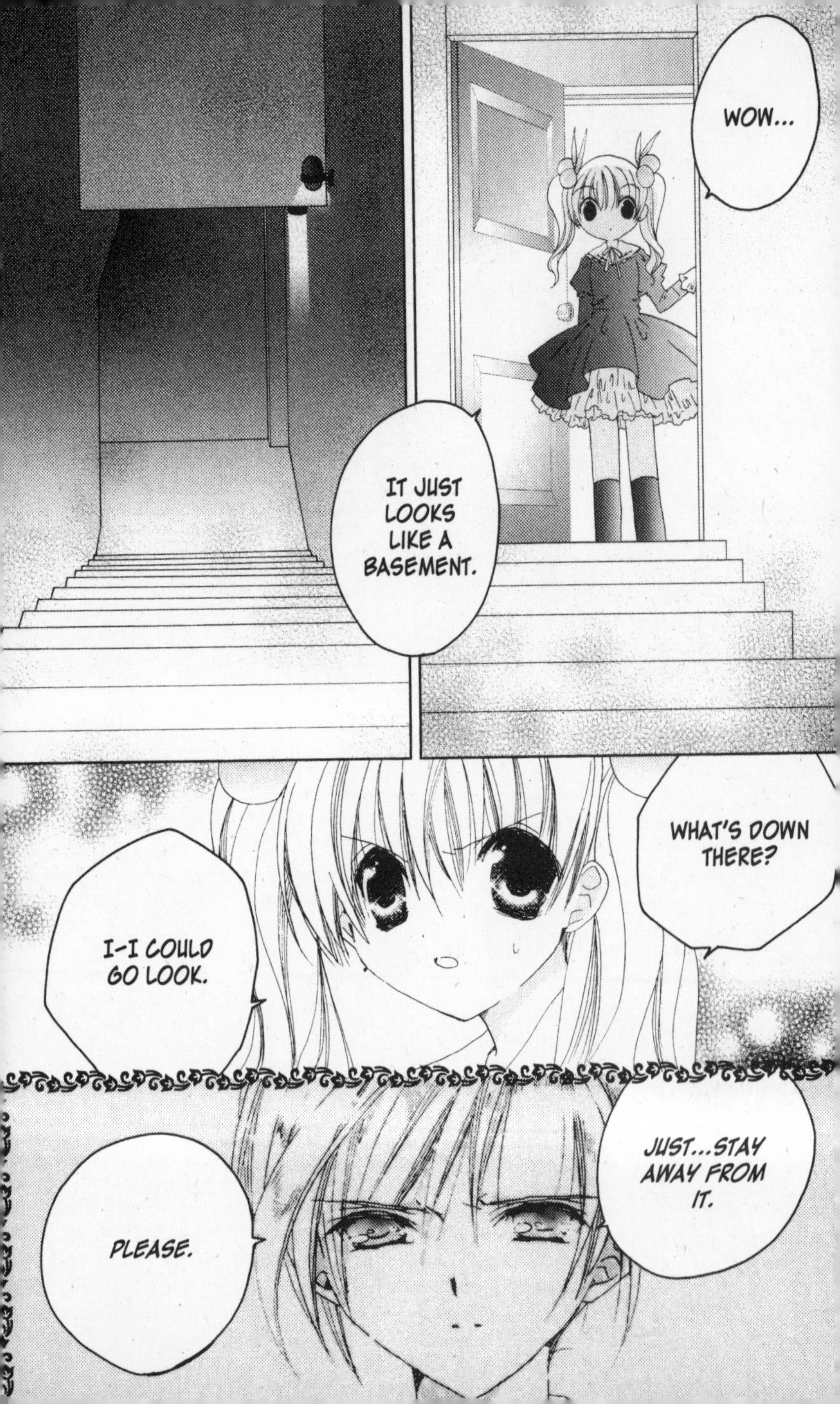
WOW...
IT JUST LOOKS LIKE A BASEMENT.
WHAT'S DOWN THERE?
I-I COULD GO LOOK.
JUST...STAY AWAY FROM IT.
PLEASE.

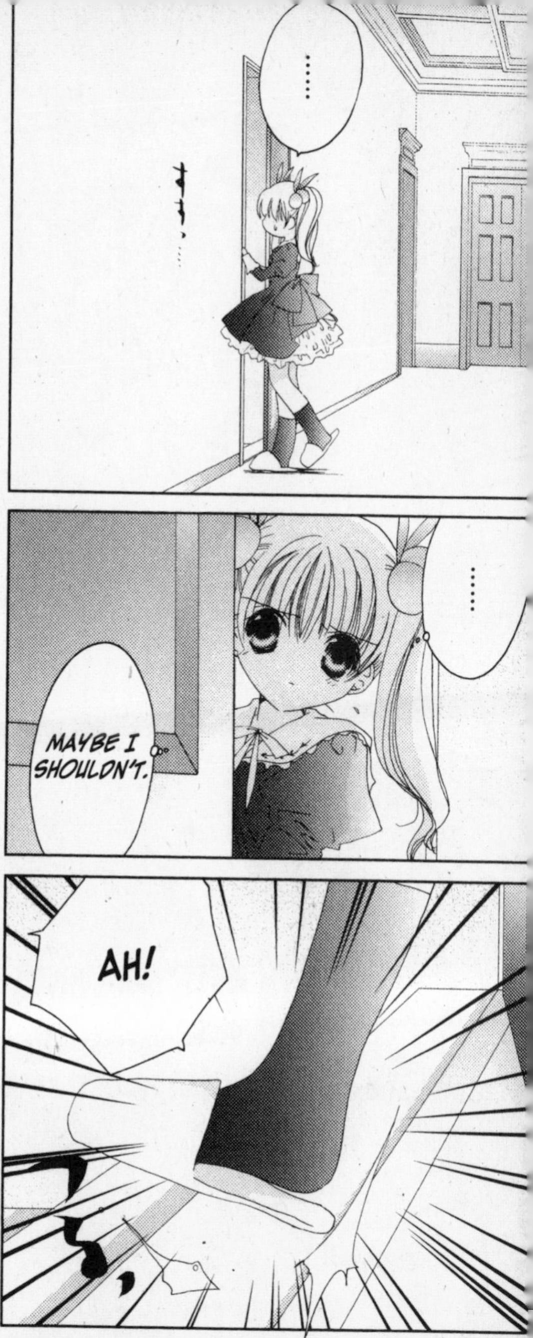
......
......
MAYBE I SHOULDN'T.
AH!
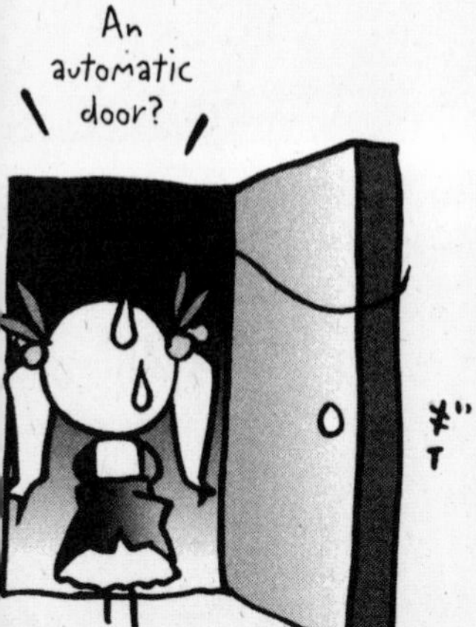
An automatic door?

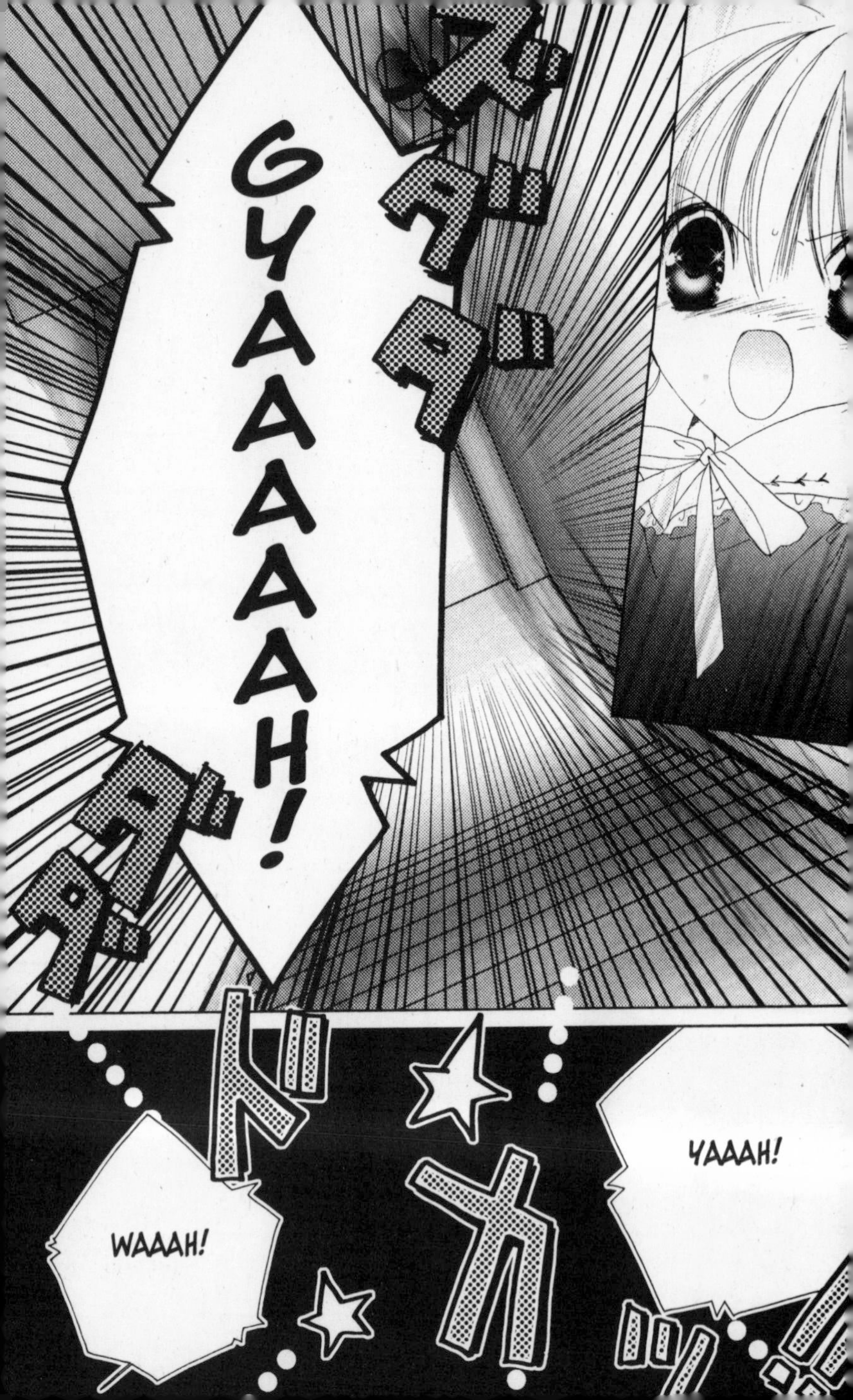
GYAAAAAH!
YAAAH!
WAAAH!

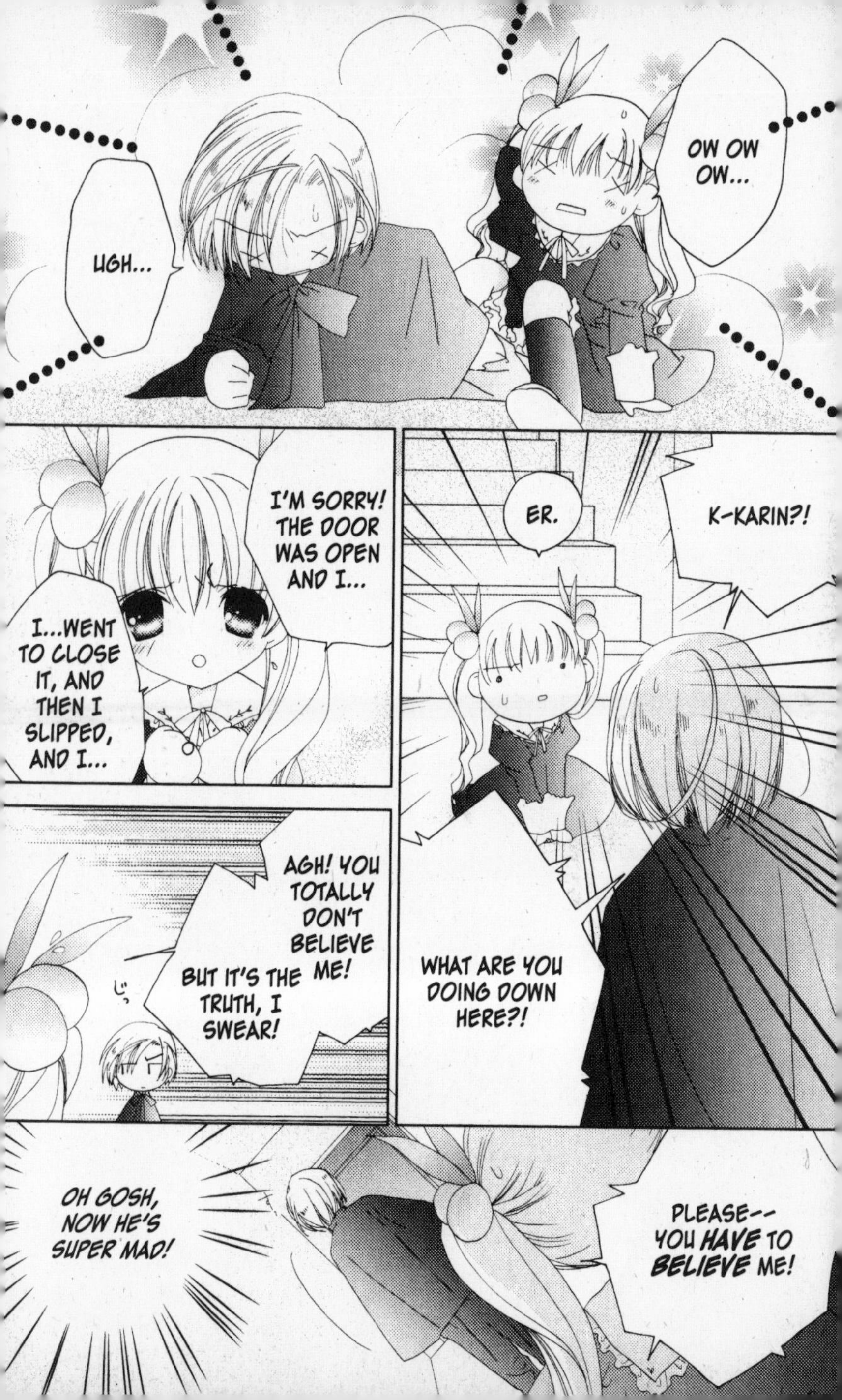
OW OW OW...
UGH...
K-KARIN?!
ER.
WHAT ARE YOU DOING DOWN HERE?!
I'M SORRY! THE DOOR WAS OPEN AND I...
I...WENT TO CLOSE IT, AND THEN I SLIPPED, AND I...
AGH! YOU TOTALLY DON'T BELIEVE ME!
BUT IT'S THE TRUTH, I SWEAR!
じっ
PLEASE-- YOU HAVE TO BELIEVE ME!
OH GOSH, NOW HE'S SUPER MAD!

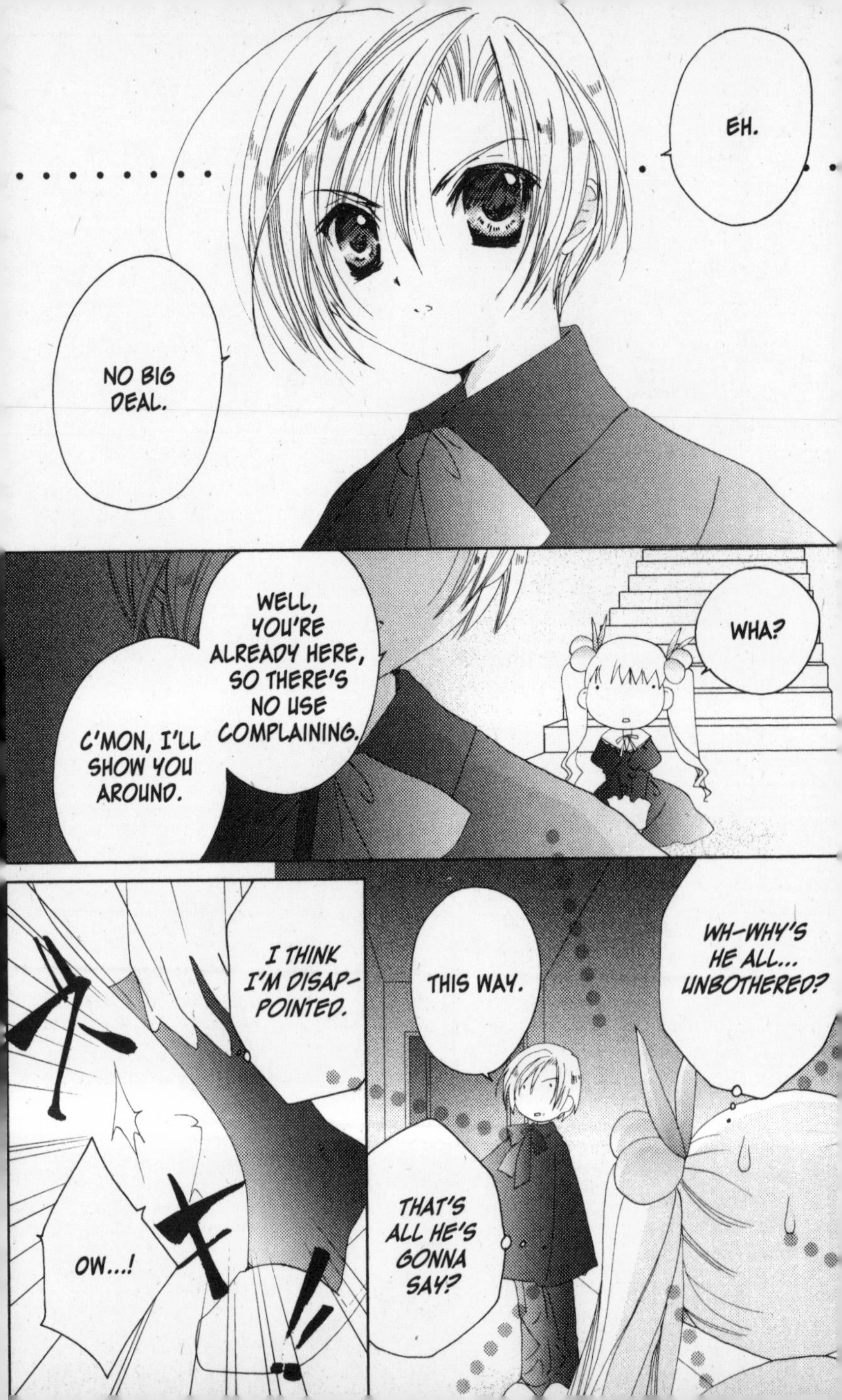
EH.
NO BIG DEAL.
WHA?
WELL, YOU'RE ALREADY HERE, SO THERE'S NO USE COMPLAINING.
C'MON, I'LL SHOW YOU AROUND.
WH-WHY'S HE ALL... UNBOTHERED?
THIS WAY.
THAT'S ALL HE'S GONNA SAY?
I THINK I'M DISAP-POINTED.
OW...!

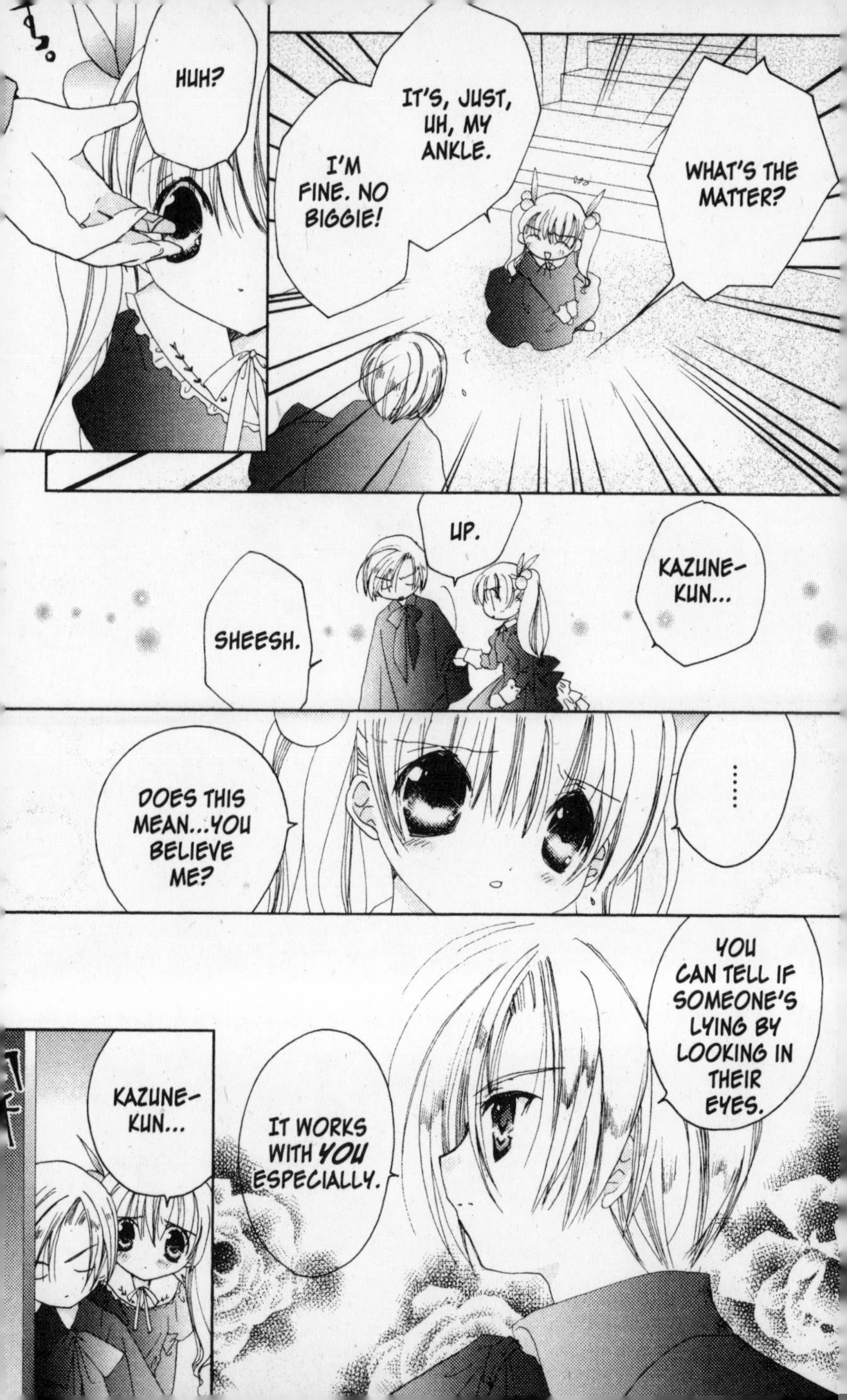
WHAT'S THE MATTER?
IT'S, JUST, UH, MY ANKLE.
I'M FINE. NO BIGGIE!
HUH?
KAZUNE-KUN...
UP.
SHEESH.
......
DOES THIS MEAN...YOU BELIEVE ME?
YOU CAN TELL IF SOMEONE'S LYING BY LOOKING IN THEIR EYES.
IT WORKS WITH *YOU* ESPECIALLY.
KAZUNE-KUN...

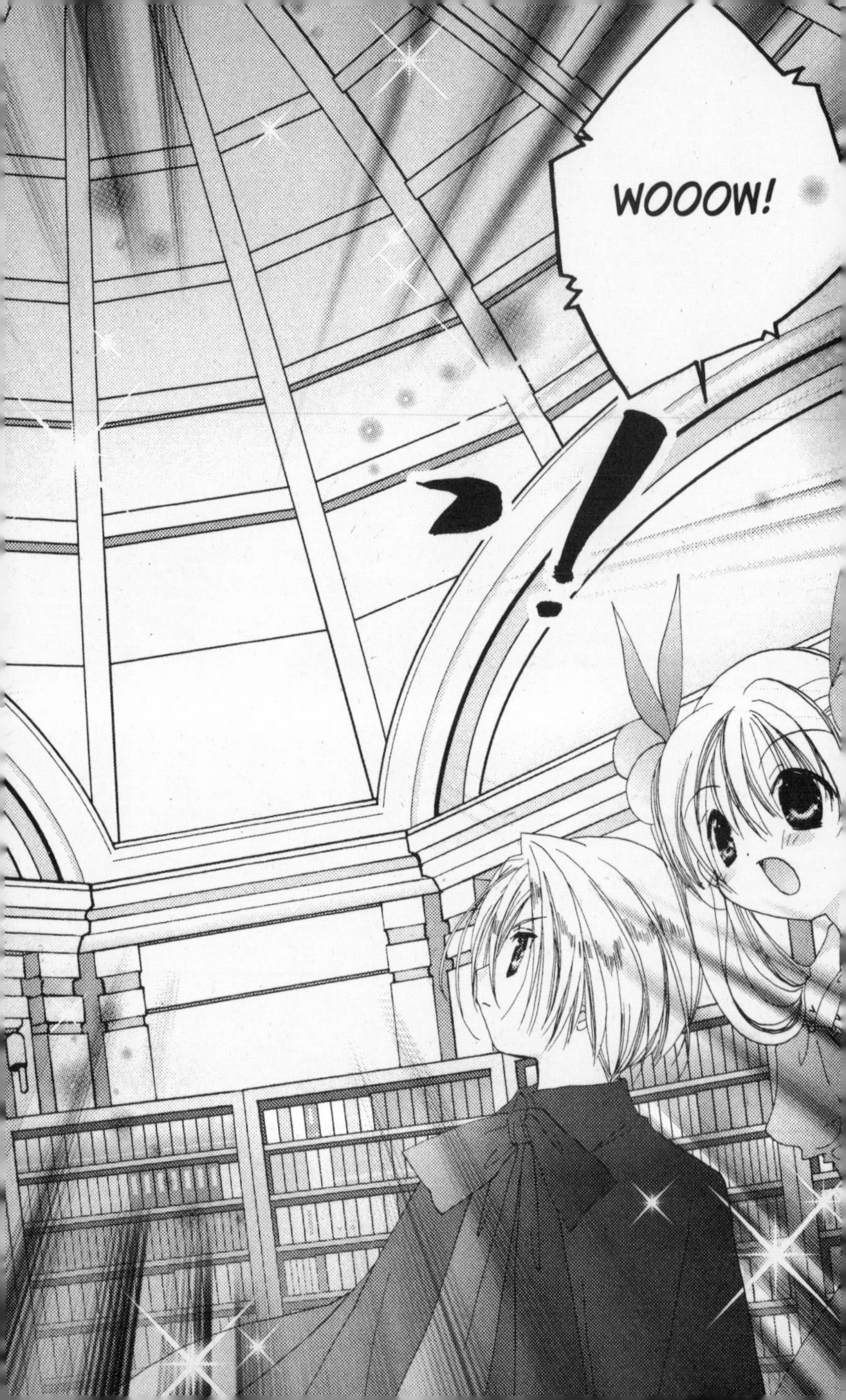
WOOOW!

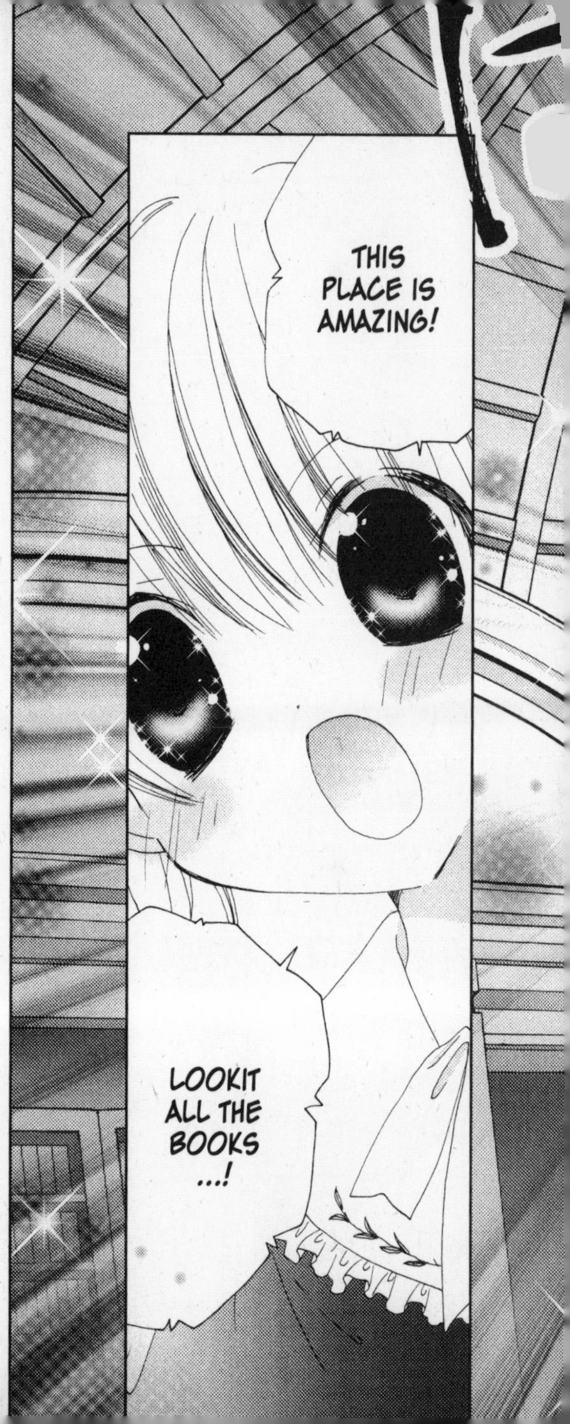
THIS PLACE IS AMAZING!
LOOKIT ALL THE BOOKS ...!

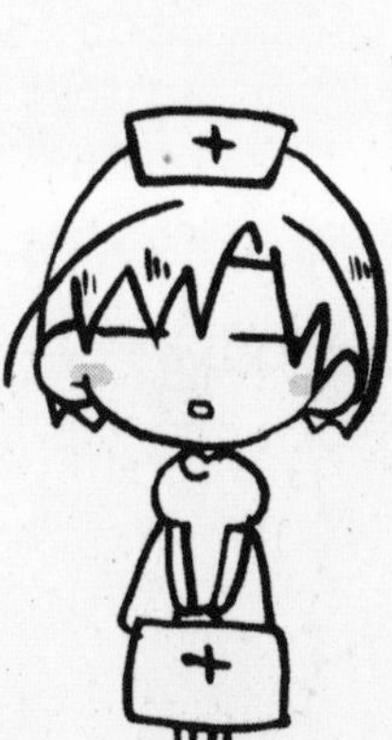

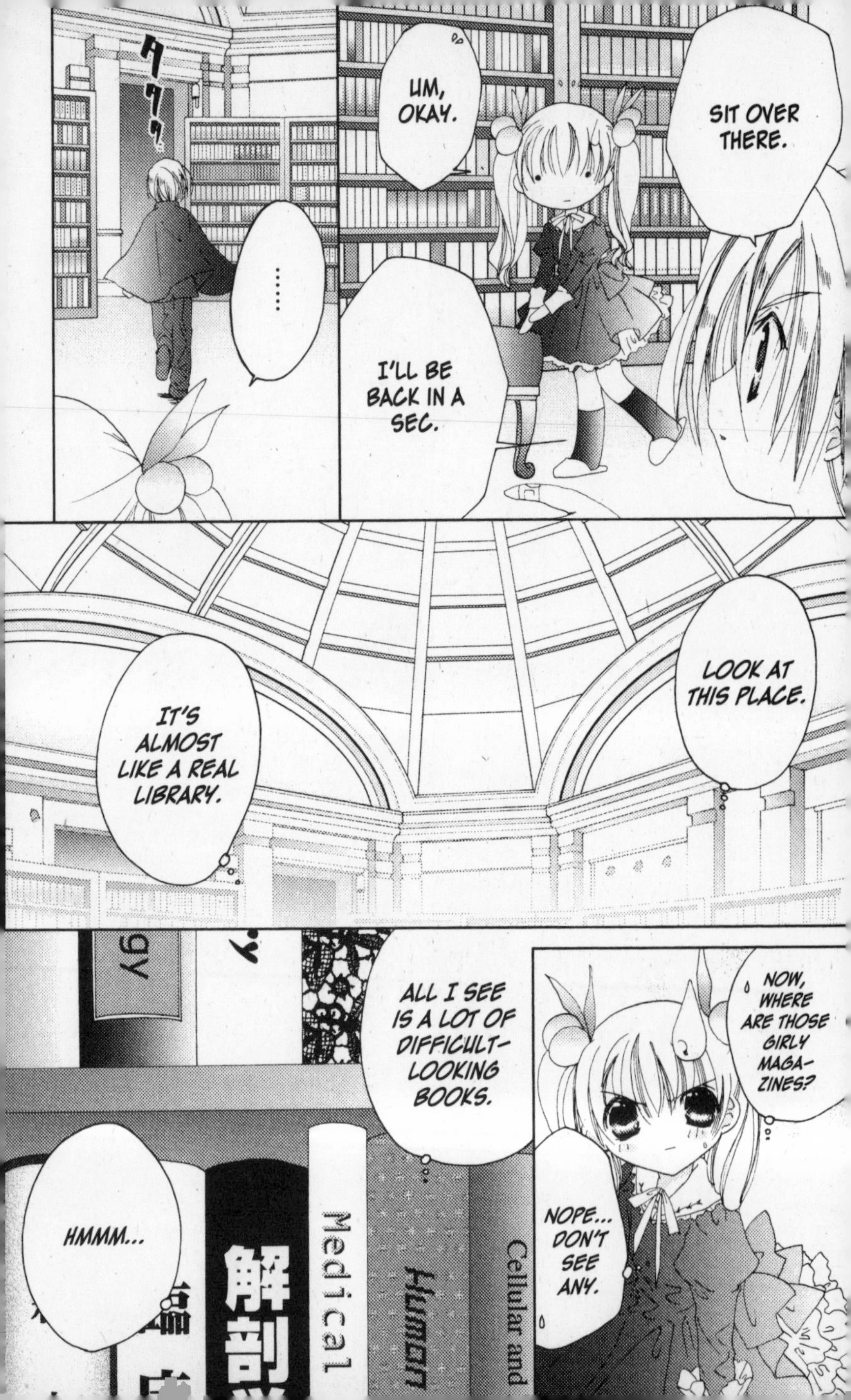
SIT OVER THERE.
UM, OKAY.
I'LL BE BACK IN A SEC.
......
タタタ
LOOK AT THIS PLACE.
IT'S ALMOST LIKE A REAL LIBRARY.
NOW, WHERE ARE THOSE GIRLY MAGAZINES?
NOPE... DON'T SEE ANY.
Cellular and
ALL I SEE IS A LOT OF DIFFICULT-LOOKING BOOKS.
Human
Medical
解剖
gy
HMMM...

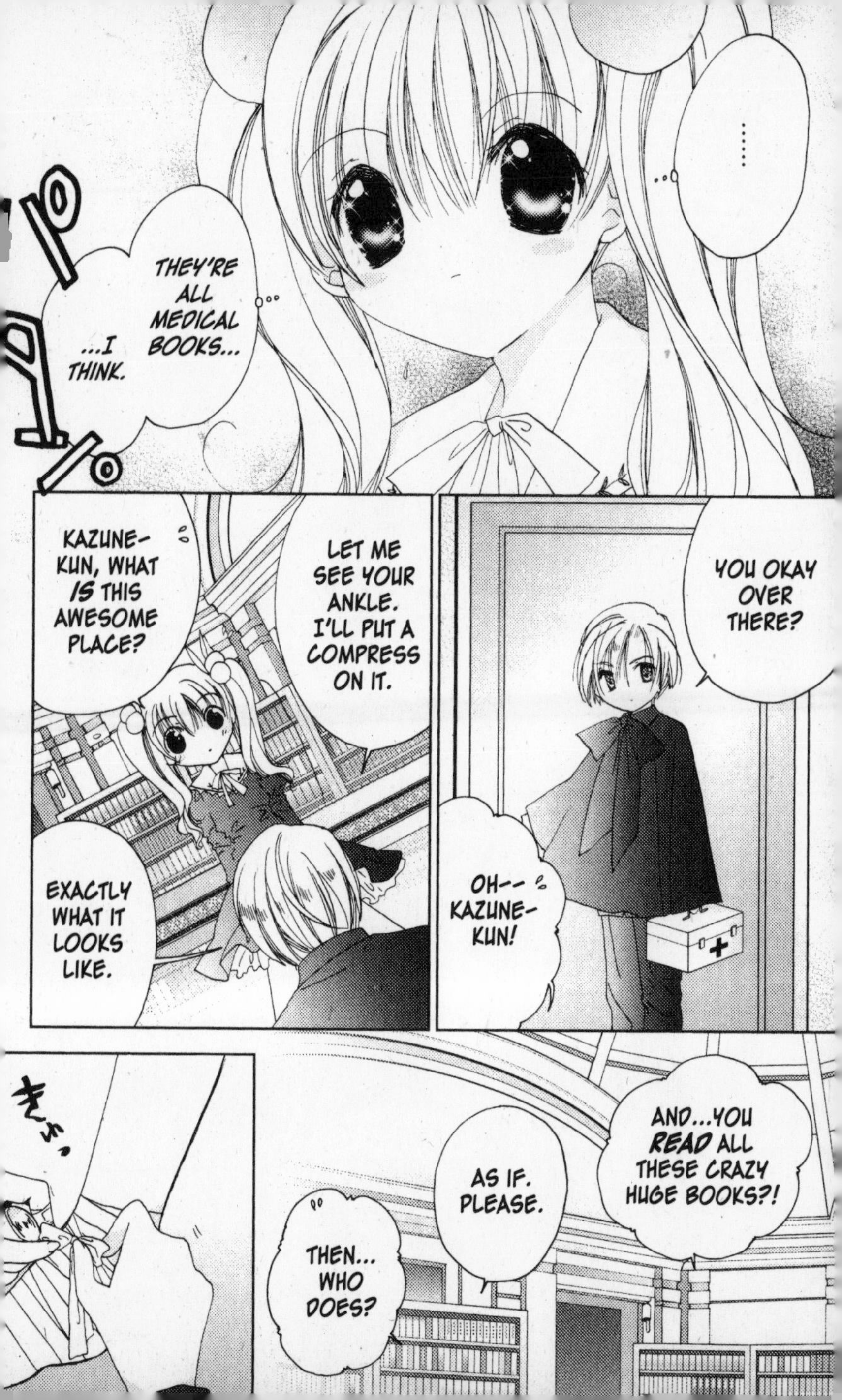
......
THEY'RE ALL MEDICAL BOOKS... ...I THINK.
YOU OKAY OVER THERE?
OH-- KAZUNE-KUN!
LET ME SEE YOUR ANKLE. I'LL PUT A COMPRESS ON IT.
KAZUNE-KUN, WHAT *IS* THIS AWESOME PLACE?
EXACTLY WHAT IT LOOKS LIKE.
AND...YOU *READ* ALL THESE CRAZY HUGE BOOKS?!
AS IF. PLEASE.
THEN... WHO DOES?

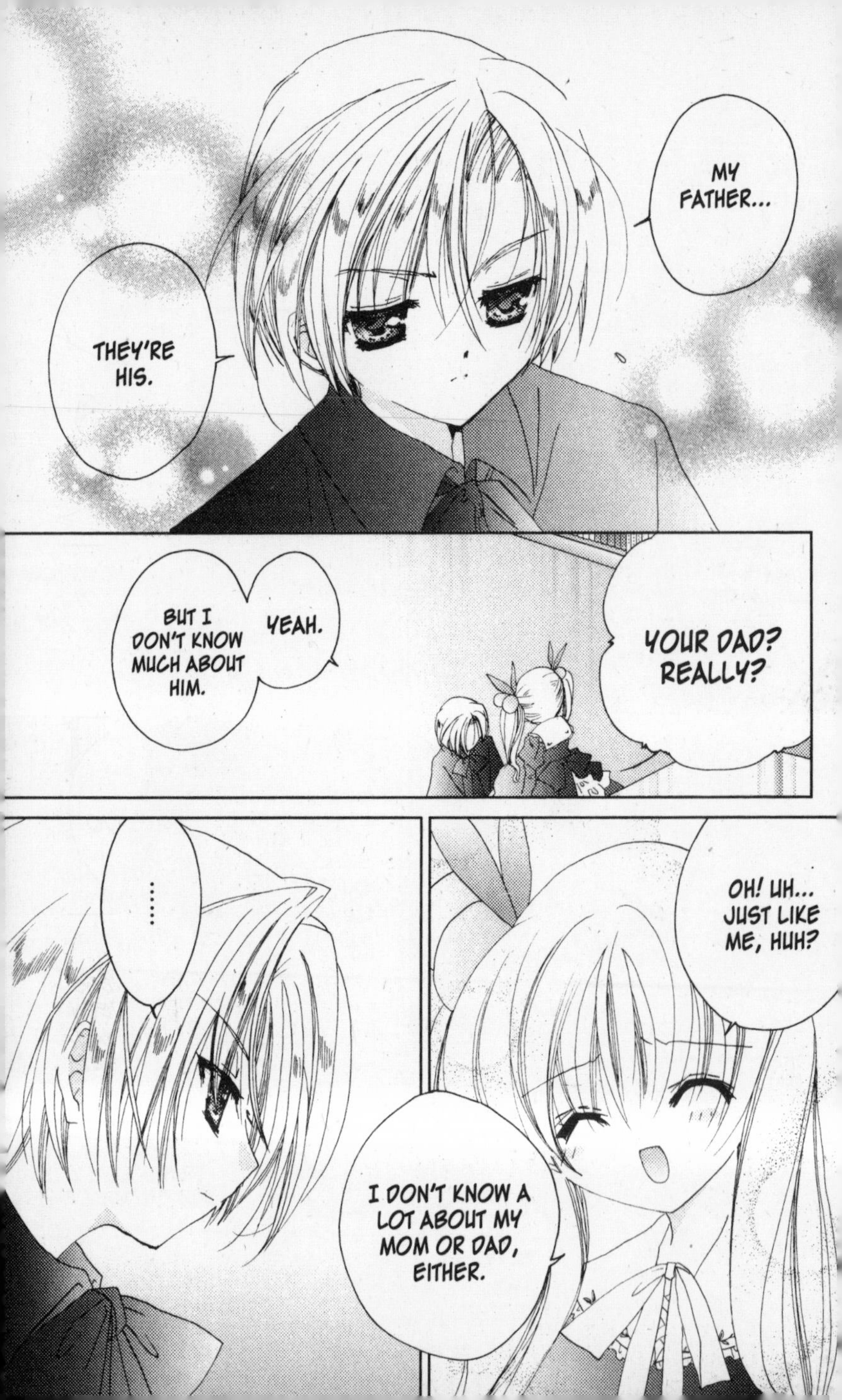
MY FATHER...
THEY'RE HIS.
YOUR DAD? REALLY?
YEAH.
BUT I DON'T KNOW MUCH ABOUT HIM.
OH! UH... JUST LIKE ME, HUH?
I DON'T KNOW A LOT ABOUT MY MOM OR DAD, EITHER.
......

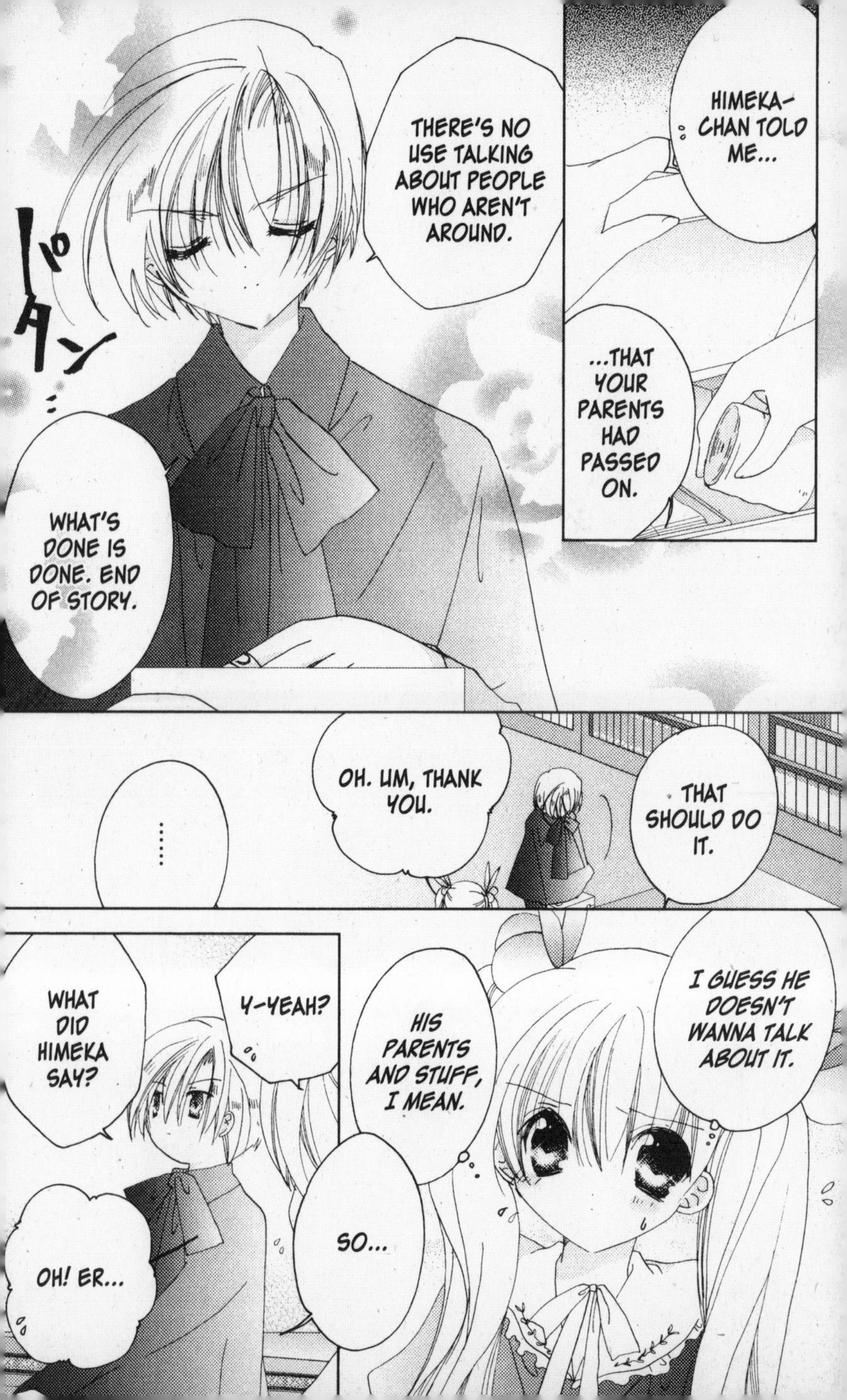
HIMEKA-CHAN TOLD ME...
...THAT YOUR PARENTS HAD PASSED ON.
THERE'S NO USE TALKING ABOUT PEOPLE WHO AREN'T AROUND.
パタン
WHAT'S DONE IS DONE. END OF STORY.
THAT SHOULD DO IT.
OH. UM, THANK YOU.
......
I GUESS HE DOESN'T WANNA TALK ABOUT IT.
HIS PARENTS AND STUFF, I MEAN.
SO...
Y-YEAH?
WHAT DID HIMEKA SAY?
OH! ER...

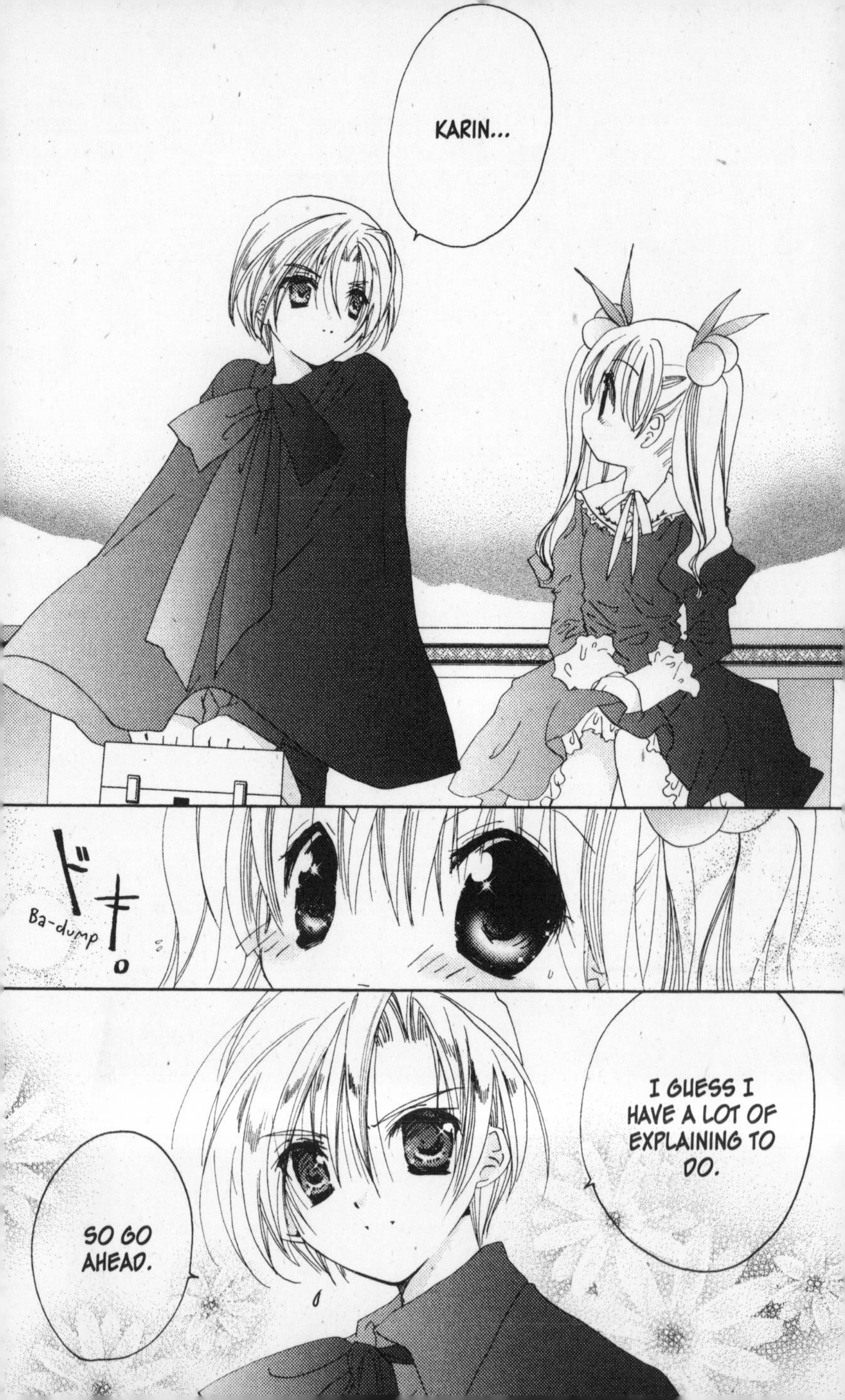
KARIN...
ドキ
Ba-dump
I GUESS I HAVE A LOT OF EXPLAINING TO DO.
SO GO AHEAD.

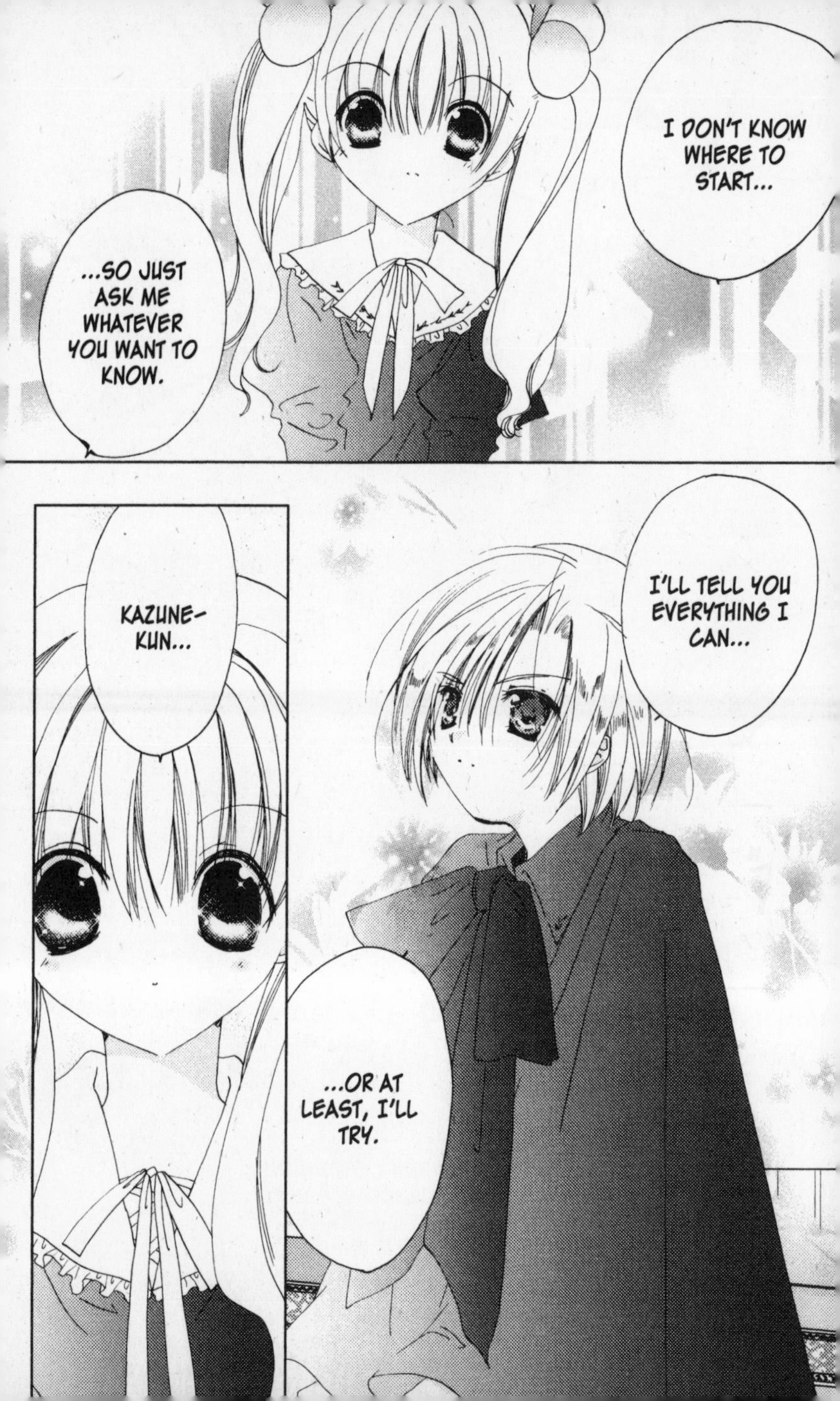
I DON'T KNOW WHERE TO START...
...SO JUST ASK ME WHATEVER YOU WANT TO KNOW.
I'LL TELL YOU EVERYTHING I CAN...
...OR AT LEAST, I'LL TRY.
KAZUNE-KUN...

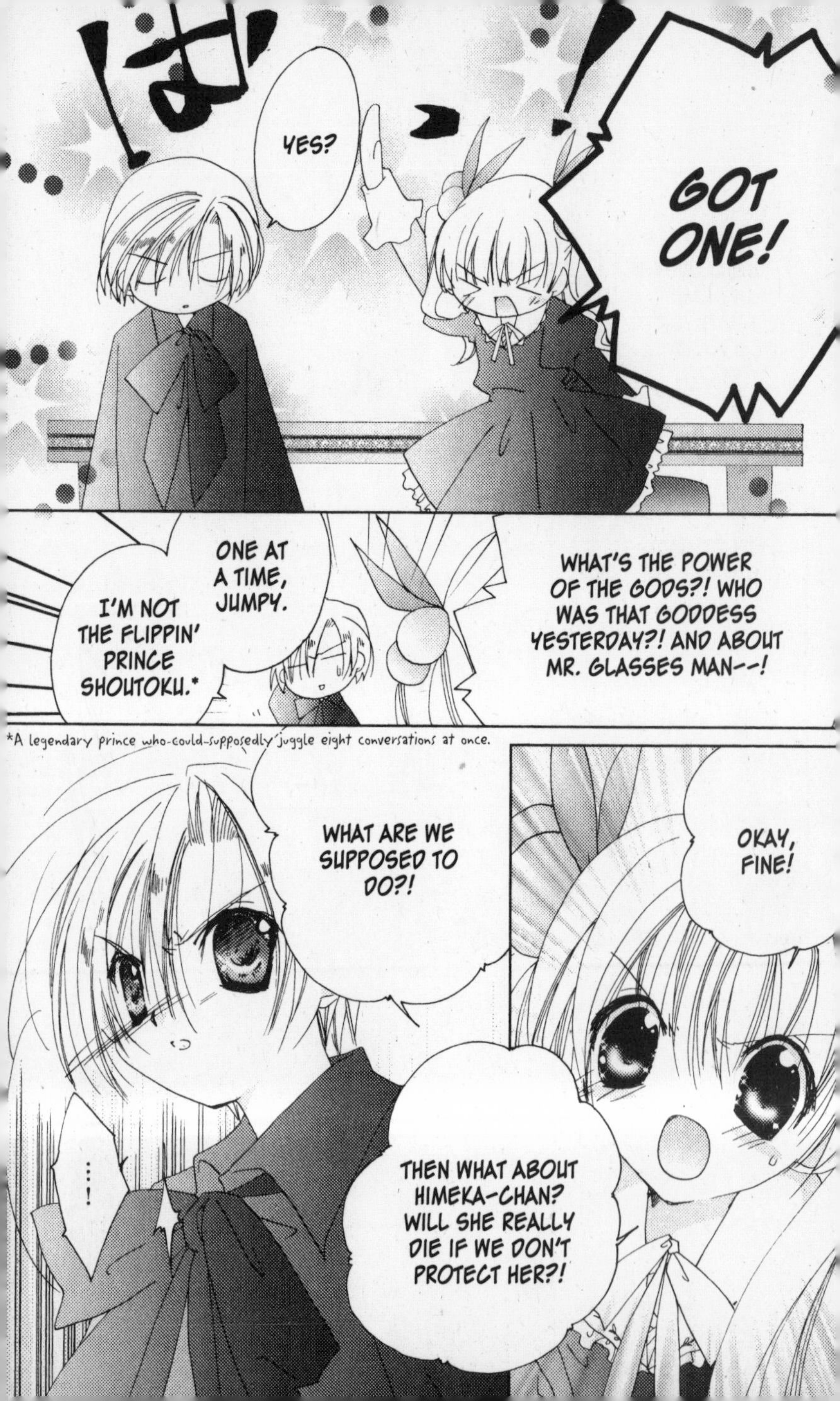
GOT ONE!
ぱ!
YES?
WHAT'S THE POWER OF THE GODS?! WHO WAS THAT GODDESS YESTERDAY?! AND ABOUT MR. GLASSES MAN--!
ONE AT A TIME, JUMPY.
I'M NOT THE FLIPPIN' PRINCE SHOUTOKU.*
OKAY, FINE!
THEN WHAT ABOUT HIMEKA-CHAN? WILL SHE REALLY DIE IF WE DON'T PROTECT HER?!
WHAT ARE WE SUPPOSED TO DO?!
...!

*A legendary prince who could supposedly juggle eight conversations at once.

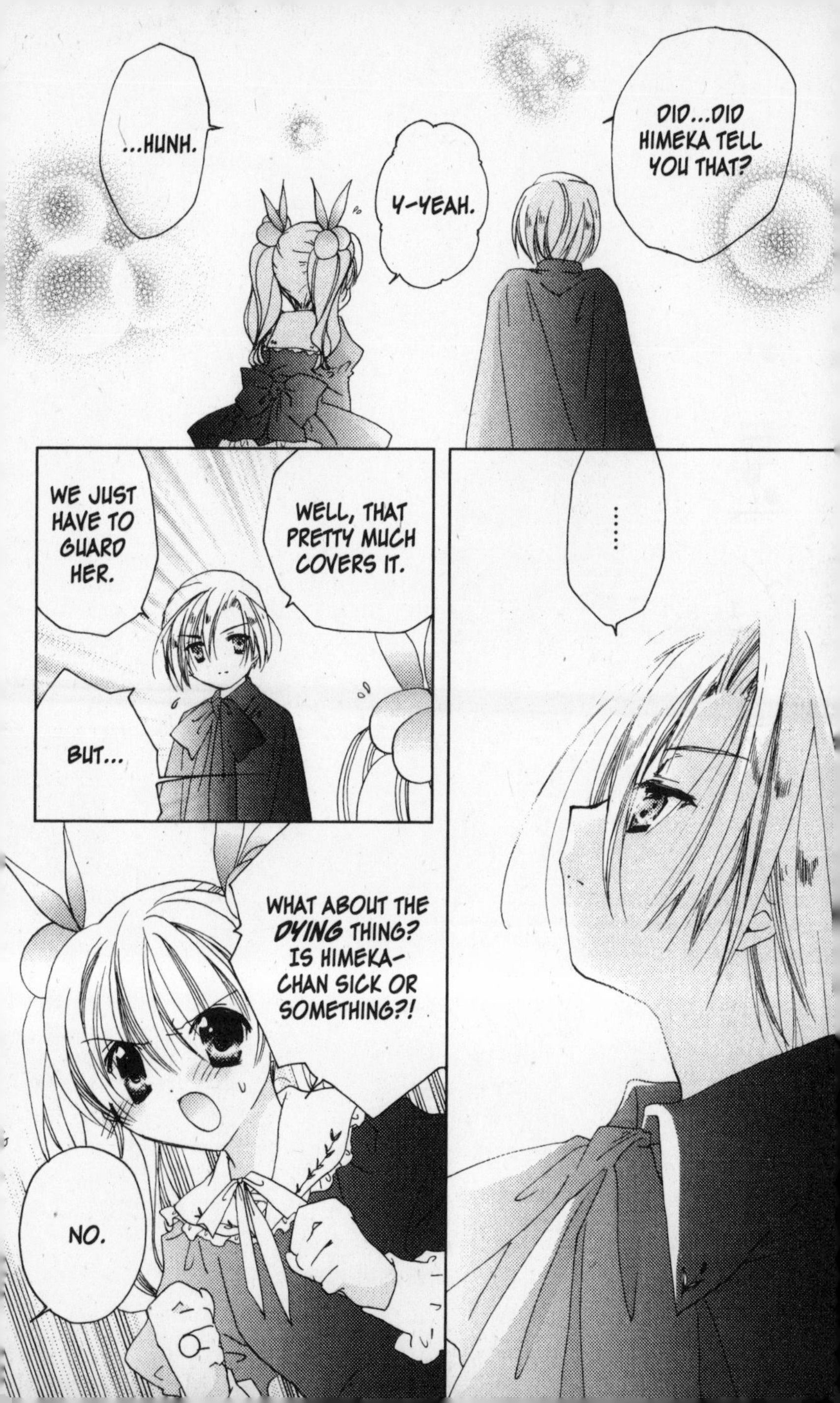
DID...DID HIMEKA TELL YOU THAT?
Y-YEAH.
...HUNH.
......
WELL, THAT PRETTY MUCH COVERS IT.
WE JUST HAVE TO GUARD HER.
BUT...
WHAT ABOUT THE *DYING* THING? IS HIMEKA-CHAN SICK OR SOMETHING?!
NO.

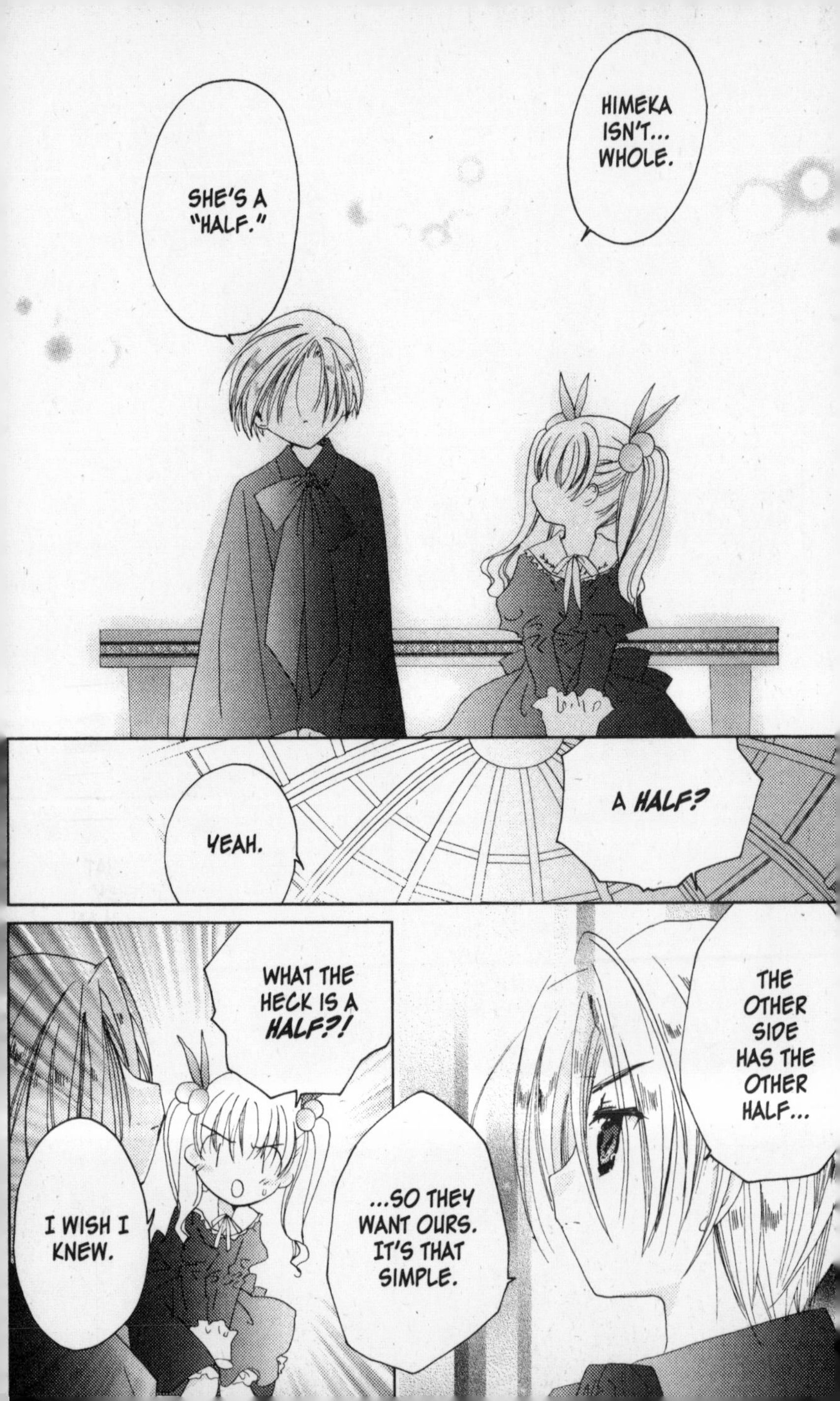
HIMEKA ISN'T... WHOLE.
SHE'S A "HALF."
A HALF?
YEAH.
THE OTHER SIDE HAS THE OTHER HALF...
...SO THEY WANT OURS. IT'S THAT SIMPLE.
WHAT THE HECK IS A HALF?!
I WISH I KNEW.

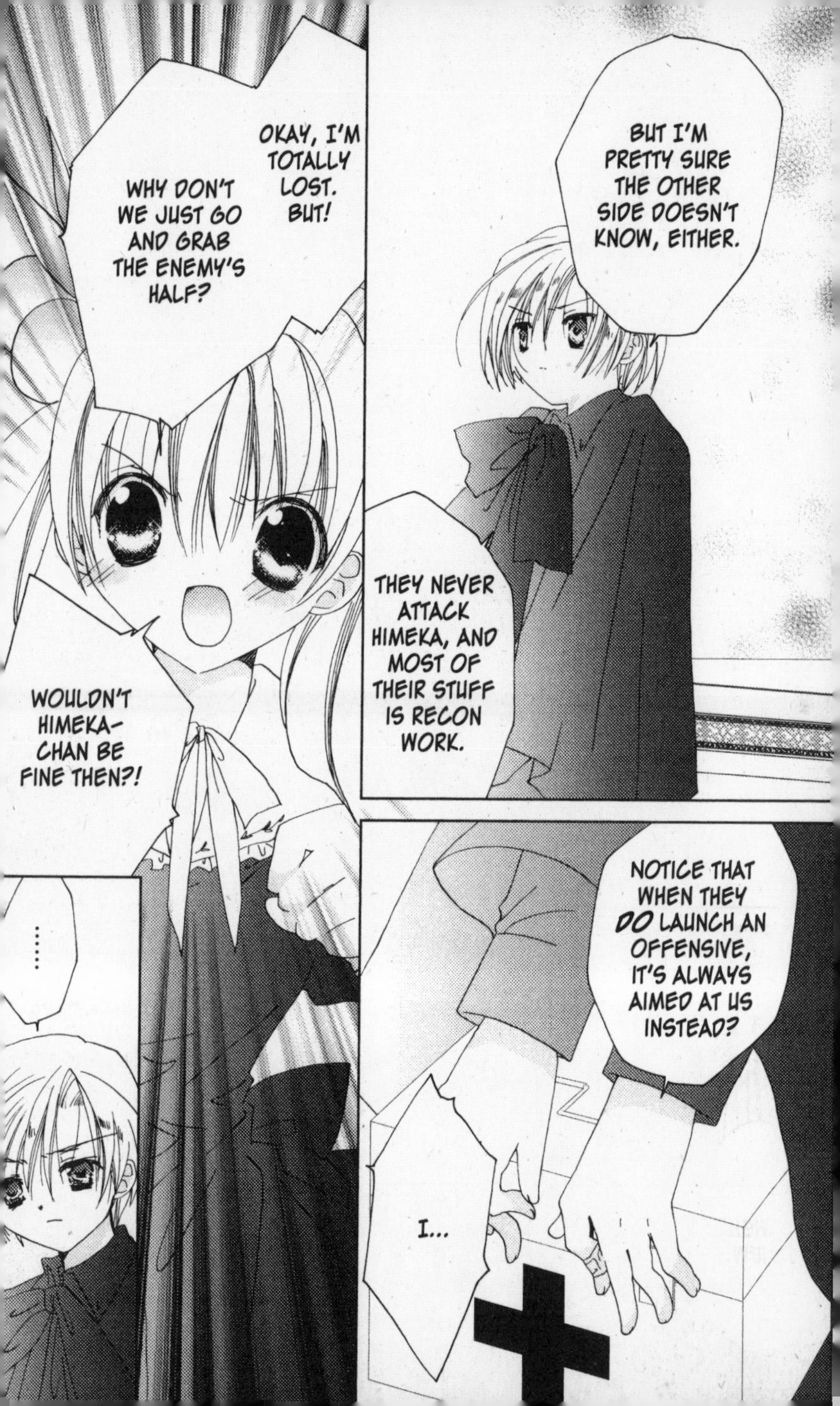
BUT I'M PRETTY SURE THE OTHER SIDE DOESN'T KNOW, EITHER.
THEY NEVER ATTACK HIMEKA, AND MOST OF THEIR STUFF IS RECON WORK.
OKAY, I'M TOTALLY LOST. BUT!
WHY DON'T WE JUST GO AND GRAB THE ENEMY'S HALF?
WOULDN'T HIMEKA-CHAN BE FINE THEN?!
NOTICE THAT WHEN THEY DO LAUNCH AN OFFENSIVE, IT'S ALWAYS AIMED AT US INSTEAD?
I...
......

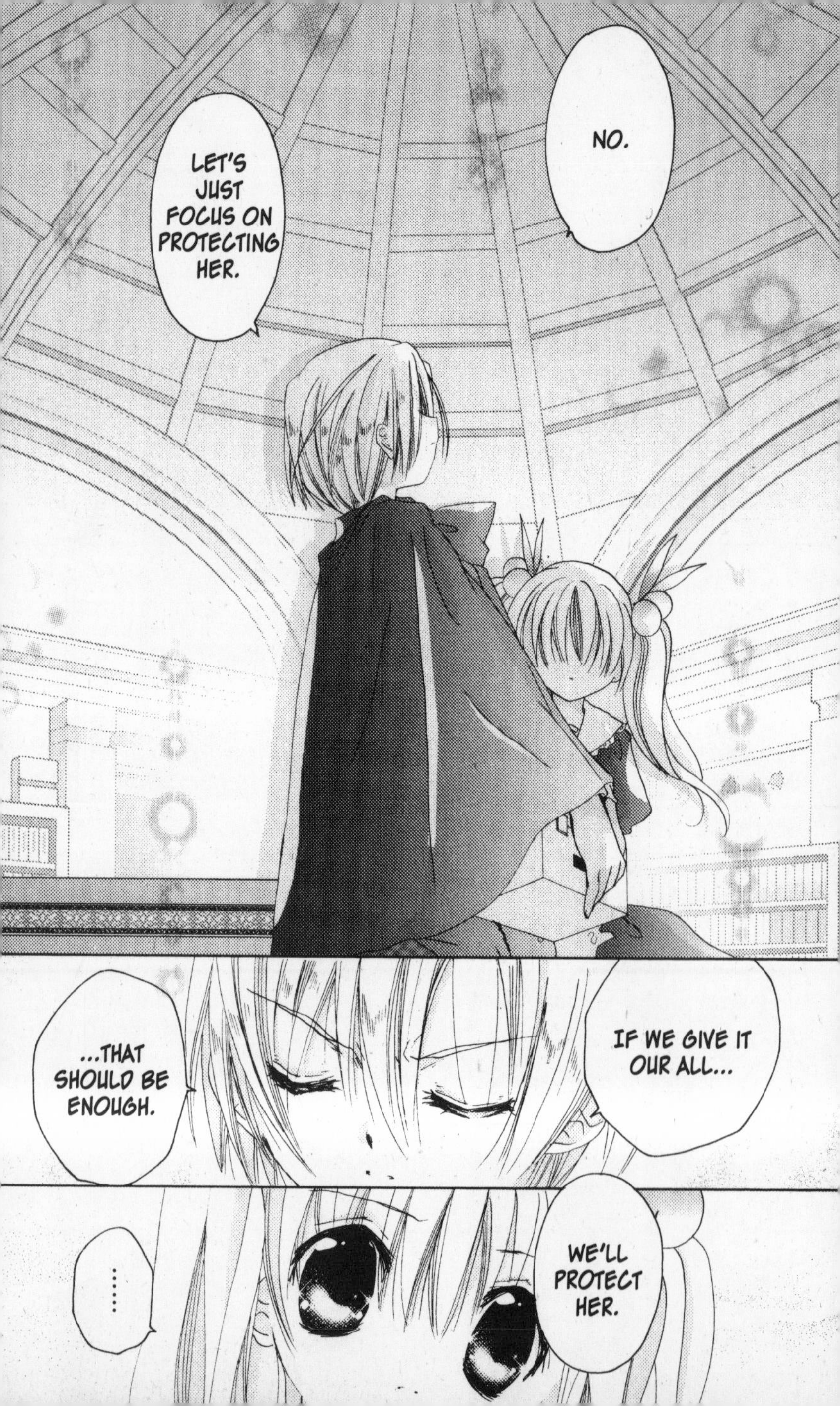
NO.
LET'S JUST FOCUS ON PROTECTING HER.
IF WE GIVE IT OUR ALL...
...THAT SHOULD BE ENOUGH.
WE'LL PROTECT HER.
......

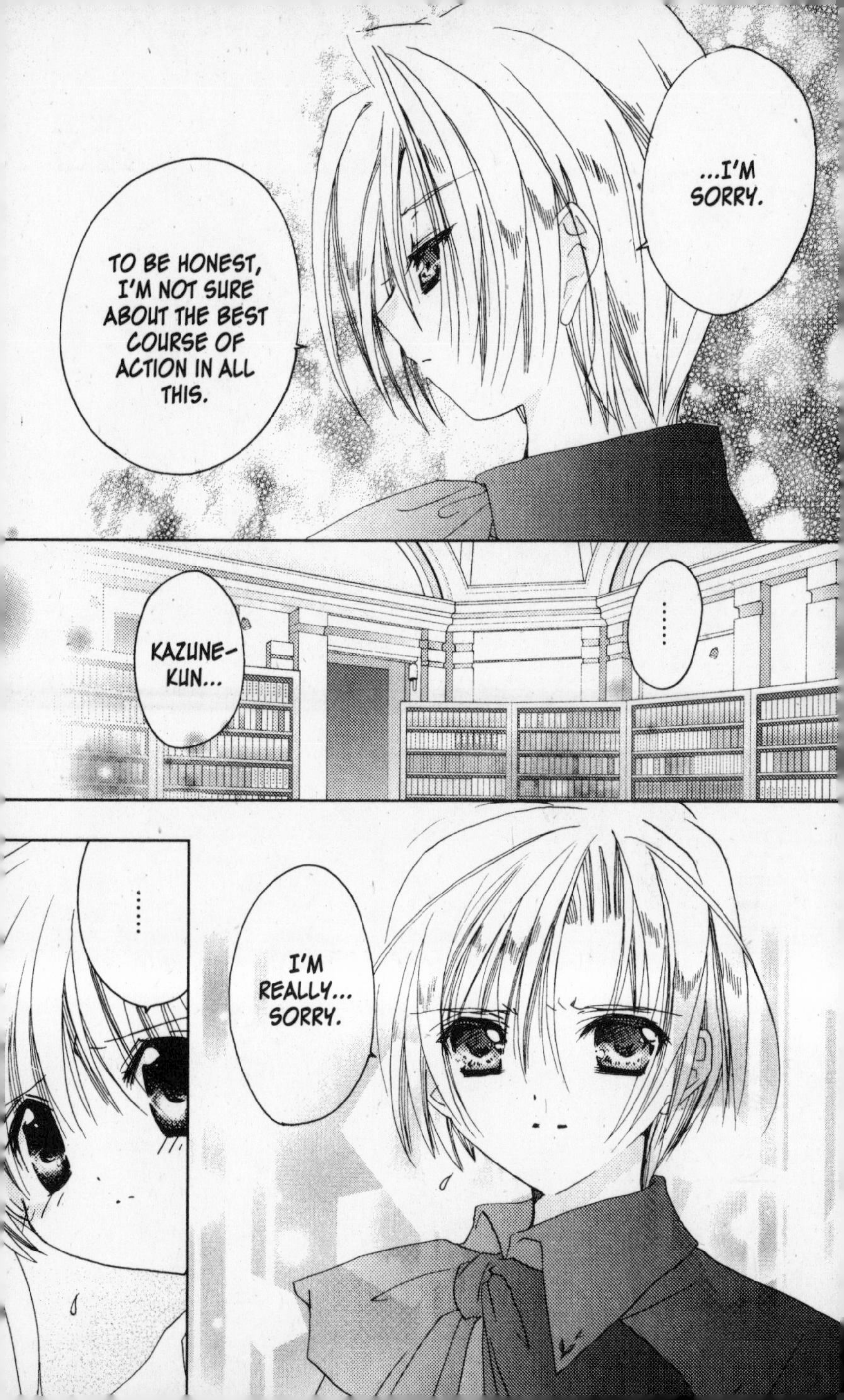
...I'M SORRY.
TO BE HONEST, I'M NOT SURE ABOUT THE BEST COURSE OF ACTION IN ALL THIS.
......
KAZUNE-KUN...
I'M REALLY... SORRY.
......

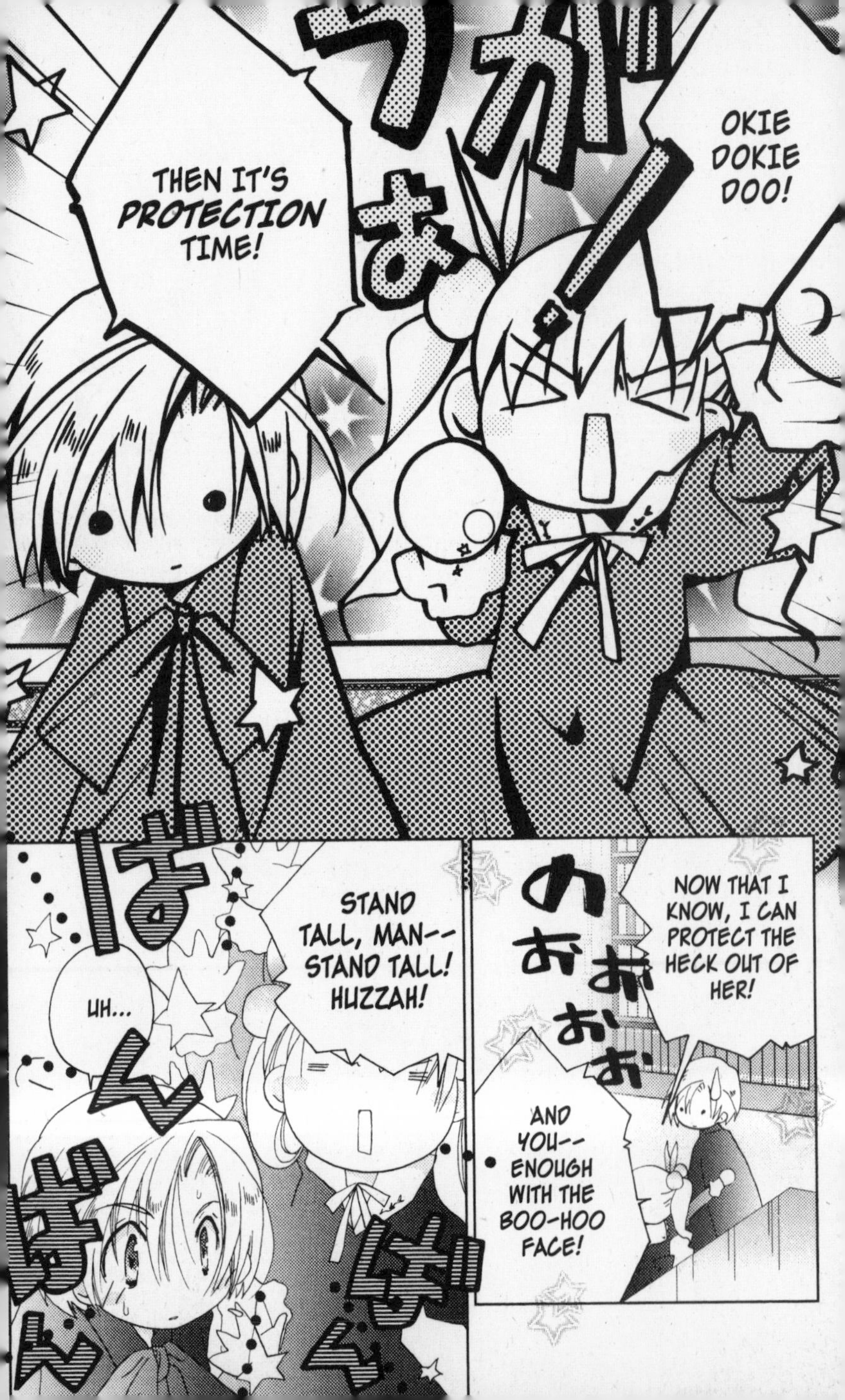
OKIE DOKIE DOO!
うがお！
THEN IT'S *PROTECTION* TIME!
めおおおお
NOW THAT I KNOW, I CAN PROTECT THE HECK OUT OF HER!
AND YOU-- ENOUGH WITH THE BOO-HOO FACE!
ばんばん
STAND TALL, MAN-- STAND TALL! HUZZAH!
UH...
ばんばん

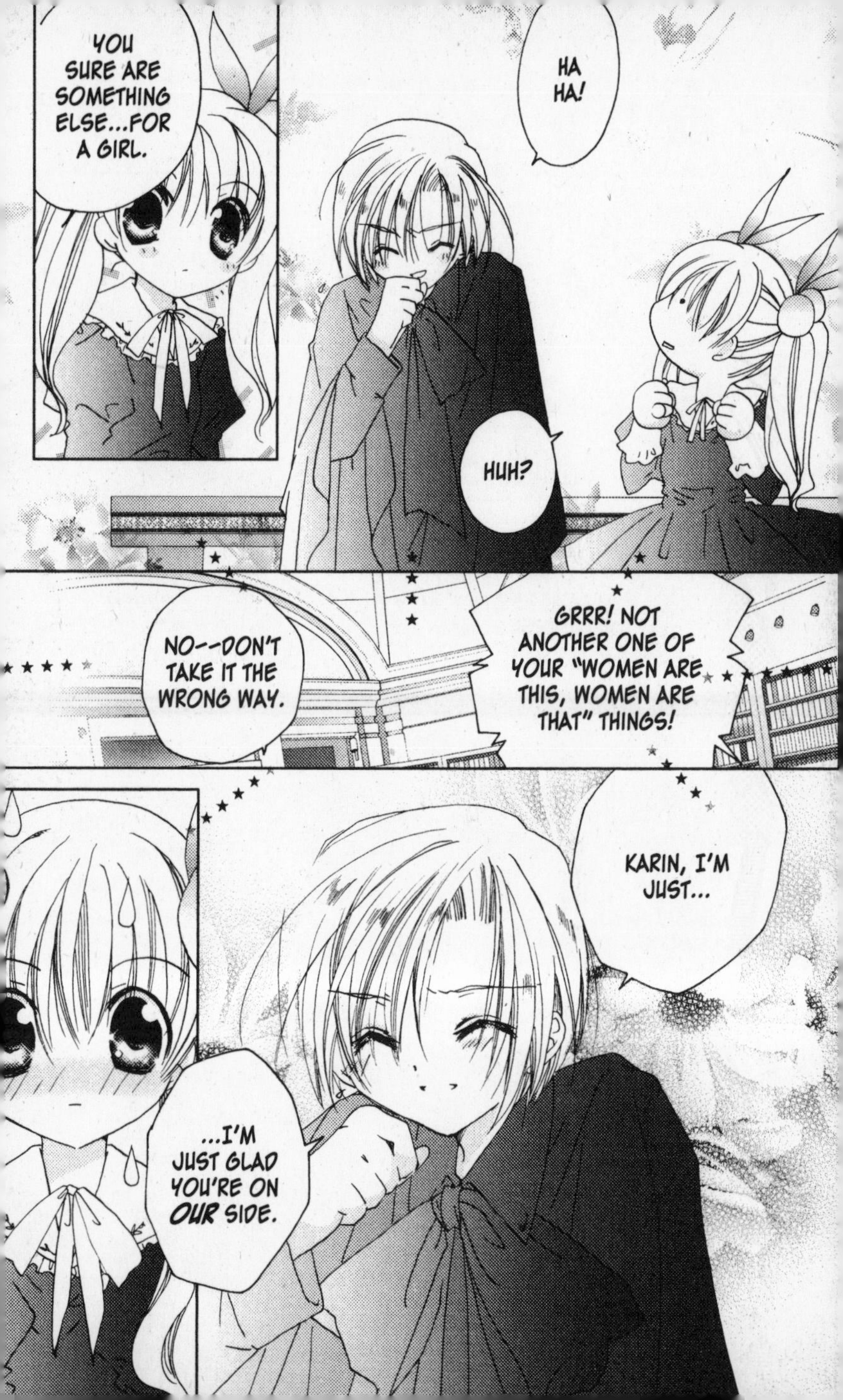
HA HA!
HUH?
YOU SURE ARE SOMETHING ELSE...FOR A GIRL.
GRRR! NOT ANOTHER ONE OF YOUR "WOMEN ARE THIS, WOMEN ARE THAT" THINGS!
NO--DON'T TAKE IT THE WRONG WAY.
KARIN, I'M JUST...
...I'M JUST GLAD YOU'RE ON **OUR** SIDE.

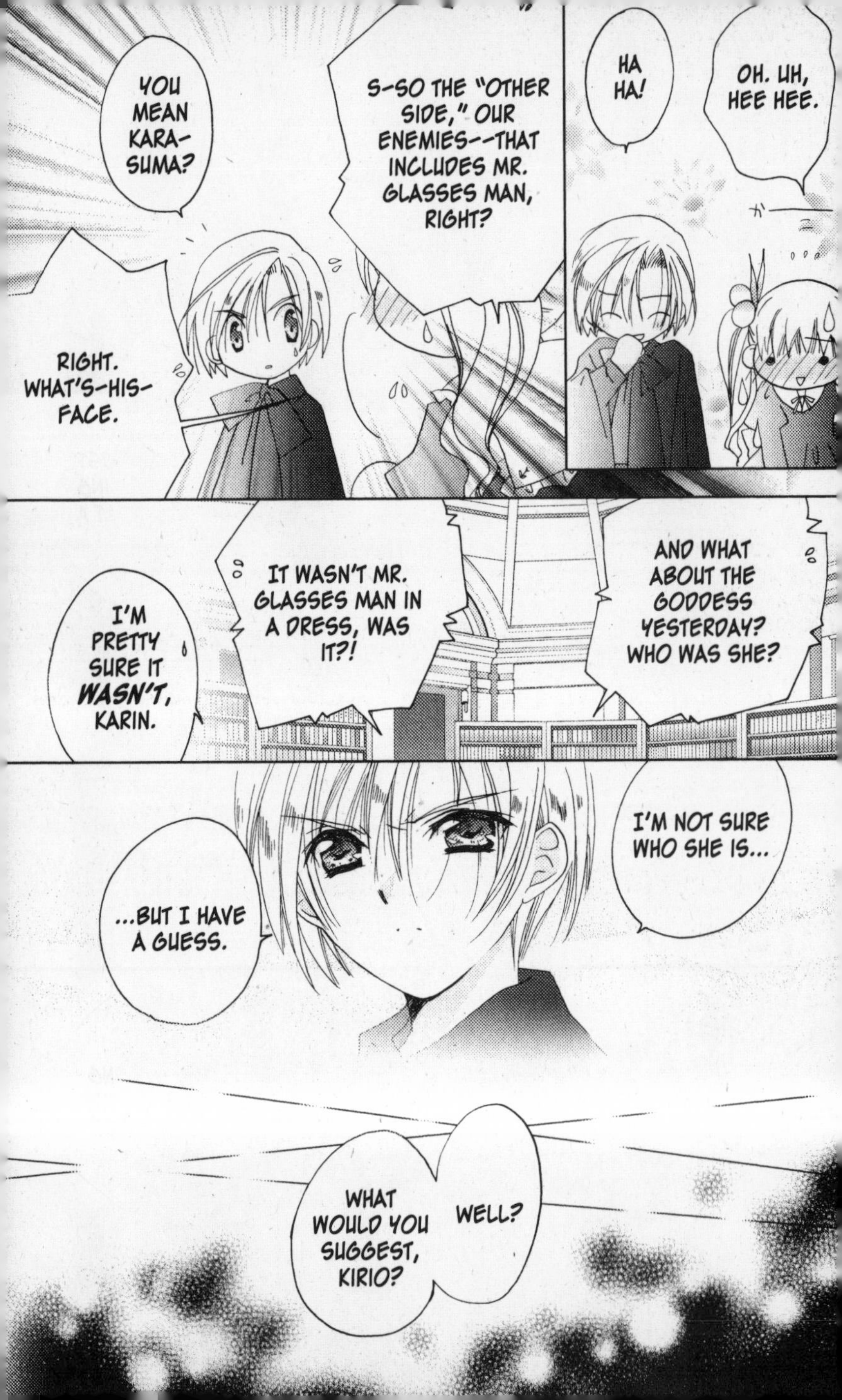
OH. UH, HEE HEE.
HA HA!
S-SO THE "OTHER SIDE," OUR ENEMIES--THAT INCLUDES MR. GLASSES MAN, RIGHT?
YOU MEAN KARASUMA?
RIGHT. WHAT'S-HIS-FACE.
AND WHAT ABOUT THE GODDESS YESTERDAY? WHO WAS SHE?
IT WASN'T MR. GLASSES MAN IN A DRESS, WAS IT?!
I'M PRETTY SURE IT *WASN'T*, KARIN.
I'M NOT SURE WHO SHE IS...
...BUT I HAVE A GUESS.
WELL?
WHAT WOULD YOU SUGGEST, KIRIO?

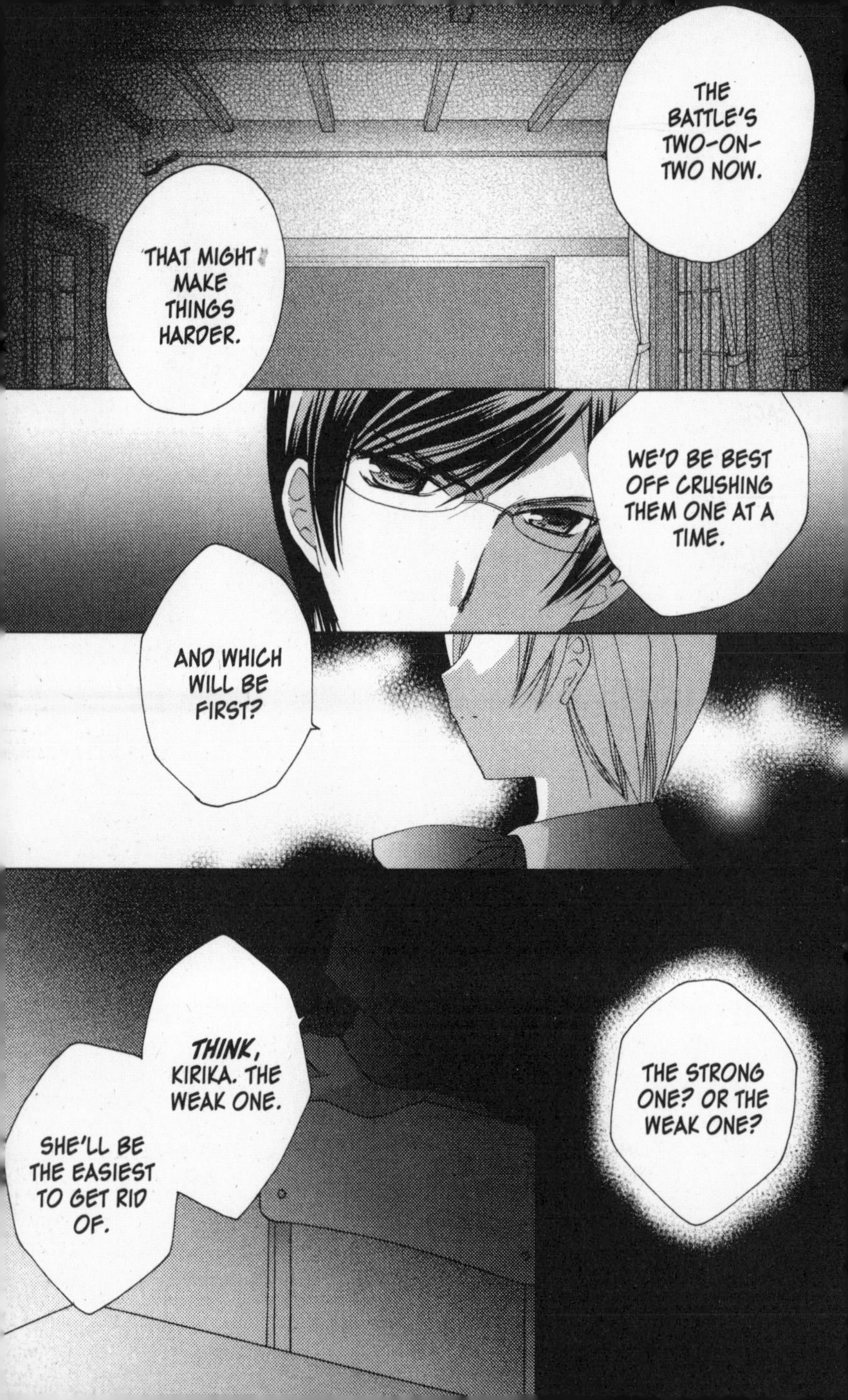
THE BATTLE'S TWO-ON-TWO NOW.
THAT MIGHT MAKE THINGS HARDER.
WE'D BE BEST OFF CRUSHING THEM ONE AT A TIME.
AND WHICH WILL BE FIRST?
THE STRONG ONE? OR THE WEAK ONE?
THINK, KIRIKA. THE WEAK ONE.
SHE'LL BE THE EASIEST TO GET RID OF.

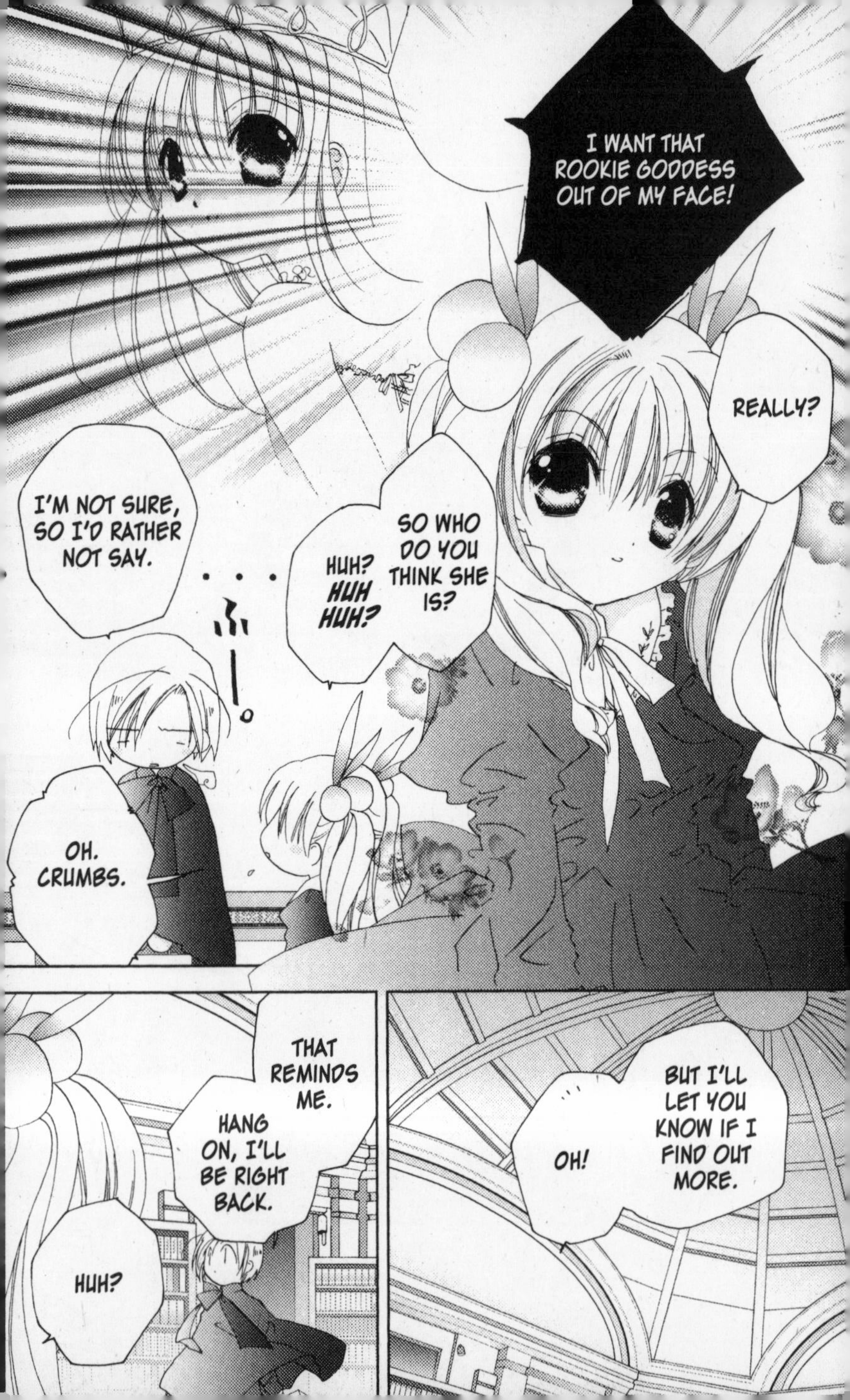
I WANT THAT ROOKIE GODDESS OUT OF MY FACE!
REALLY?
SO WHO DO YOU THINK SHE IS?
HUH? HUH HUH?
I'M NOT SURE, SO I'D RATHER NOT SAY.
. . .
ふー。
OH. CRUMBS.
BUT I'LL LET YOU KNOW IF I FIND OUT MORE.
OH!
THAT REMINDS ME.
HANG ON, I'LL BE RIGHT BACK.
HUH?

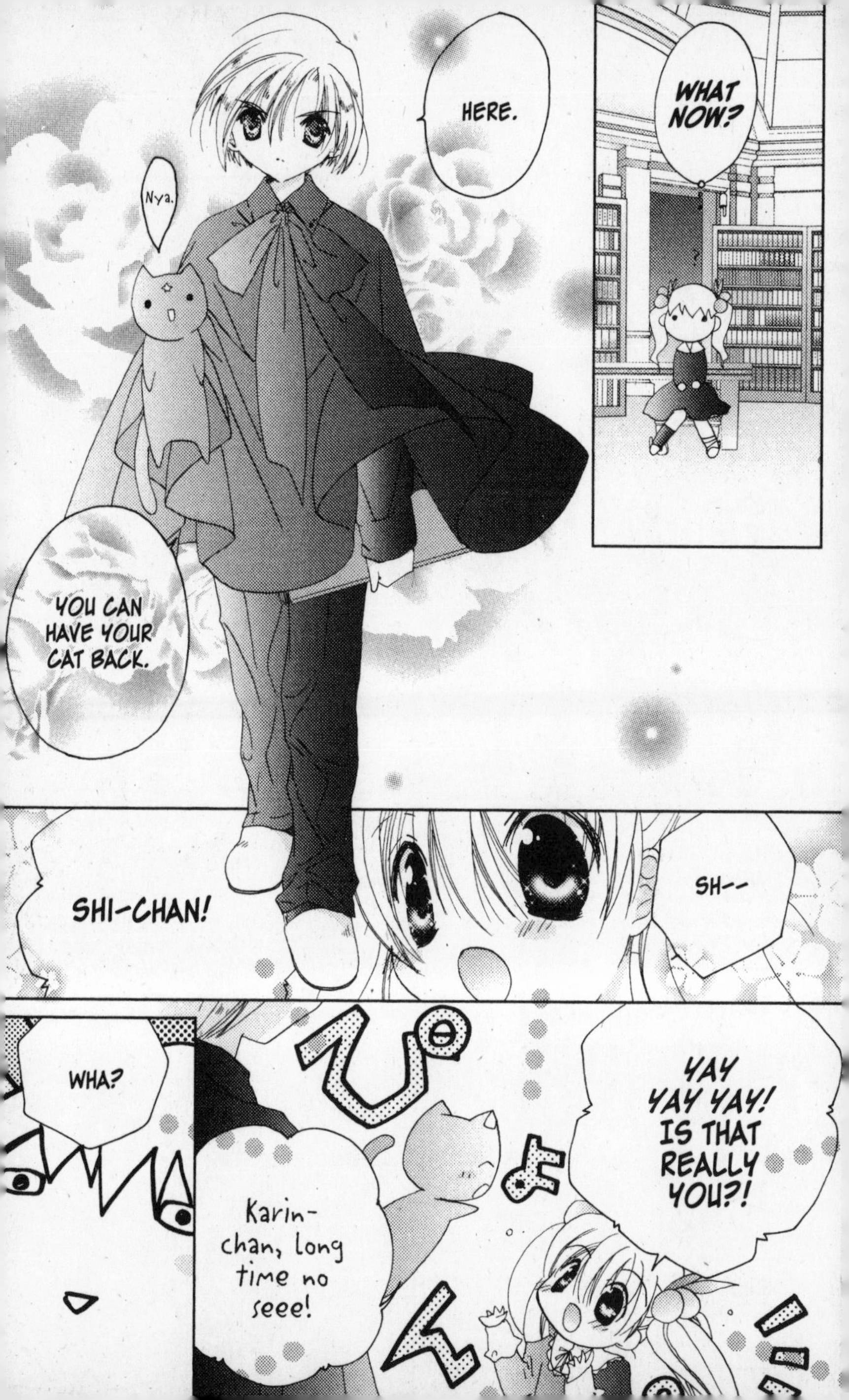
WHAT NOW?
HERE.
Nya.
YOU CAN HAVE YOUR CAT BACK.
SH--
SHI-CHAN!
YAY YAY YAY! IS THAT REALLY YOU?!
Karin-chan, long time no seee!
WHA?

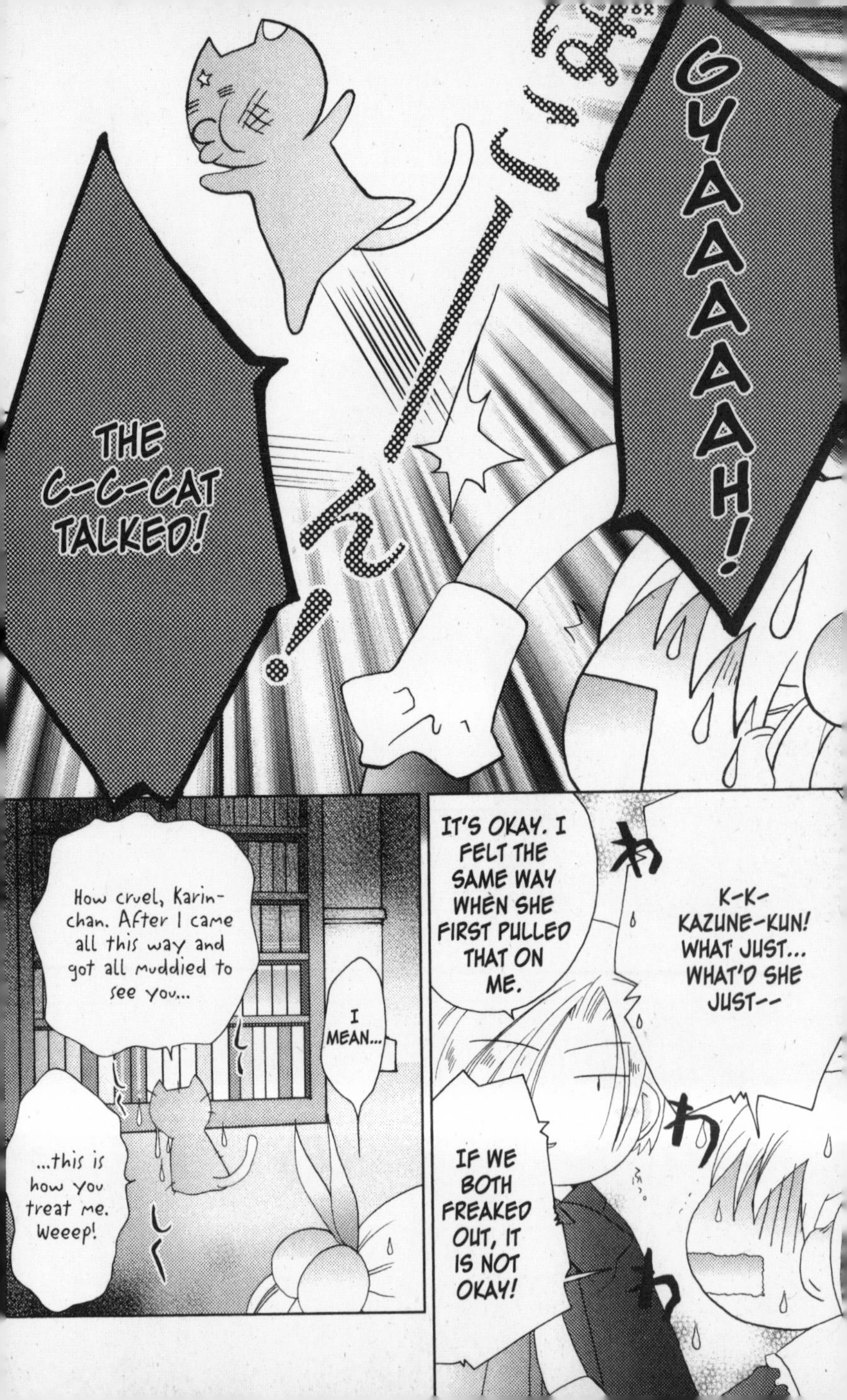
GYAAAAAH!
THE C-C-CAT TALKED!
K-K-KAZUNE-KUN! WHAT JUST... WHAT'D SHE JUST--
IT'S OKAY. I FELT THE SAME WAY WHEN SHE FIRST PULLED THAT ON ME.
IF WE BOTH FREAKED OUT, IT IS NOT OKAY!
I MEAN...
How cruel, Karin-chan. After I came all this way and got all muddied to see you...
...this is how you treat me. Weeep!

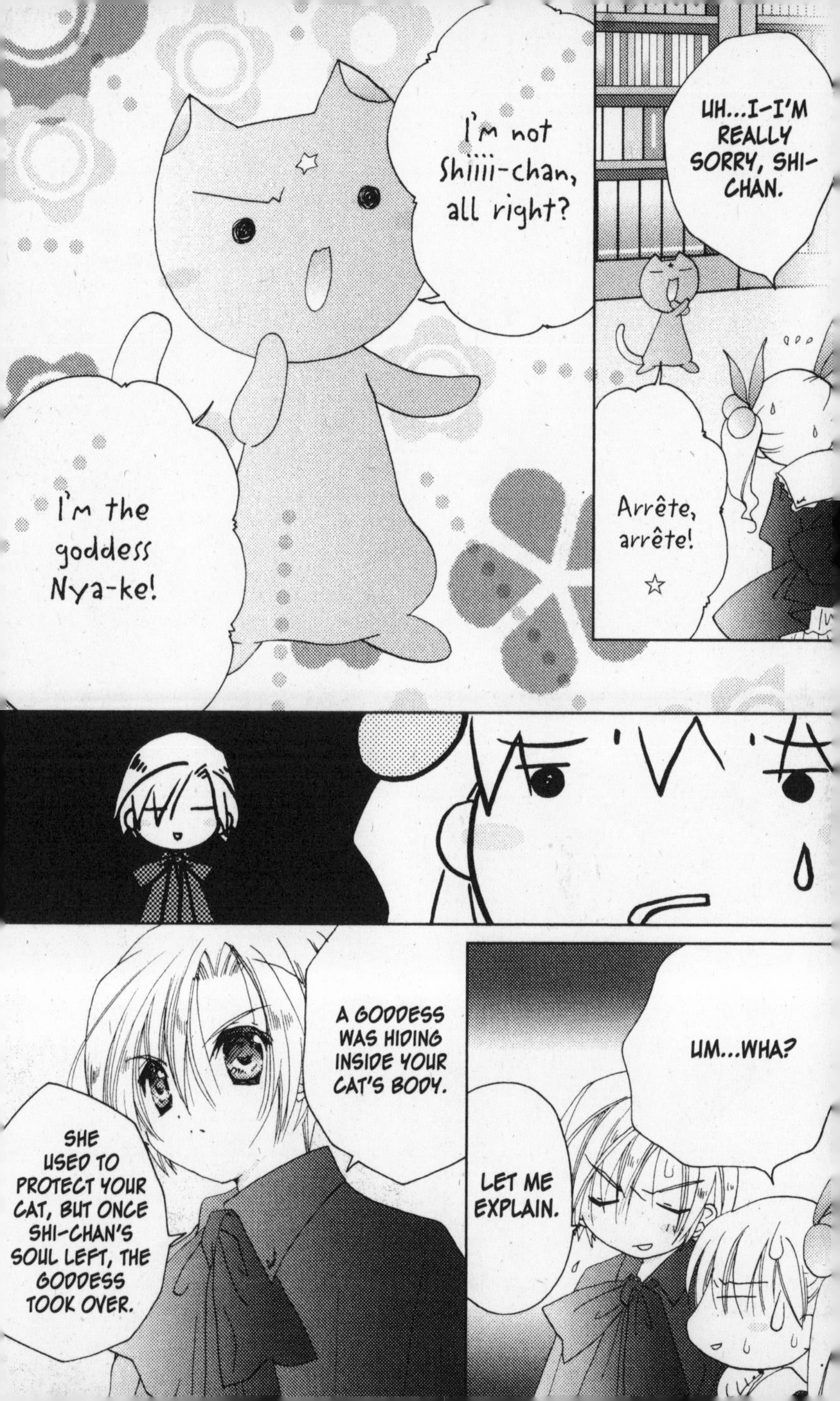
UH...I-I'M REALLY SORRY, SHI-CHAN.
Arrête, arrête!
I'm not Shiiii-chan, all right?
I'm the goddess Nya-ke!
UM...WHA?
LET ME EXPLAIN.
A GODDESS WAS HIDING INSIDE YOUR CAT'S BODY.
SHE USED TO PROTECT YOUR CAT, BUT ONCE SHI-CHAN'S SOUL LEFT, THE GODDESS TOOK OVER.

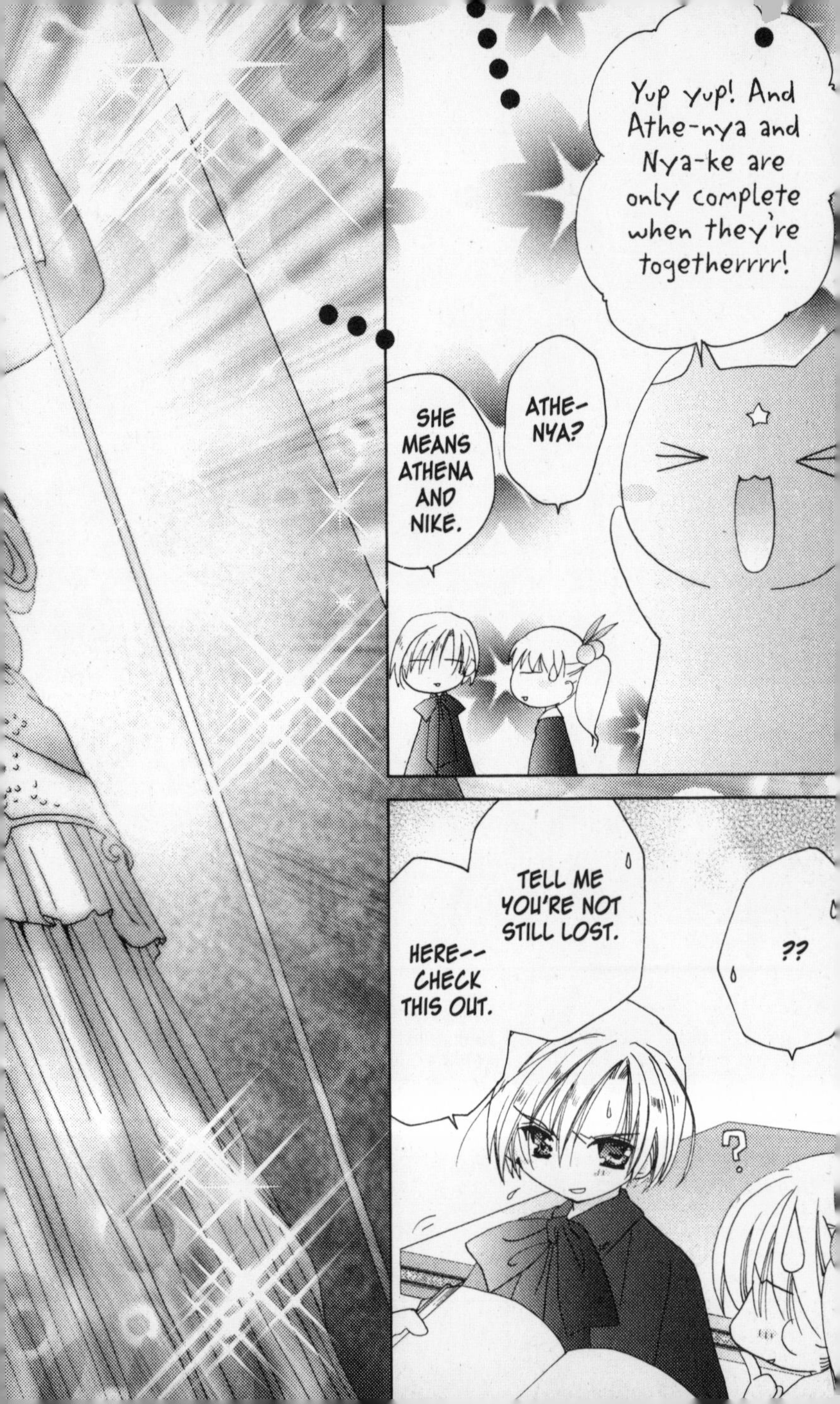

Yup yup! And Athe-nya and Nya-ke are only complete when they're togetherrrr!
ATHE-NYA?
SHE MEANS ATHENA AND NIKE.
??
TELL ME YOU'RE NOT STILL LOST.
HERE-- CHECK THIS OUT.

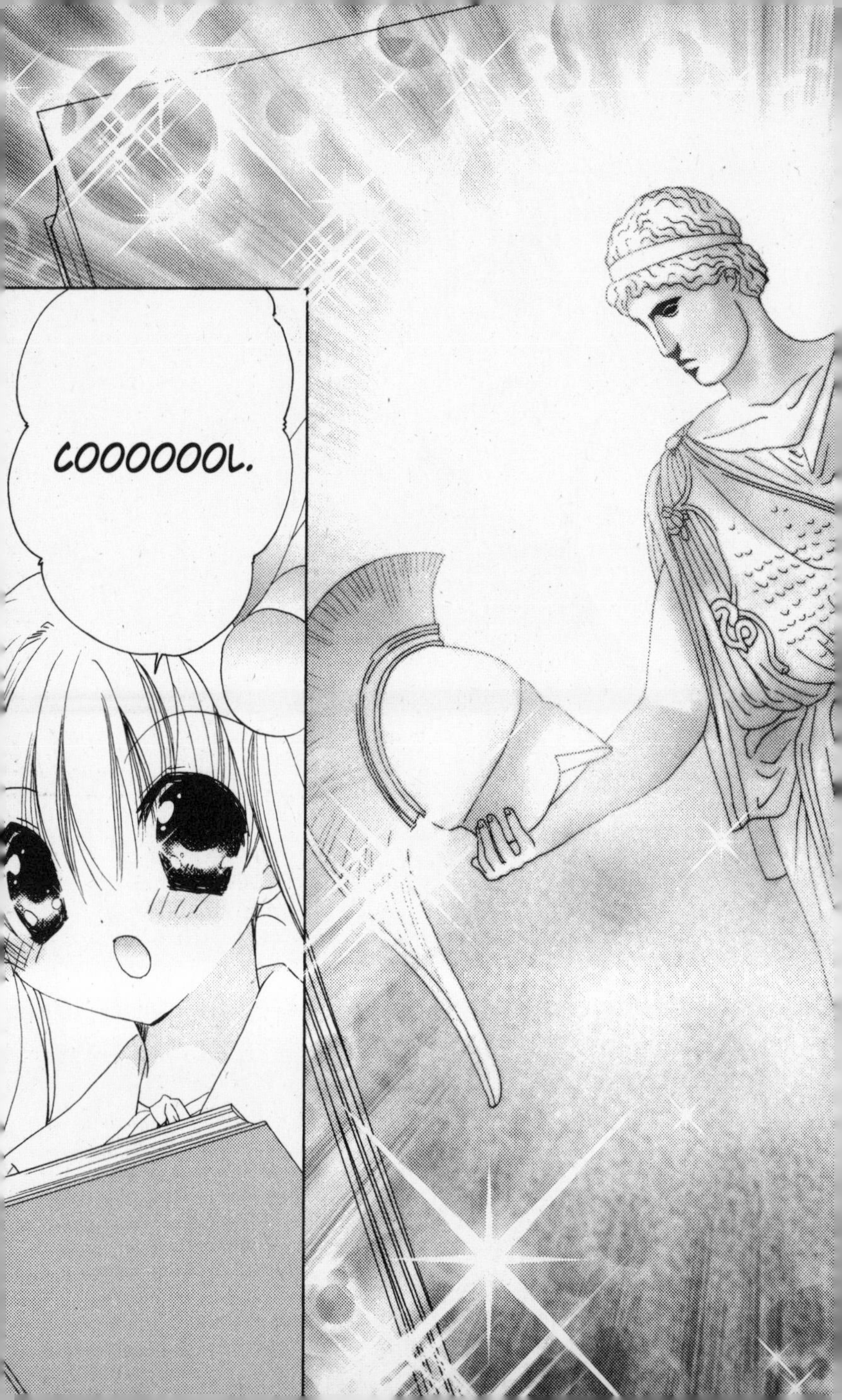
COOOOOOL.

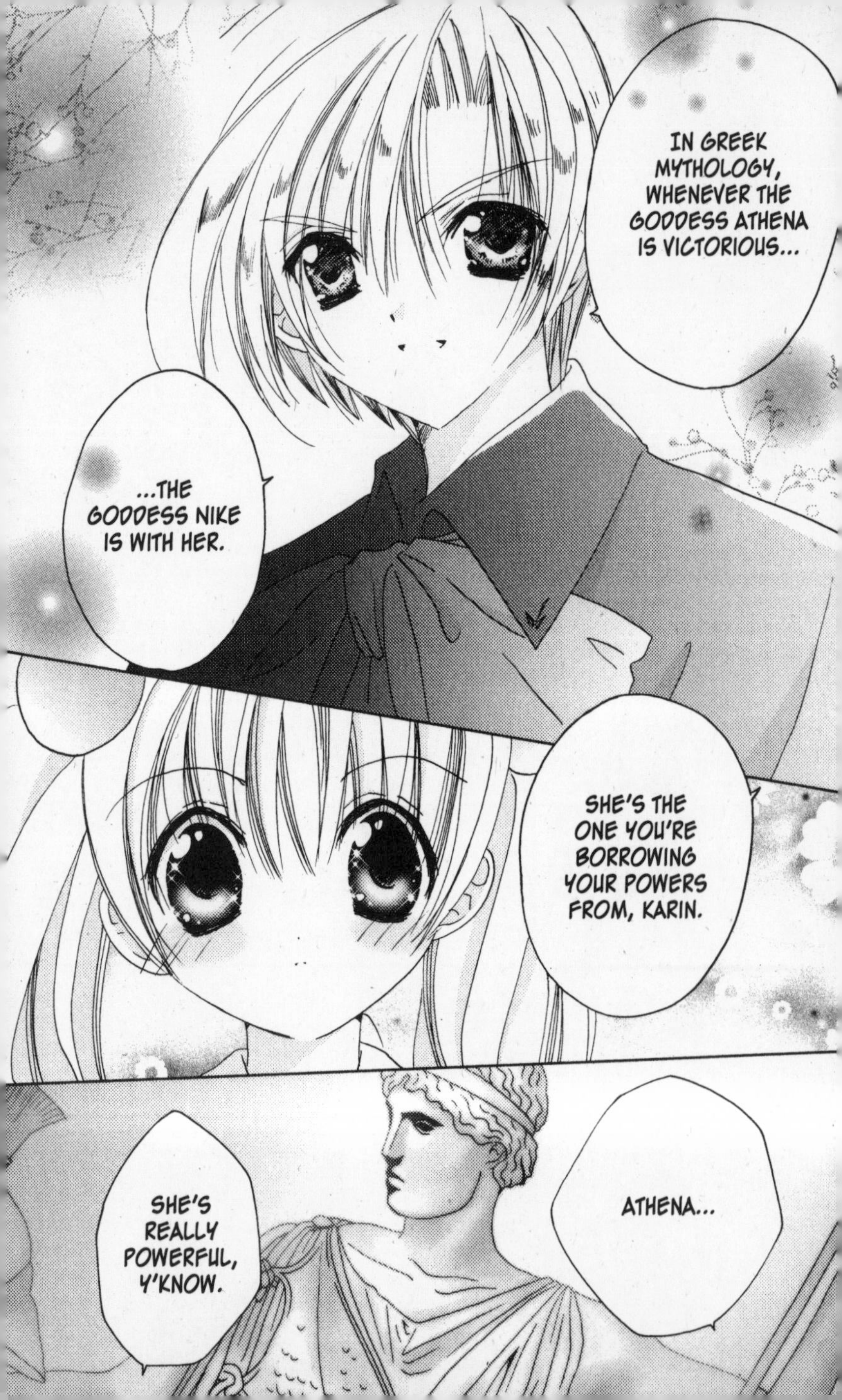
IN GREEK MYTHOLOGY, WHENEVER THE GODDESS ATHENA IS VICTORIOUS...
...THE GODDESS NIKE IS WITH HER.
SHE'S THE ONE YOU'RE BORROWING YOUR POWERS FROM, KARIN.
ATHENA...
SHE'S REALLY POWERFUL, Y'KNOW.

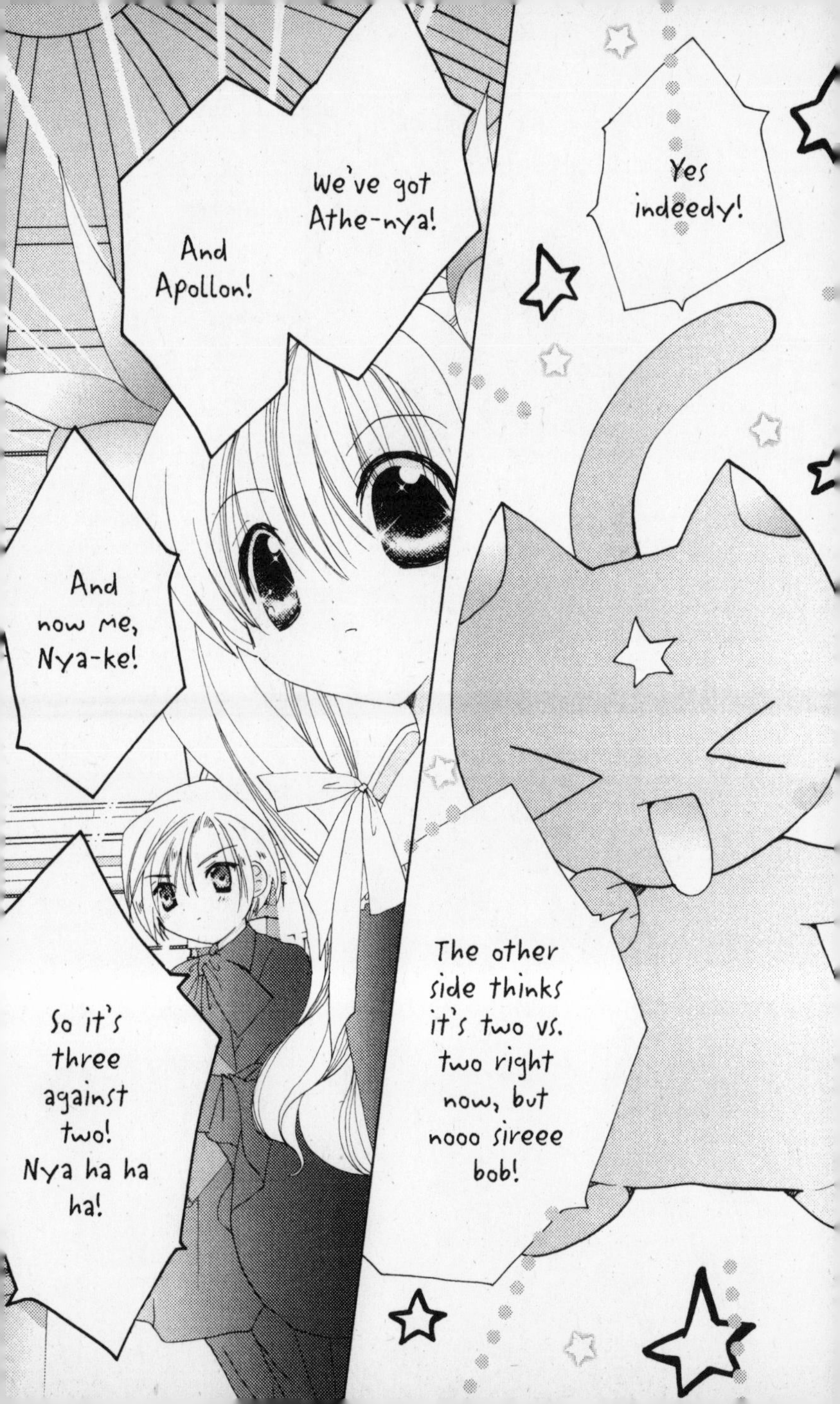

Yes indeedy!
The other side thinks it's two vs. two right now, but nooo sireee bob!
We've got Athe-nya!
And Apollon!
And now me, Nya-ke!
So it's three against two! Nya ha ha ha!

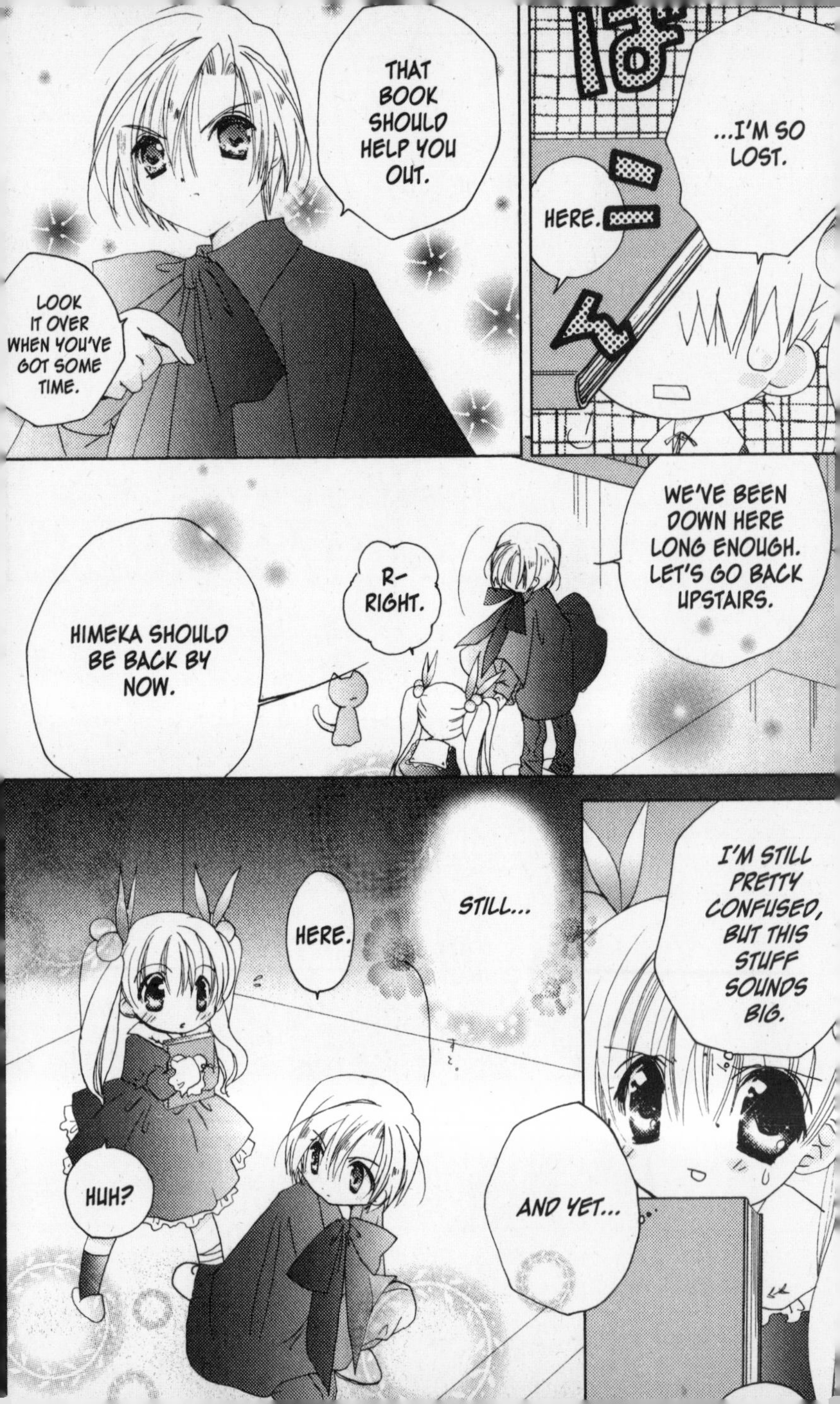
...I'M SO LOST.
HERE.
THAT BOOK SHOULD HELP YOU OUT.
LOOK IT OVER WHEN YOU'VE GOT SOME TIME.
WE'VE BEEN DOWN HERE LONG ENOUGH. LET'S GO BACK UPSTAIRS.
R-RIGHT.
HIMEKA SHOULD BE BACK BY NOW.
I'M STILL PRETTY CONFUSED, BUT THIS STUFF SOUNDS BIG.
AND YET...
STILL...
HERE.
HUH?

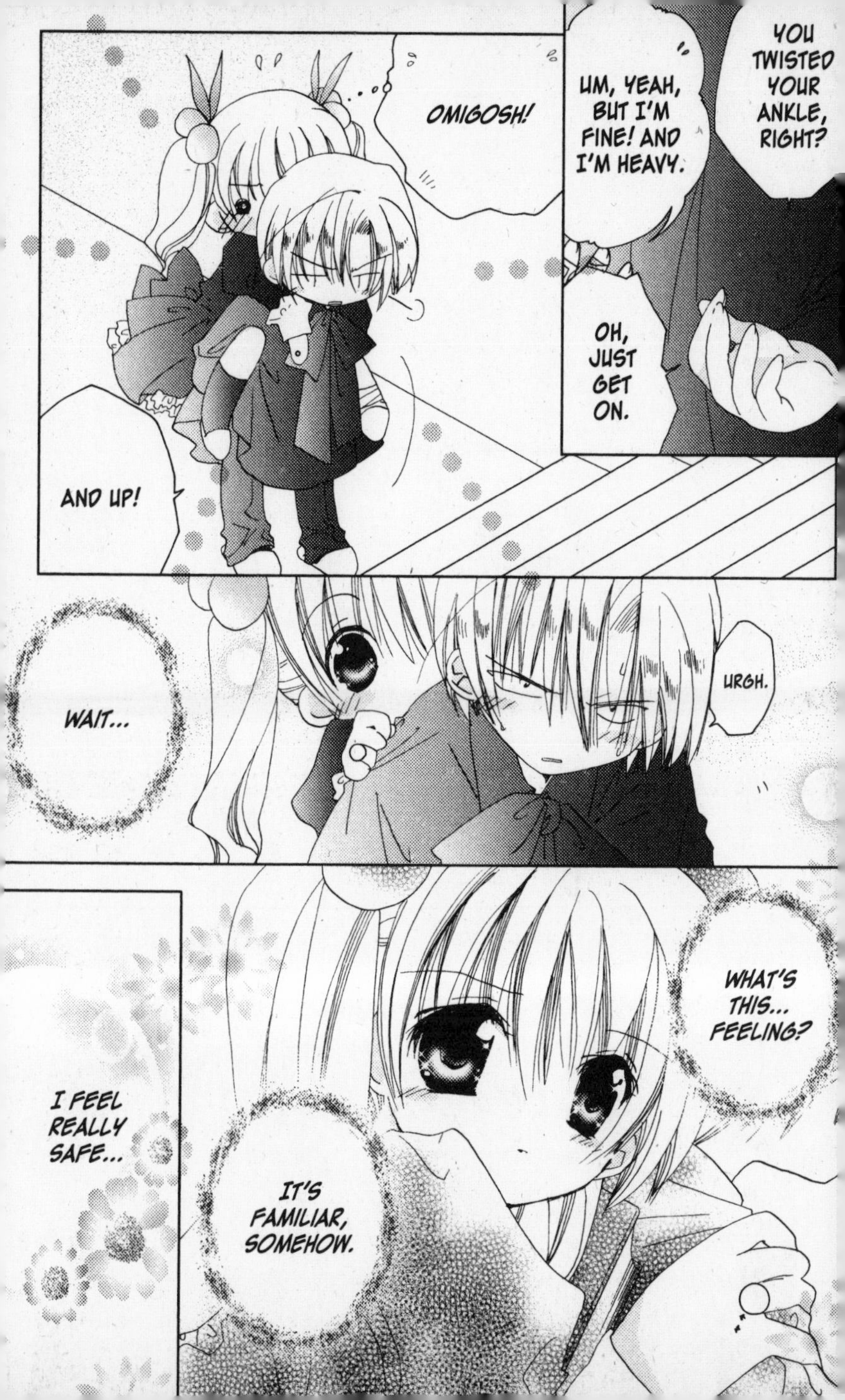
YOU TWISTED YOUR ANKLE, RIGHT?
UM, YEAH, BUT I'M FINE! AND I'M HEAVY.
OH, JUST GET ON.
OMIGOSH!
AND UP!
URGH.
WAIT...
WHAT'S THIS... FEELING?
IT'S FAMILIAR, SOMEHOW.
I FEEL REALLY SAFE...

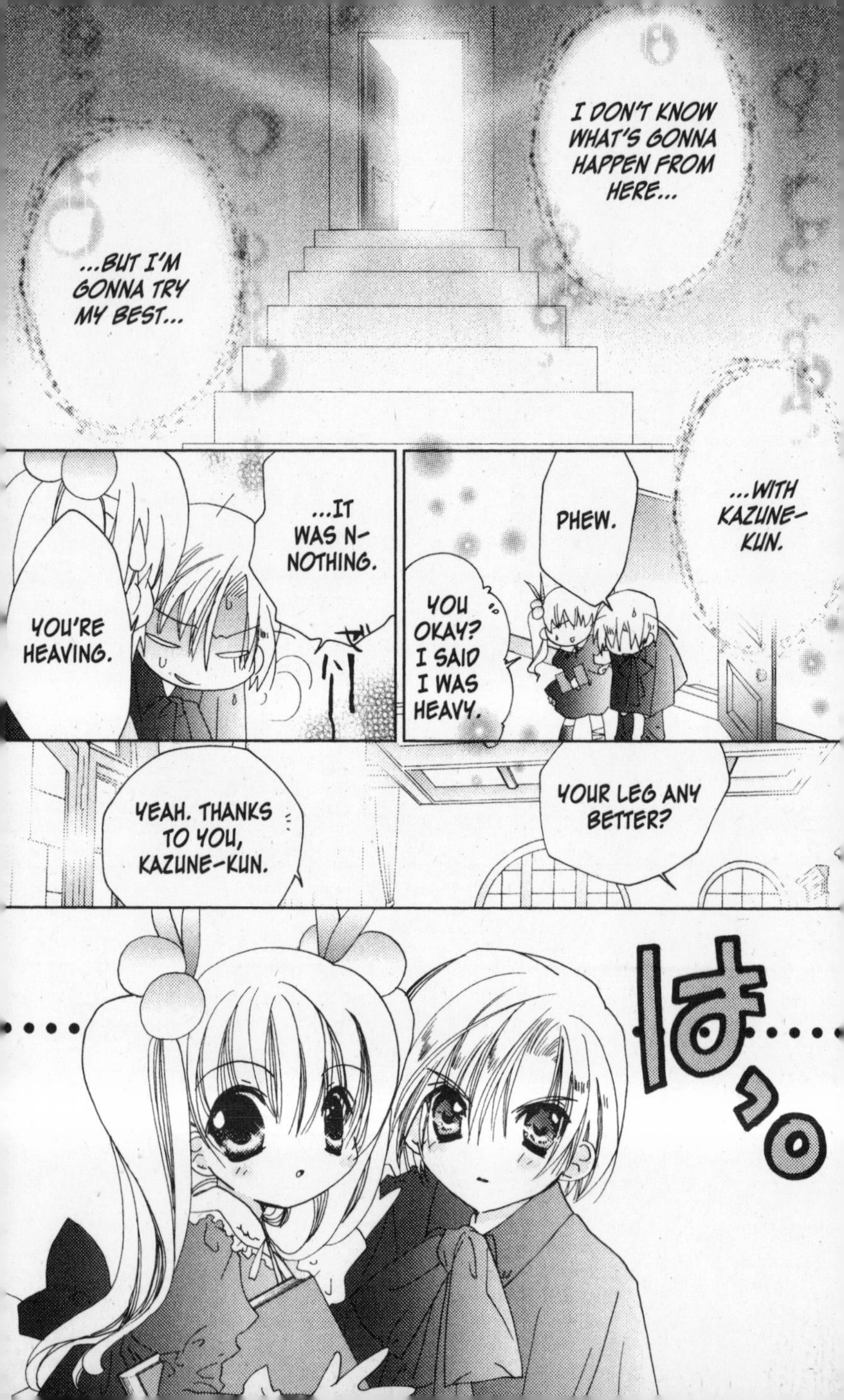
I DON'T KNOW WHAT'S GONNA HAPPEN FROM HERE...
...BUT I'M GONNA TRY MY BEST...
...WITH KAZUNE-KUN.
PHEW.
YOU OKAY? I SAID I WAS HEAVY.
...IT WAS N-NOTHING.
YOU'RE HEAVING.
YOUR LEG ANY BETTER?
YEAH. THANKS TO YOU, KAZUNE-KUN.
はっ。....
....

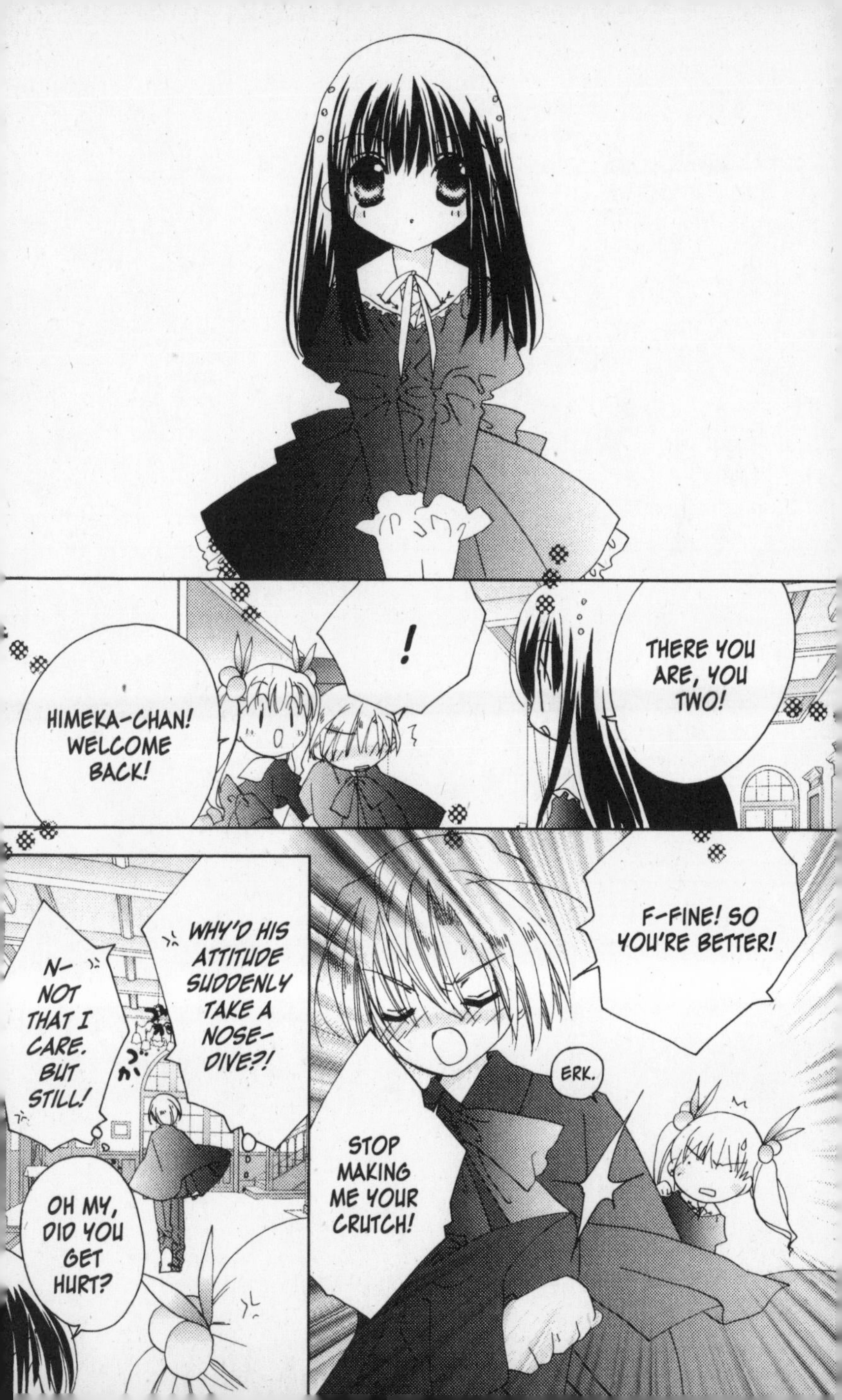
THERE YOU ARE, YOU TWO!
!
HIMEKA-CHAN! WELCOME BACK!
F-FINE! SO YOU'RE BETTER!
ERK.
STOP MAKING ME YOUR CRUTCH!
WHY'D HIS ATTITUDE SUDDENLY TAKE A NOSE-DIVE?!
N-NOT THAT I CARE. BUT STILL!
OH MY, DID YOU GET HURT?

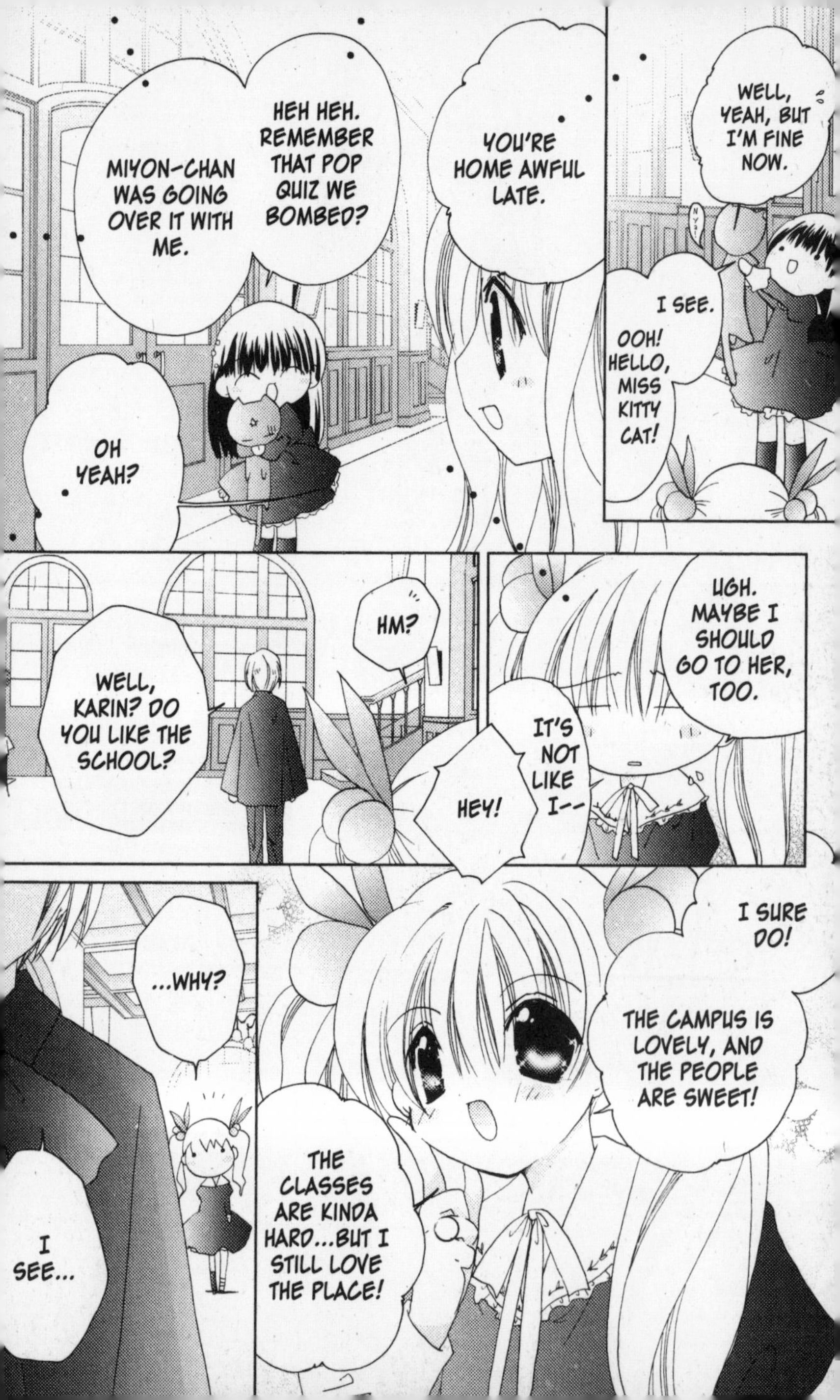
WELL, YEAH, BUT I'M FINE NOW.
I SEE.
OOH! HELLO, MISS KITTY CAT!
YOU'RE HOME AWFUL LATE.
HEH HEH. REMEMBER THAT POP QUIZ WE BOMBED?
MIYON-CHAN WAS GOING OVER IT WITH ME.
OH YEAH?
UGH. MAYBE I SHOULD GO TO HER, TOO.
IT'S NOT LIKE I--
HEY!
HM?
WELL, KARIN? DO YOU LIKE THE SCHOOL?
I SURE DO!
THE CAMPUS IS LOVELY, AND THE PEOPLE ARE SWEET!
THE CLASSES ARE KINDA HARD...BUT I STILL LOVE THE PLACE!
...WHY?
I SEE...

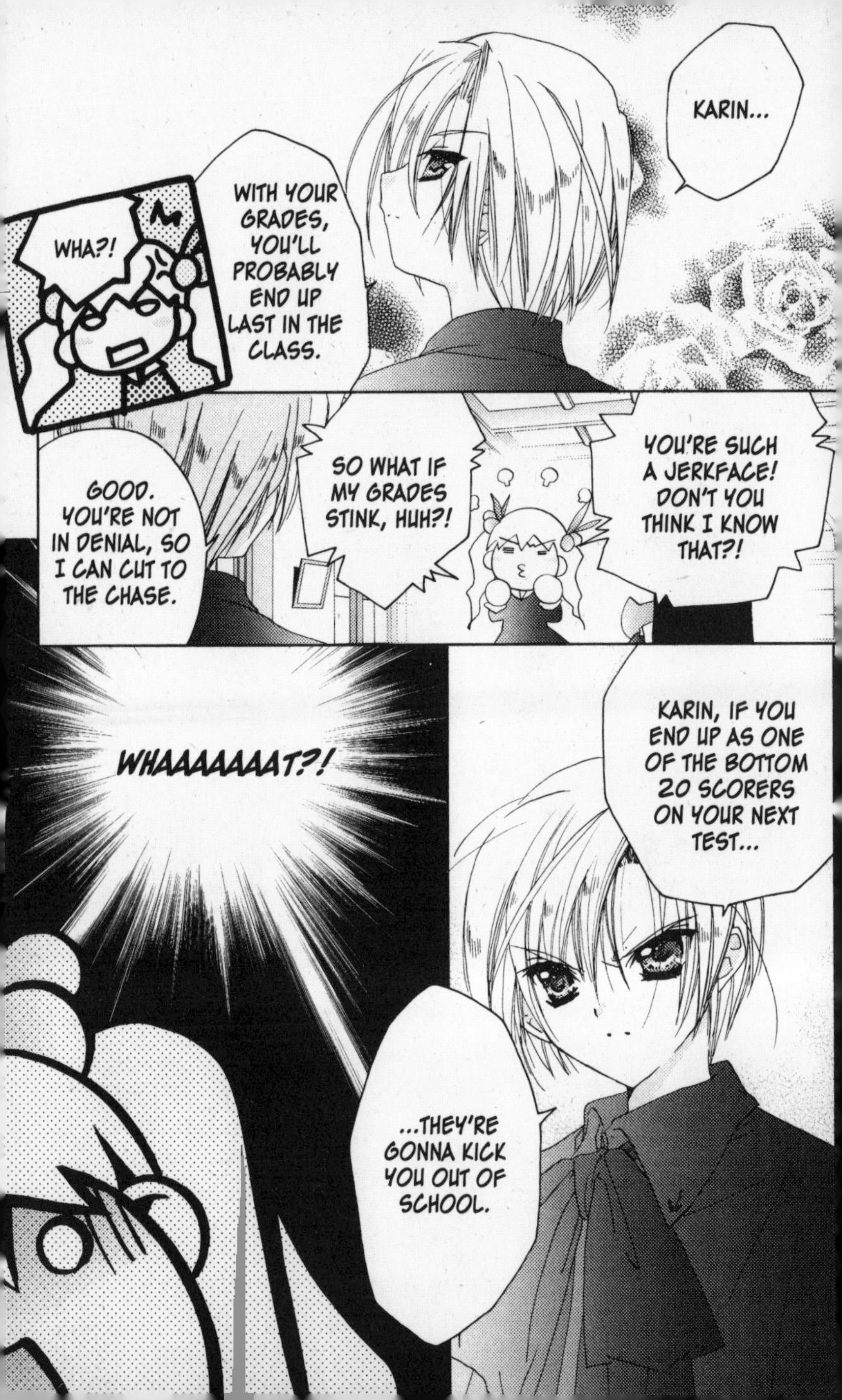
KARIN...
WITH YOUR GRADES, YOU'LL PROBABLY END UP LAST IN THE CLASS.
WHA?!
YOU'RE SUCH A JERKFACE! DON'T YOU THINK I KNOW THAT?!
SO WHAT IF MY GRADES STINK, HUH?!
GOOD. YOU'RE NOT IN DENIAL, SO I CAN CUT TO THE CHASE.
KARIN, IF YOU END UP AS ONE OF THE BOTTOM 20 SCORERS ON YOUR NEXT TEST...
...THEY'RE GONNA KICK YOU OUT OF SCHOOL.
WHAAAAAAAT?!

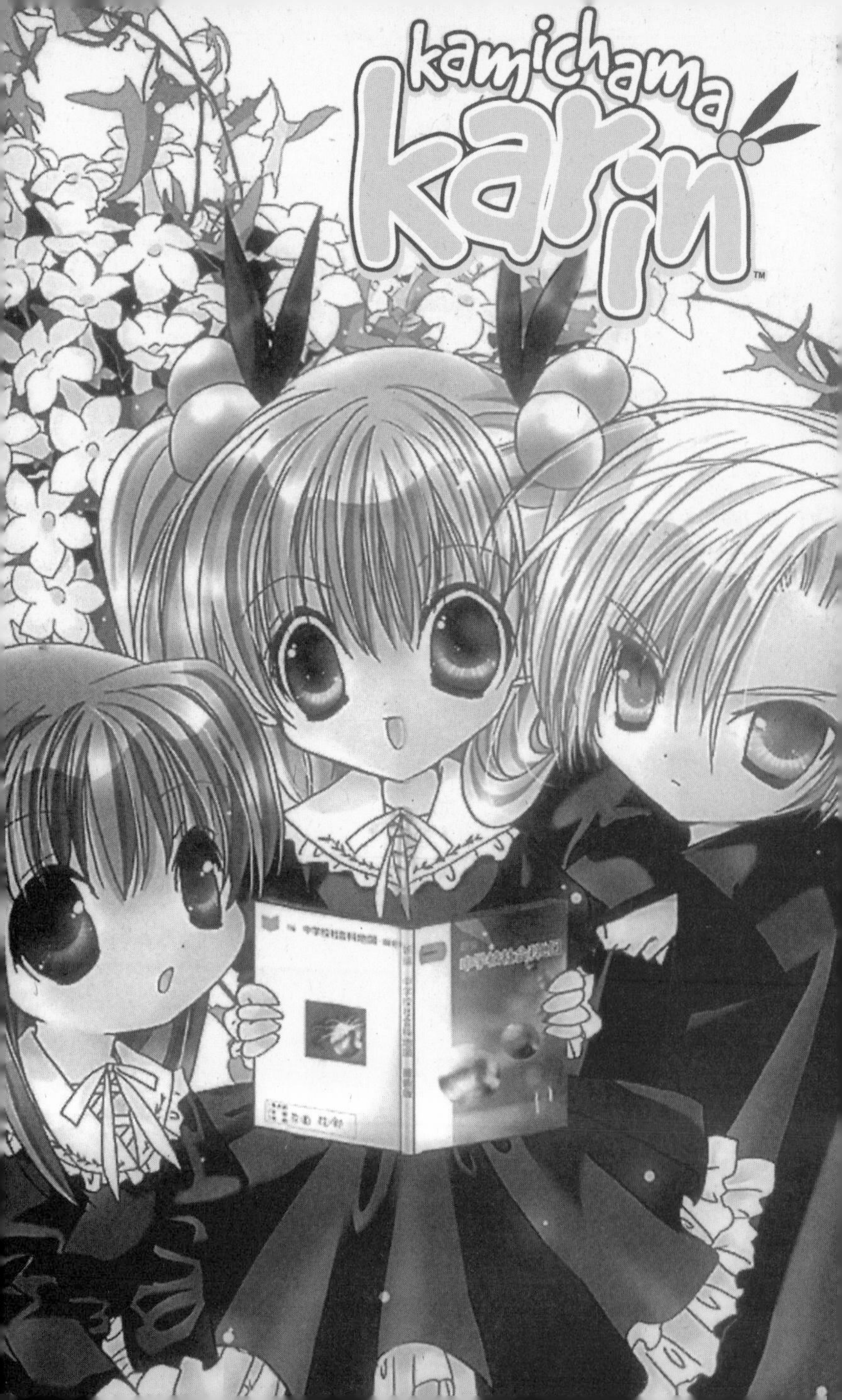
kamichama karin™

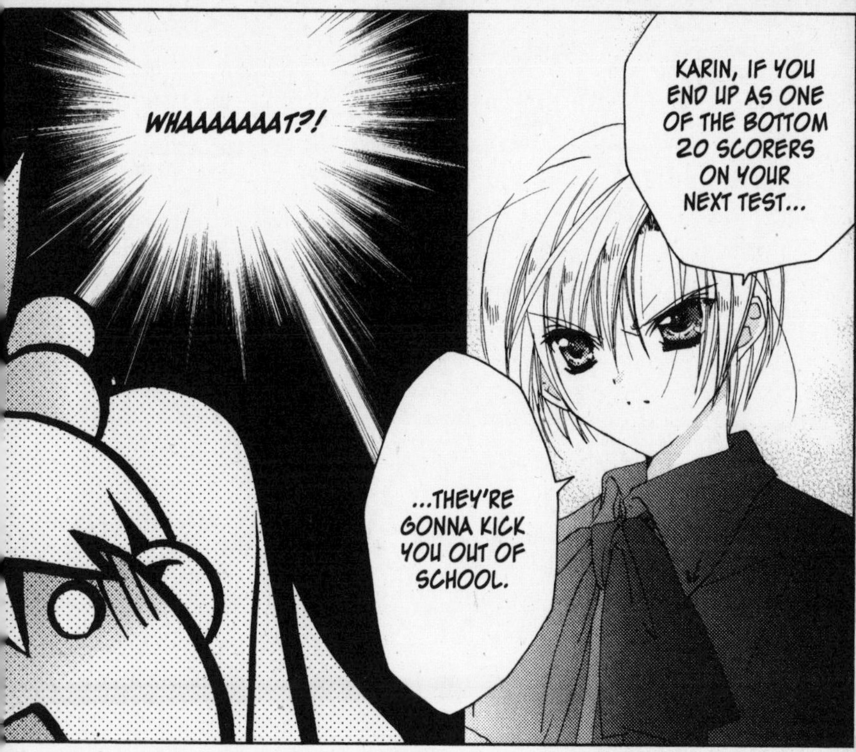
KARIN, IF YOU END UP AS ONE OF THE BOTTOM 20 SCORERS ON YOUR NEXT TEST...
...THEY'RE GONNA KICK YOU OUT OF SCHOOL.
WHAAAAAAAT?!

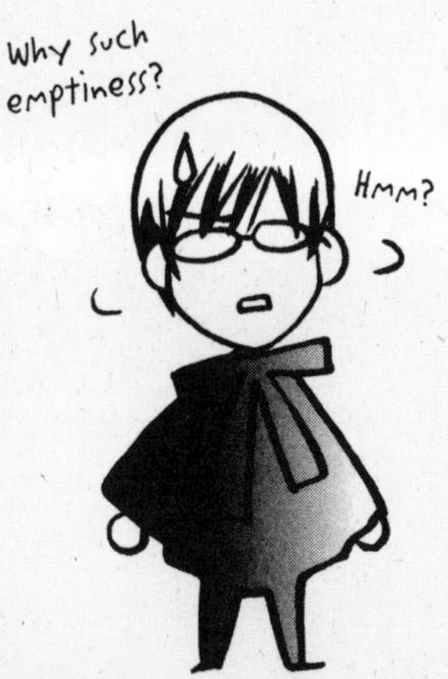
Why such emptiness?
Hmm?

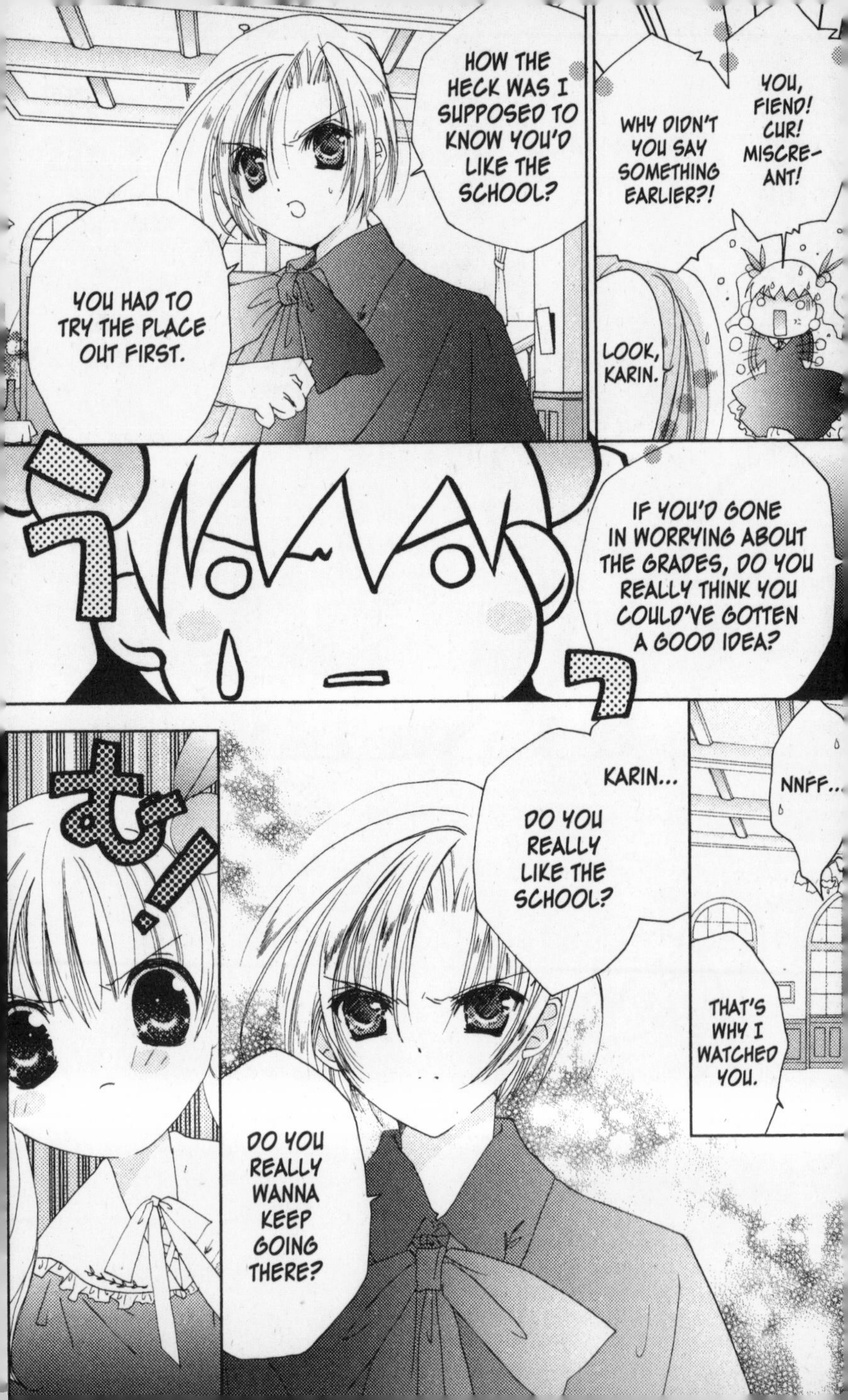
YOU, FIEND! CUR! MISCRE-ANT!
WHY DIDN'T YOU SAY SOMETHING EARLIER?!
LOOK, KARIN.
HOW THE HECK WAS I SUPPOSED TO KNOW YOU'D LIKE THE SCHOOL?
YOU HAD TO TRY THE PLACE OUT FIRST.
IF YOU'D GONE IN WORRYING ABOUT THE GRADES, DO YOU REALLY THINK YOU COULD'VE GOTTEN A GOOD IDEA?
う
NNFF...
THAT'S WHY I WATCHED YOU.
KARIN...
DO YOU REALLY LIKE THE SCHOOL?
む!
DO YOU REALLY WANNA KEEP GOING THERE?

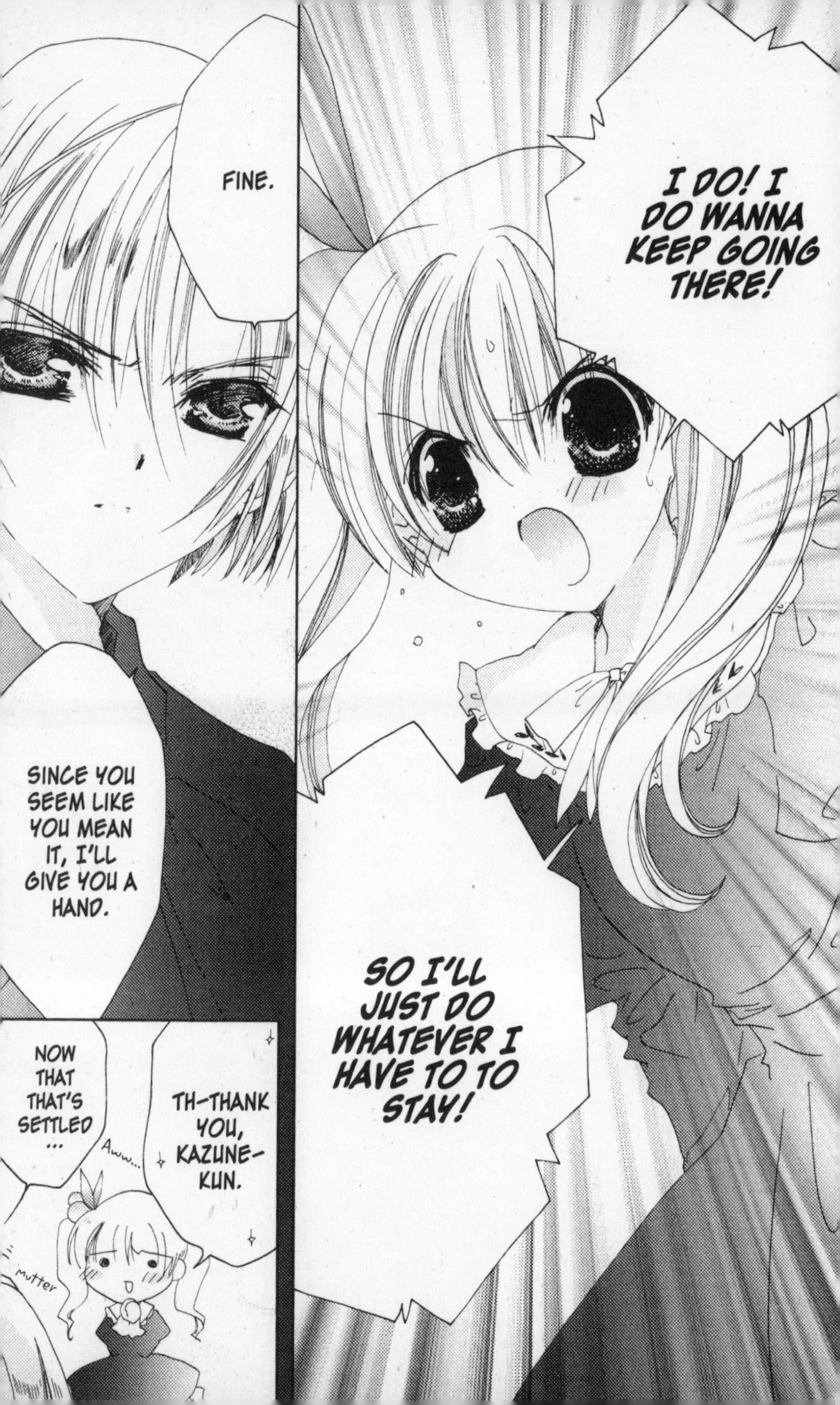
I DO! I DO WANNA KEEP GOING THERE!
SO I'LL JUST DO WHATEVER I HAVE TO TO STAY!
FINE.
SINCE YOU SEEM LIKE YOU MEAN IT, I'LL GIVE YOU A HAND.
TH-THANK YOU, KAZUNE-KUN.
NOW THAT THAT'S SETTLED ...
Aww...
mutter

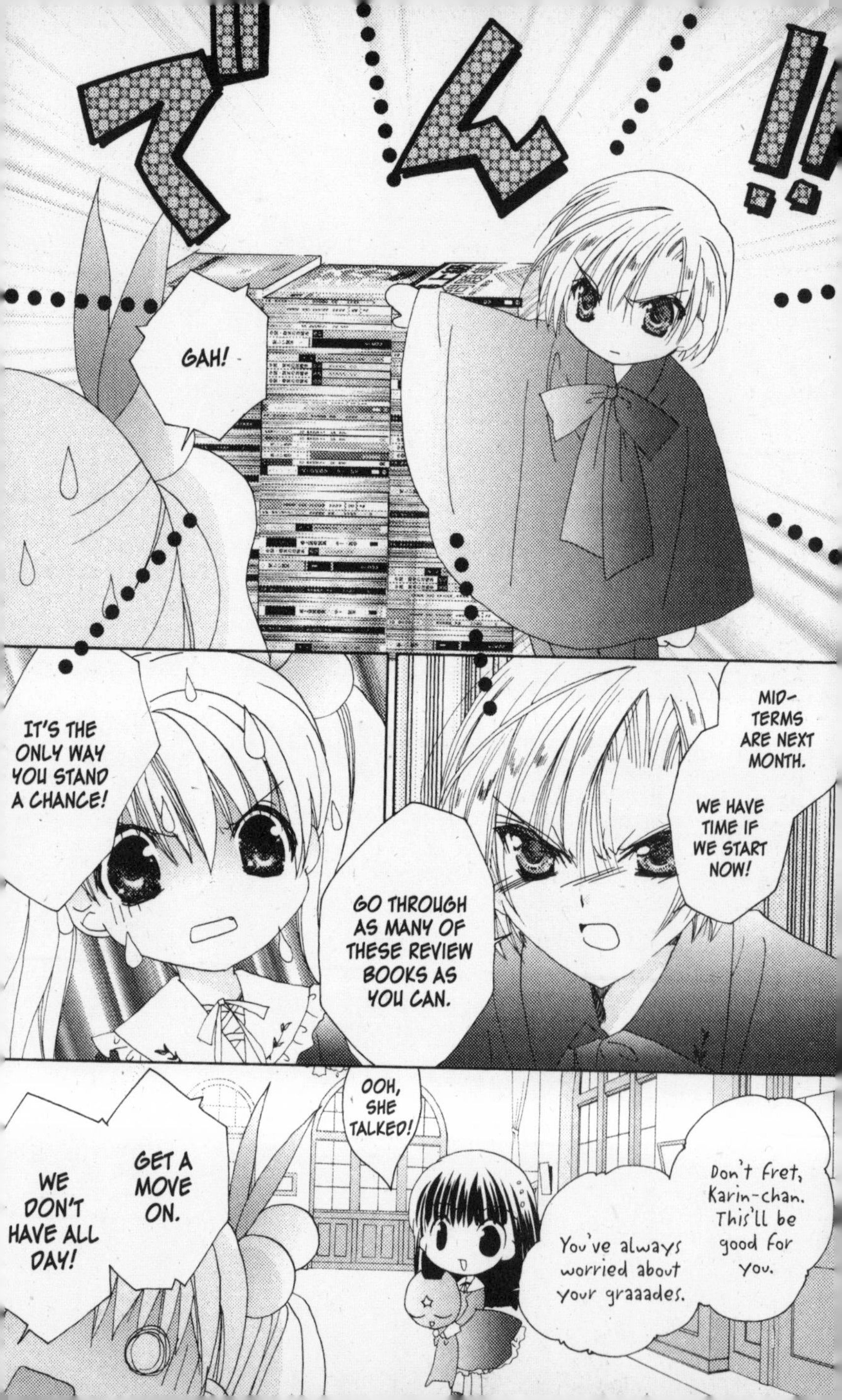

ずん……!!
GAH!
MID-TERMS ARE NEXT MONTH.
WE HAVE TIME IF WE START NOW!
GO THROUGH AS MANY OF THESE REVIEW BOOKS AS YOU CAN.
IT'S THE ONLY WAY YOU STAND A CHANCE!
Don't fret, Karin-chan. This'll be good for you.
You've always worried about your graaades.
OOH, SHE TALKED!
GET A MOVE ON.
WE DON'T HAVE ALL DAY!

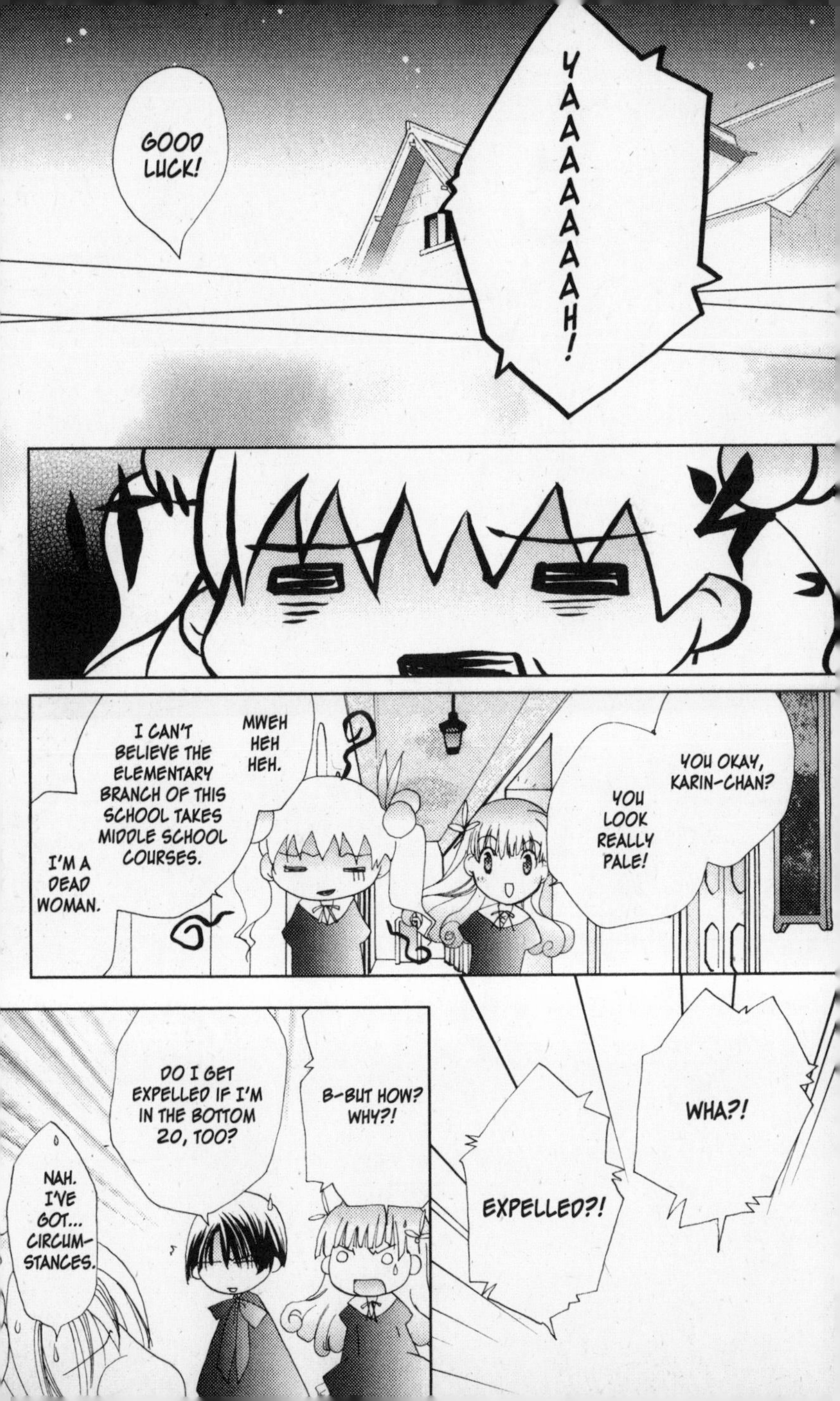
YAAAAAAAH!
GOOD LUCK!
YOU OKAY, KARIN-CHAN?
YOU LOOK REALLY PALE!
MWEH HEH HEH.
I CAN'T BELIEVE THE ELEMENTARY BRANCH OF THIS SCHOOL TAKES MIDDLE SCHOOL COURSES.
I'M A DEAD WOMAN.
WHA?!
EXPELLED?!
B-BUT HOW? WHY?!
DO I GET EXPELLED IF I'M IN THE BOTTOM 20, TOO?
NAH. I'VE GOT... CIRCUMSTANCES.

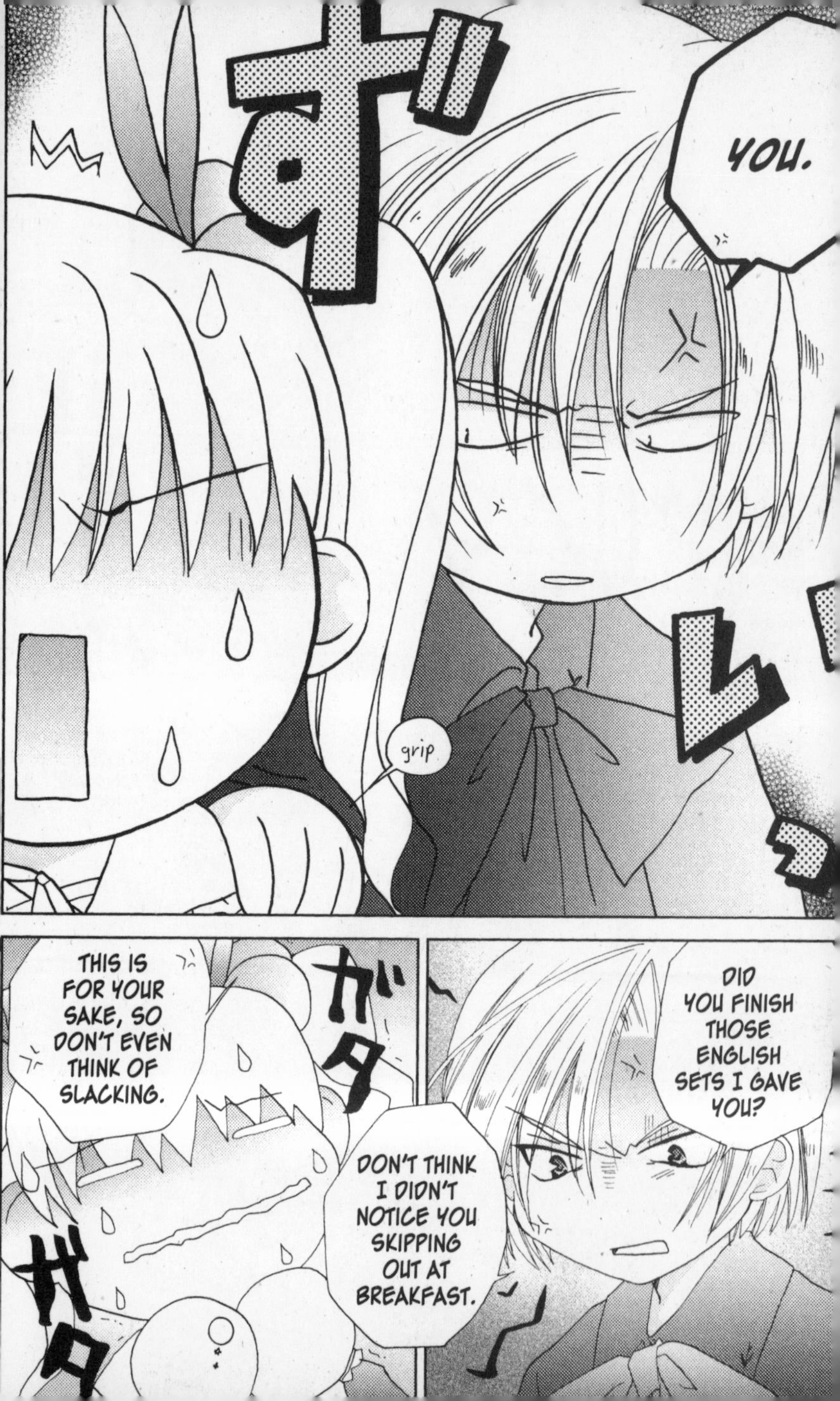
YOU.
grip
DID YOU FINISH THOSE ENGLISH SETS I GAVE YOU?
DON'T THINK I DIDN'T NOTICE YOU SKIPPING OUT AT BREAKFAST.
THIS IS FOR YOUR SAKE, SO DON'T EVEN THINK OF SLACKING.
ガタ
ガタ

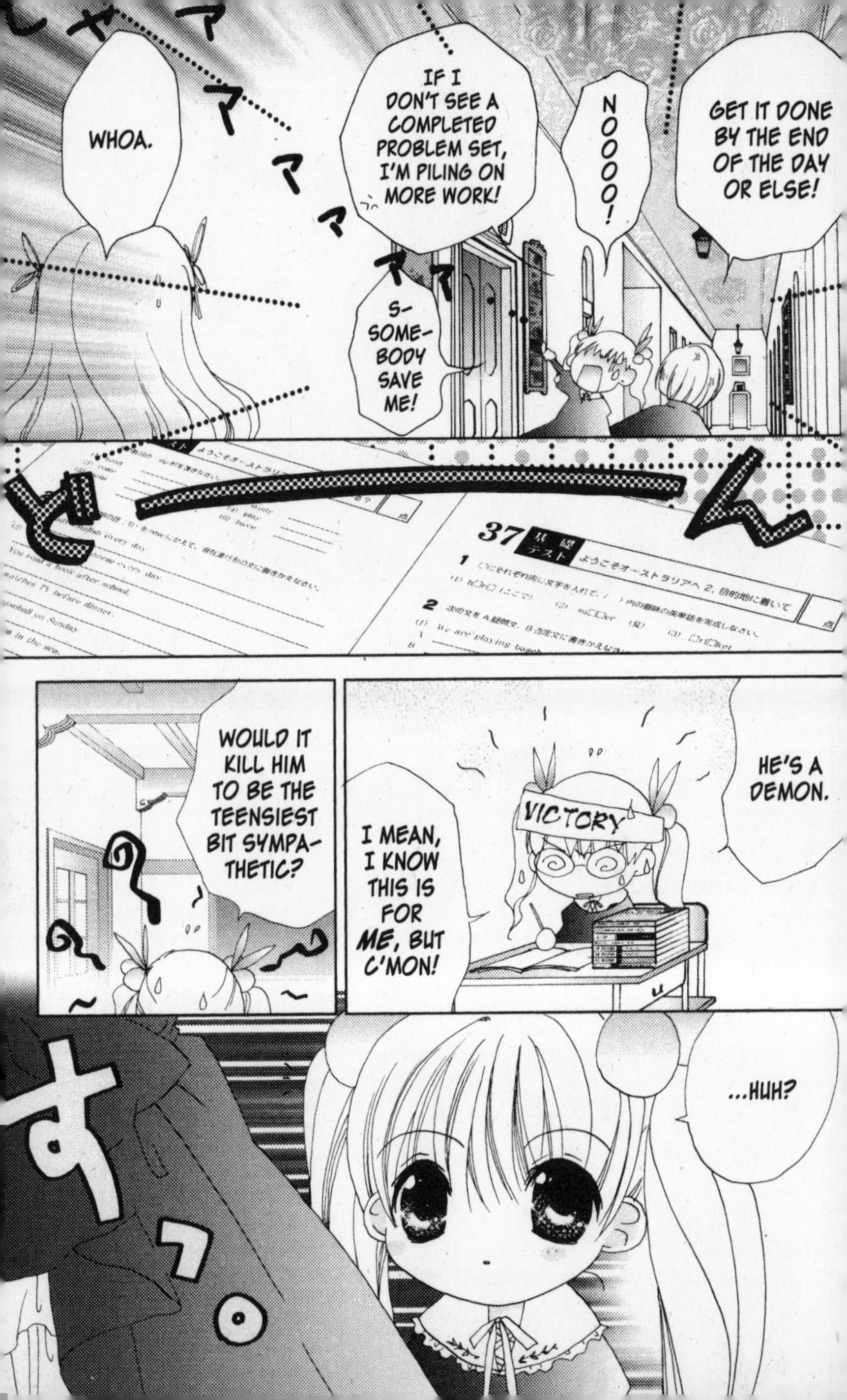
GET IT DONE BY THE END OF THE DAY OR ELSE!
NOOOOO!
IF I DON'T SEE A COMPLETED PROBLEM SET, I'M PILING ON MORE WORK!
S-SOMEBODY SAVE ME!
WHOA.
どーーーーん
37 基礎テスト ようこそオーストラリアへ 2. 目的地に着いて
HE'S A DEMON.
VICTORY
I MEAN, I KNOW THIS IS FOR *ME*, BUT C'MON!
WOULD IT KILL HIM TO BE THE TEENSIEST BIT SYMPATHETIC?
...HUH?
すっ

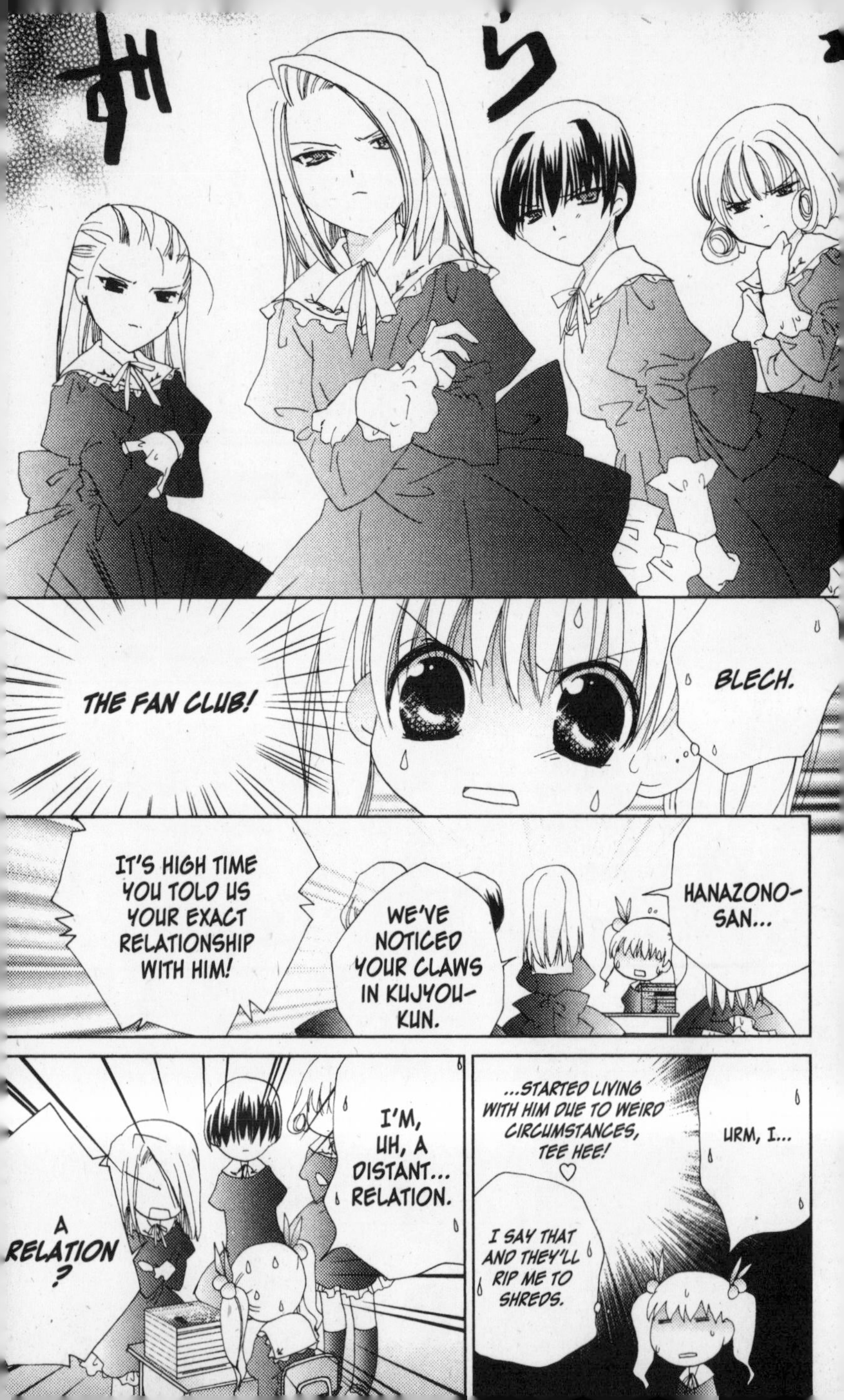
ずら
BLECH.
THE FAN CLUB!
HANAZONO-SAN...
WE'VE NOTICED YOUR CLAWS IN KUJYOU-KUN.
IT'S HIGH TIME YOU TOLD US YOUR EXACT RELATIONSHIP WITH HIM!
URM, I...
...STARTED LIVING WITH HIM DUE TO WEIRD CIRCUMSTANCES, TEE HEE! ♡
I SAY THAT AND THEY'LL RIP ME TO SHREDS.
I'M, UH, A DISTANT... RELATION.
A RELATION?

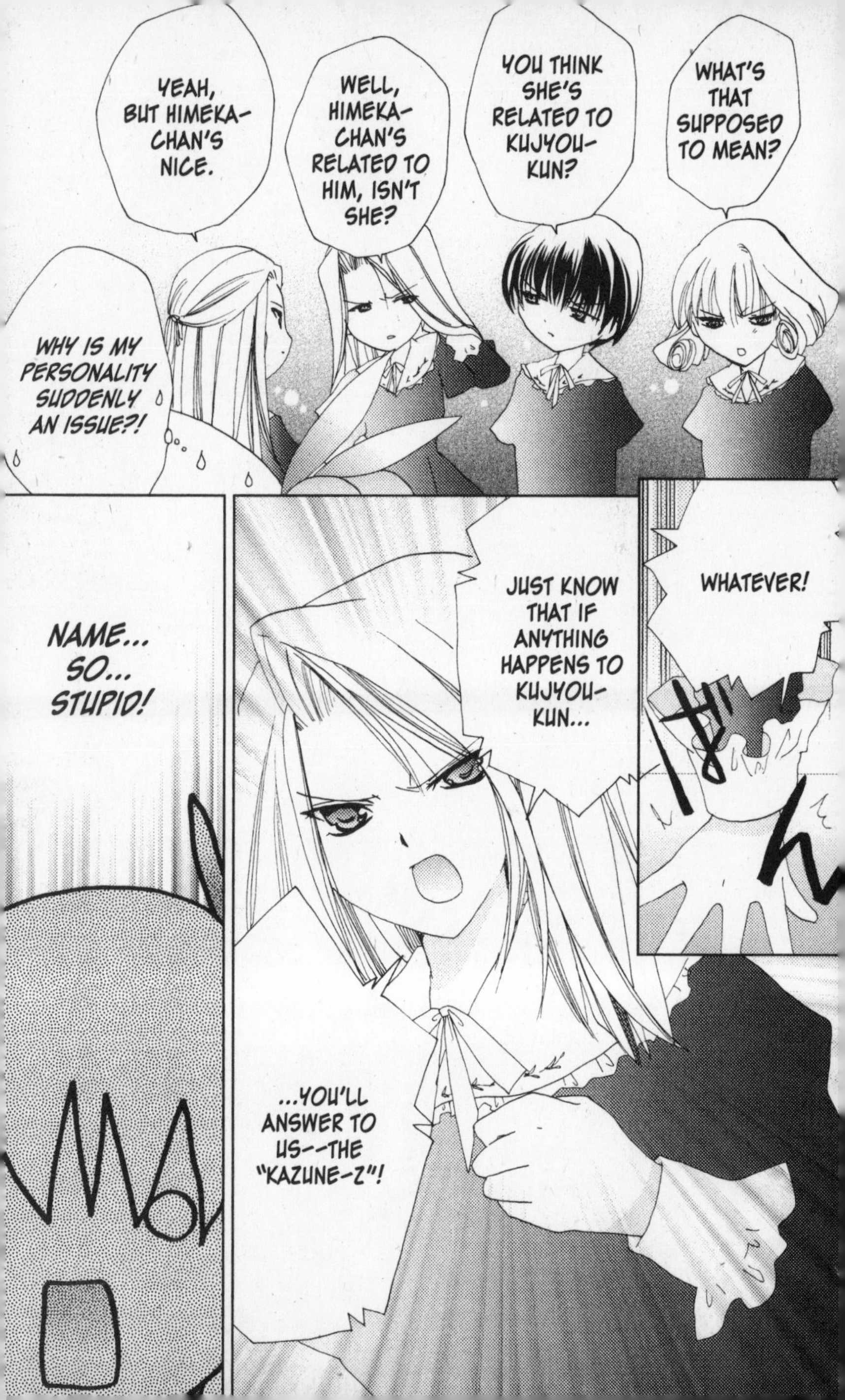
WHAT'S THAT SUPPOSED TO MEAN?
YOU THINK SHE'S RELATED TO KUJYOU-KUN?
WELL, HIMEKA-CHAN'S RELATED TO HIM, ISN'T SHE?
YEAH, BUT HIMEKA-CHAN'S NICE.
WHY IS MY PERSONALITY SUDDENLY AN ISSUE?!
WHATEVER!
JUST KNOW THAT IF ANYTHING HAPPENS TO KUJYOU-KUN...
...YOU'LL ANSWER TO US--THE "KAZUNE-Z"!
NAME... SO... STUPID!

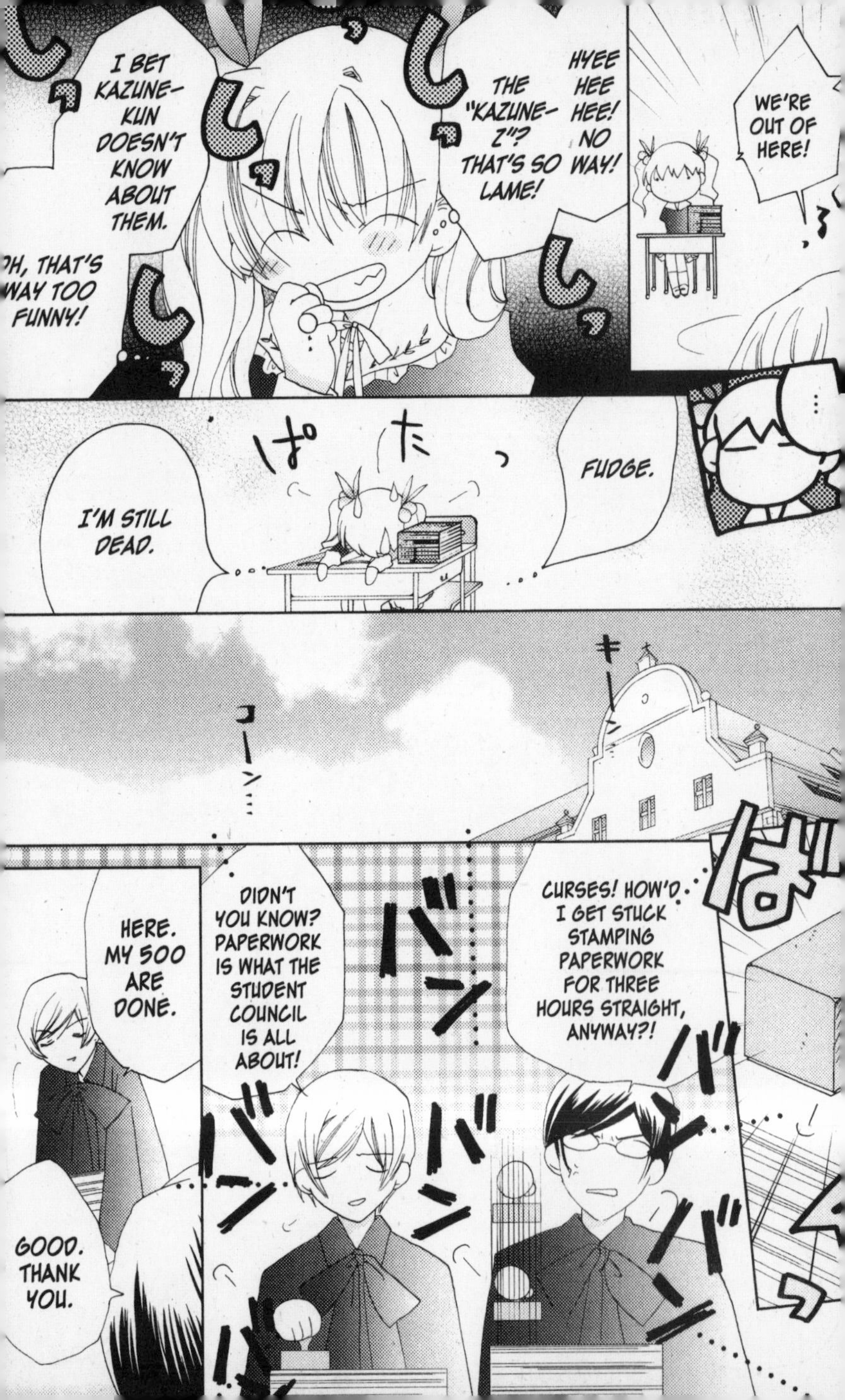
WE'RE OUT OF HERE!
HYEE HEE HEE! NO WAY!
THE "KAZUNE-Z"? THAT'S SO LAME!
I BET KAZUNE-KUN DOESN'T KNOW ABOUT THEM.
OH, THAT'S WAY TOO FUNNY!
...
FUDGE.
I'M STILL DEAD.
CURSES! HOW'D I GET STUCK STAMPING PAPERWORK FOR THREE HOURS STRAIGHT, ANYWAY?!
DIDN'T YOU KNOW? PAPERWORK IS WHAT THE STUDENT COUNCIL IS ALL ABOUT!
HERE. MY 500 ARE DONE.
GOOD. THANK YOU.

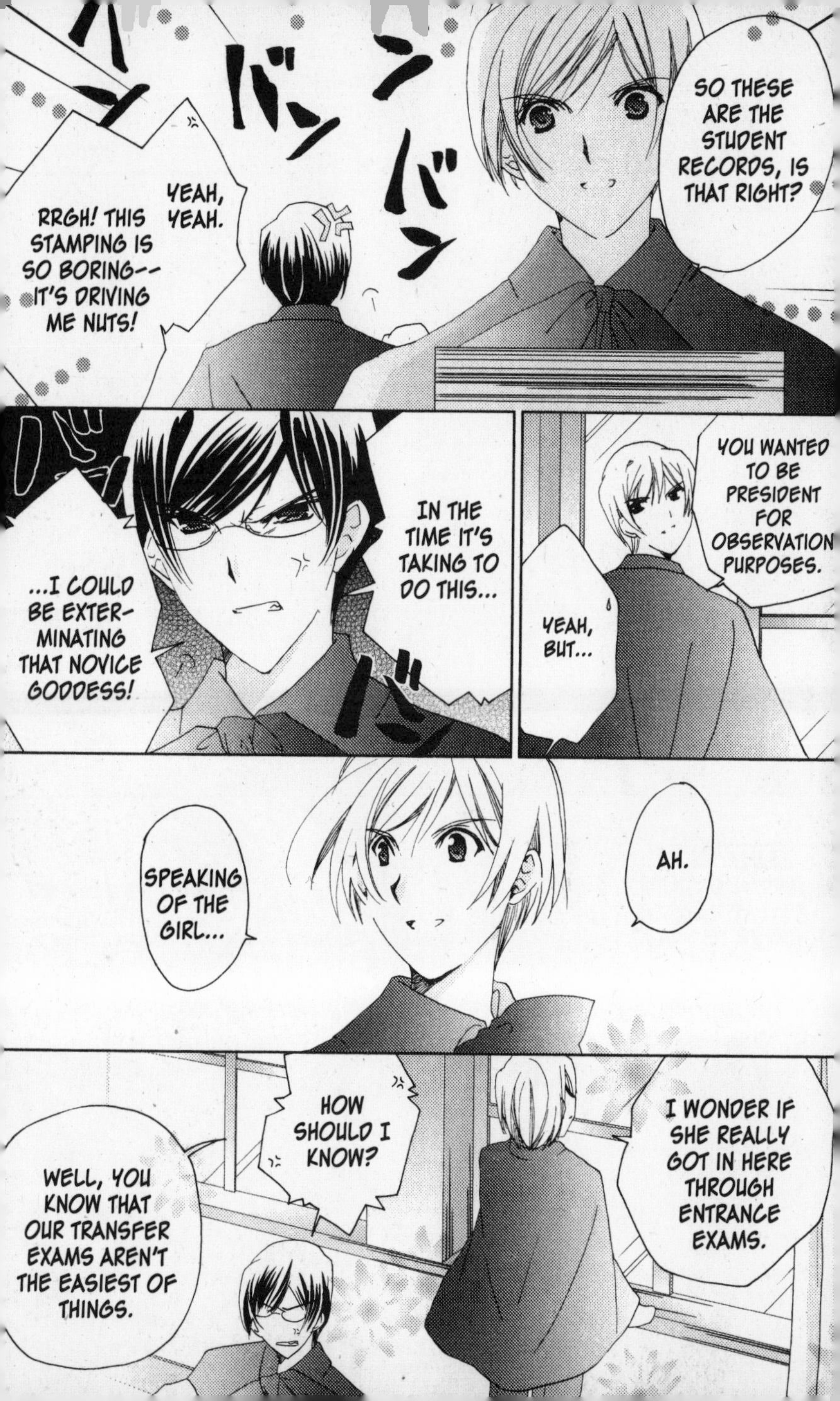
SO THESE ARE THE STUDENT RECORDS, IS THAT RIGHT?
バンッ
バンッ
YEAH, YEAH.
RRGH! THIS STAMPING IS SO BORING--IT'S DRIVING ME NUTS!
YOU WANTED TO BE PRESIDENT FOR OBSERVATION PURPOSES.
YEAH, BUT...
IN THE TIME IT'S TAKING TO DO THIS...
...I COULD BE EXTER-MINATING THAT NOVICE GODDESS!
AH.
SPEAKING OF THE GIRL...
I WONDER IF SHE REALLY GOT IN HERE THROUGH ENTRANCE EXAMS.
HOW SHOULD I KNOW?
WELL, YOU KNOW THAT OUR TRANSFER EXAMS AREN'T THE EASIEST OF THINGS.

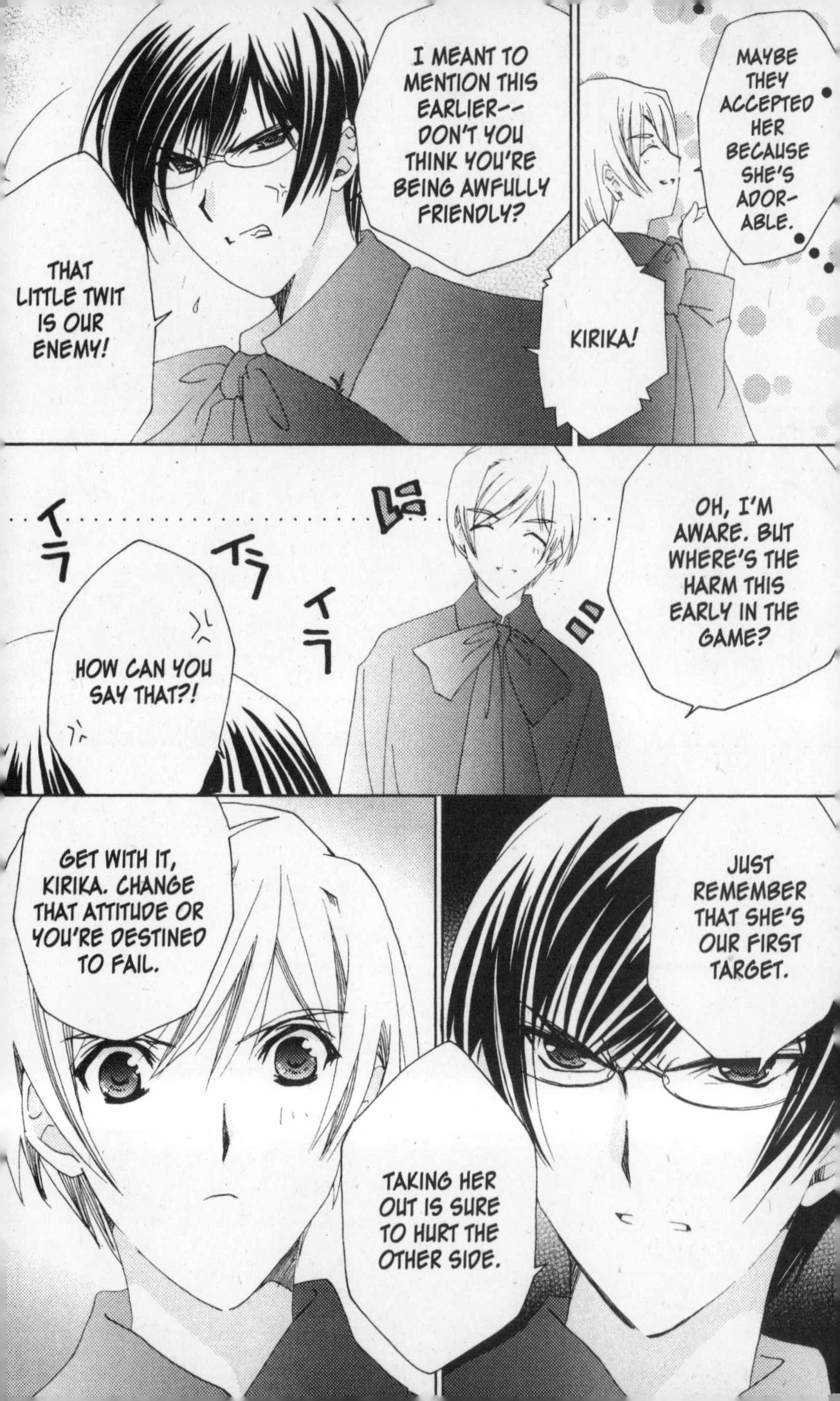
MAYBE THEY ACCEPTED HER BECAUSE SHE'S ADOR-ABLE.
KIRIKA!
I MEANT TO MENTION THIS EARLIER-- DON'T YOU THINK YOU'RE BEING AWFULLY FRIENDLY?
THAT LITTLE TWIT IS OUR ENEMY!
OH, I'M AWARE. BUT WHERE'S THE HARM THIS EARLY IN THE GAME?
イラ
イラ
イラ
HOW CAN YOU SAY THAT?!
JUST REMEMBER THAT SHE'S OUR FIRST TARGET.
TAKING HER OUT IS SURE TO HURT THE OTHER SIDE.
GET WITH IT, KIRIKA. CHANGE THAT ATTITUDE OR YOU'RE DESTINED TO FAIL.

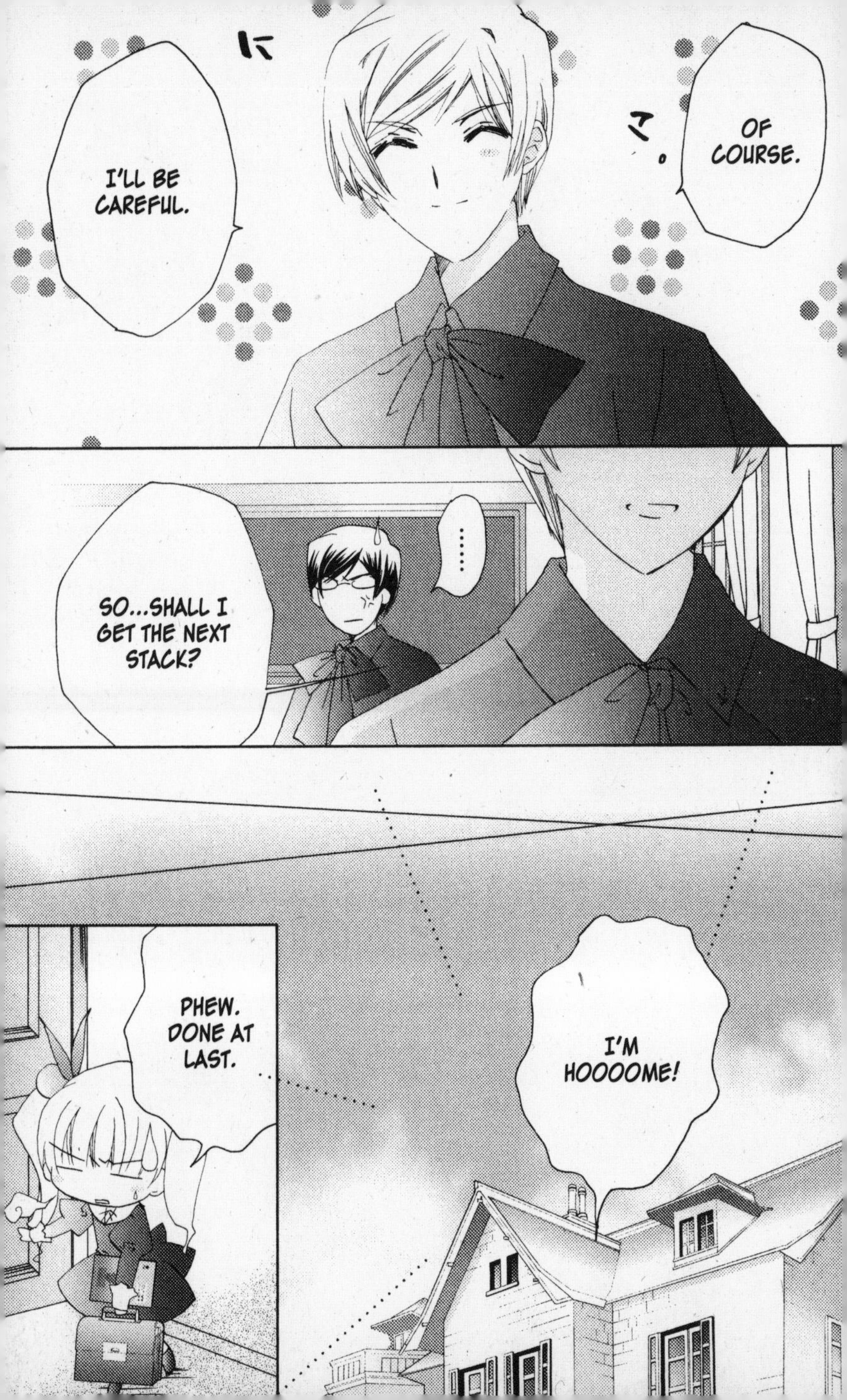
OF COURSE.
にこ。
I'LL BE CAREFUL.
......
SO...SHALL I GET THE NEXT STACK?
I'M HOOOOME!
PHEW. DONE AT LAST.

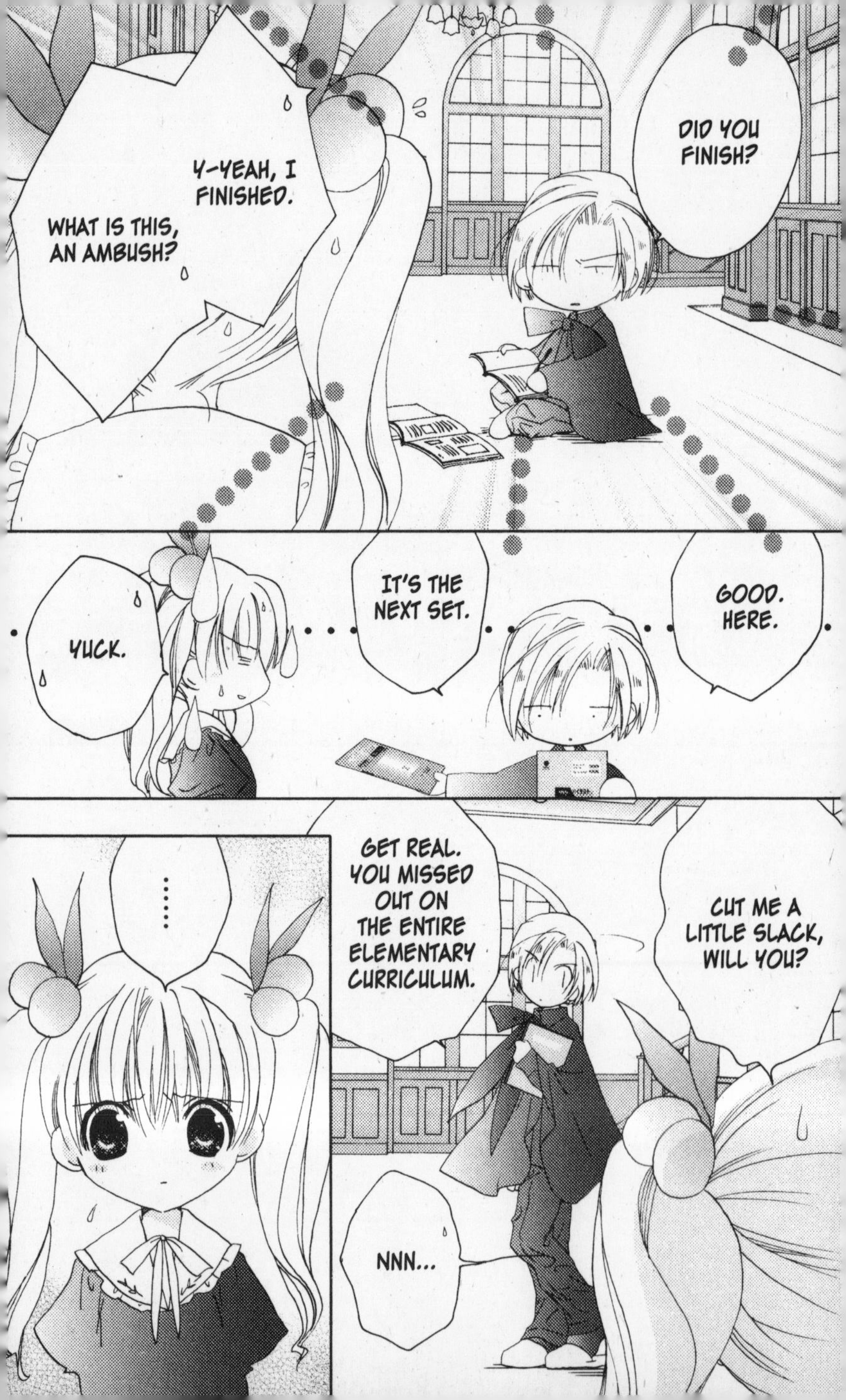
DID YOU FINISH?
Y-YEAH, I FINISHED.
WHAT IS THIS, AN AMBUSH?
GOOD. HERE.
IT'S THE NEXT SET.
YUCK.
CUT ME A LITTLE SLACK, WILL YOU?
GET REAL. YOU MISSED OUT ON THE ENTIRE ELEMENTARY CURRICULUM.
NNN...
......

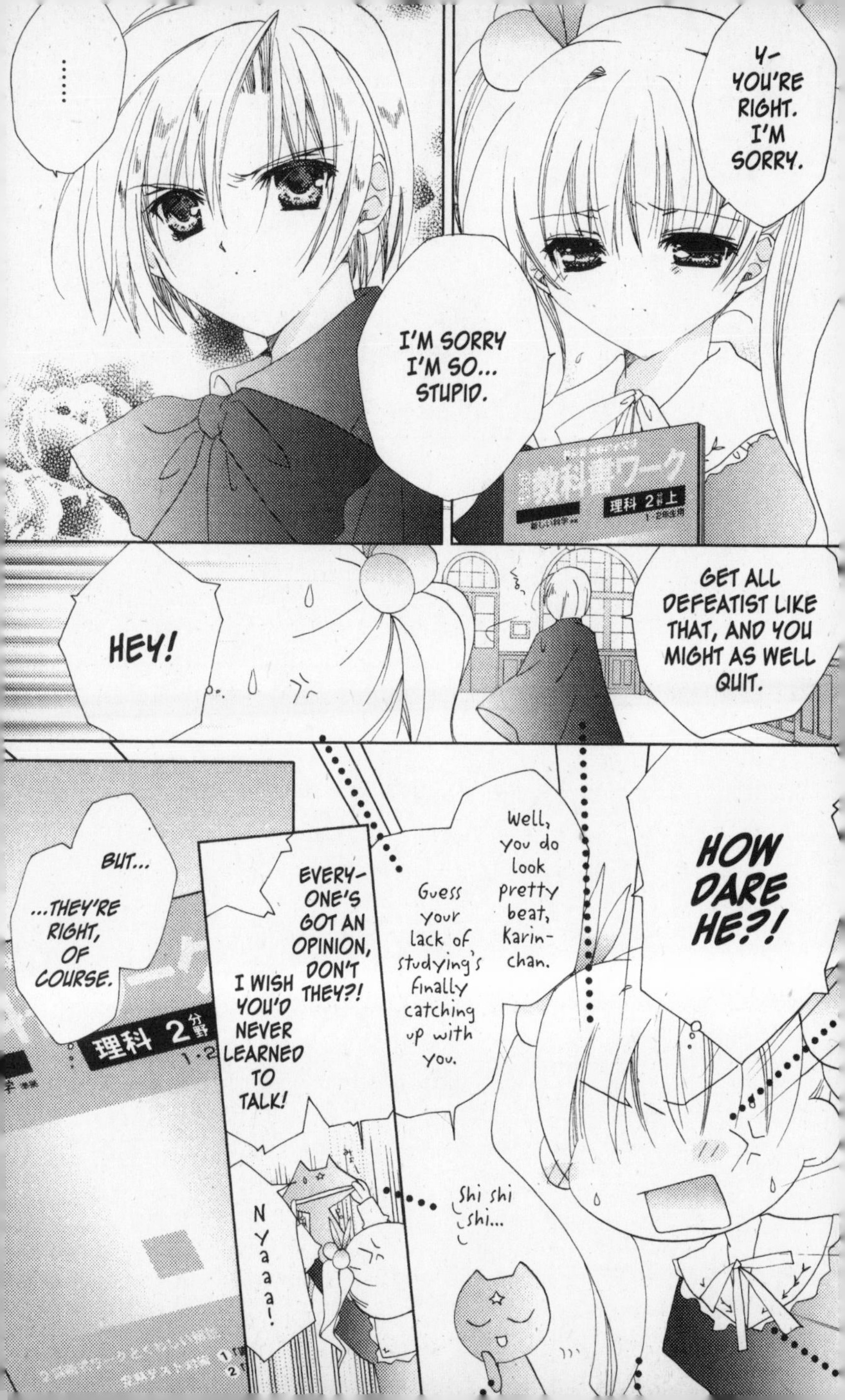

Y-YOU'RE RIGHT. I'M SORRY.
I'M SORRY I'M SO... STUPID.
教科書ワーク
理科 2分野上
......
GET ALL DEFEATIST LIKE THAT, AND YOU MIGHT AS WELL QUIT.
HEY!
HOW DARE HE?!
Well, you do look pretty beat, Karin-chan.
Guess your lack of studying's finally catching up with you.
Shi shi shi...
EVERYONE'S GOT AN OPINION, DON'T THEY?!
I WISH YOU'D NEVER LEARNED TO TALK!
Nyaaa!
BUT...
...THEY'RE RIGHT, OF COURSE.
理科 2分野

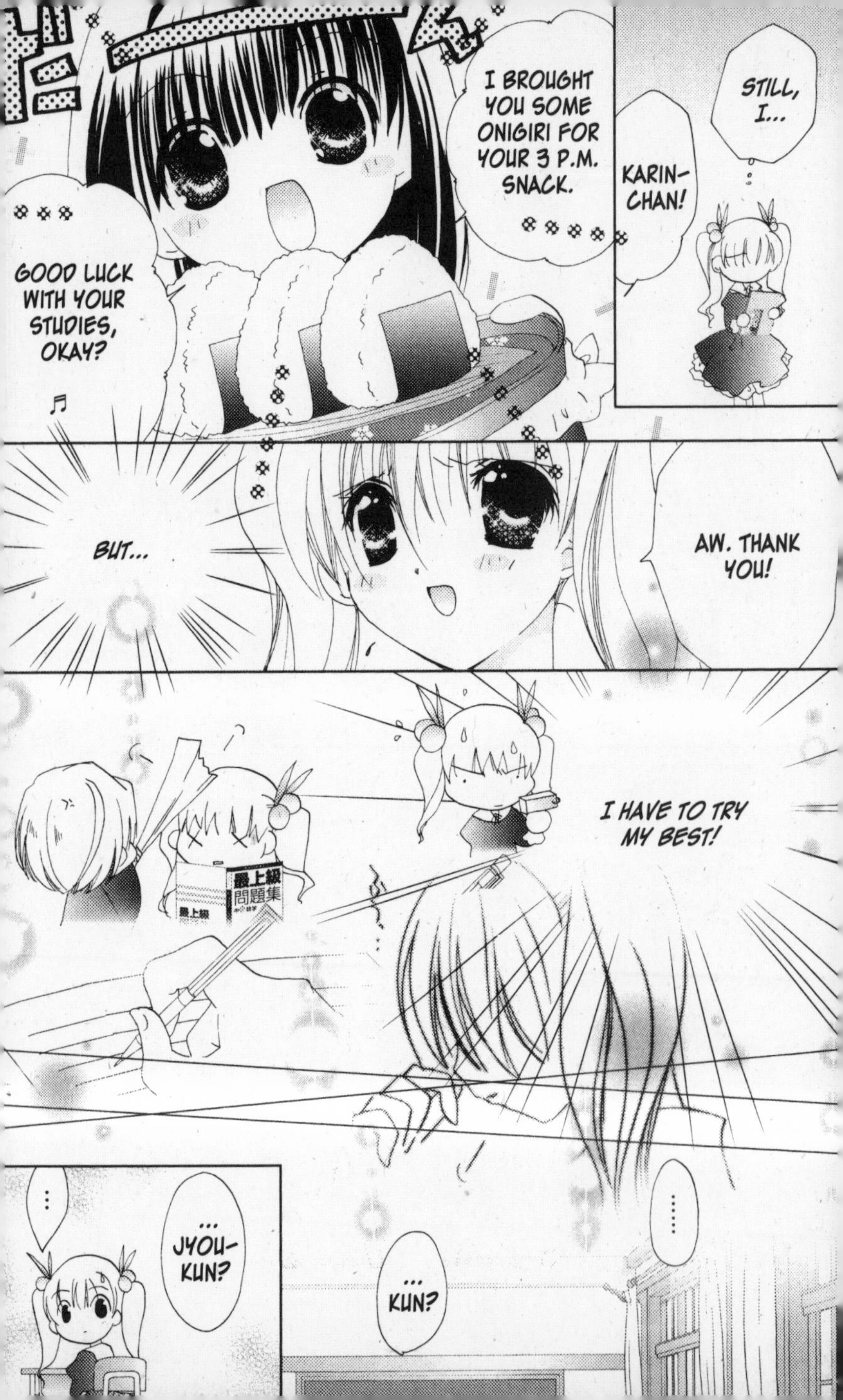
STILL, I...
KARIN-CHAN!
I BROUGHT YOU SOME ONIGIRI FOR YOUR 3 P.M. SNACK.
GOOD LUCK WITH YOUR STUDIES, OKAY?
AW. THANK YOU!
BUT...
I HAVE TO TRY MY BEST!
最上級
問題集
......
...KUN?
...JYOU-KUN?
...

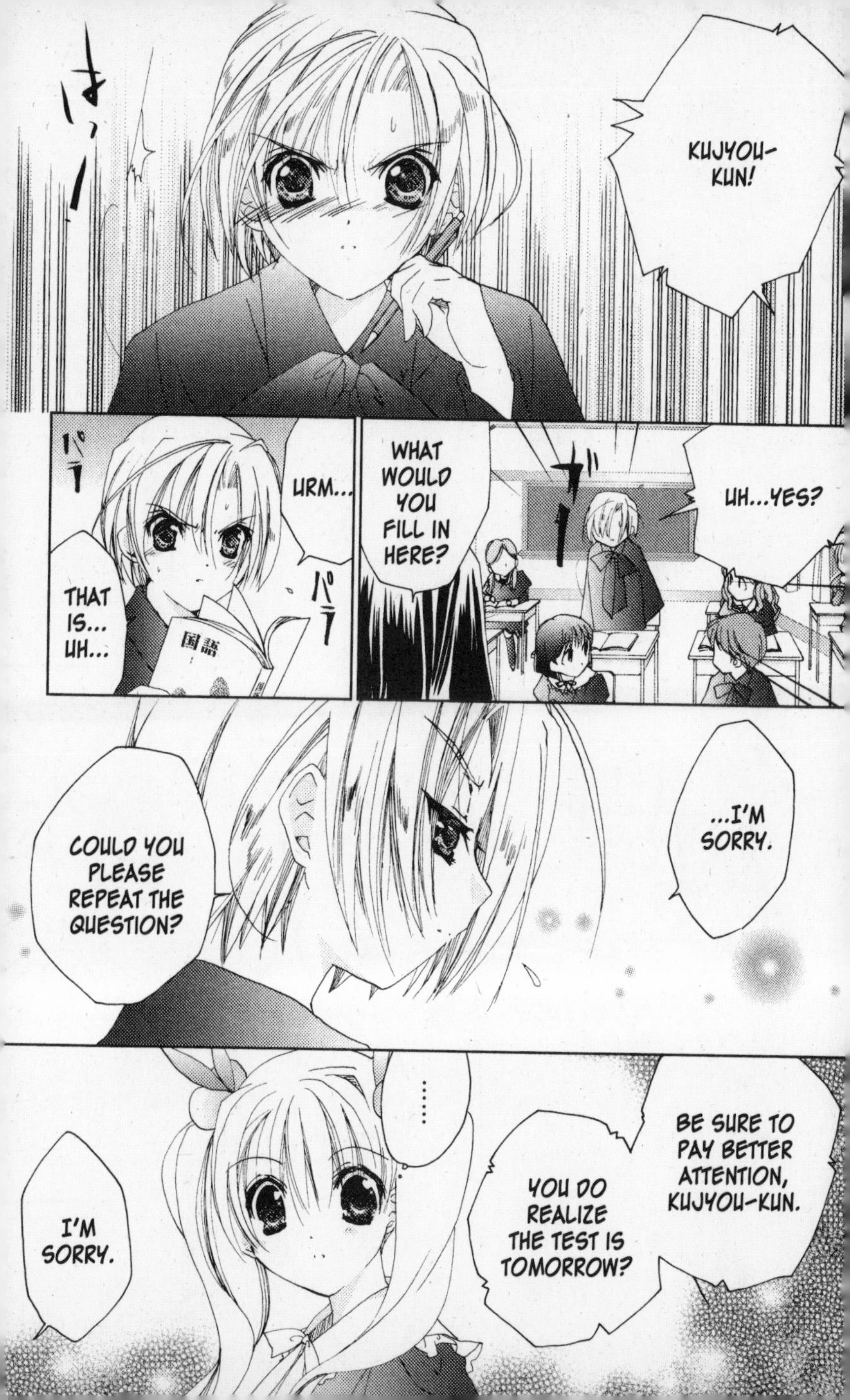
KUJYOU-KUN!
はっ
UH...YES?
WHAT WOULD YOU FILL IN HERE?
URM...
パラ
THAT IS... UH...
国語
...I'M SORRY.
COULD YOU PLEASE REPEAT THE QUESTION?
BE SURE TO PAY BETTER ATTENTION, KUJYOU-KUN.
YOU DO REALIZE THE TEST IS TOMORROW?
......
I'M SORRY.

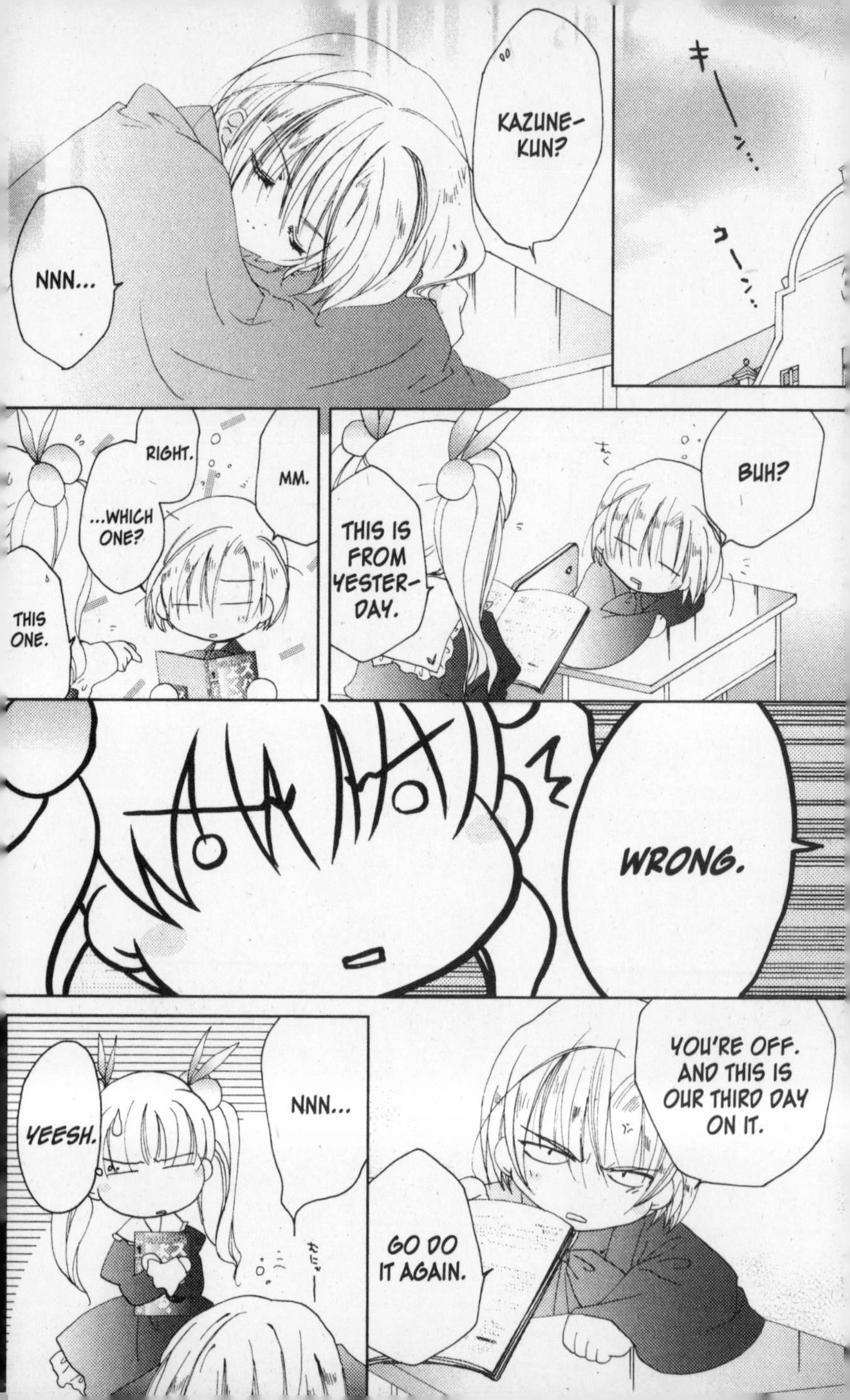

キーン…
コーン…
KAZUNE-KUN?
NNN...
BUH?
THIS IS FROM YESTER-DAY.
MM.
RIGHT.
...WHICH ONE?
THIS ONE.
WRONG.
YOU'RE OFF. AND THIS IS OUR THIRD DAY ON IT.
GO DO IT AGAIN.
NNN...
YEESH.

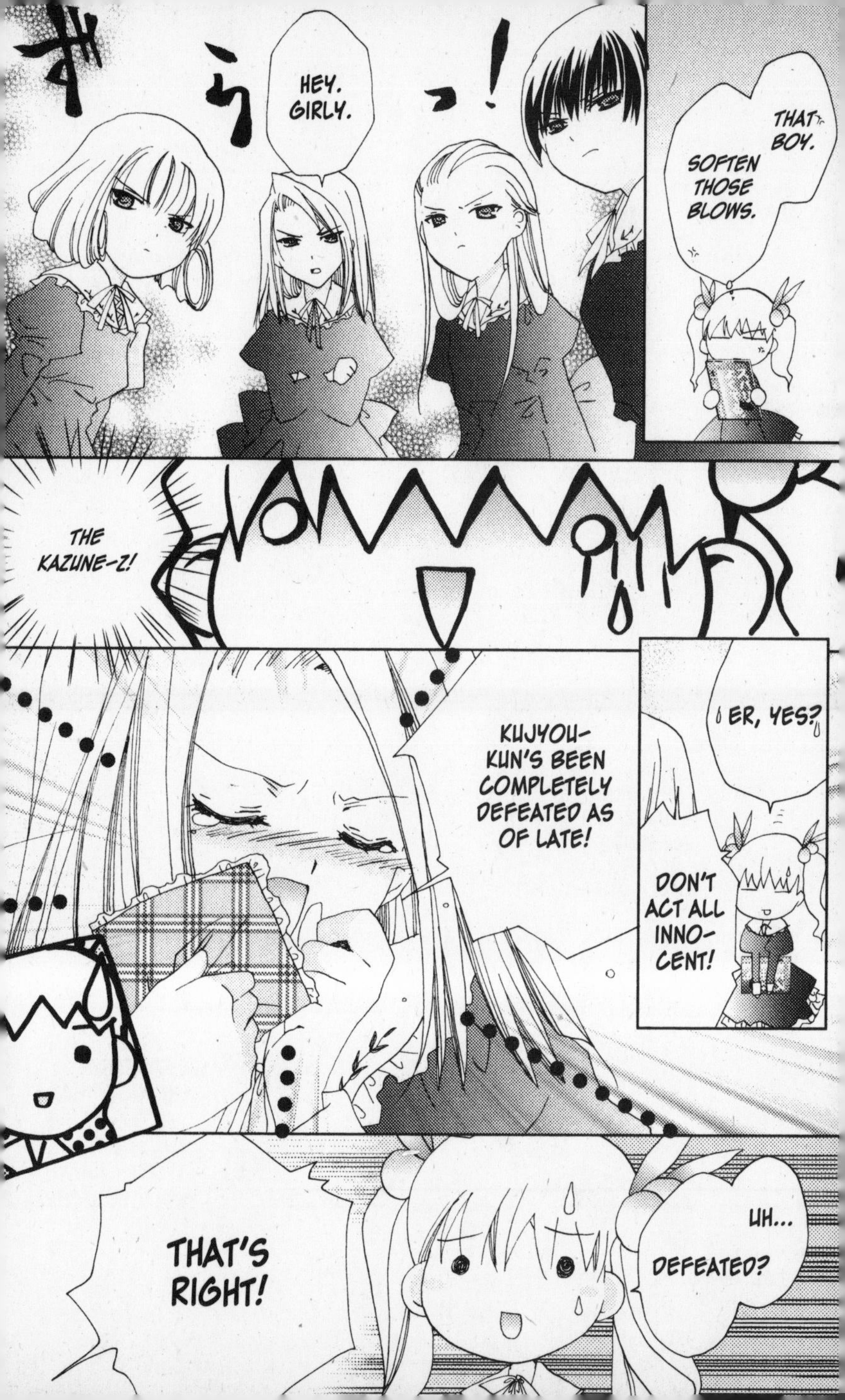
THAT BOY.
SOFTEN THOSE BLOWS.
HEY. GIRLY.
ずらっ!
THE KAZUNE-Z!
ER, YES?
DON'T ACT ALL INNO-CENT!
KUJYOU-KUN'S BEEN COMPLETELY DEFEATED AS OF LATE!
UH... DEFEATED?
THAT'S RIGHT!

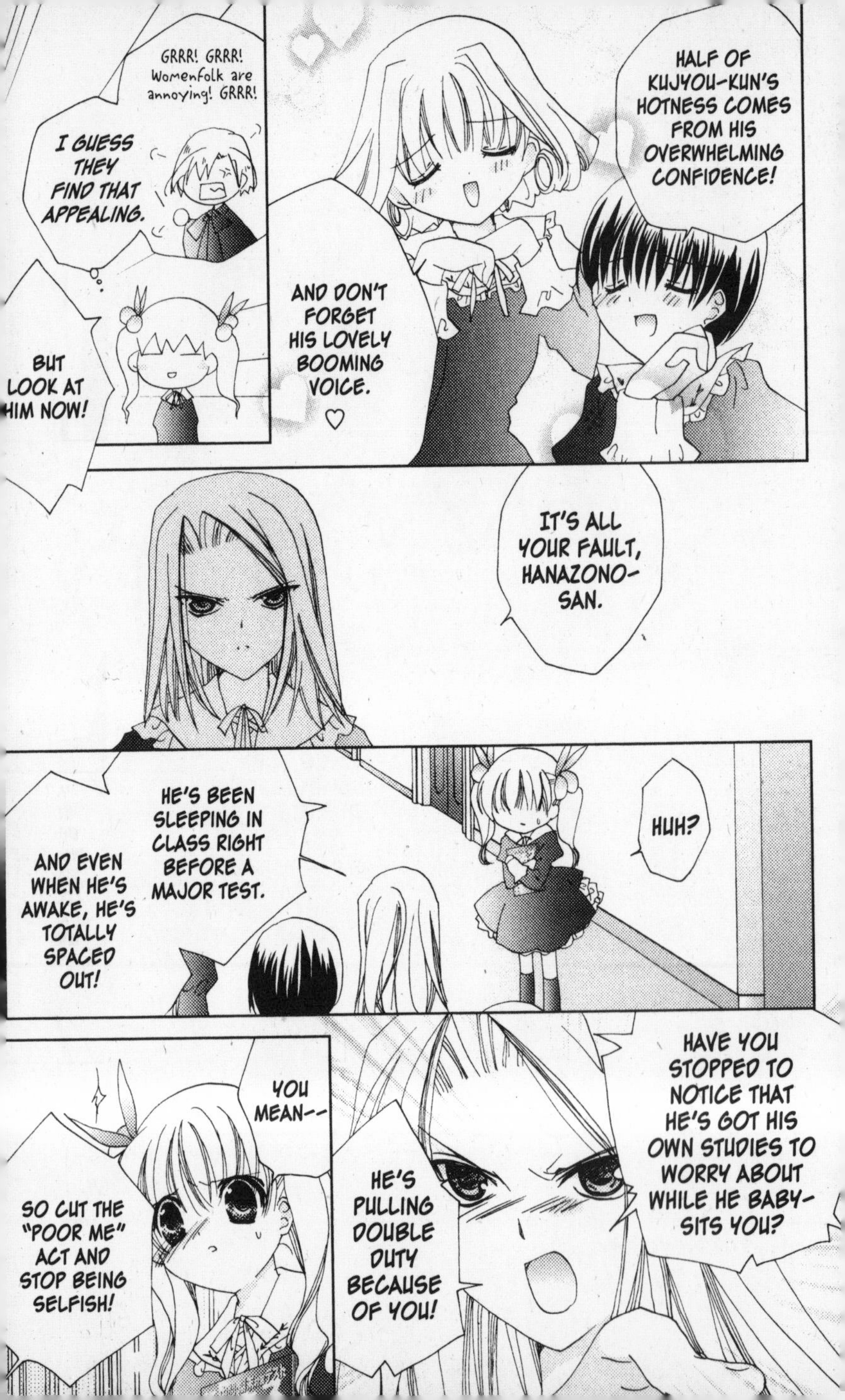
HALF OF KUJYOU-KUN'S HOTNESS COMES FROM HIS OVERWHELMING CONFIDENCE!
AND DON'T FORGET HIS LOVELY BOOMING VOICE. ♡
GRRR! GRRR! Womenfolk are annoying! GRRR!
I GUESS THEY FIND THAT APPEALING.
BUT LOOK AT HIM NOW!
IT'S ALL YOUR FAULT, HANAZONO-SAN.
HUH?
HE'S BEEN SLEEPING IN CLASS RIGHT BEFORE A MAJOR TEST.
AND EVEN WHEN HE'S AWAKE, HE'S TOTALLY SPACED OUT!
HAVE YOU STOPPED TO NOTICE THAT HE'S GOT HIS OWN STUDIES TO WORRY ABOUT WHILE HE BABY-SITS YOU?
HE'S PULLING DOUBLE DUTY BECAUSE OF YOU!
YOU MEAN--
SO CUT THE "POOR ME" ACT AND STOP BEING SELFISH!

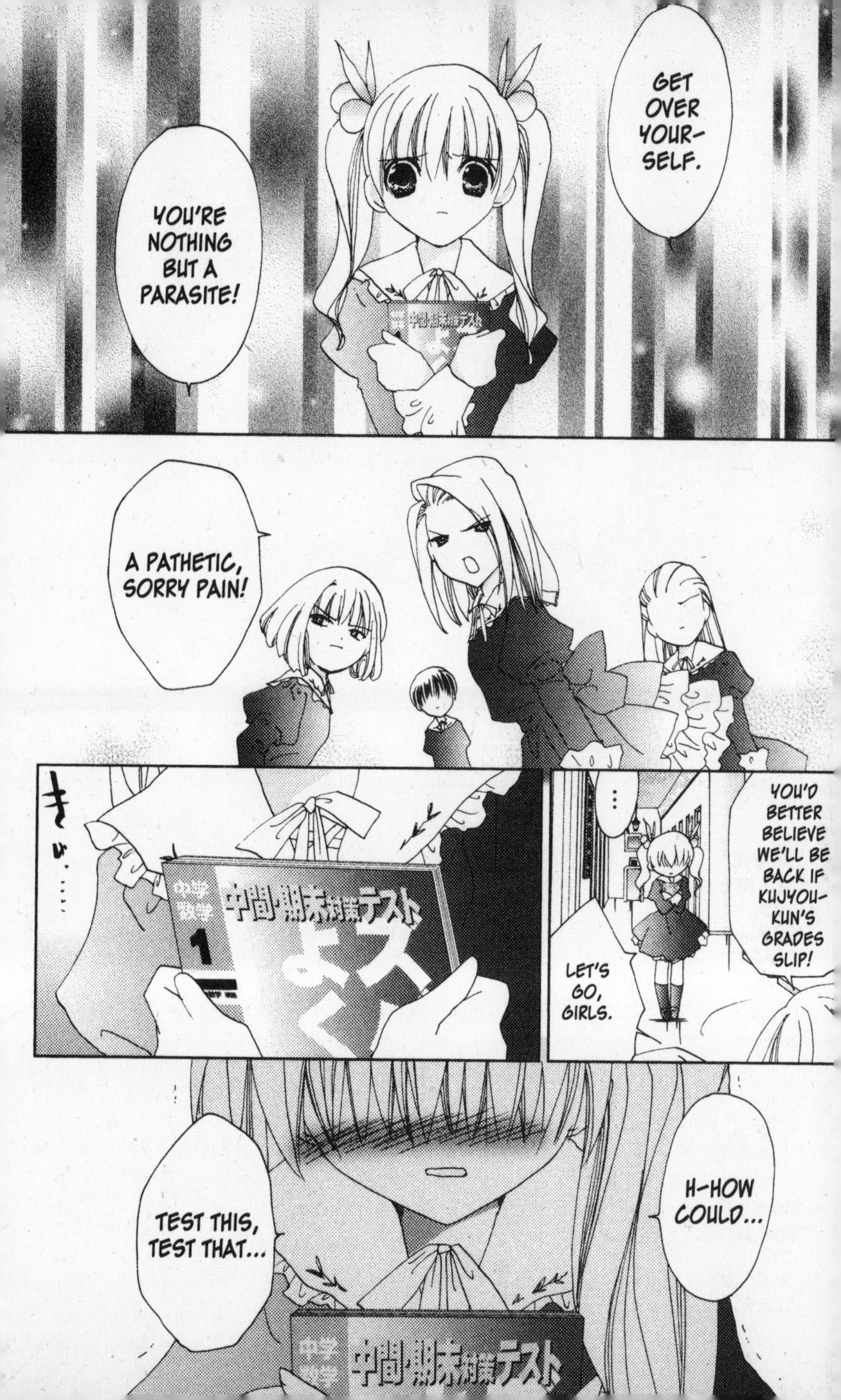
GET OVER YOUR-SELF.
YOU'RE NOTHING BUT A PARASITE!
A PATHETIC, SORRY PAIN!
YOU'D BETTER BELIEVE WE'LL BE BACK IF KUJYOU-KUN'S GRADES SLIP!
...
LET'S GO, GIRLS.
H-HOW COULD...
TEST THIS, TEST THAT...

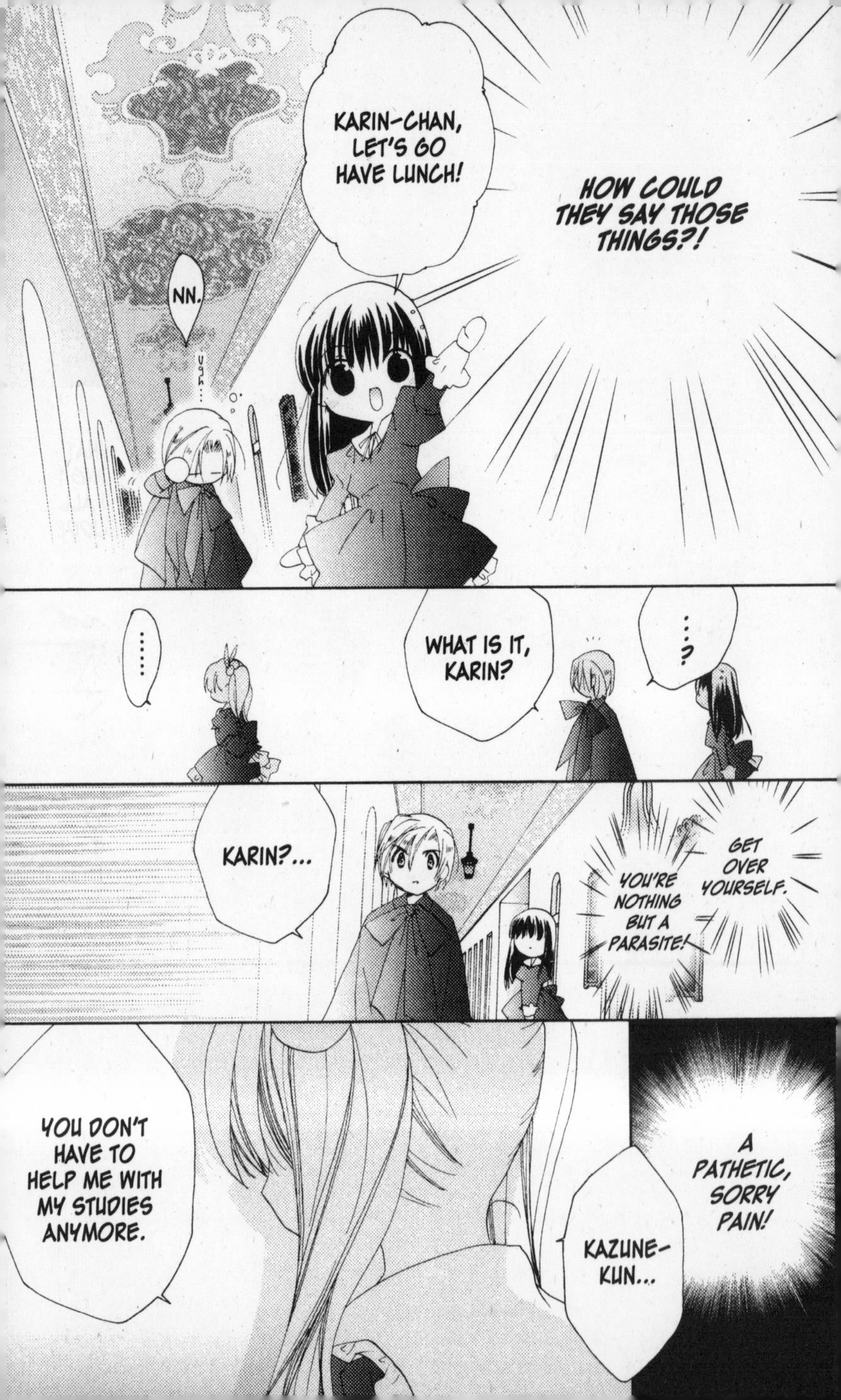
HOW COULD THEY SAY THOSE THINGS?!
KARIN-CHAN, LET'S GO HAVE LUNCH!
NN.
ugh...
...?
WHAT IS IT, KARIN?
......
GET OVER YOURSELF.
YOU'RE NOTHING BUT A PARASITE!
KARIN?...
A PATHETIC, SORRY PAIN!
KAZUNE-KUN...
YOU DON'T HAVE TO HELP ME WITH MY STUDIES ANYMORE.

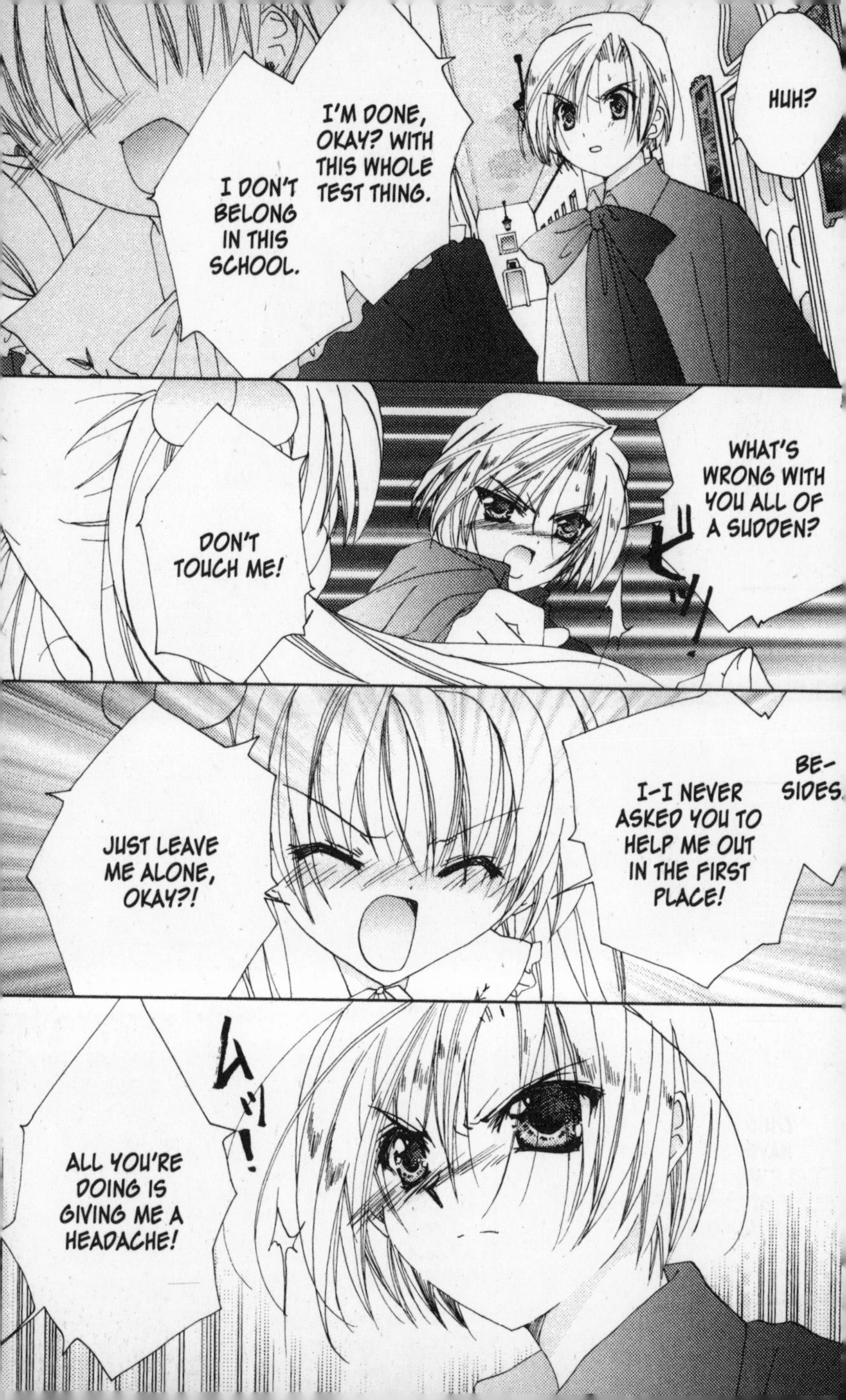
HUH?
I'M DONE, OKAY? WITH THIS WHOLE TEST THING.
I DON'T BELONG IN THIS SCHOOL.
WHAT'S WRONG WITH YOU ALL OF A SUDDEN?
DON'T TOUCH ME!
BE-SIDES.
I-I NEVER ASKED YOU TO HELP ME OUT IN THE FIRST PLACE!
JUST LEAVE ME ALONE, OKAY?!
ムッ!
ALL YOU'RE DOING IS GIVING ME A HEADACHE!

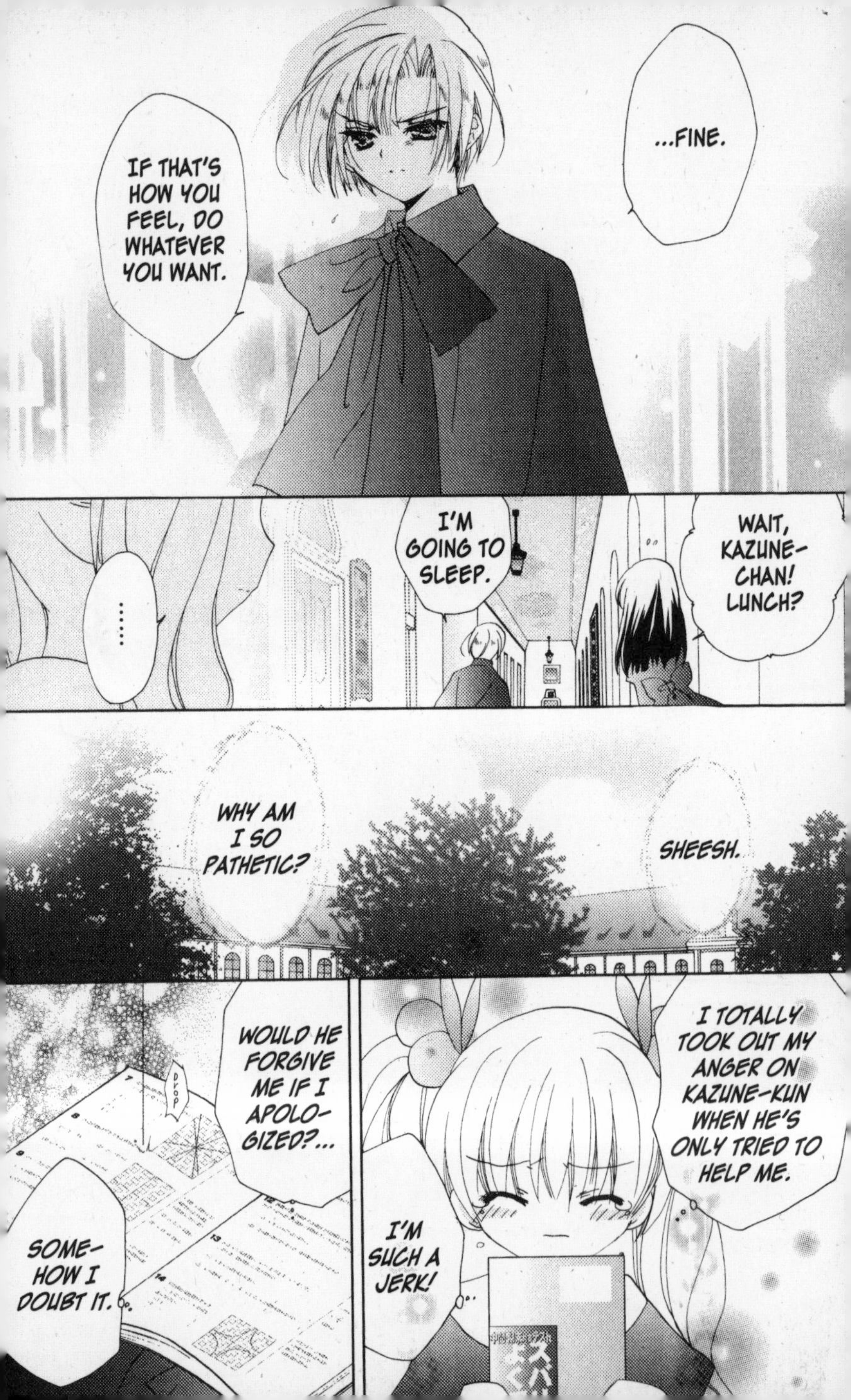
...FINE.
IF THAT'S HOW YOU FEEL, DO WHATEVER YOU WANT.
WAIT, KAZUNE-CHAN! LUNCH?
I'M GOING TO SLEEP.
......
SHEESH.
WHY AM I SO PATHETIC?
I TOTALLY TOOK OUT MY ANGER ON KAZUNE-KUN WHEN HE'S ONLY TRIED TO HELP ME.
I'M SUCH A JERK!
WOULD HE FORGIVE ME IF I APOLOGIZED?...
drop
SOMEHOW I DOUBT IT.

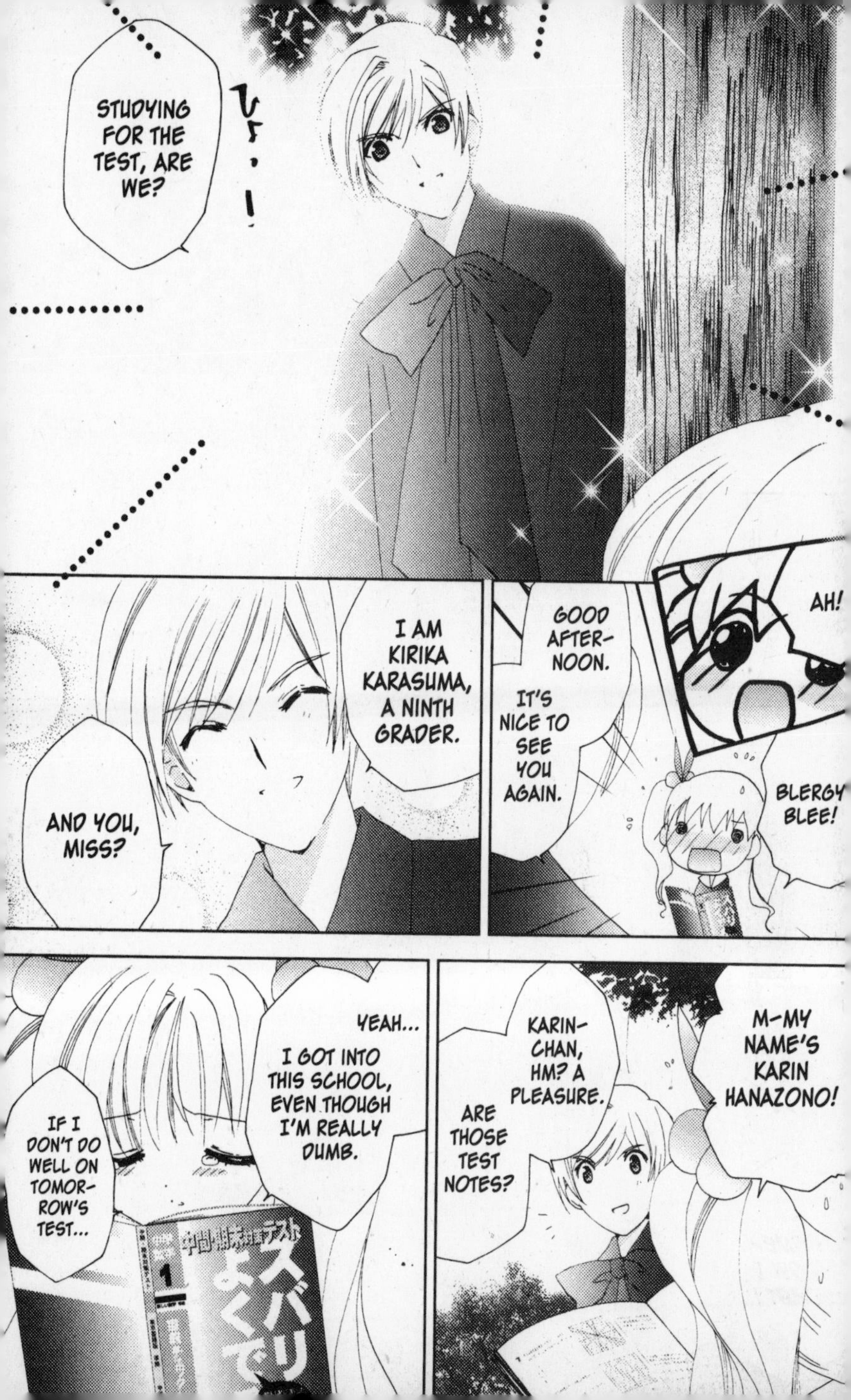
STUDYING FOR THE TEST, ARE WE?
AH!
BLERGY BLEE!
GOOD AFTERNOON.
IT'S NICE TO SEE YOU AGAIN.
I AM KIRIKA KARASUMA, A NINTH GRADER.
AND YOU, MISS?
M-MY NAME'S KARIN HANAZONO!
KARIN-CHAN, HM? A PLEASURE.
ARE THOSE TEST NOTES?
YEAH...
I GOT INTO THIS SCHOOL, EVEN THOUGH I'M REALLY DUMB.
IF I DON'T DO WELL ON TOMORROW'S TEST...

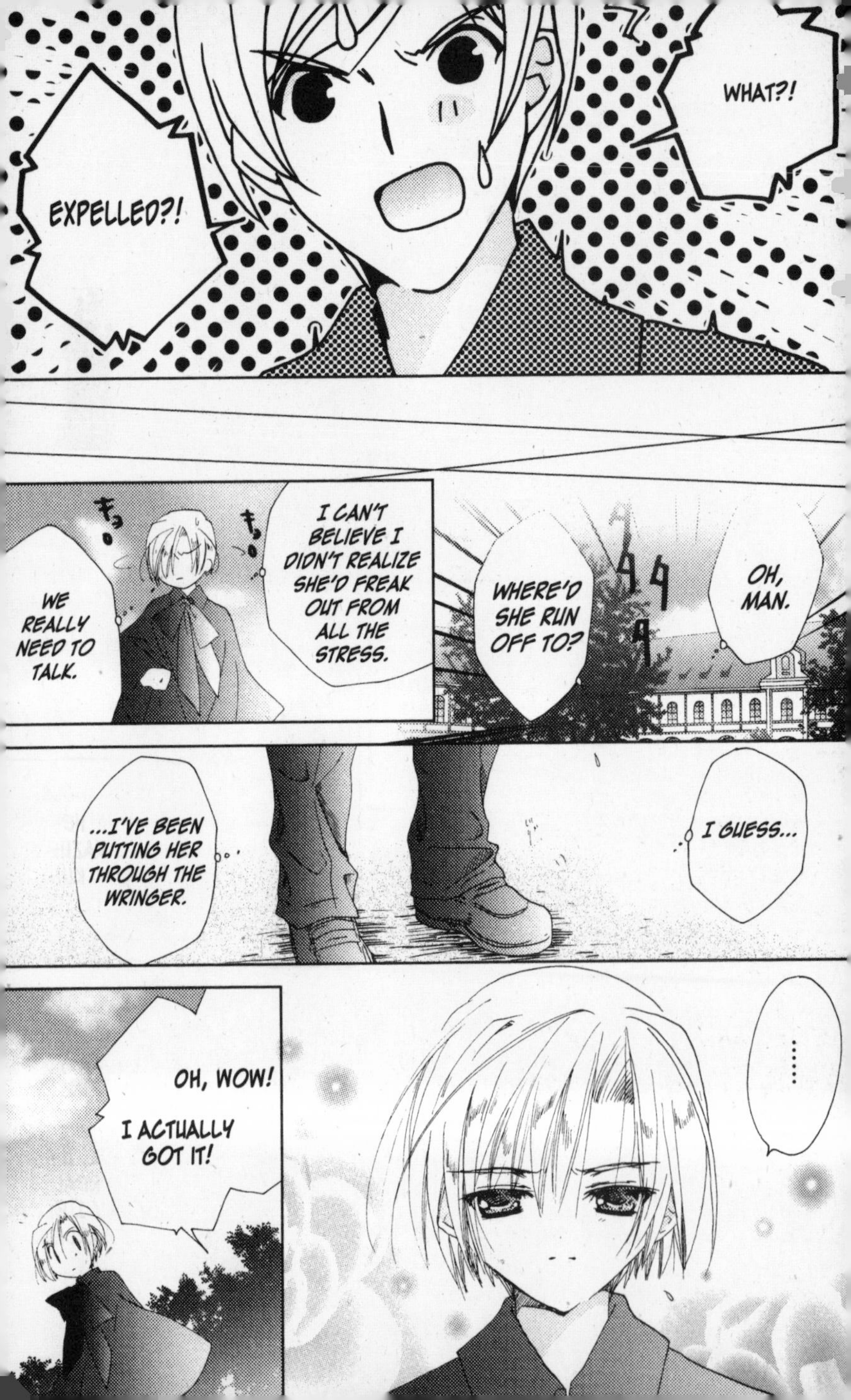
WHAT?!
EXPELLED?!
OH, MAN.
WHERE'D SHE RUN OFF TO?
I CAN'T BELIEVE I DIDN'T REALIZE SHE'D FREAK OUT FROM ALL THE STRESS.
WE REALLY NEED TO TALK.
I GUESS...
...I'VE BEEN PUTTING HER THROUGH THE WRINGER.
......
OH, WOW!
I ACTUALLY GOT IT!

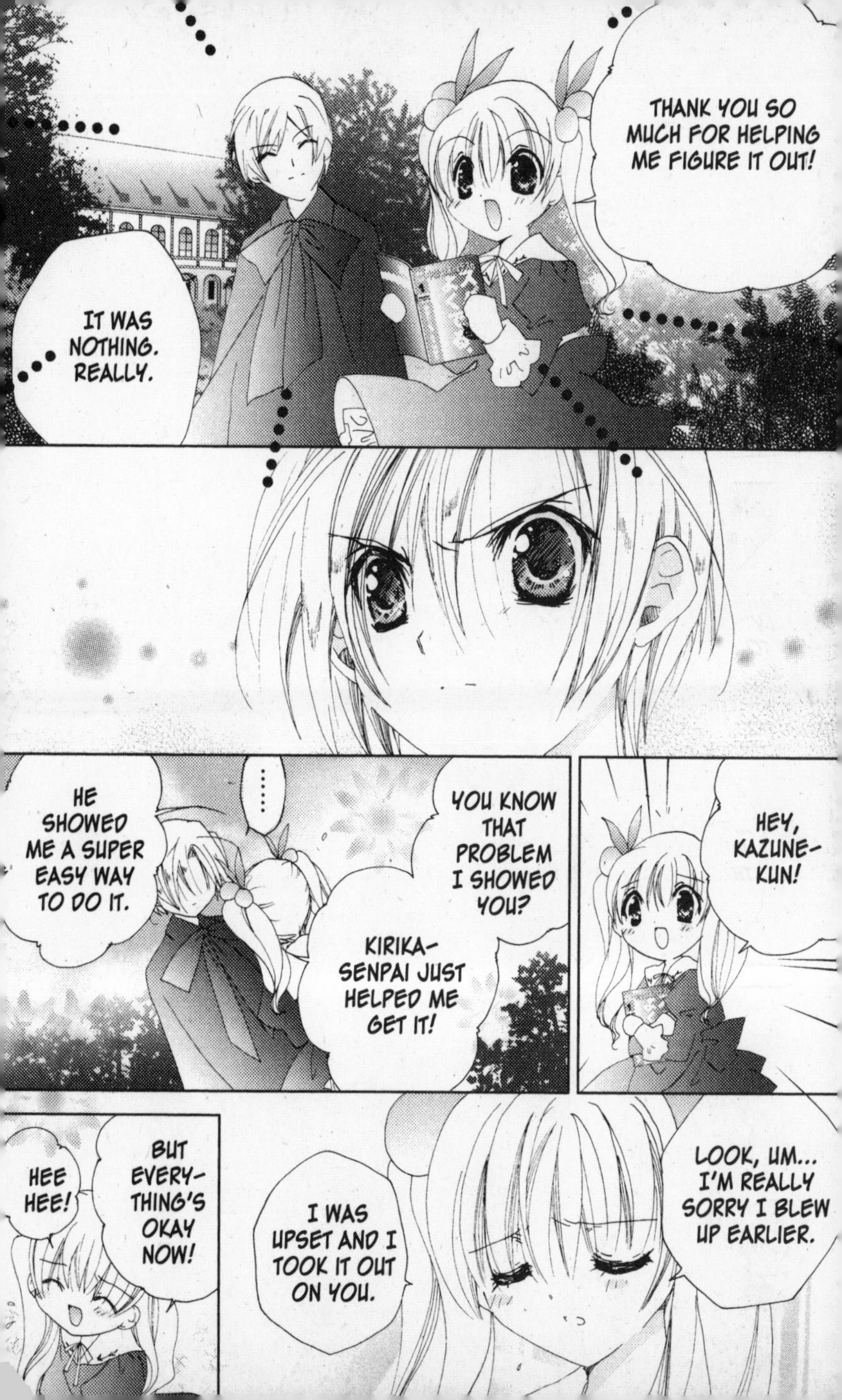

THANK YOU SO MUCH FOR HELPING ME FIGURE IT OUT!
IT WAS NOTHING. REALLY.
HEY, KAZUNE-KUN!
YOU KNOW THAT PROBLEM I SHOWED YOU?
KIRIKA-SENPAI JUST HELPED ME GET IT!
......
HE SHOWED ME A SUPER EASY WAY TO DO IT.
LOOK, UM... I'M REALLY SORRY I BLEW UP EARLIER.
I WAS UPSET AND I TOOK IT OUT ON YOU.
BUT EVERYTHING'S OKAY NOW!
HEE HEE!

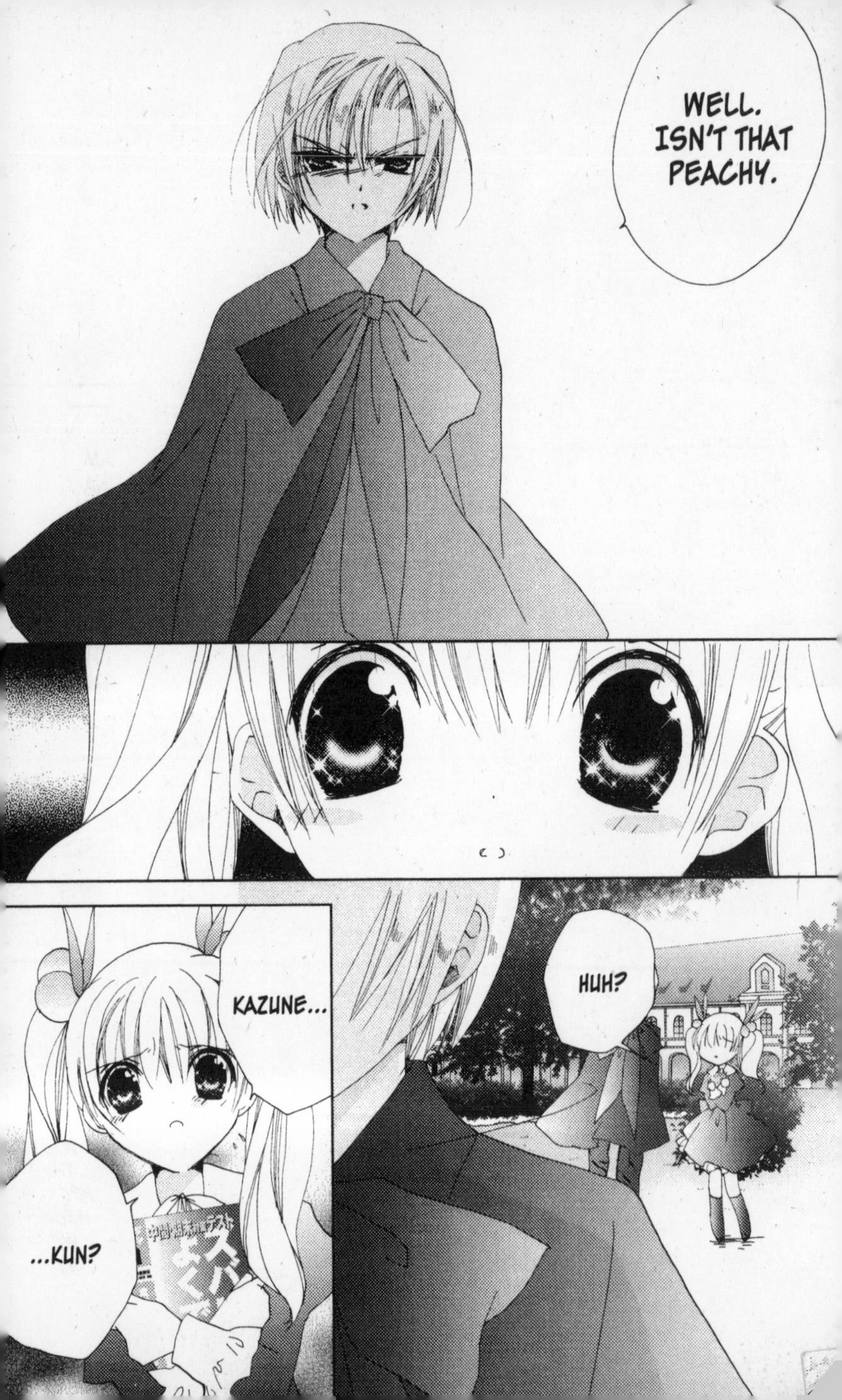
WELL. ISN'T THAT PEACHY.
HUH?
KAZUNE...
...KUN?

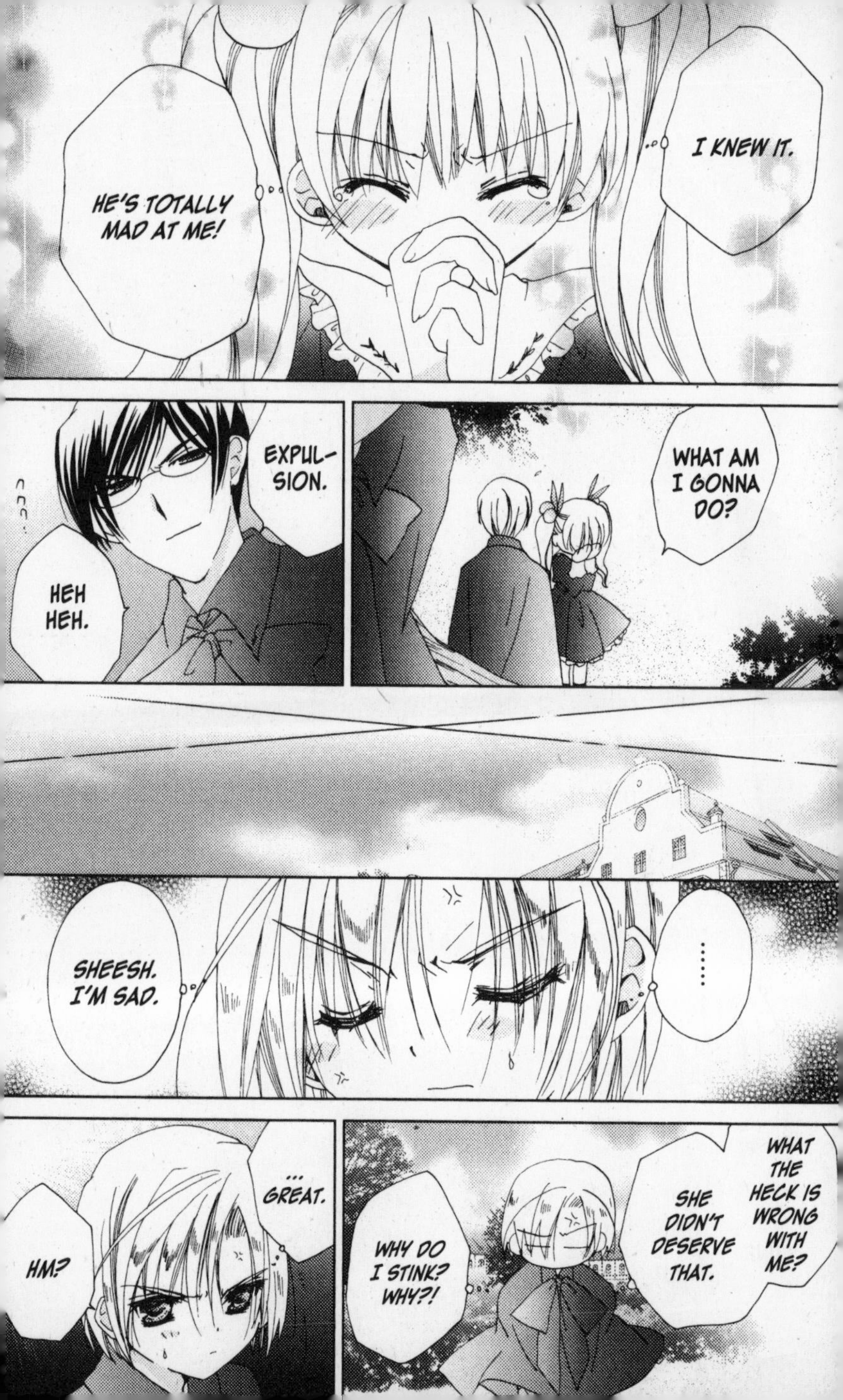
I KNEW IT.
HE'S TOTALLY MAD AT ME!
WHAT AM I GONNA DO?
EXPUL-SION.
HEH HEH.
......
SHEESH. I'M SAD.
WHAT THE HECK IS WRONG WITH ME?
SHE DIDN'T DESERVE THAT.
WHY DO I STINK? WHY?!
... GREAT.
HM?

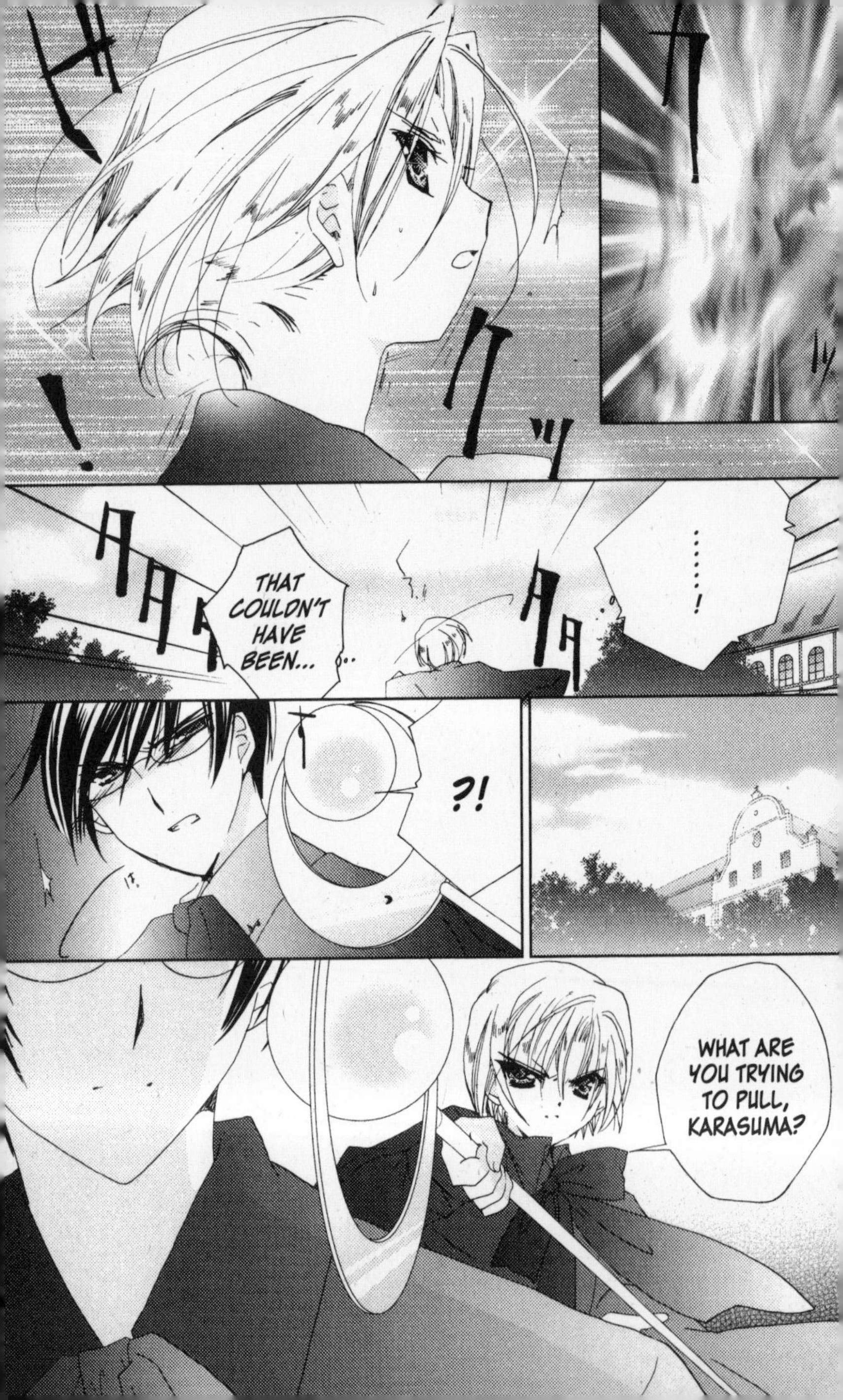
......!
THAT COULDN'T HAVE BEEN...
?!
WHAT ARE YOU TRYING TO PULL, KARASUMA?

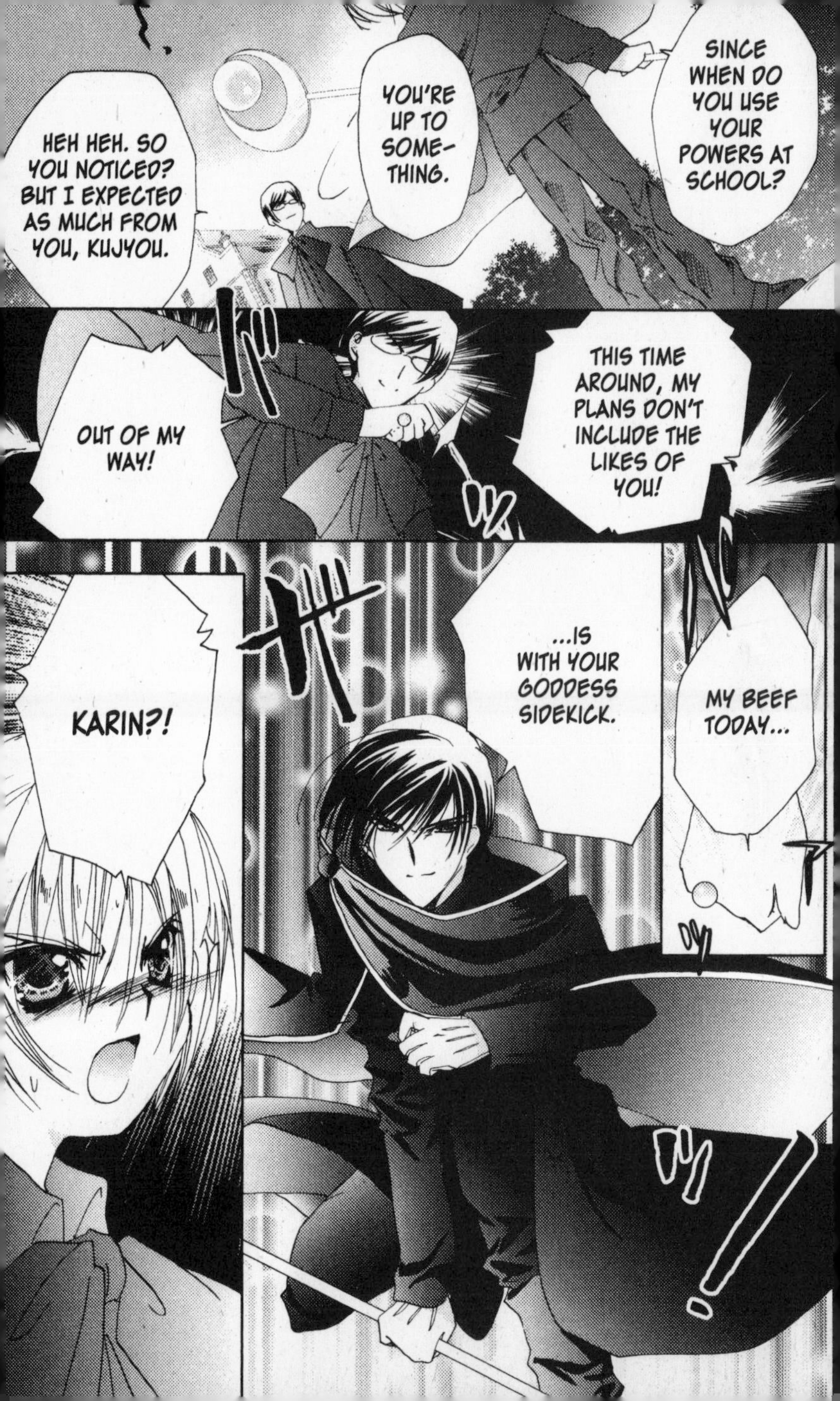
SINCE WHEN DO YOU USE YOUR POWERS AT SCHOOL?
YOU'RE UP TO SOME-THING.
HEH HEH. SO YOU NOTICED? BUT I EXPECTED AS MUCH FROM YOU, KUJYOU.
THIS TIME AROUND, MY PLANS DON'T INCLUDE THE LIKES OF YOU!
OUT OF MY WAY!
MY BEEF TODAY...
...IS WITH YOUR GODDESS SIDEKICK.
KARIN?!

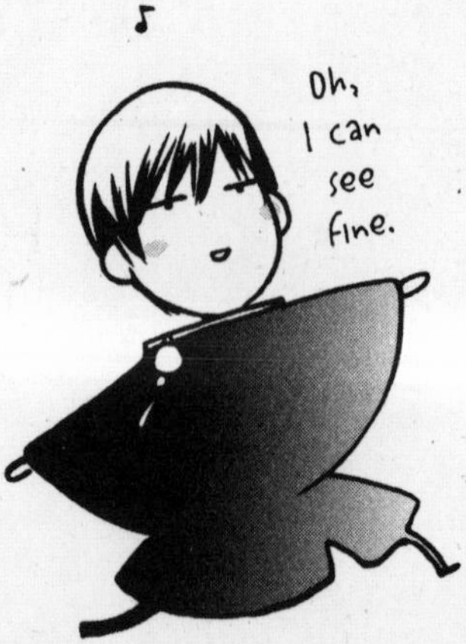
Oh, I can see fine.

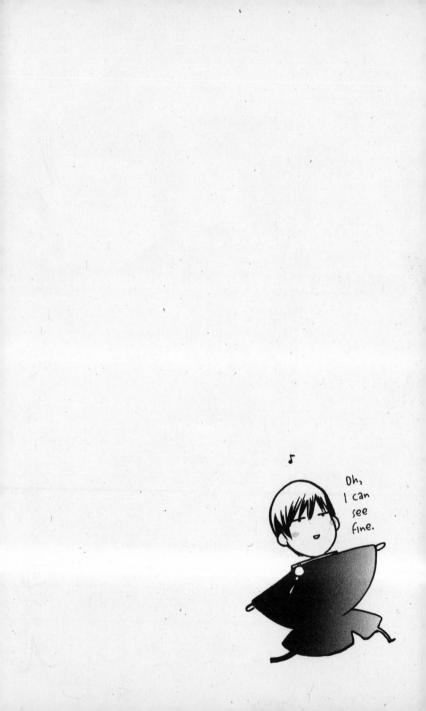

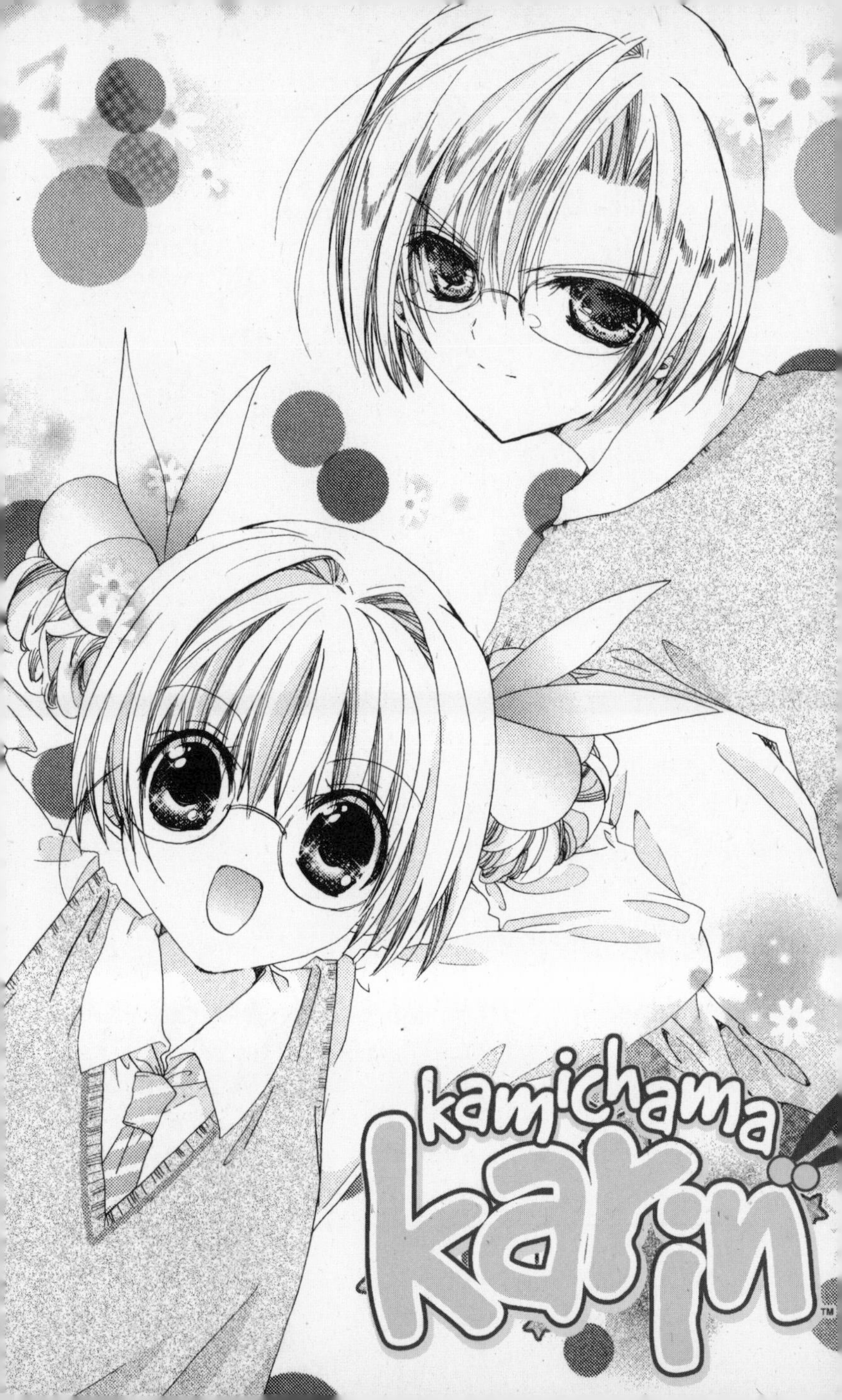
kamichama karin™

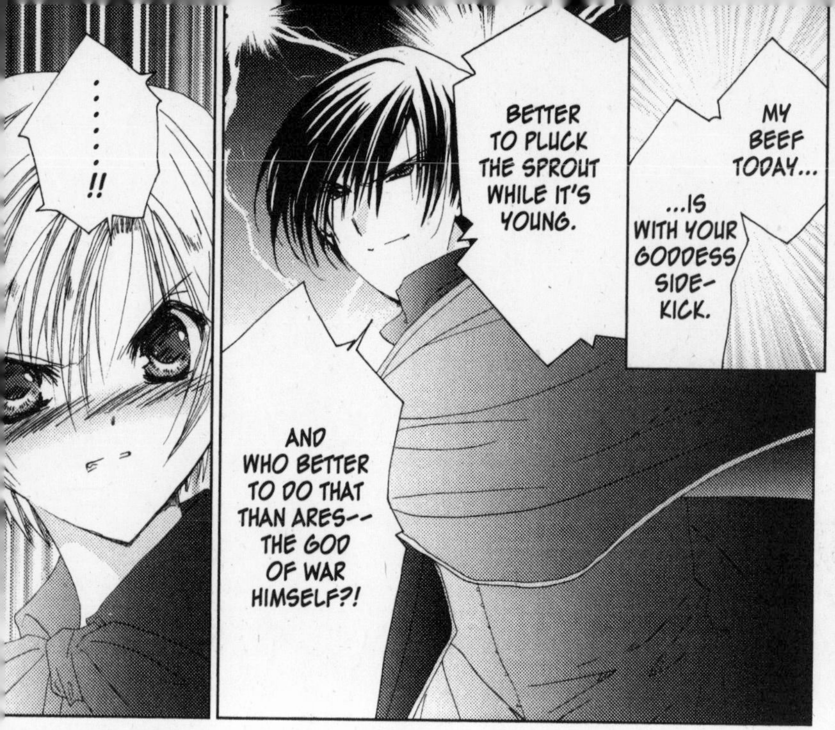
MY BEEF TODAY...
...IS WITH YOUR GODDESS SIDE-KICK.
BETTER TO PLUCK THE SPROUT WHILE IT'S YOUNG.
AND WHO BETTER TO DO THAT THAN ARES-- THE GOD OF WAR HIMSELF?!
......!!

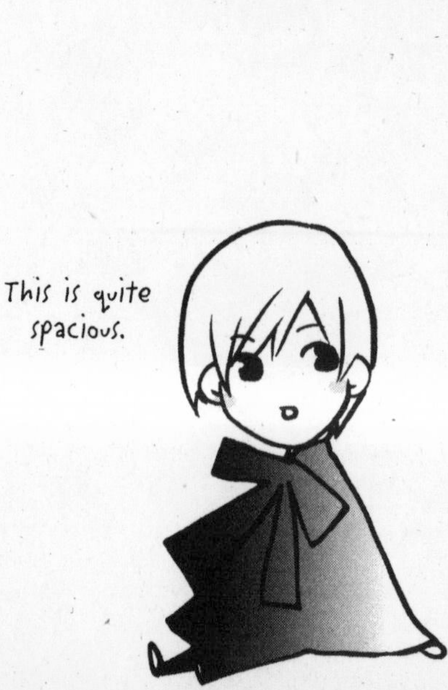
This is quite spacious.

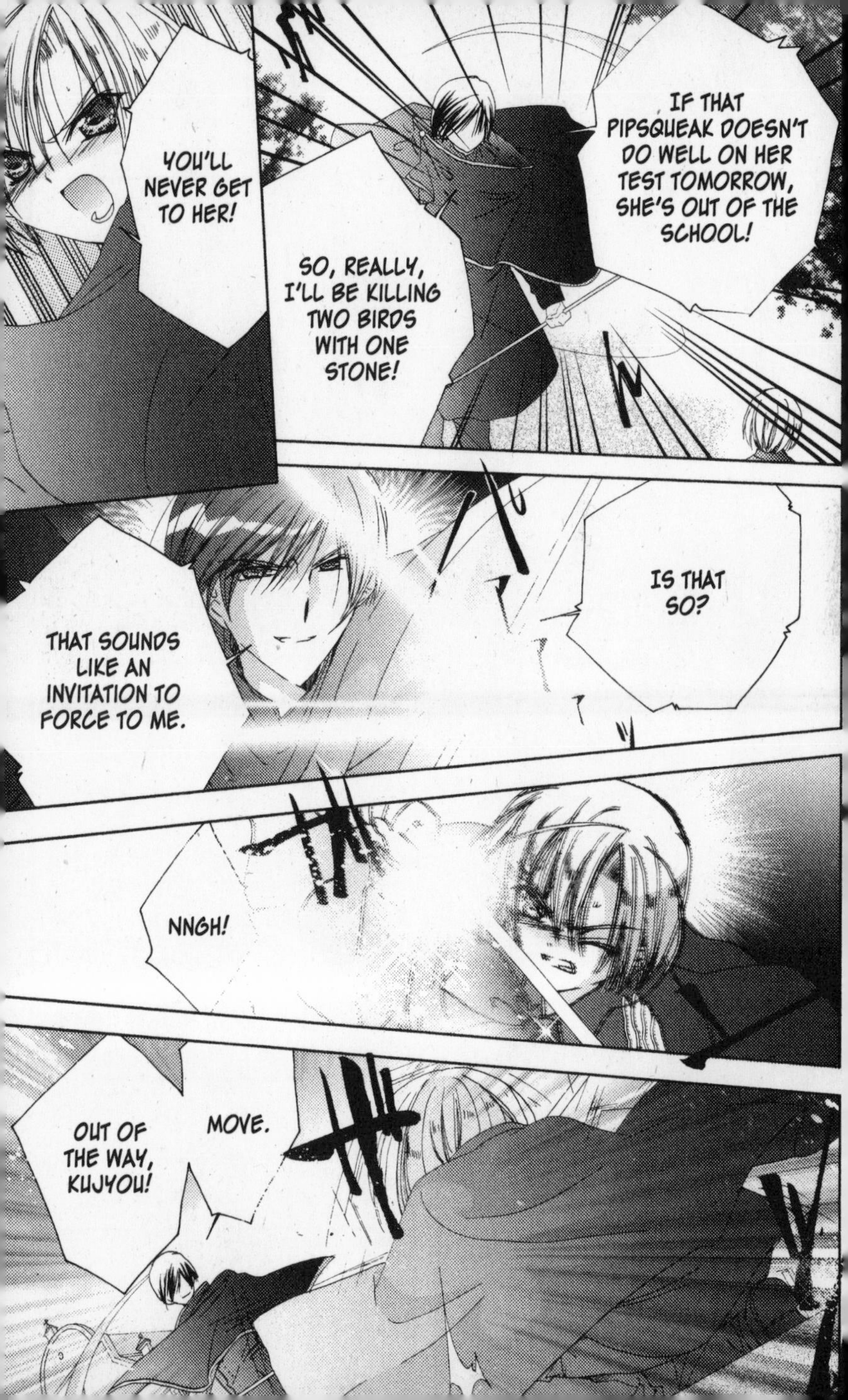
IF THAT PIPSQUEAK DOESN'T DO WELL ON HER TEST TOMORROW, SHE'S OUT OF THE SCHOOL!
SO, REALLY, I'LL BE KILLING TWO BIRDS WITH ONE STONE!
YOU'LL NEVER GET TO HER!
IS THAT SO?
THAT SOUNDS LIKE AN INVITATION TO FORCE TO ME.
NNGH!
MOVE.
OUT OF THE WAY, KUJYOU!

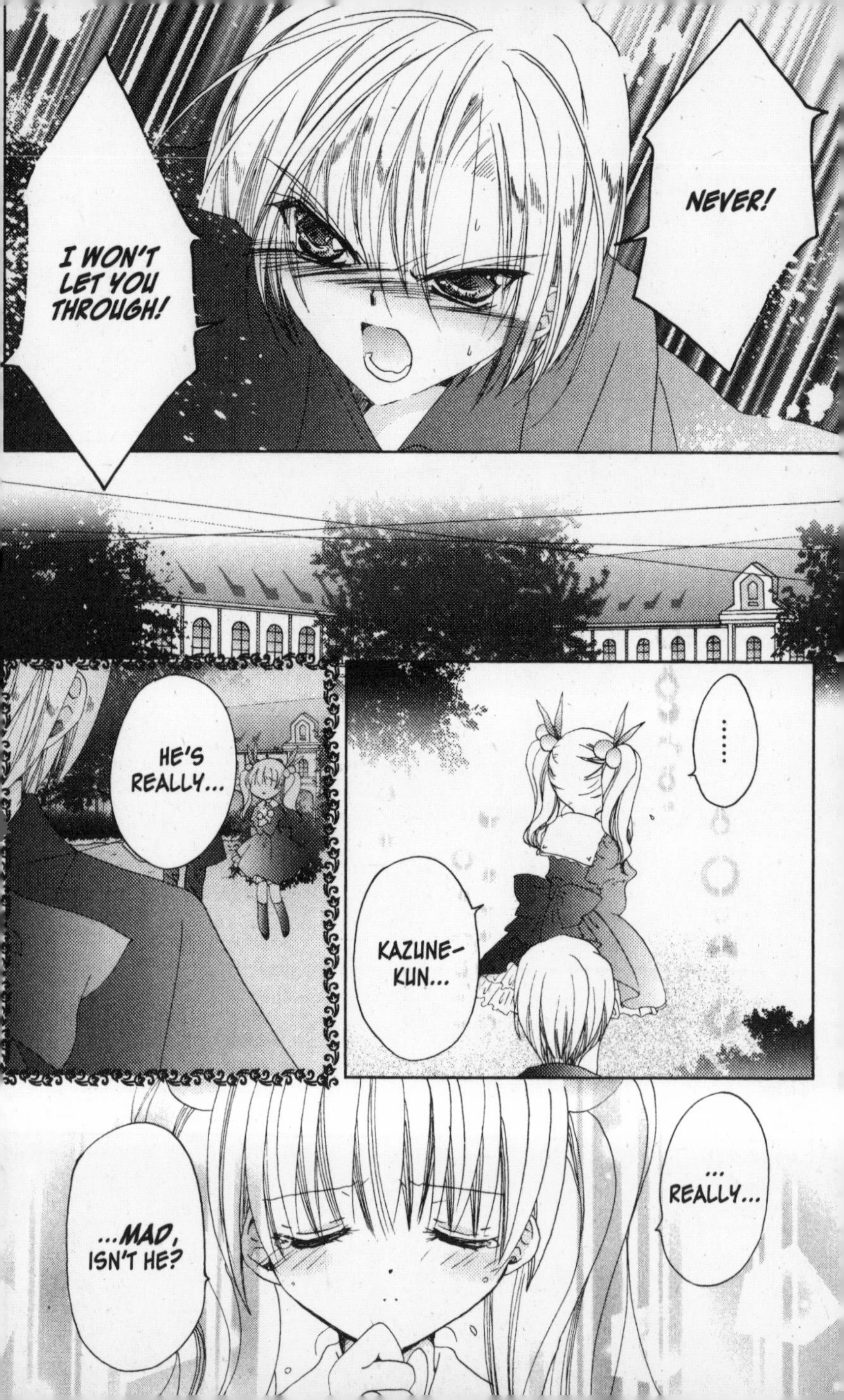
NEVER!
I WON'T LET YOU THROUGH!
......
KAZUNE-KUN...
HE'S REALLY...
... REALLY...
...MAD, ISN'T HE?

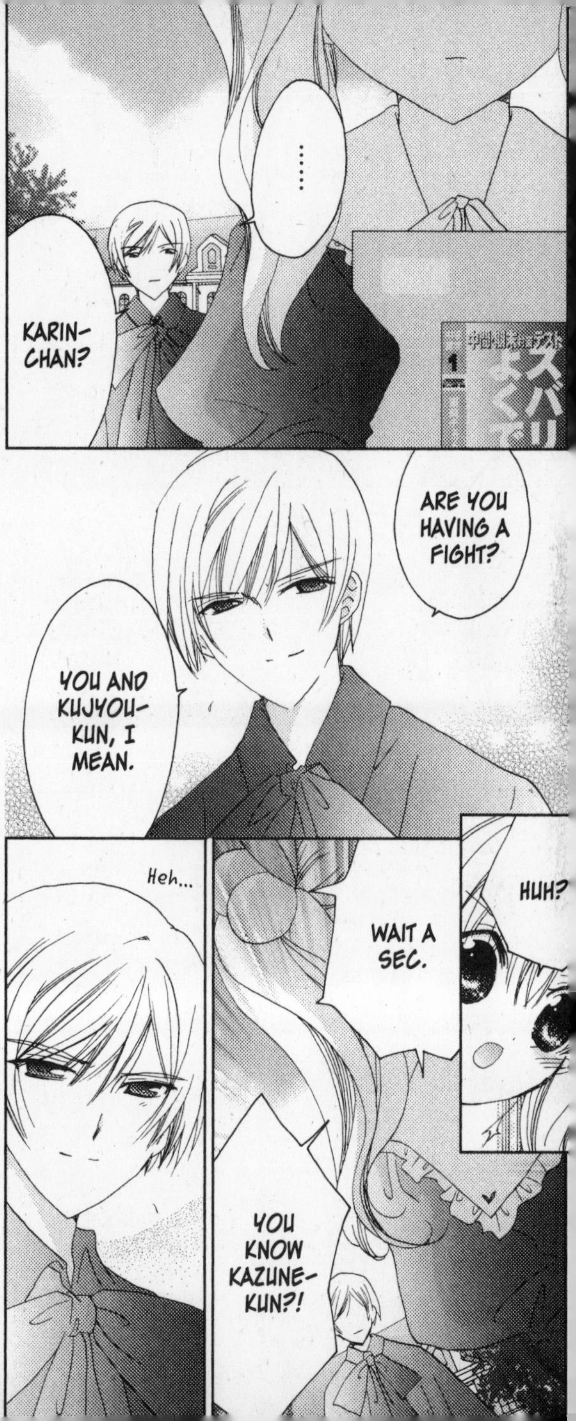
......
KARIN-CHAN?
ARE YOU HAVING A FIGHT?
YOU AND KUJYOU-KUN, I MEAN.
HUH?
WAIT A SEC.
YOU KNOW KAZUNE-KUN?!
Heh...

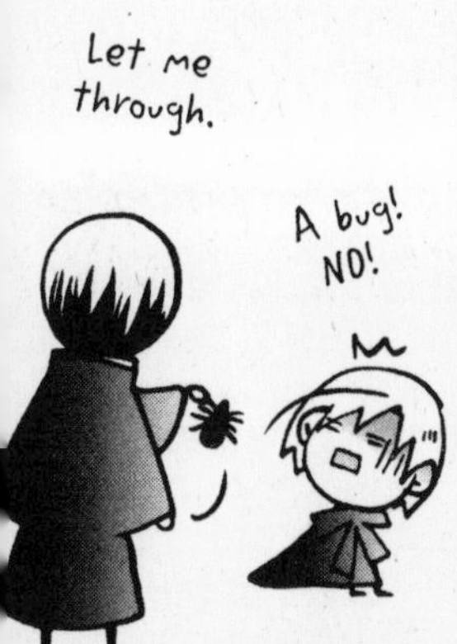
Let me through.
A bug! NO!

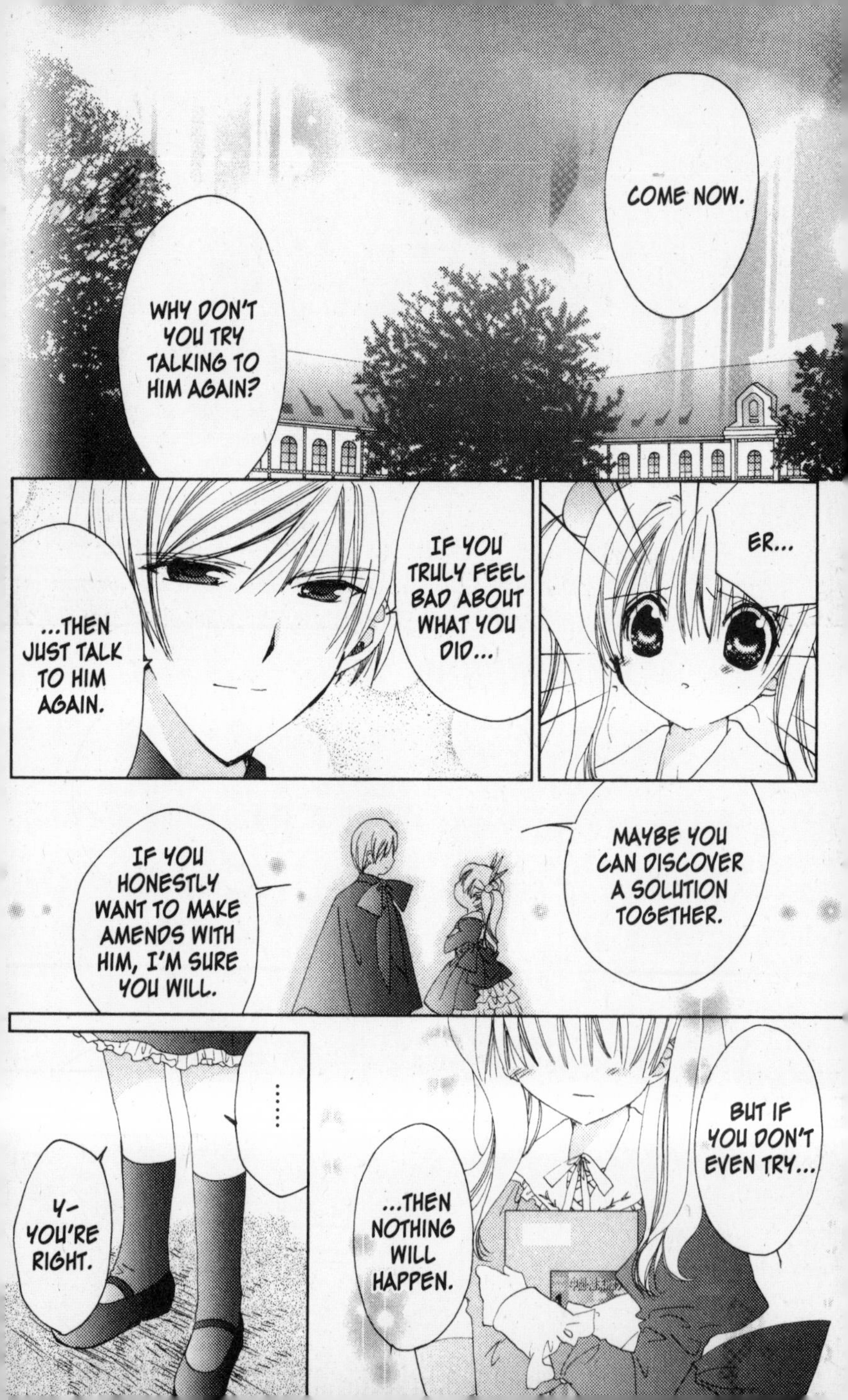
COME NOW.
WHY DON'T YOU TRY TALKING TO HIM AGAIN?
ER...
IF YOU TRULY FEEL BAD ABOUT WHAT YOU DID...
...THEN JUST TALK TO HIM AGAIN.
MAYBE YOU CAN DISCOVER A SOLUTION TOGETHER.
IF YOU HONESTLY WANT TO MAKE AMENDS WITH HIM, I'M SURE YOU WILL.
BUT IF YOU DON'T EVEN TRY...
...THEN NOTHING WILL HAPPEN.
......
Y- YOU'RE RIGHT.

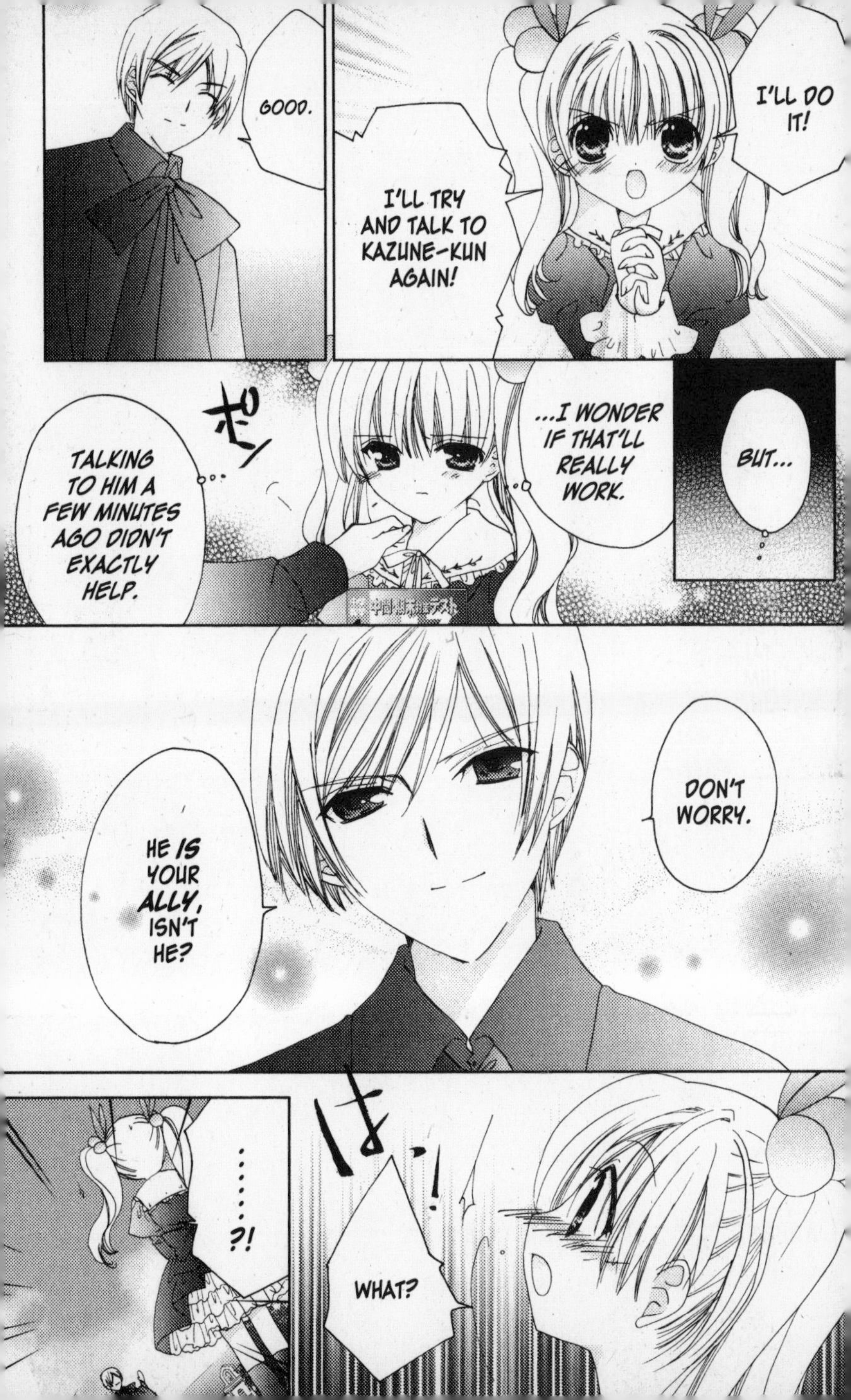
I'LL DO IT!
I'LL TRY AND TALK TO KAZUNE-KUN AGAIN!
GOOD.
BUT...
...I WONDER IF THAT'LL REALLY WORK.
TALKING TO HIM A FEW MINUTES AGO DIDN'T EXACTLY HELP.
DON'T WORRY.
HE IS YOUR ALLY, ISN'T HE?
WHAT?
......?!

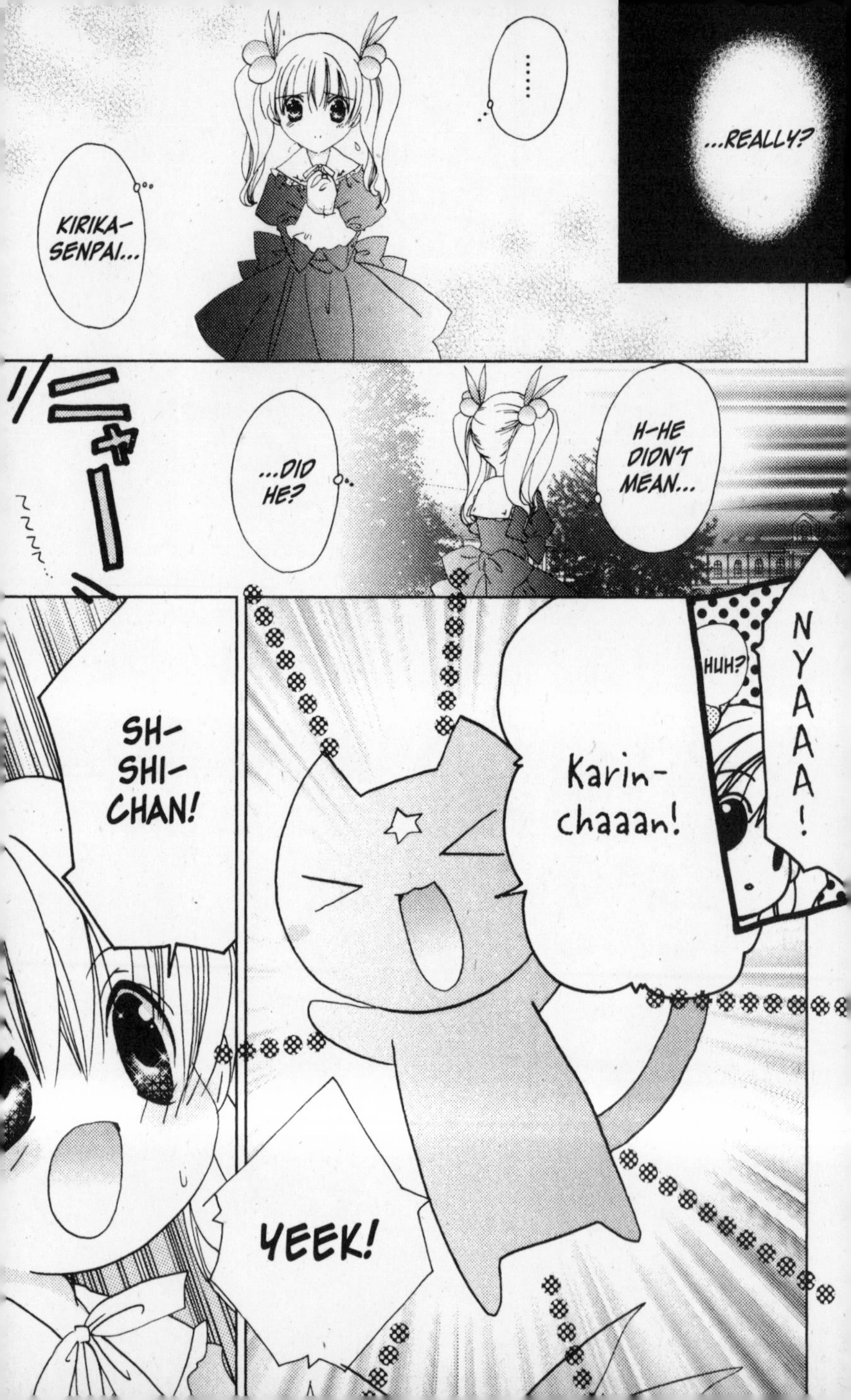
...REALLY?
......
KIRIKA-SENPAI...
H-HE DIDN'T MEAN...
...DID HE?
NYAAAA!
HUH?
Karin-chaaan!
SH-SHI-CHAN!
YEEK!

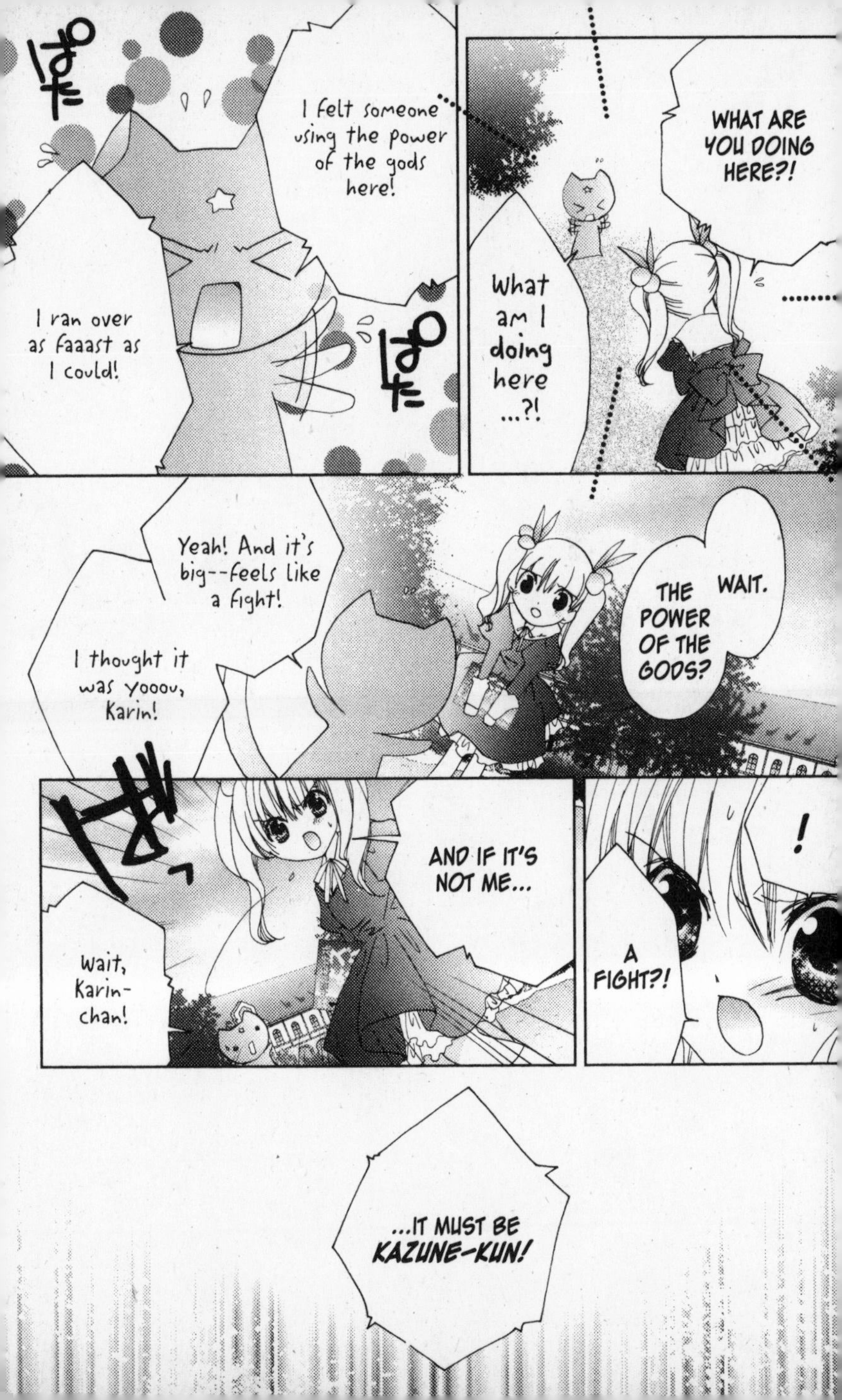
WHAT ARE YOU DOING HERE?!
What am I doing here...?!
I felt someone using the power of the gods here!
I ran over as faaast as I could!
WAIT.
THE POWER OF THE GODS?
Yeah! And it's big--feels like a fight!
I thought it was yooou, Karin!
A FIGHT?!
AND IF IT'S NOT ME...
Wait, Karin-chan!
...IT MUST BE KAZUNE-KUN!

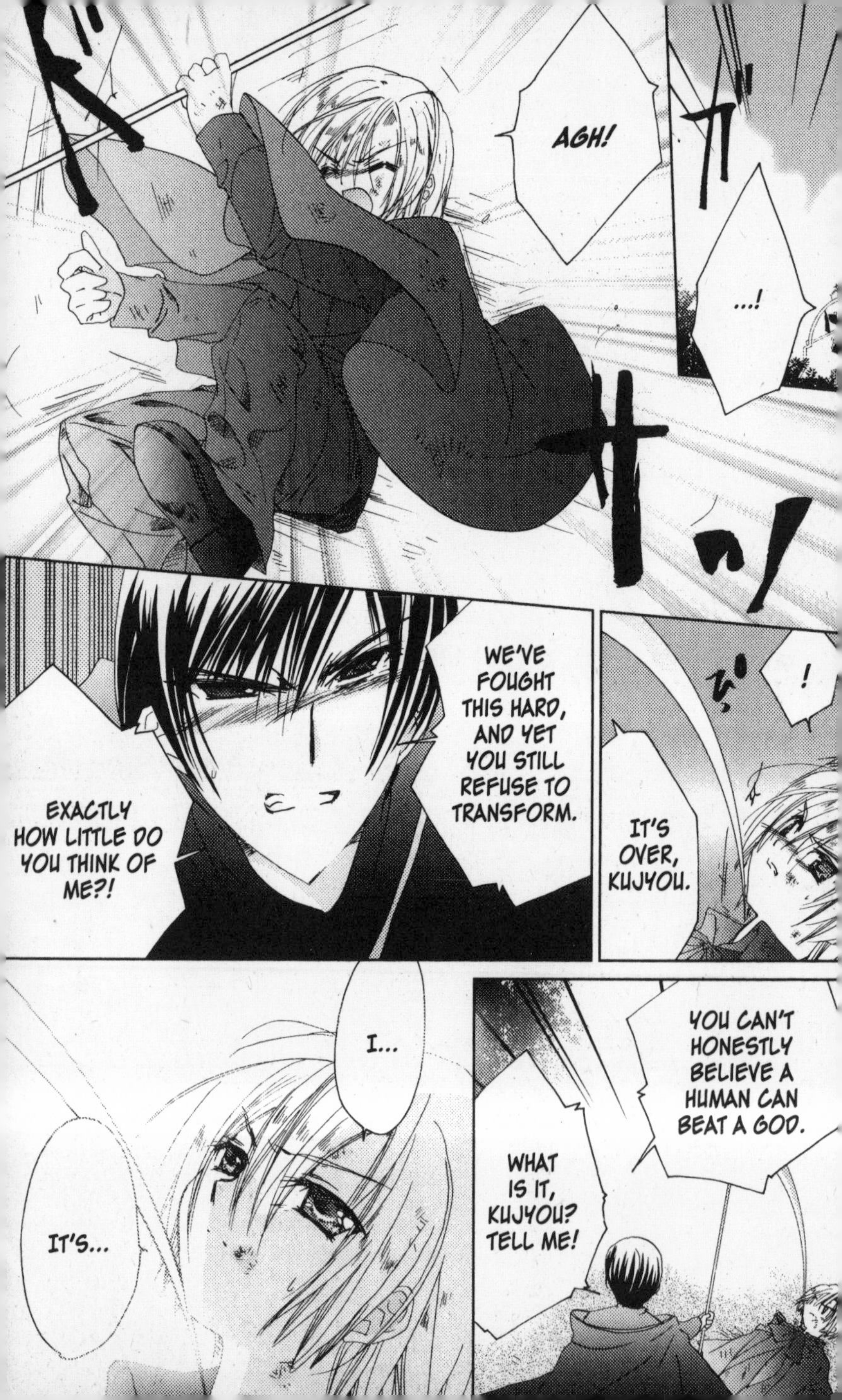
...!
AGH!
!
IT'S OVER, KUJYOU.
WE'VE FOUGHT THIS HARD, AND YET YOU STILL REFUSE TO TRANSFORM.
EXACTLY HOW LITTLE DO YOU THINK OF ME?!
YOU CAN'T HONESTLY BELIEVE A HUMAN CAN BEAT A GOD.
WHAT IS IT, KUJYOU? TELL ME!
I...
IT'S...

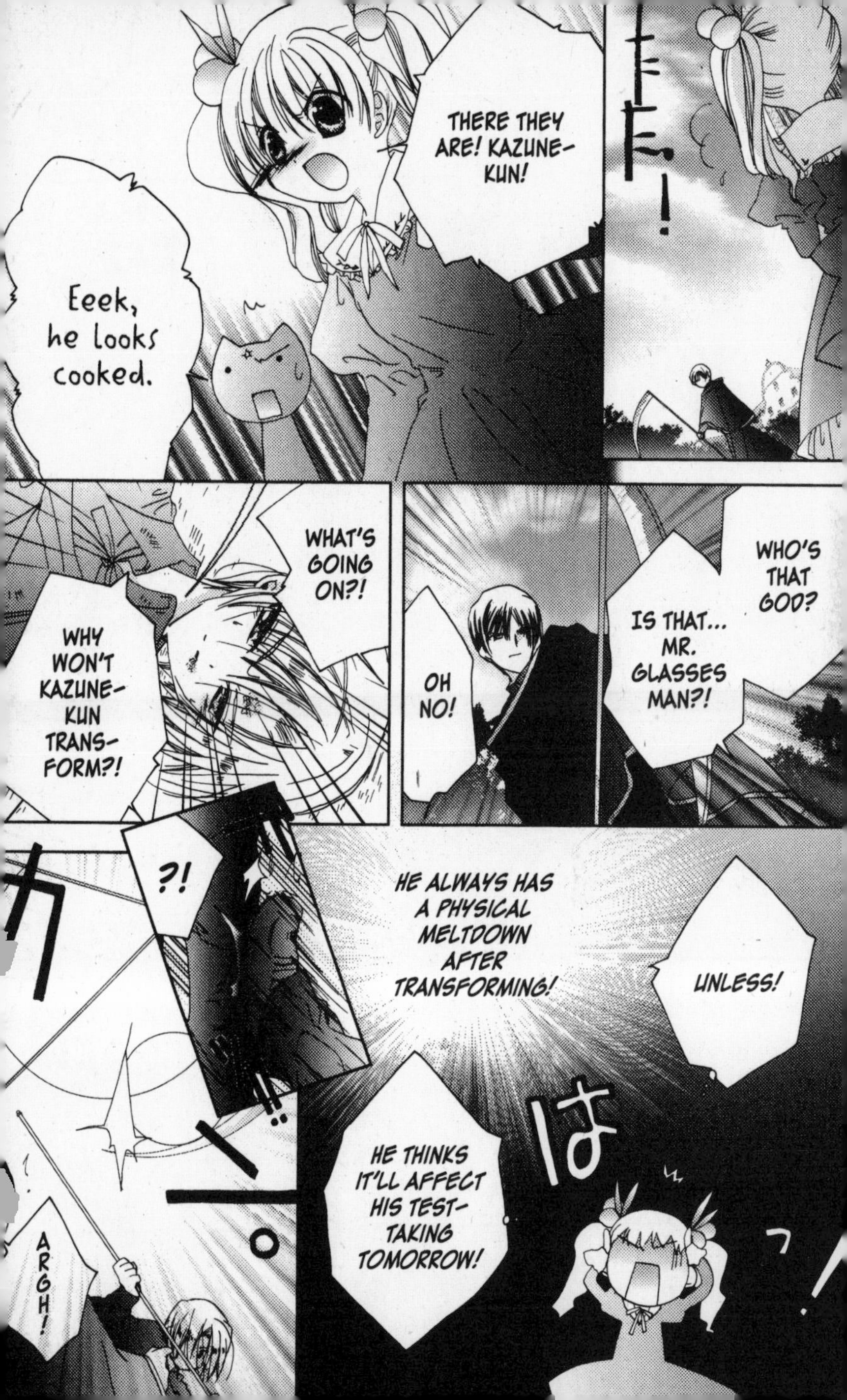
THERE THEY ARE! KAZUNE-KUN!
Eeek, he looks cooked.
WHO'S THAT GOD?
IS THAT... MR. GLASSES MAN?!
OH NO!
WHAT'S GOING ON?!
WHY WON'T KAZUNE-KUN TRANSFORM?!
UNLESS!
はっ!
HE ALWAYS HAS A PHYSICAL MELTDOWN AFTER TRANSFORMING!
HE THINKS IT'LL AFFECT HIS TEST-TAKING TOMORROW!
?!
ARGH!

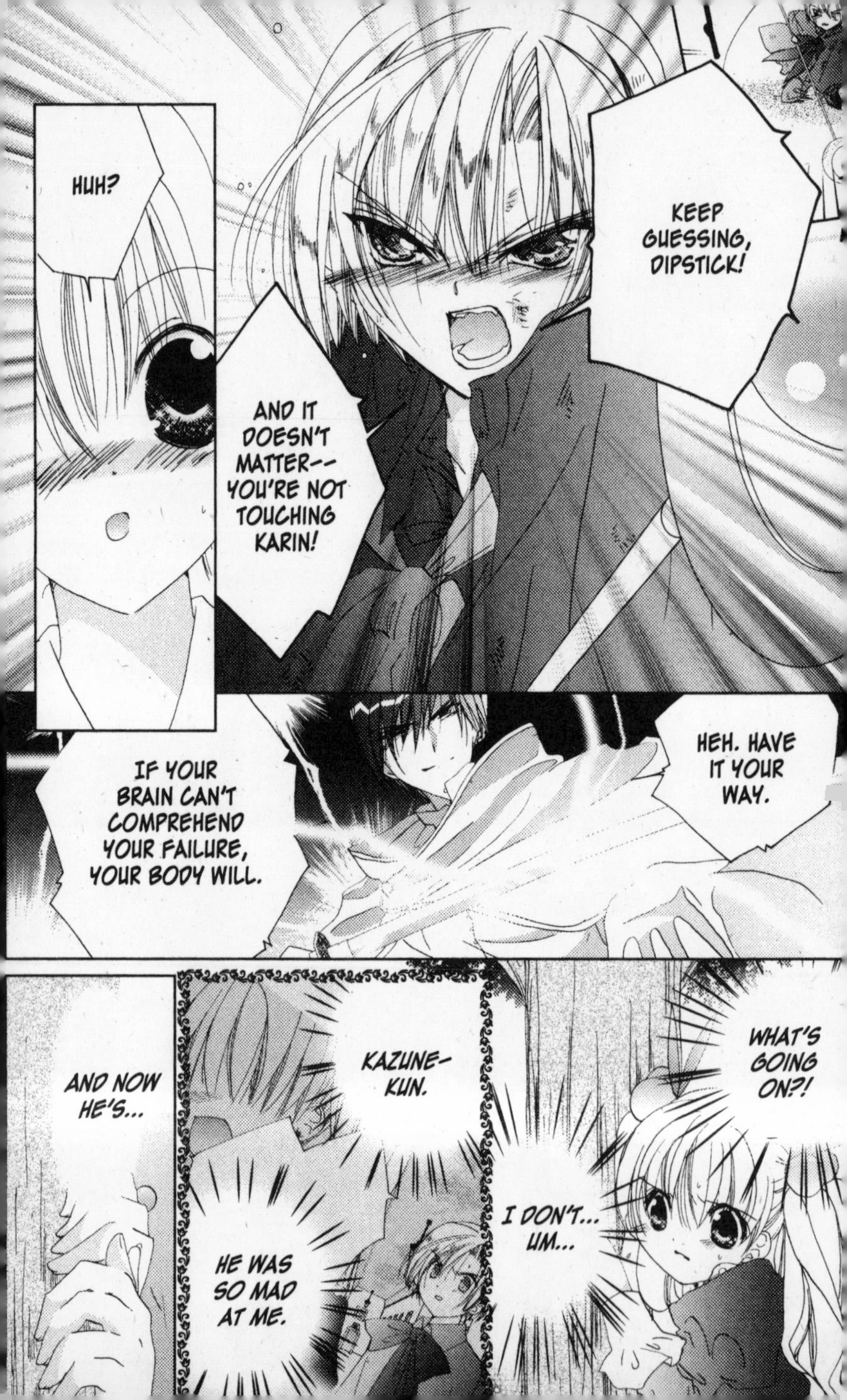
KEEP GUESSING, DIPSTICK!
AND IT DOESN'T MATTER--YOU'RE NOT TOUCHING KARIN!
HUH?
HEH. HAVE IT YOUR WAY.
IF YOUR BRAIN CAN'T COMPREHEND YOUR FAILURE, YOUR BODY WILL.
WHAT'S GOING ON?!
I DON'T... UM...
KAZUNE-KUN.
HE WAS SO MAD AT ME.
AND NOW HE'S...

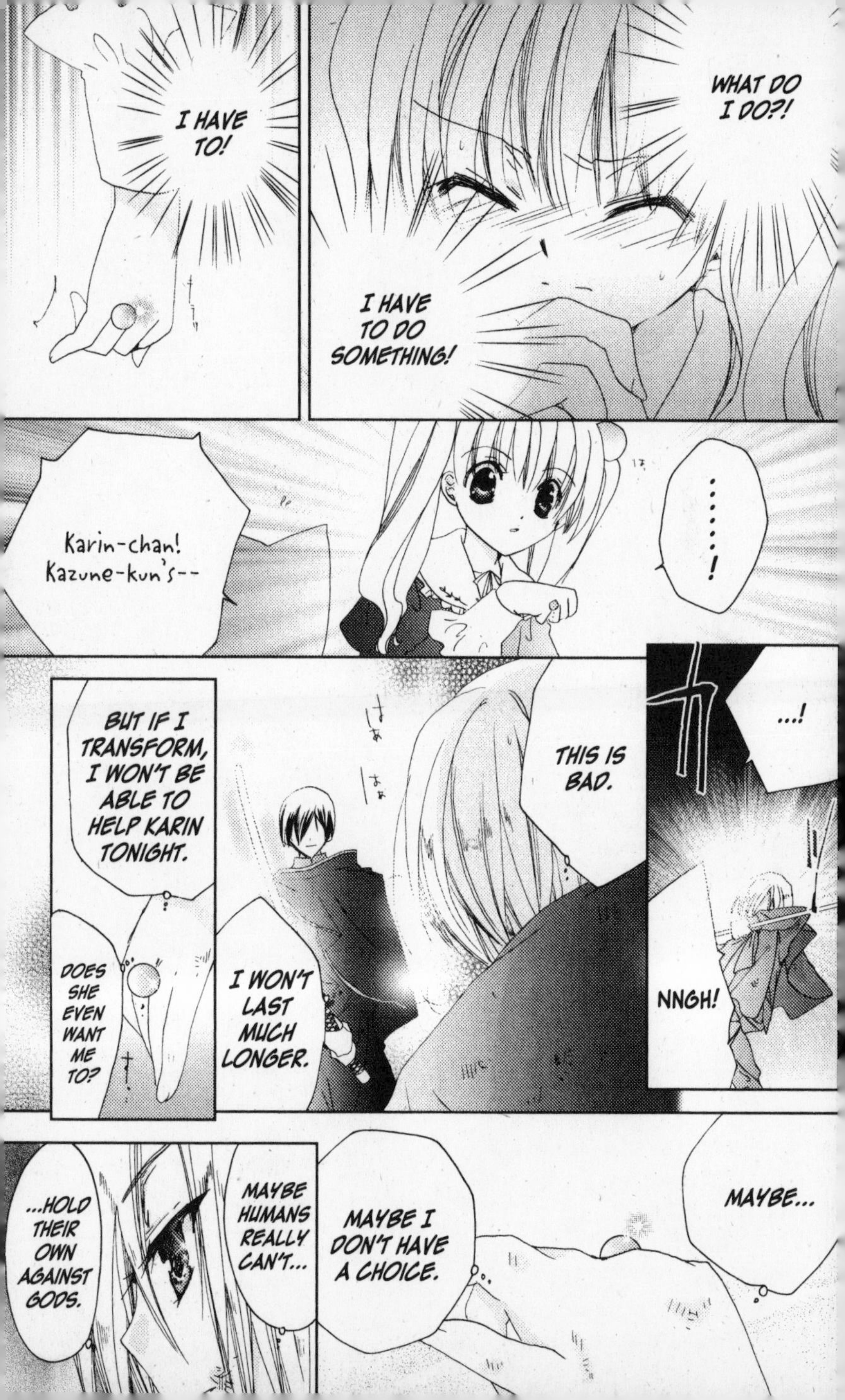
WHAT DO I DO?!
I HAVE TO DO SOMETHING!
I HAVE TO!
......!
Karin-chan! Kazune-kun's--
...!
NNGH!
THIS IS BAD.
I WON'T LAST MUCH LONGER.
BUT IF I TRANSFORM, I WON'T BE ABLE TO HELP KARIN TONIGHT.
DOES SHE EVEN WANT ME TO?
MAYBE...
MAYBE I DON'T HAVE A CHOICE.
MAYBE HUMANS REALLY CAN'T...
...HOLD THEIR OWN AGAINST GODS.

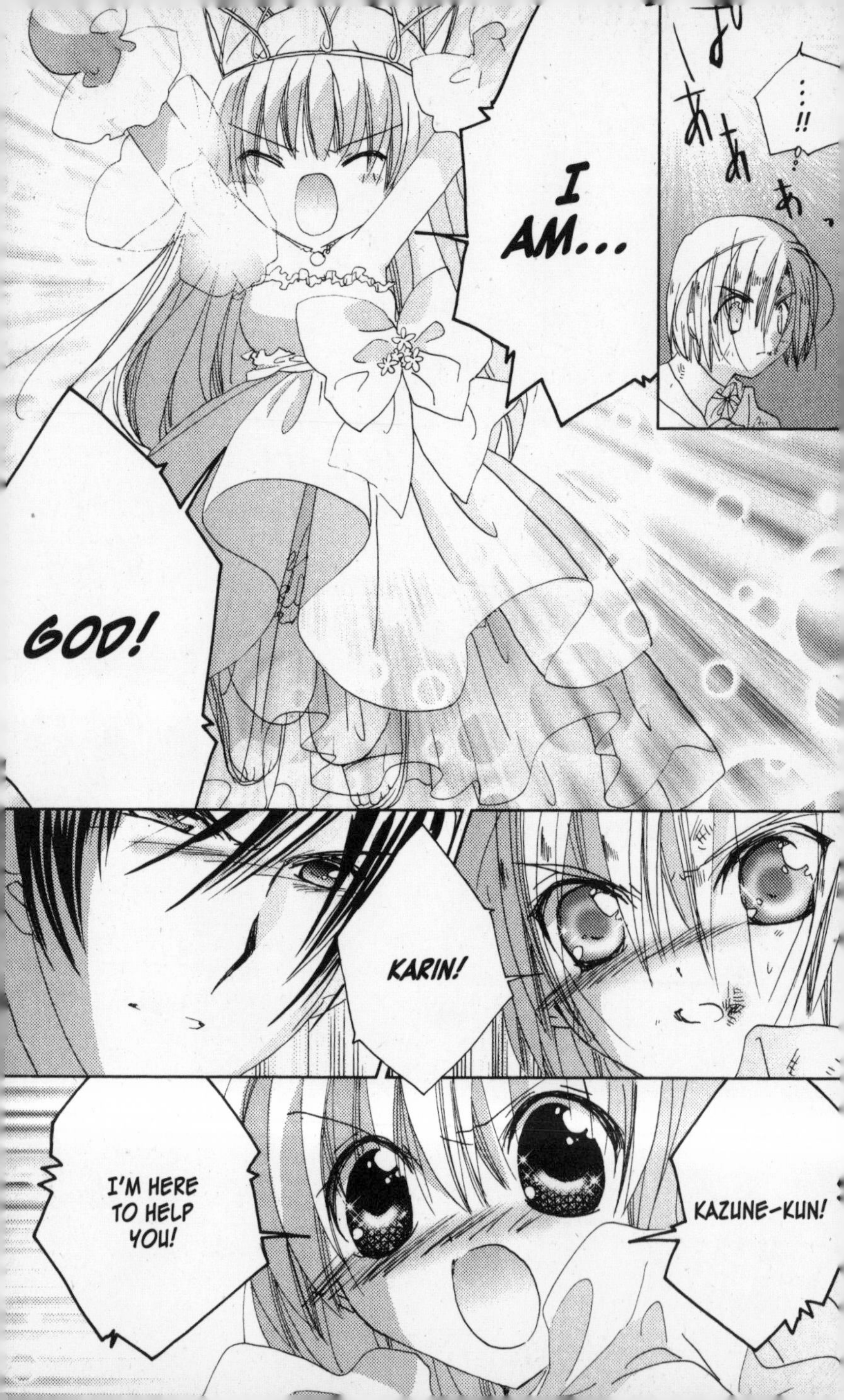

...!!?
I AM...
GOD!
KARIN!
KAZUNE-KUN!
I'M HERE TO HELP YOU!

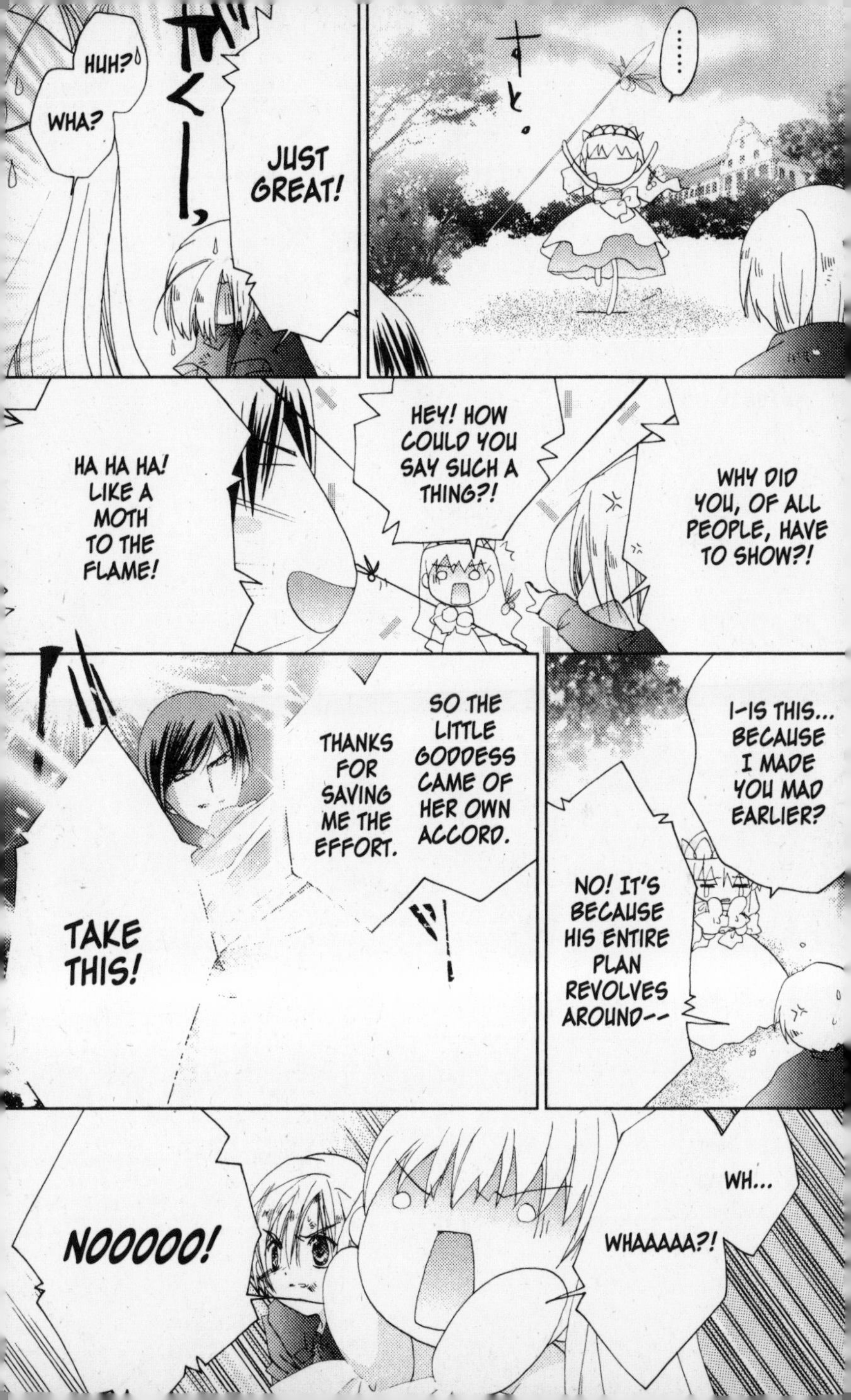
……
HUH?
WHA?
JUST GREAT!
WHY DID YOU, OF ALL PEOPLE, HAVE TO SHOW?!
HEY! HOW COULD YOU SAY SUCH A THING?!
HA HA HA! LIKE A MOTH TO THE FLAME!
I-IS THIS... BECAUSE I MADE YOU MAD EARLIER?
NO! IT'S BECAUSE HIS ENTIRE PLAN REVOLVES AROUND--
SO THE LITTLE GODDESS CAME OF HER OWN ACCORD.
THANKS FOR SAVING ME THE EFFORT.
TAKE THIS!
WH...
WHAAAAA?!
NOOOOO!

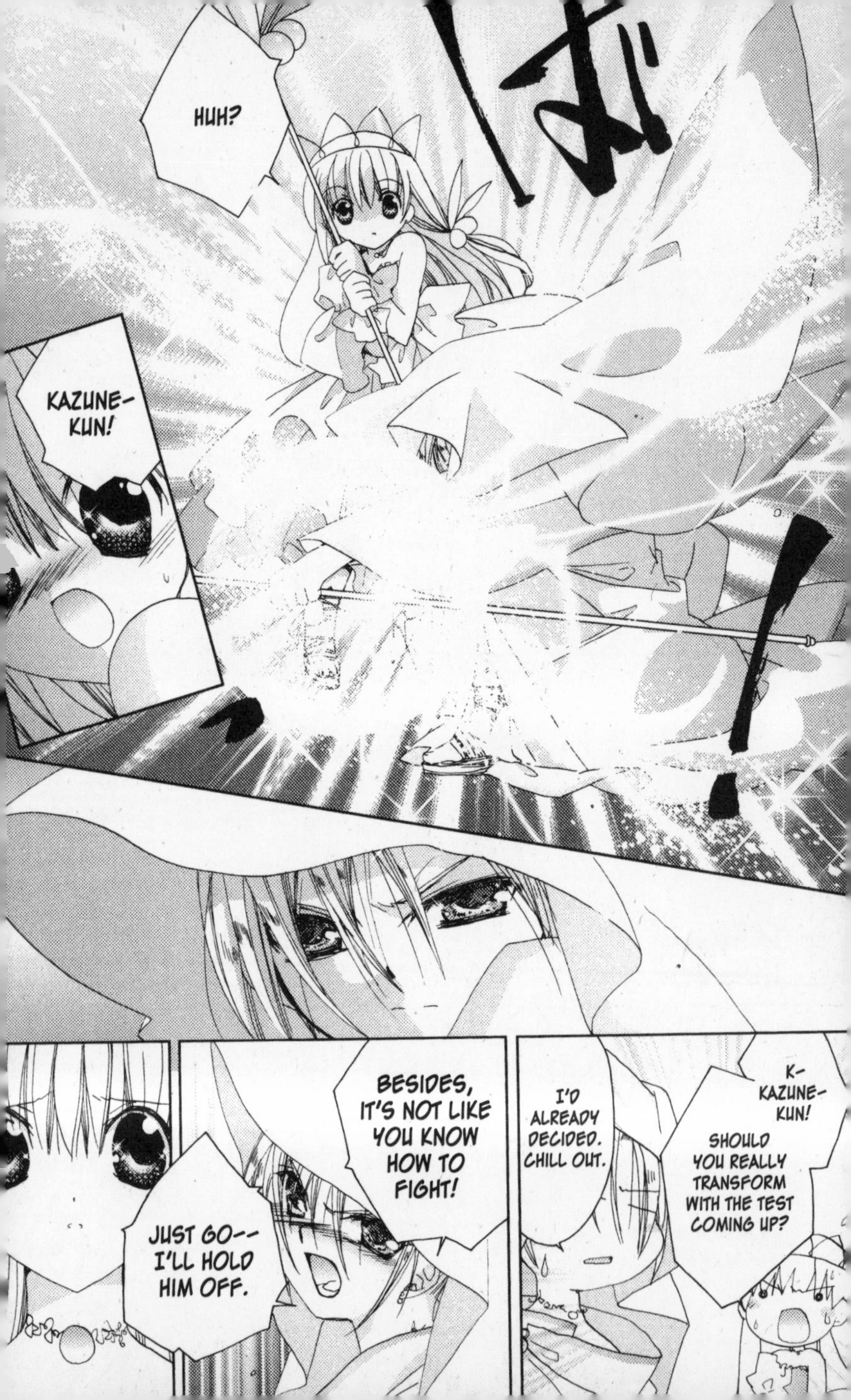
HUH?
KAZUNE-KUN!
K-KAZUNE-KUN!
SHOULD YOU REALLY TRANSFORM WITH THE TEST COMING UP?
I'D ALREADY DECIDED. CHILL OUT.
BESIDES, IT'S NOT LIKE YOU KNOW HOW TO FIGHT!
JUST GO--I'LL HOLD HIM OFF.

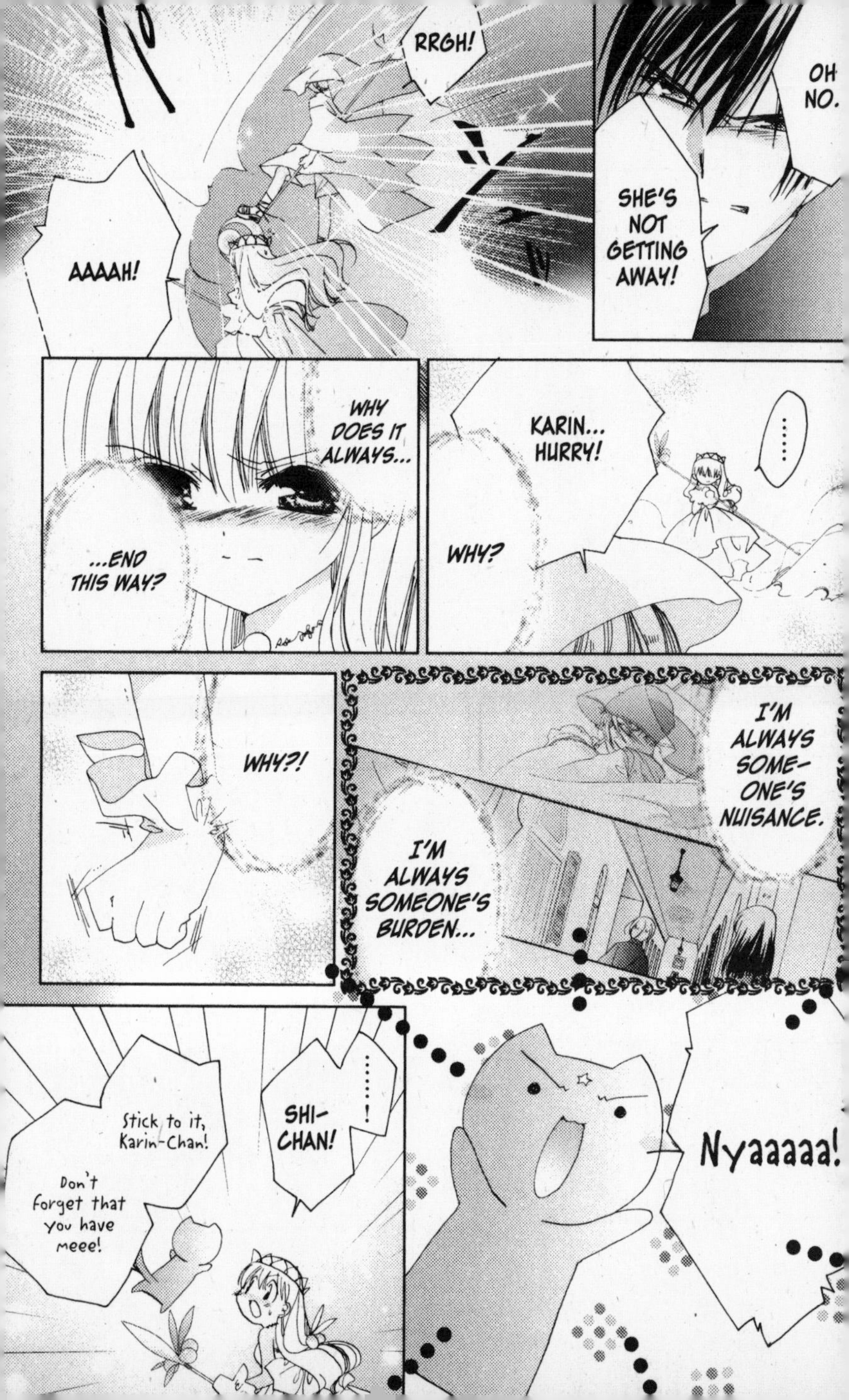
OH NO.
SHE'S NOT GETTING AWAY!
RRGH!
AAAAH!
......
KARIN... HURRY!
WHY?
WHY DOES IT ALWAYS...
...END THIS WAY?
I'M ALWAYS SOMEONE'S NUISANCE.
I'M ALWAYS SOMEONE'S BURDEN...
WHY?!
Nyaaaaa!
......!
SHI-CHAN!
Stick to it, Karin-Chan!
Don't forget that you have meee!

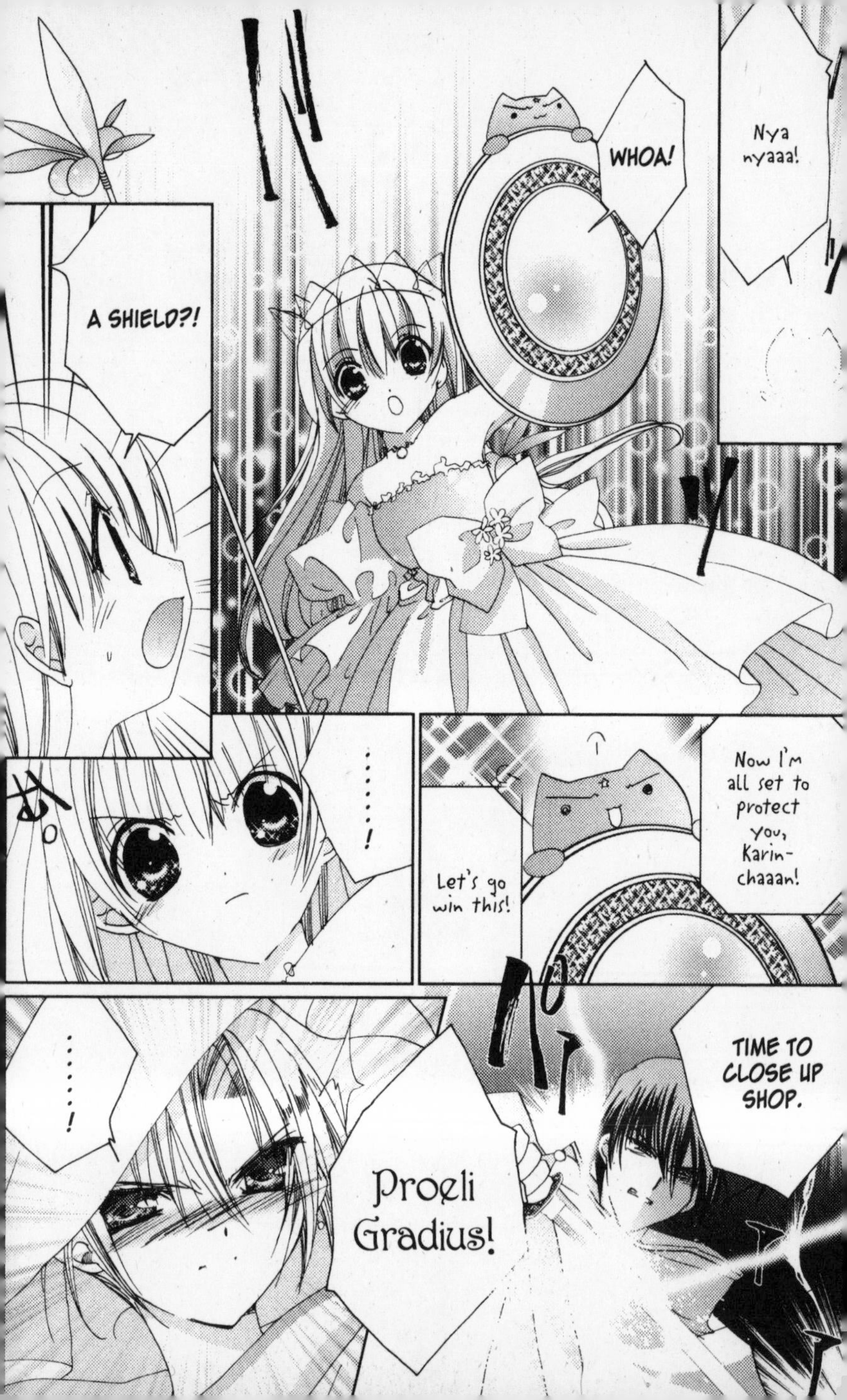
Nya nyaaa!
WHOA!
A SHIELD?!
Now I'm all set to protect you, Karin-chaaan!
Let's go win this!
......!
TIME TO CLOSE UP SHOP.
Proeli Gradius!
......!

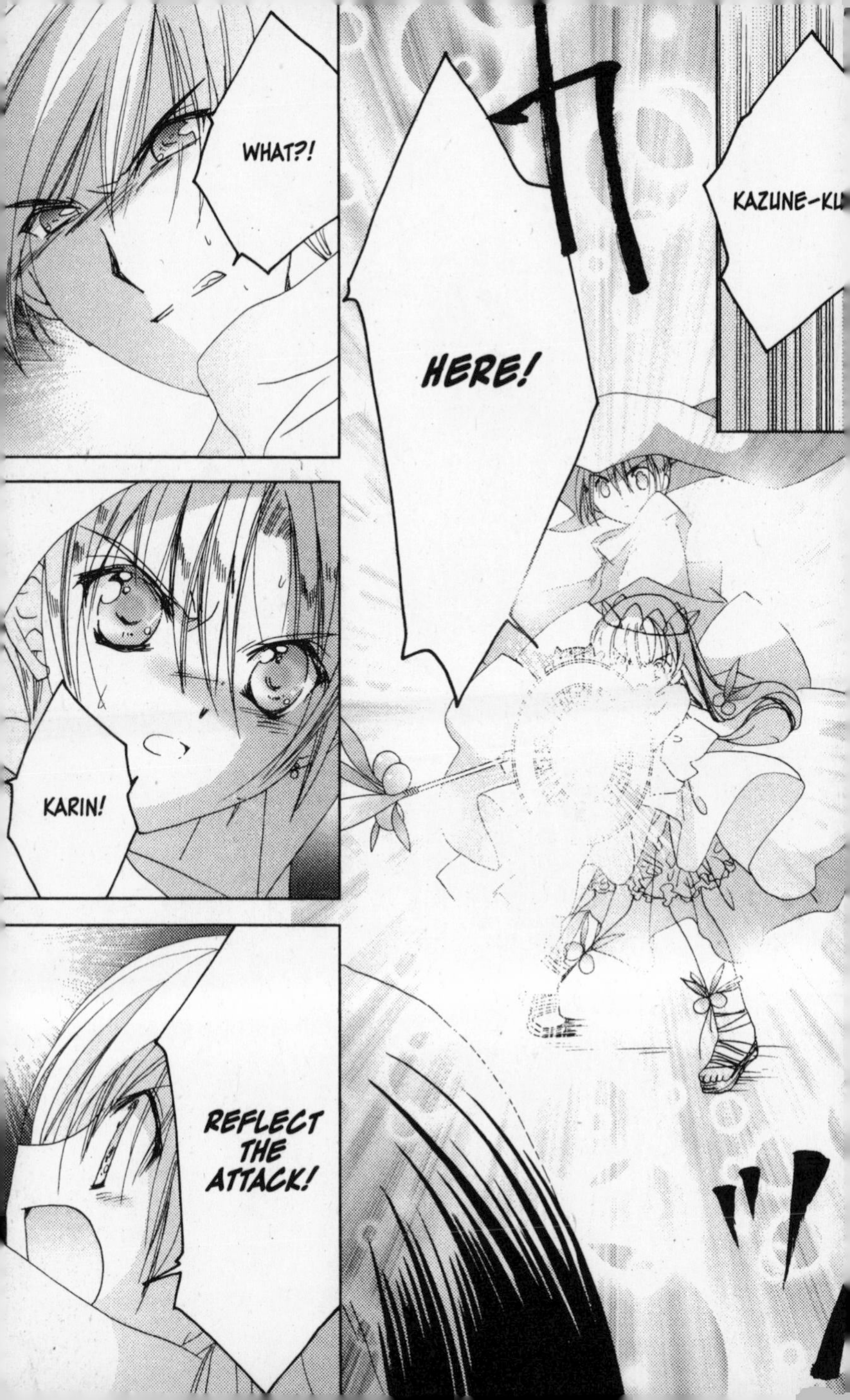
KAZUNE-KU
HERE!
WHAT?!
KARIN!
REFLECT THE ATTACK!

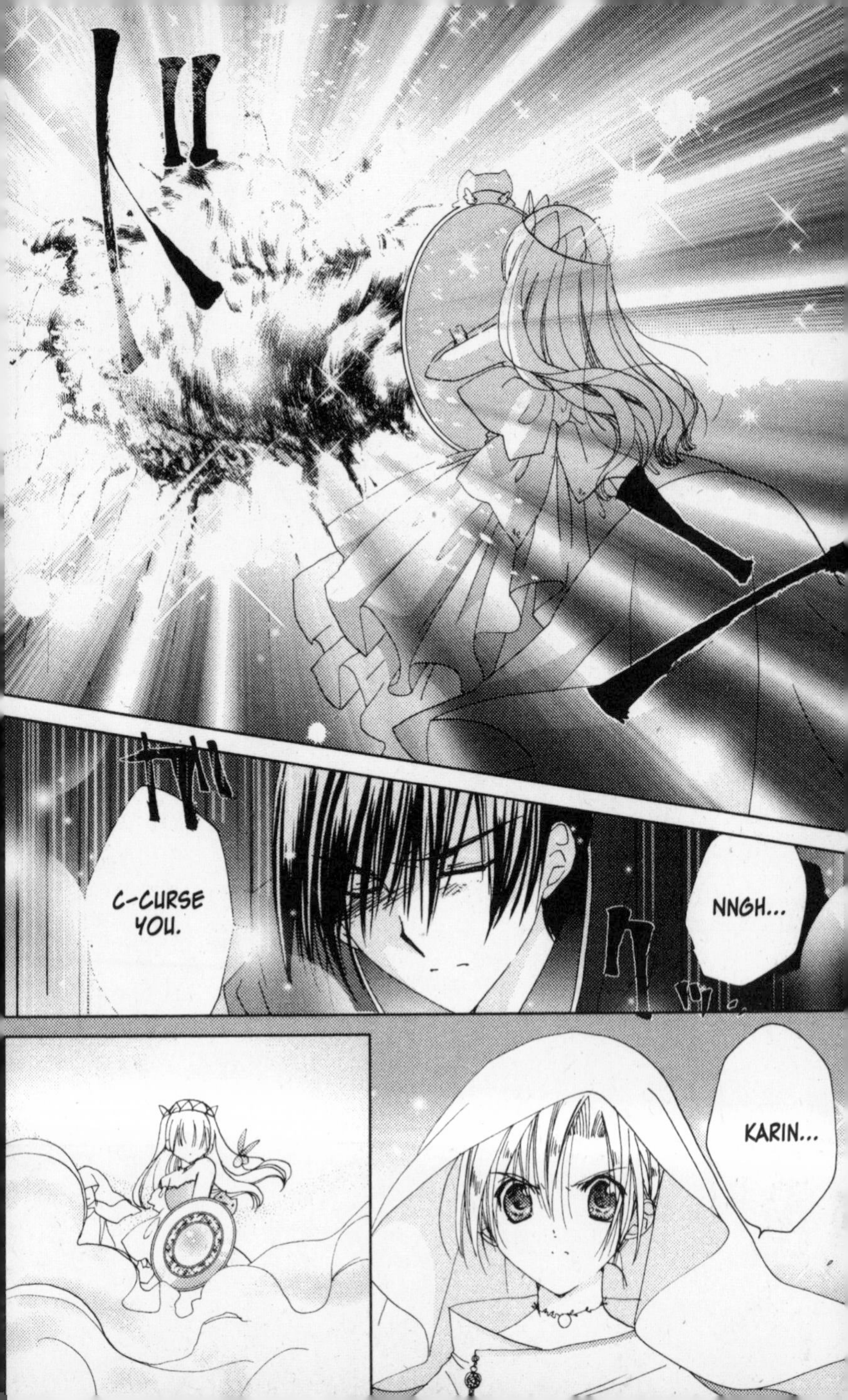
NNGH...
C-CURSE YOU.
KARIN...

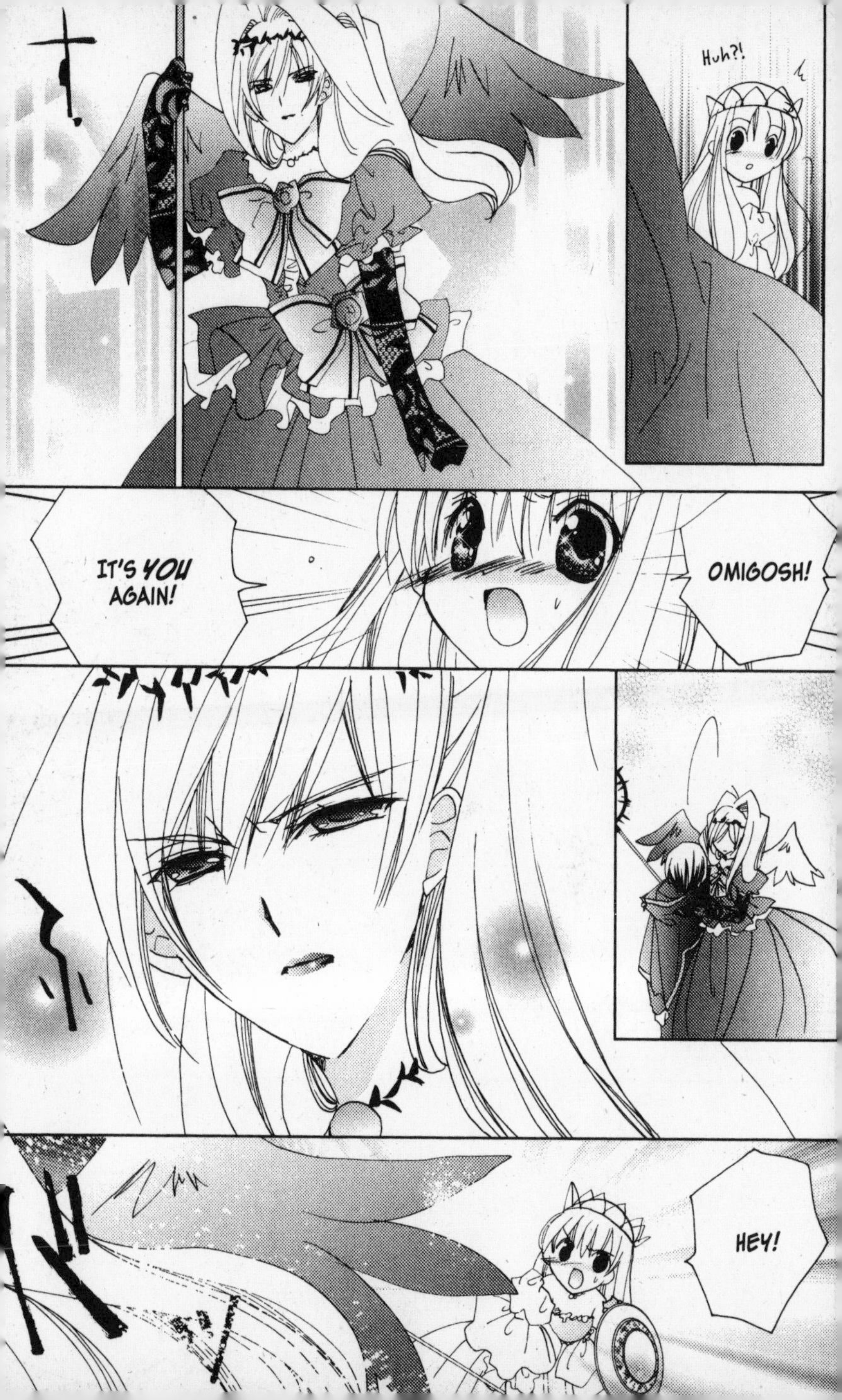
Huh?!
OMIGOSH!
IT'S YOU AGAIN!
HEY!

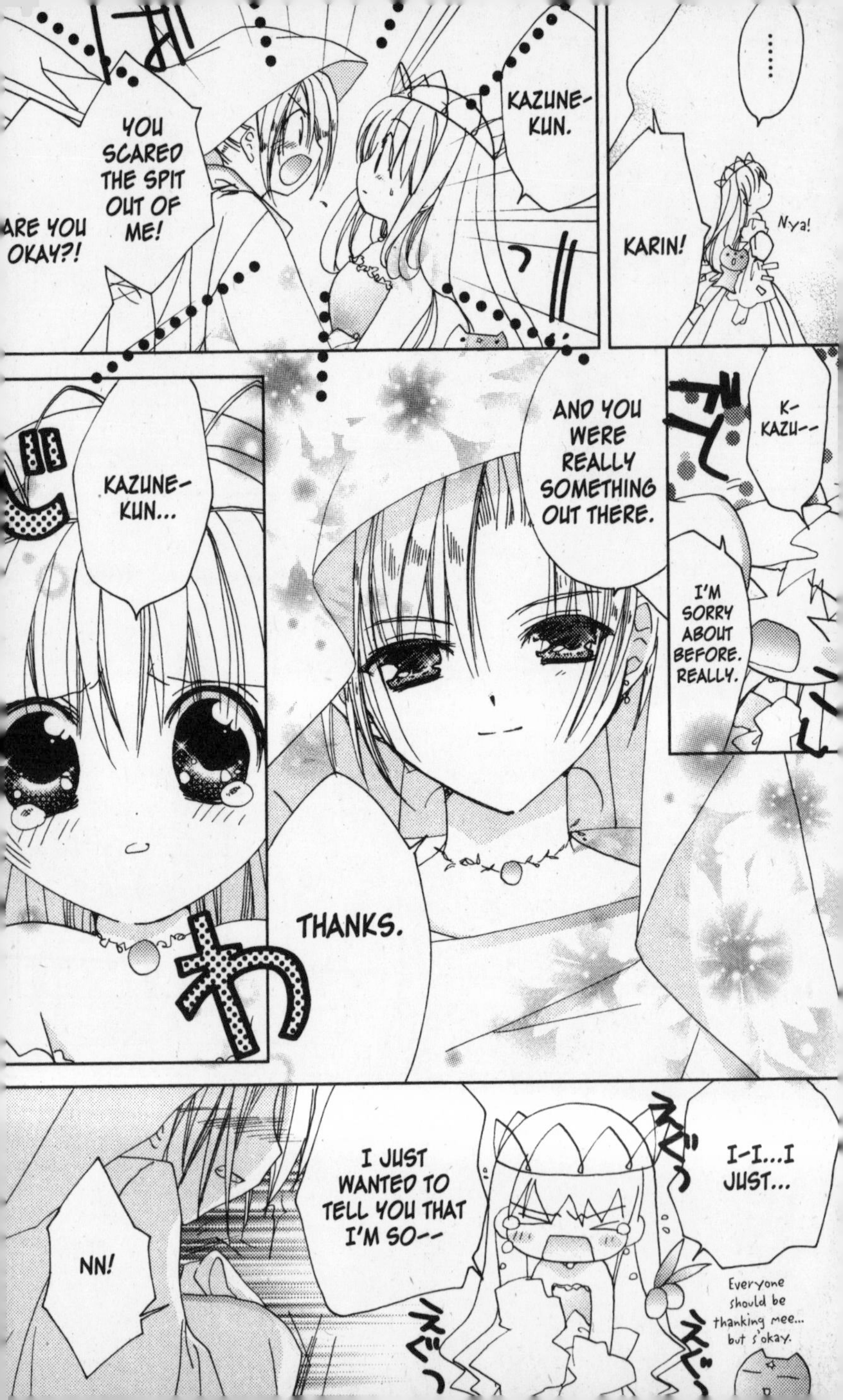
......
KARIN!
Nya!
KAZUNE-KUN.
YOU SCARED THE SPIT OUT OF ME!
ARE YOU OKAY?!
K-KAZU--
I'M SORRY ABOUT BEFORE. REALLY.
AND YOU WERE REALLY SOMETHING OUT THERE.
THANKS.
KAZUNE-KUN...
わ
I-I...I JUST...
I JUST WANTED TO TELL YOU THAT I'M SO--
Everyone should be thanking mee... but s'okay.
NN!

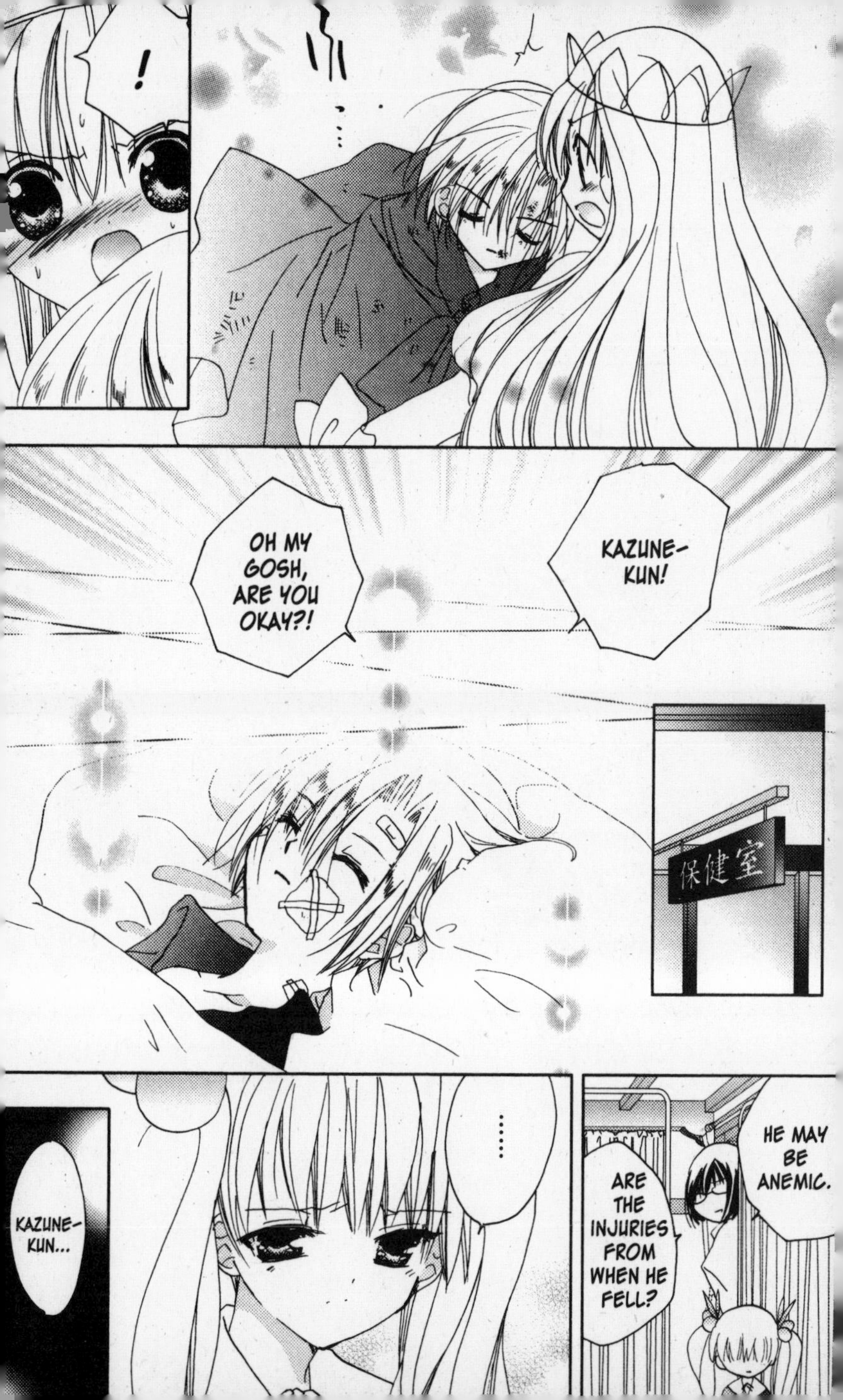

...
!
KAZUNE-KUN!
OH MY GOSH, ARE YOU OKAY?!
保健室
HE MAY BE ANEMIC.
ARE THE INJURIES FROM WHEN HE FELL?
......
KAZUNE-KUN...

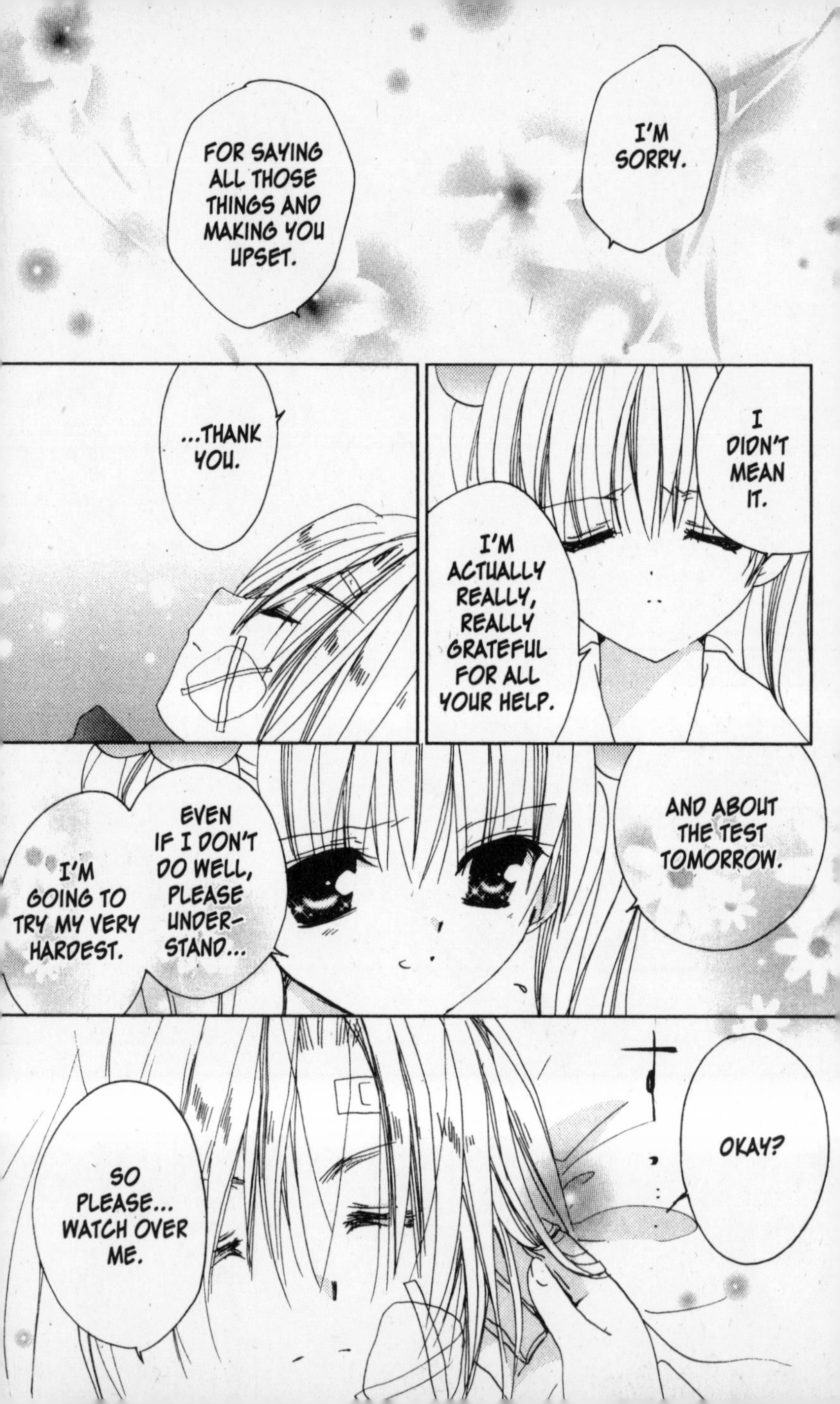
I'M SORRY.
FOR SAYING ALL THOSE THINGS AND MAKING YOU UPSET.
I DIDN'T MEAN IT.
I'M ACTUALLY REALLY, REALLY GRATEFUL FOR ALL YOUR HELP.
...THANK YOU.
AND ABOUT THE TEST TOMORROW.
EVEN IF I DON'T DO WELL, PLEASE UNDER-STAND...
I'M GOING TO TRY MY VERY HARDEST.
OKAY?
SO PLEASE... WATCH OVER ME.

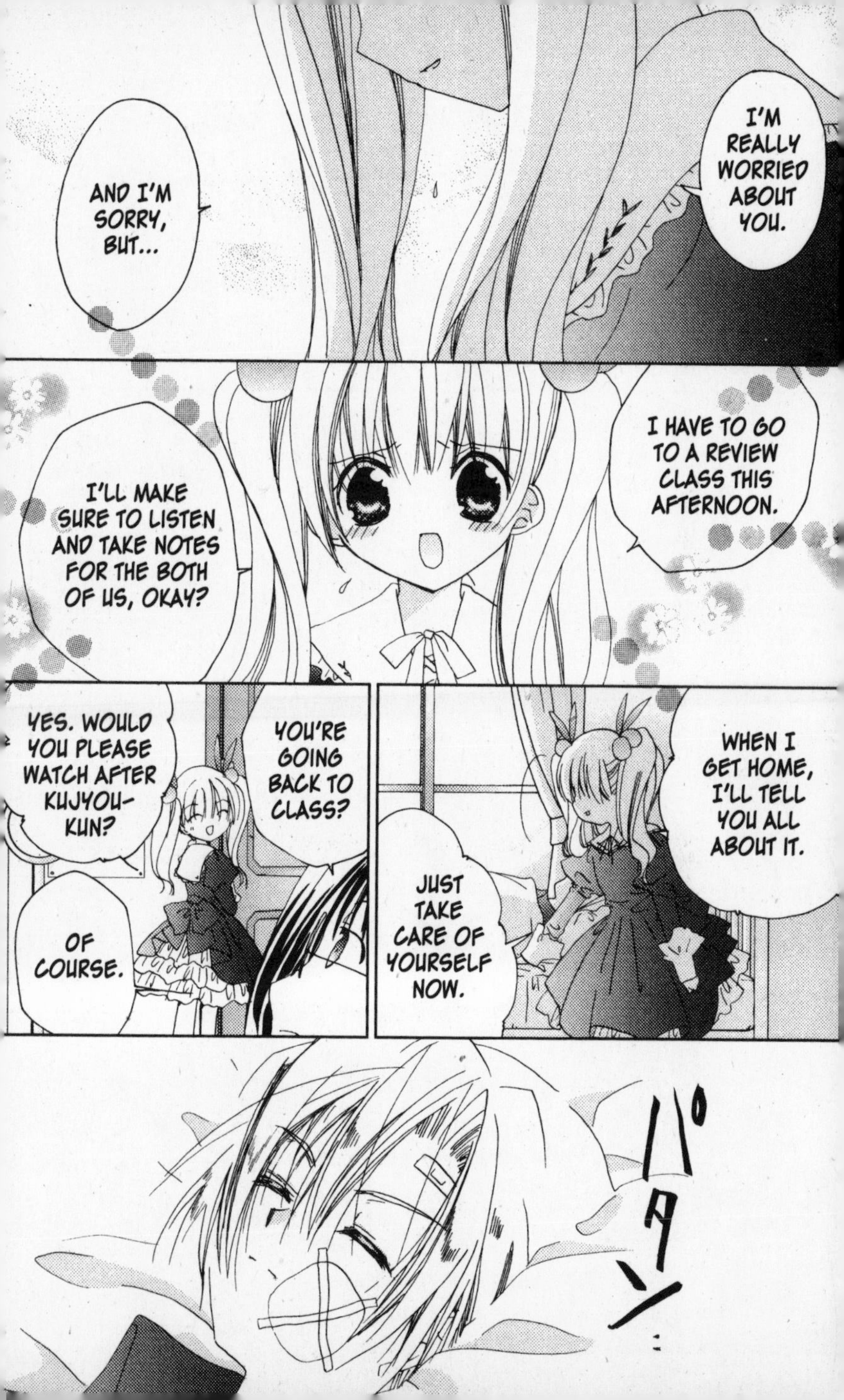
I'M REALLY WORRIED ABOUT YOU.
AND I'M SORRY, BUT...
I HAVE TO GO TO A REVIEW CLASS THIS AFTERNOON.
I'LL MAKE SURE TO LISTEN AND TAKE NOTES FOR THE BOTH OF US, OKAY?
WHEN I GET HOME, I'LL TELL YOU ALL ABOUT IT.
JUST TAKE CARE OF YOURSELF NOW.
YOU'RE GOING BACK TO CLASS?
YES. WOULD YOU PLEASE WATCH AFTER KUJYOU-KUN?
OF COURSE.
パタン

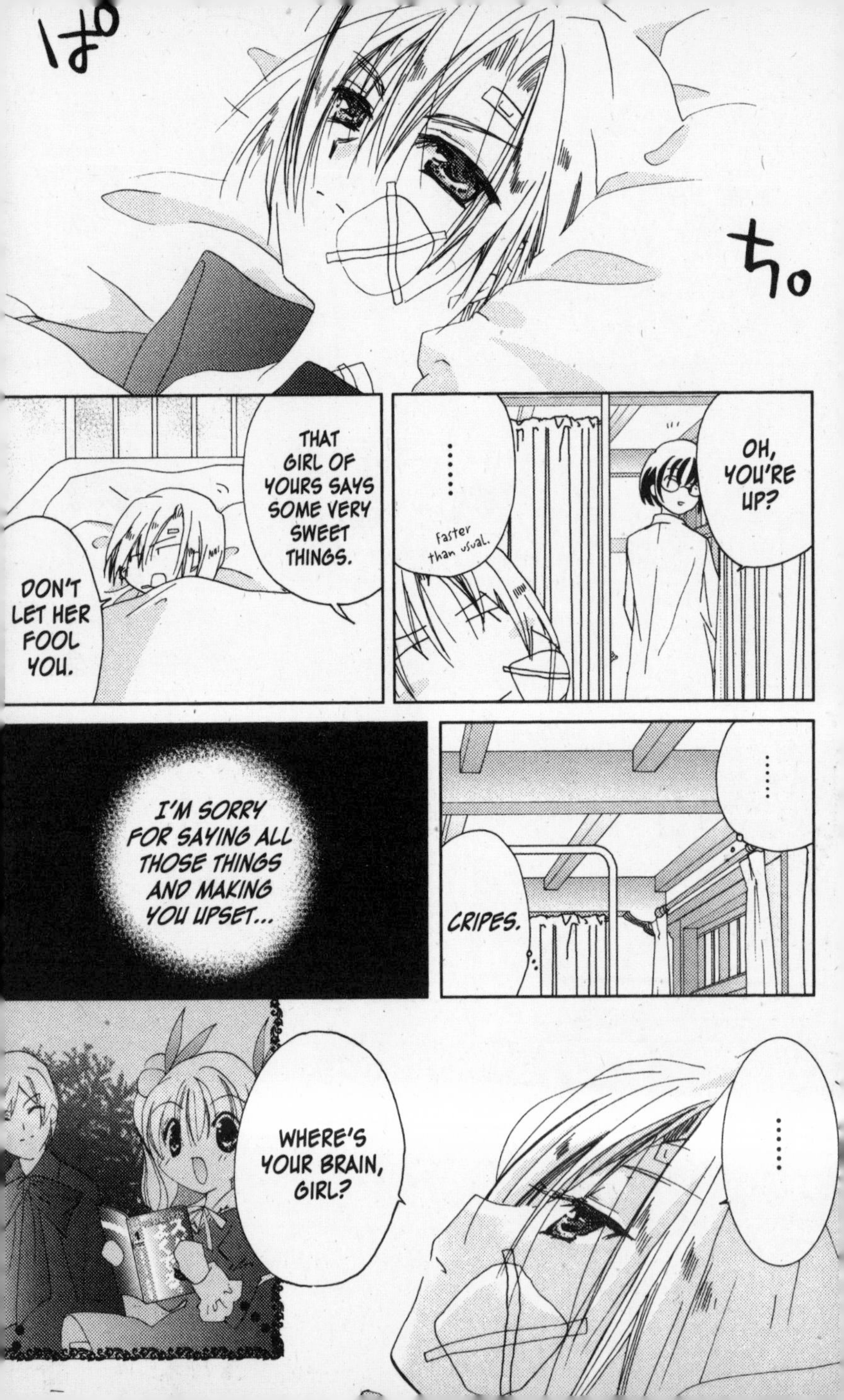
ぱち
OH, YOU'RE UP?
......
faster than usual.
THAT GIRL OF YOURS SAYS SOME VERY SWEET THINGS.
DON'T LET HER FOOL YOU.
......
CRIPES.
I'M SORRY FOR SAYING ALL THOSE THINGS AND MAKING YOU UPSET...
......
WHERE'S YOUR BRAIN, GIRL?

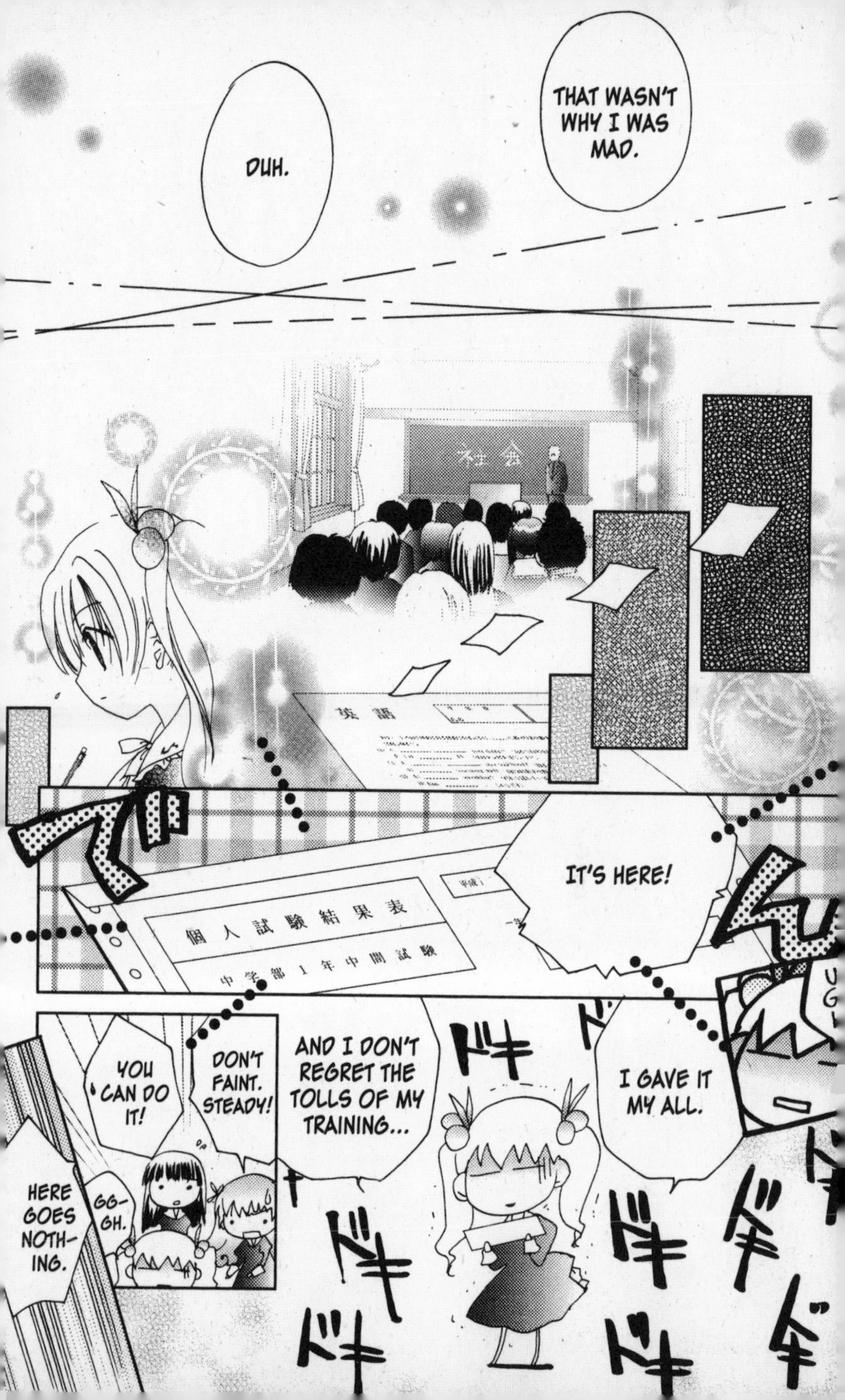
THAT WASN'T WHY I WAS MAD.
DUH.
社会
英語
個人試験結果表
中学部 1 年中間試験
IT'S HERE!
I GAVE IT MY ALL.
AND I DON'T REGRET THE TOLLS OF MY TRAINING...
DON'T FAINT. STEADY!
YOU CAN DO IT!
GG-GH.
HERE GOES NOTHING.

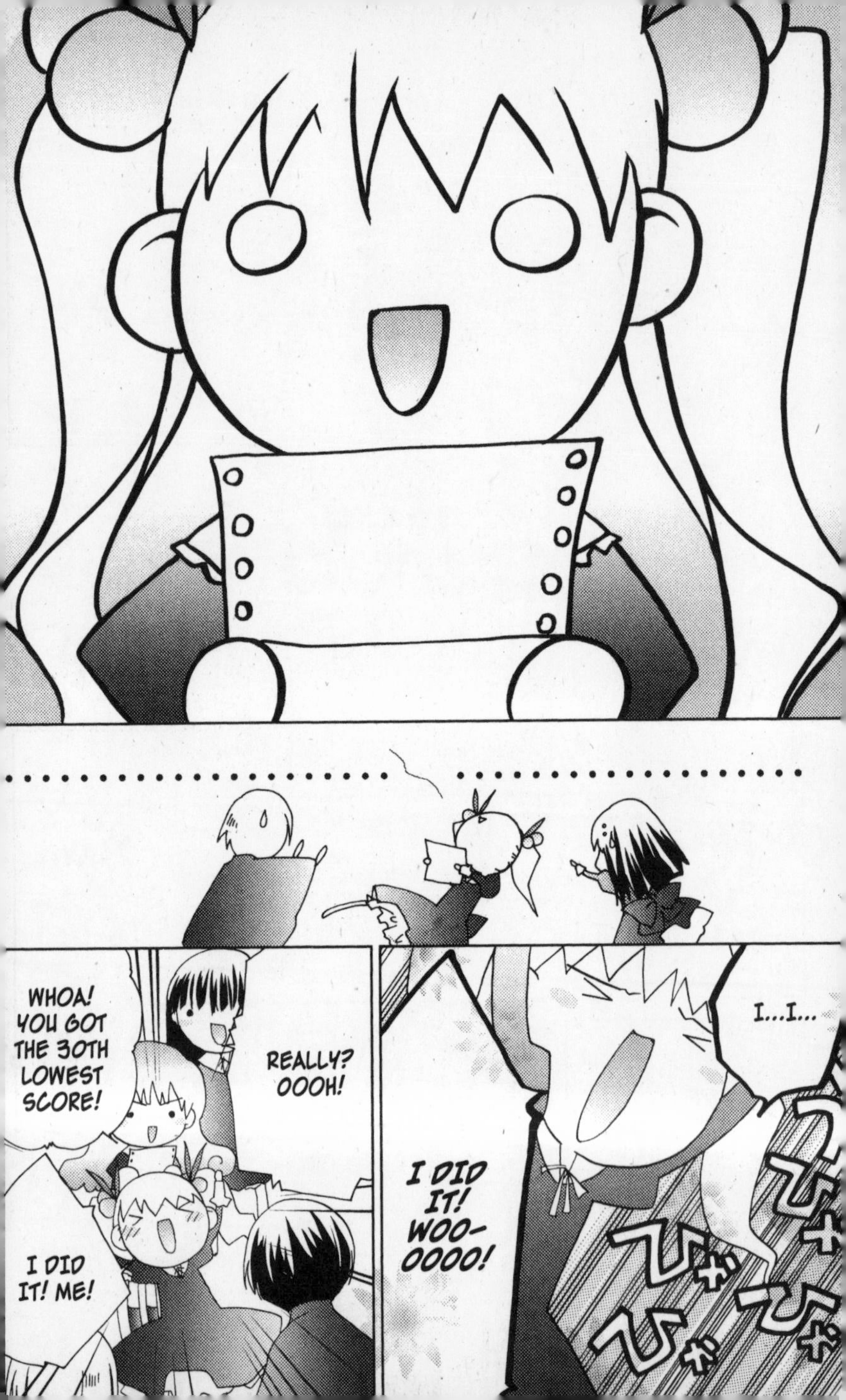

I...I...
I DID IT! WOO-OOOO!
REALLY? OOOH!
WHOA! YOU GOT THE 30TH LOWEST SCORE!
I DID IT! ME!

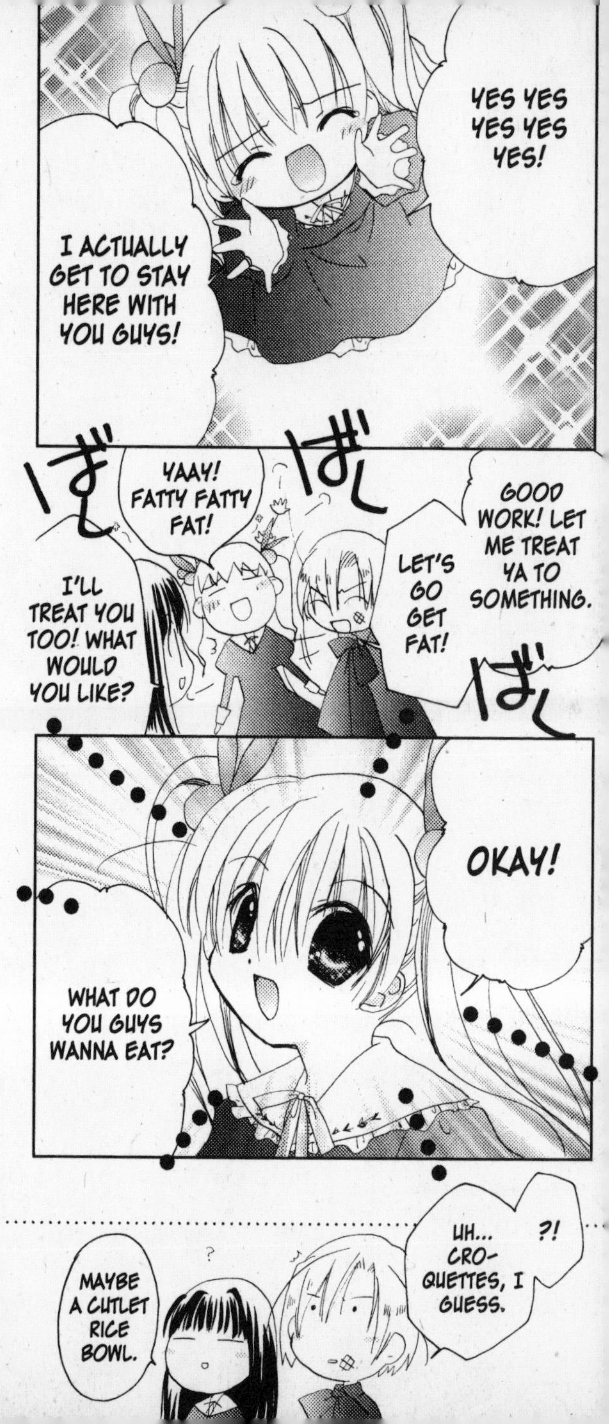
YES YES YES YES YES!
I ACTUALLY GET TO STAY HERE WITH YOU GUYS!
ばし
GOOD WORK! LET ME TREAT YA TO SOMETHING.
LET'S GO GET FAT!
ばし
YAAY! FATTY FATTY FAT!
ばし
I'LL TREAT YOU TOO! WHAT WOULD YOU LIKE?
OKAY!
WHAT DO YOU GUYS WANNA EAT?
?!
UH... CRO-QUETTES, I GUESS.
?
MAYBE A CUTLET RICE BOWL.
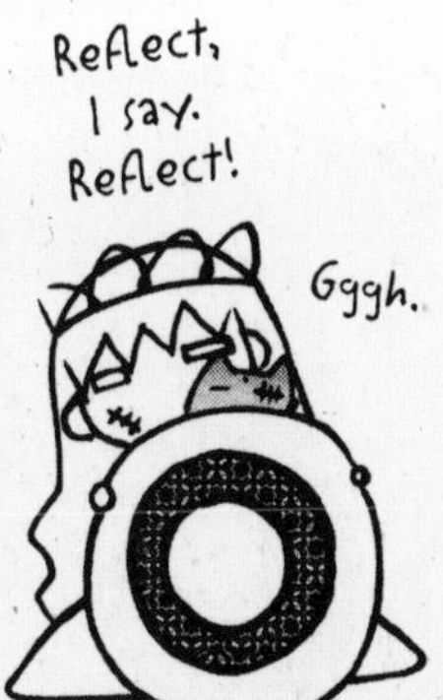
Reflect, I say. Reflect!
Gggh.

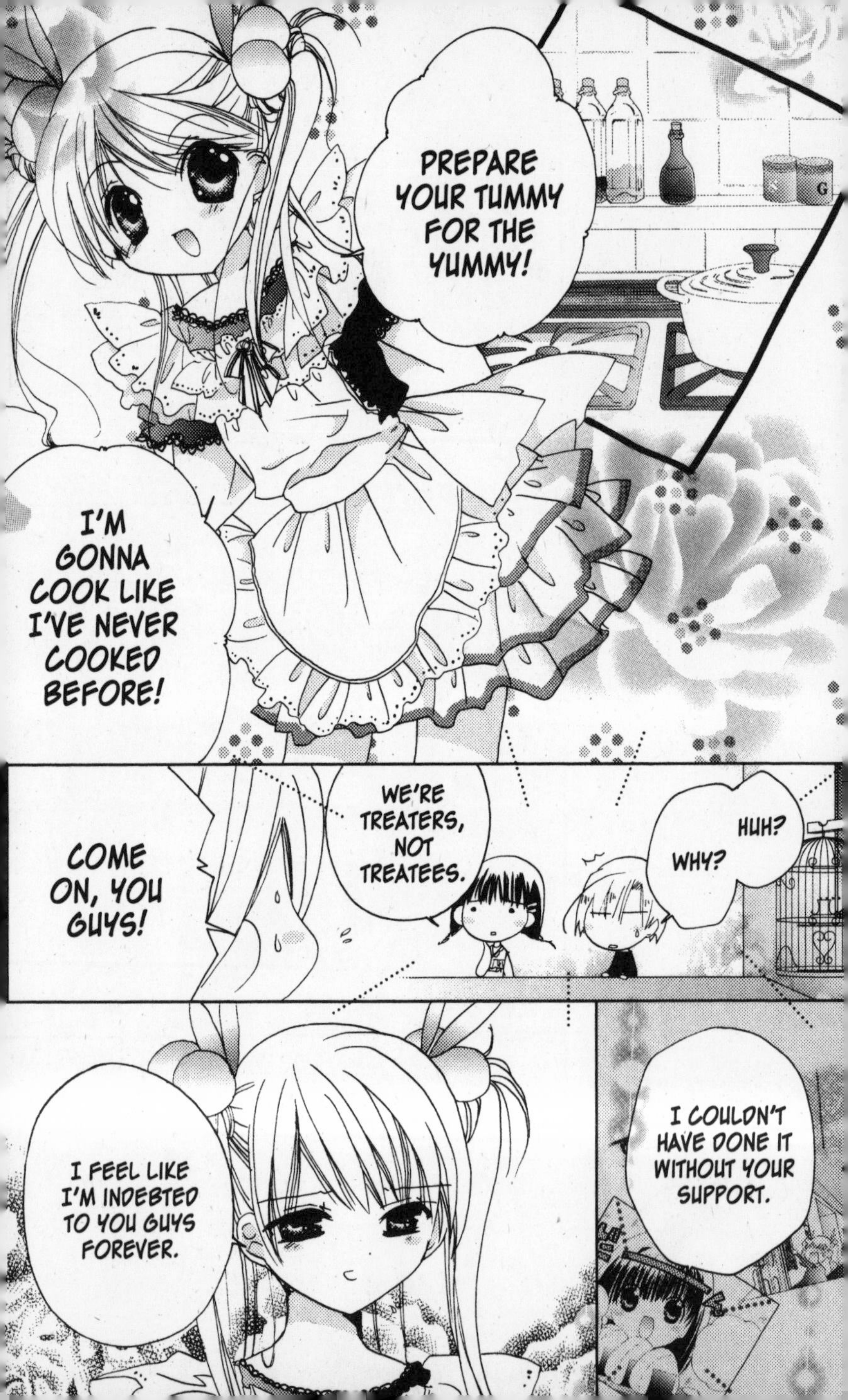
PREPARE YOUR TUMMY FOR THE YUMMY!
I'M GONNA COOK LIKE I'VE NEVER COOKED BEFORE!
HUH?
WHY?
WE'RE TREATERS, NOT TREATEES.
COME ON, YOU GUYS!
I COULDN'T HAVE DONE IT WITHOUT YOUR SUPPORT.
I FEEL LIKE I'M INDEBTED TO YOU GUYS FOREVER.

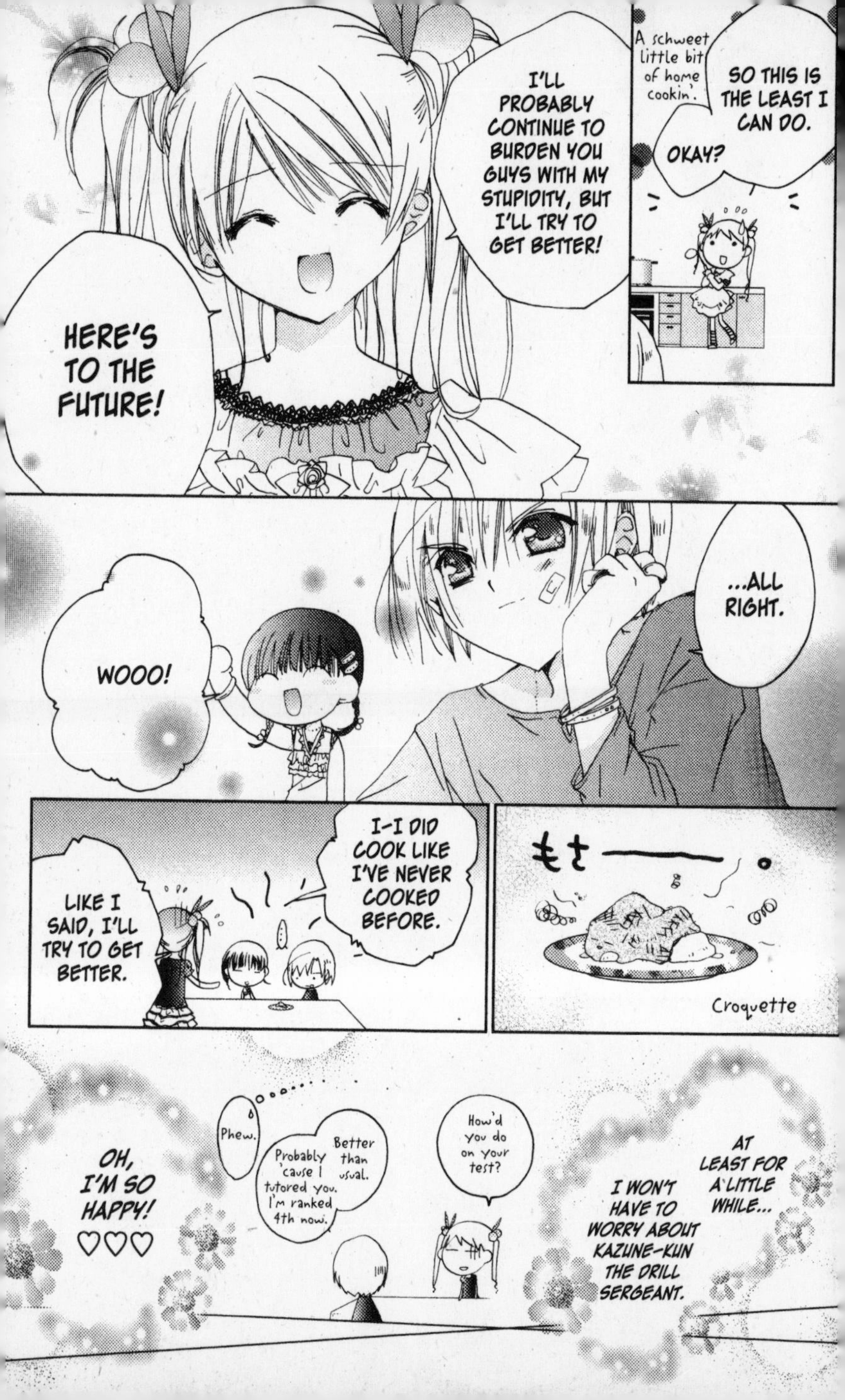
A schweet little bit of home cookin'.
SO THIS IS THE LEAST I CAN DO.
OKAY?
I'LL PROBABLY CONTINUE TO BURDEN YOU GUYS WITH MY STUPIDITY, BUT I'LL TRY TO GET BETTER!
HERE'S TO THE FUTURE!
...ALL RIGHT.
WOOO!
もさーーー。
Croquette
I-I DID COOK LIKE I'VE NEVER COOKED BEFORE.
LIKE I SAID, I'LL TRY TO GET BETTER.
AT LEAST FOR A LITTLE WHILE...
I WON'T HAVE TO WORRY ABOUT KAZUNE-KUN THE DRILL SERGEANT.
How'd you do on your test?
Better than usual.
Probably 'cause I tutored you. I'm ranked 4th now.
Phew.
OH, I'M SO HAPPY! ♡♡♡

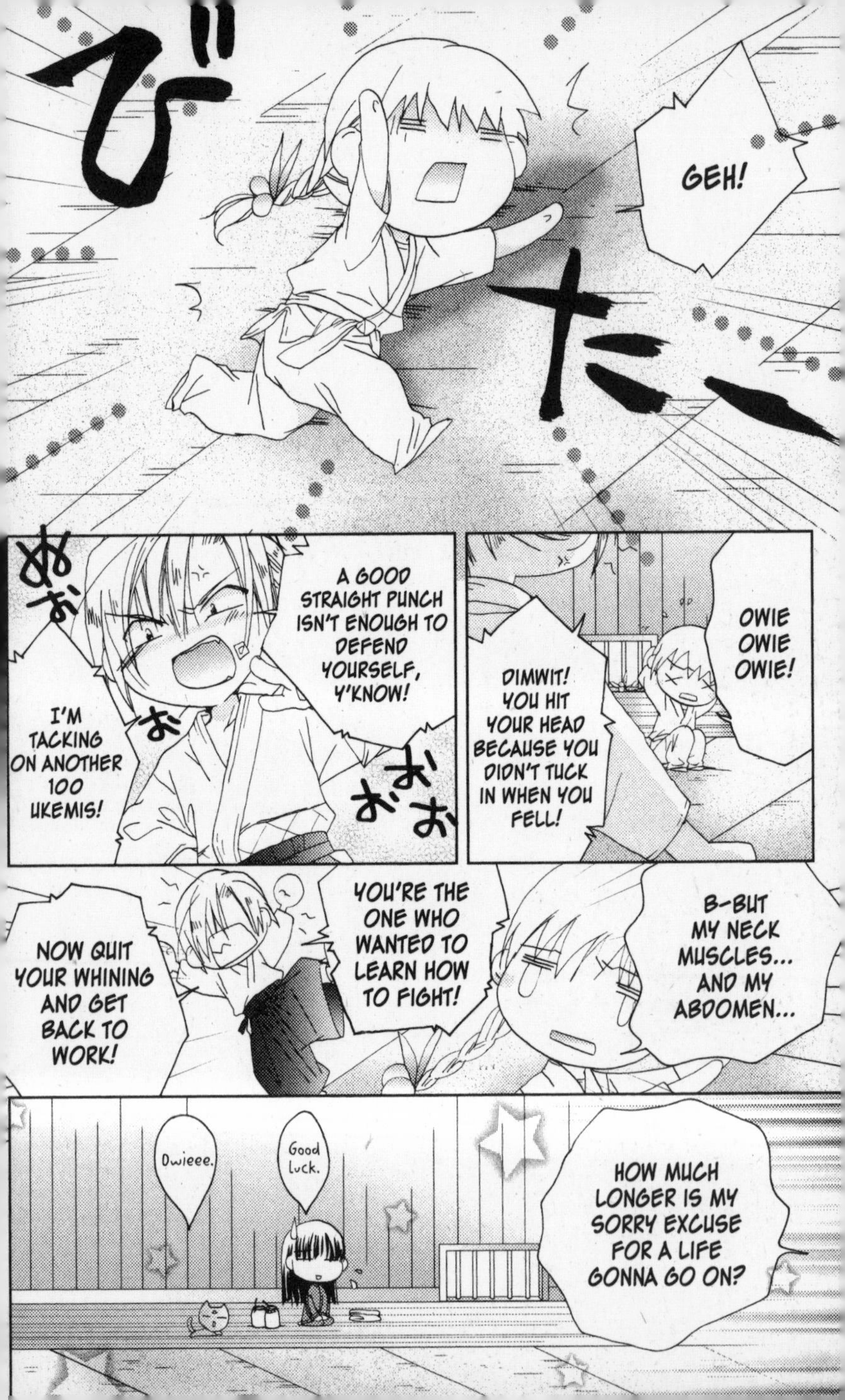
GEH!
たー
び
OWIE OWIE OWIE!
DIMWIT! YOU HIT YOUR HEAD BECAUSE YOU DIDN'T TUCK IN WHEN YOU FELL!
ぬぉ
A GOOD STRAIGHT PUNCH ISN'T ENOUGH TO DEFEND YOURSELF, Y'KNOW!
おおおお
I'M TACKING ON ANOTHER 100 UKEMIS!
B-BUT MY NECK MUSCLES... AND MY ABDOMEN...
YOU'RE THE ONE WHO WANTED TO LEARN HOW TO FIGHT!
NOW QUIT YOUR WHINING AND GET BACK TO WORK!
HOW MUCH LONGER IS MY SORRY EXCUSE FOR A LIFE GONNA GO ON?
Good luck.
Owieee.

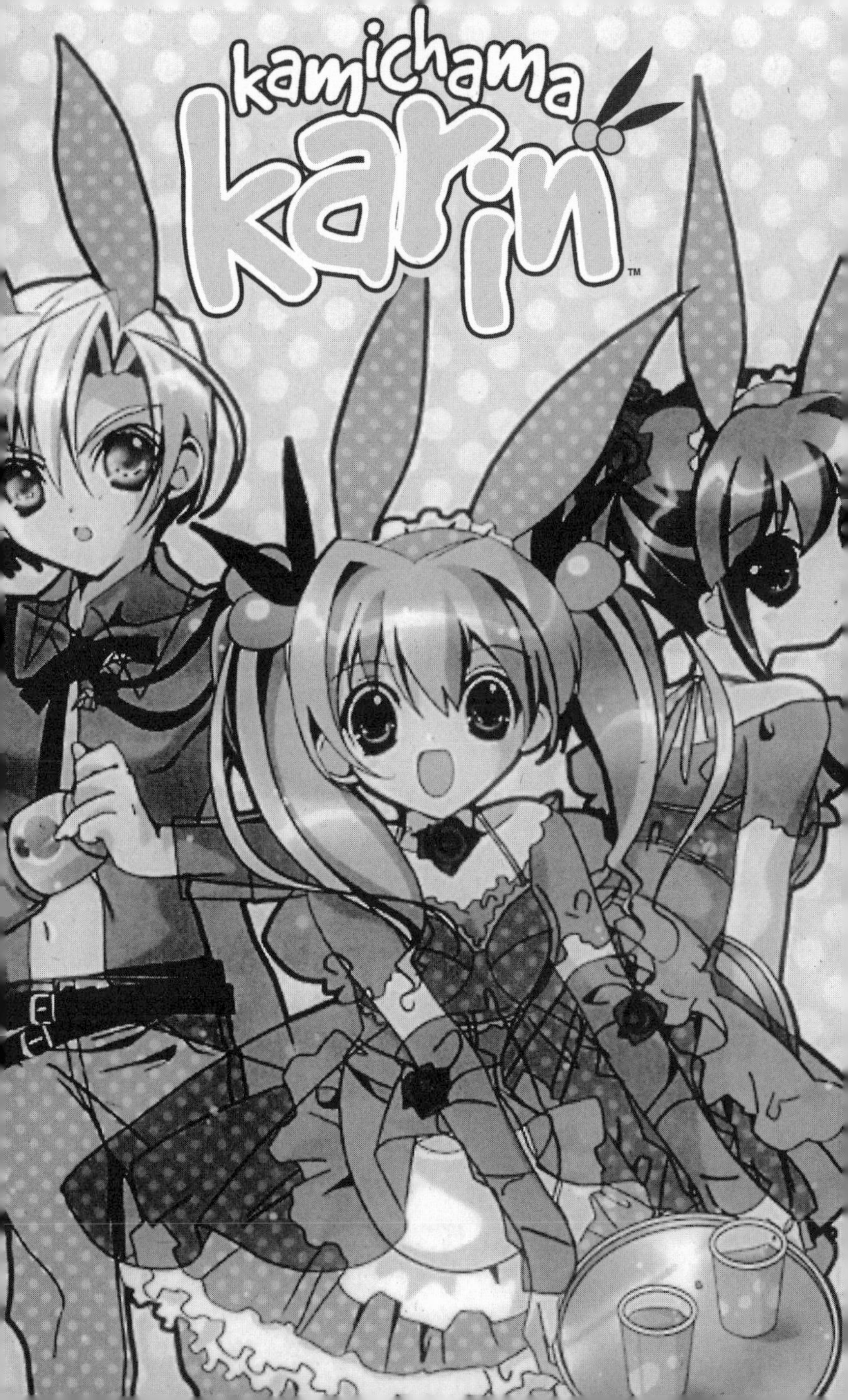
kamichama
karin™

Endurance.

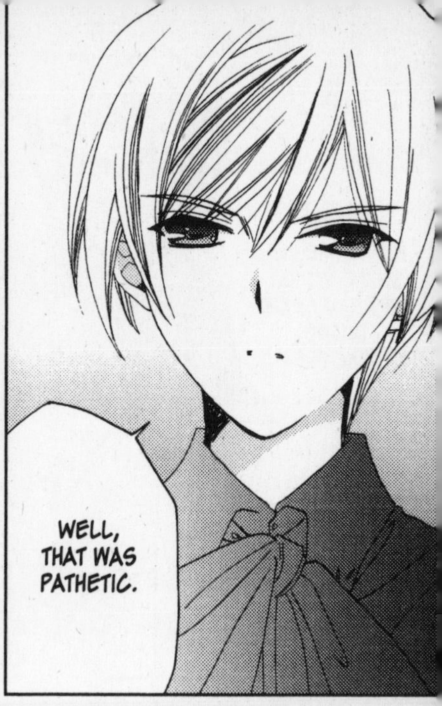
WELL, THAT WAS PATHETIC.
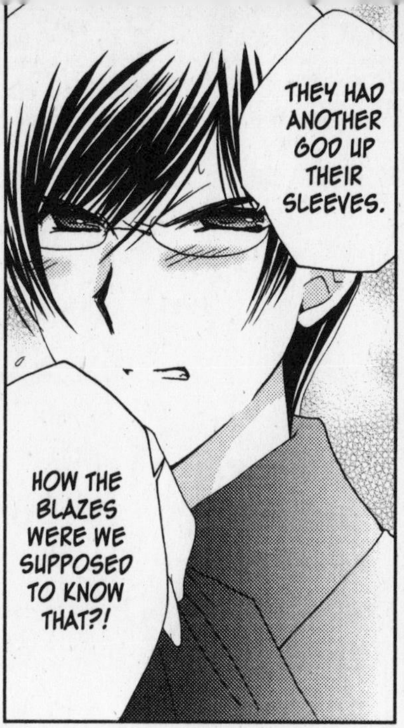
THEY HAD ANOTHER GOD UP THEIR SLEEVES.
HOW THE BLAZES WERE WE SUPPOSED TO KNOW THAT?!
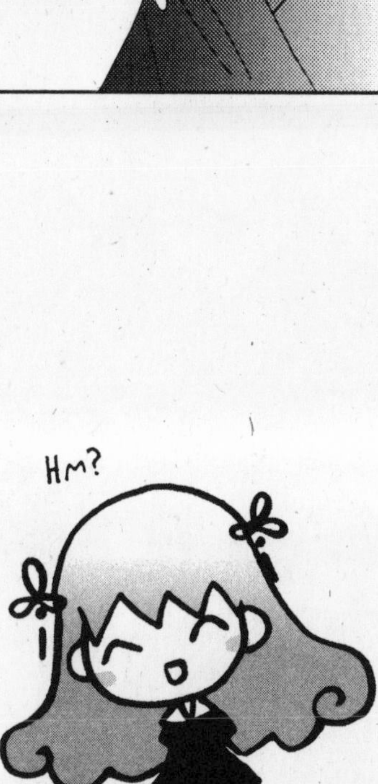
HM?

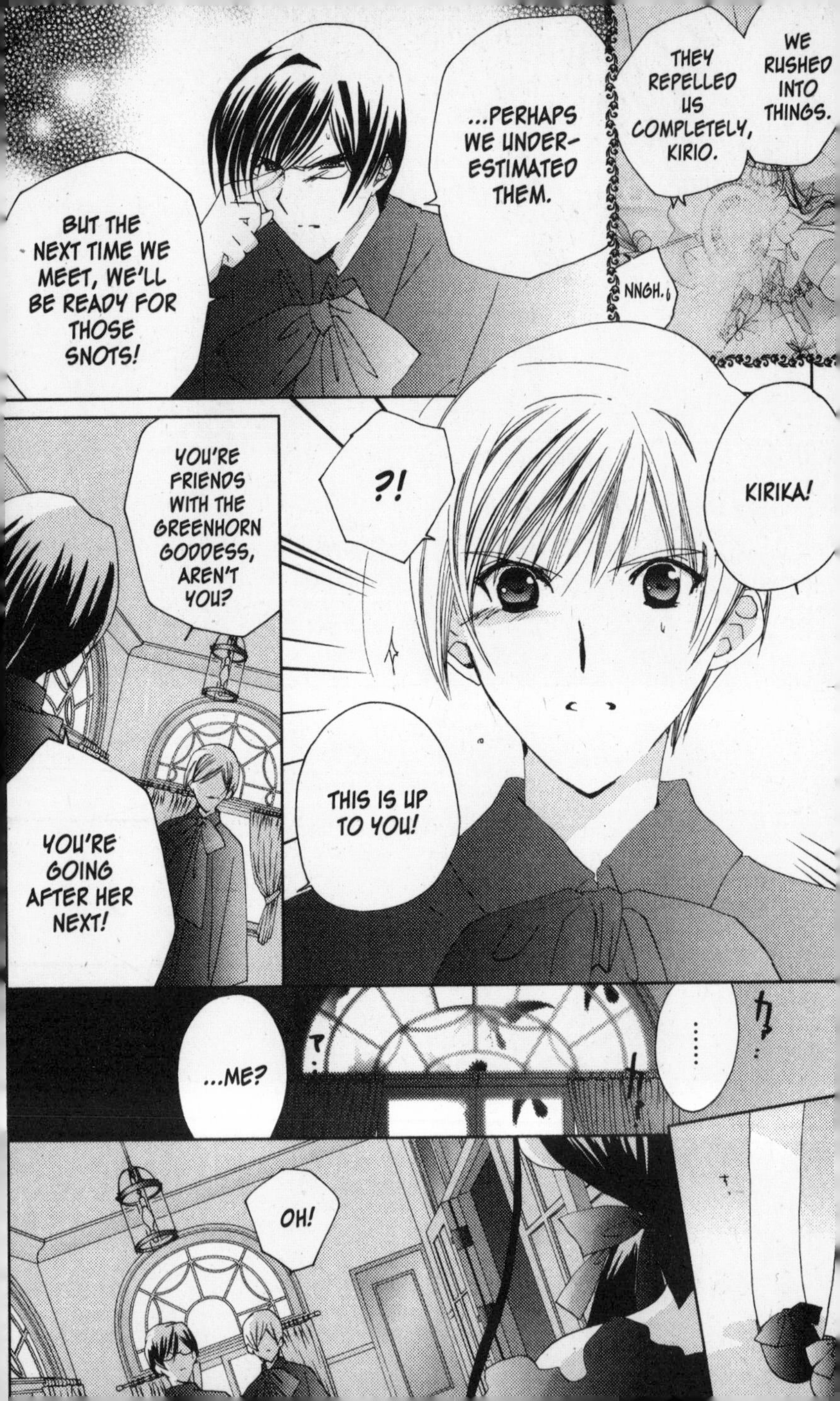
WE RUSHED INTO THINGS.
THEY REPELLED US COMPLETELY, KIRIO.
NNGH.
...PERHAPS WE UNDER-ESTIMATED THEM.
BUT THE NEXT TIME WE MEET, WE'LL BE READY FOR THOSE SNOTS!
KIRIKA!
?!
THIS IS UP TO YOU!
YOU'RE FRIENDS WITH THE GREENHORN GODDESS, AREN'T YOU?
YOU'RE GOING AFTER HER NEXT!
......
...ME?
OH!

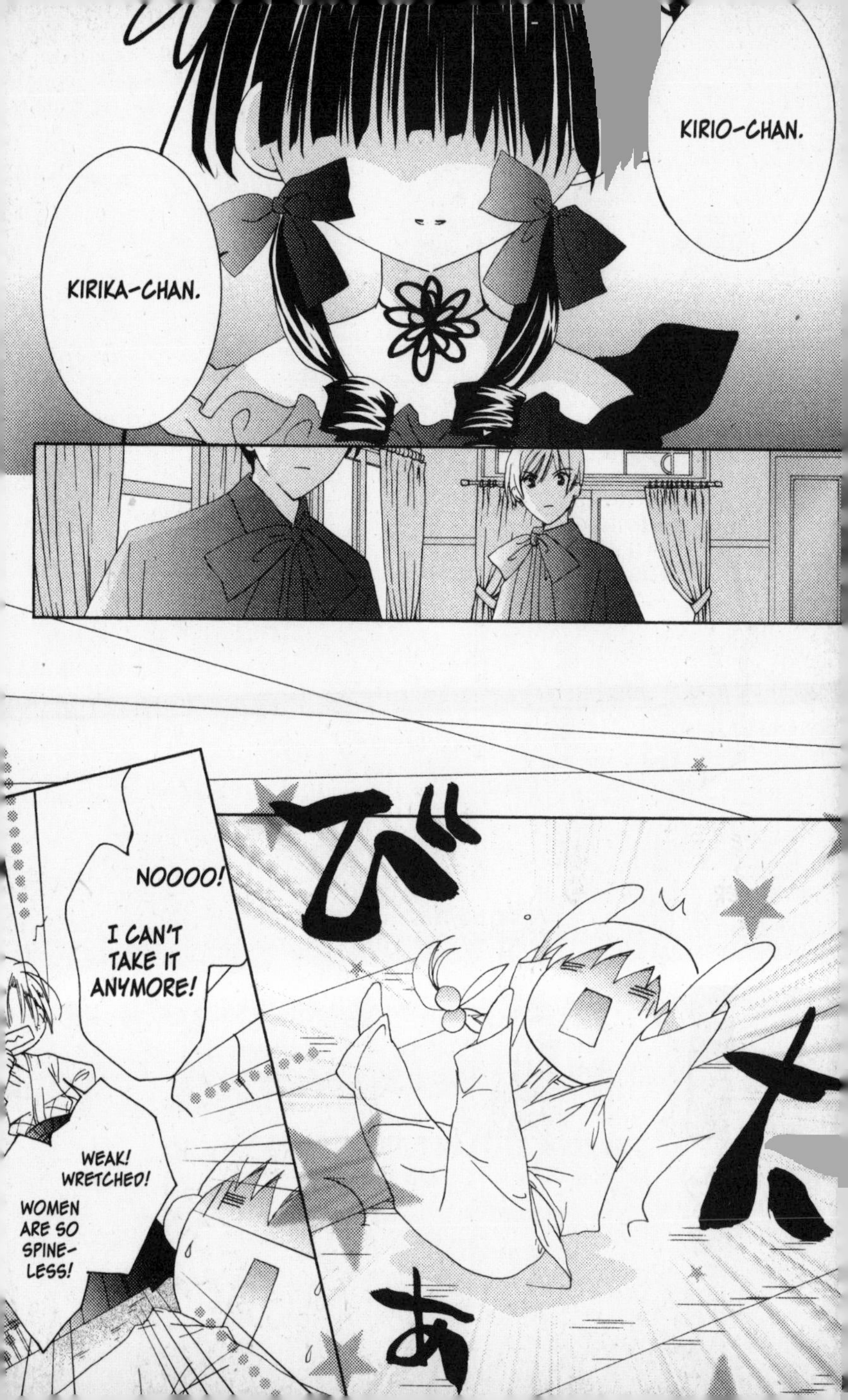
KIRIO-CHAN.
KIRIKA-CHAN.
NOOOO! I CAN'T TAKE IT ANYMORE!
WEAK! WRETCHED!
WOMEN ARE SO SPINE-LESS!

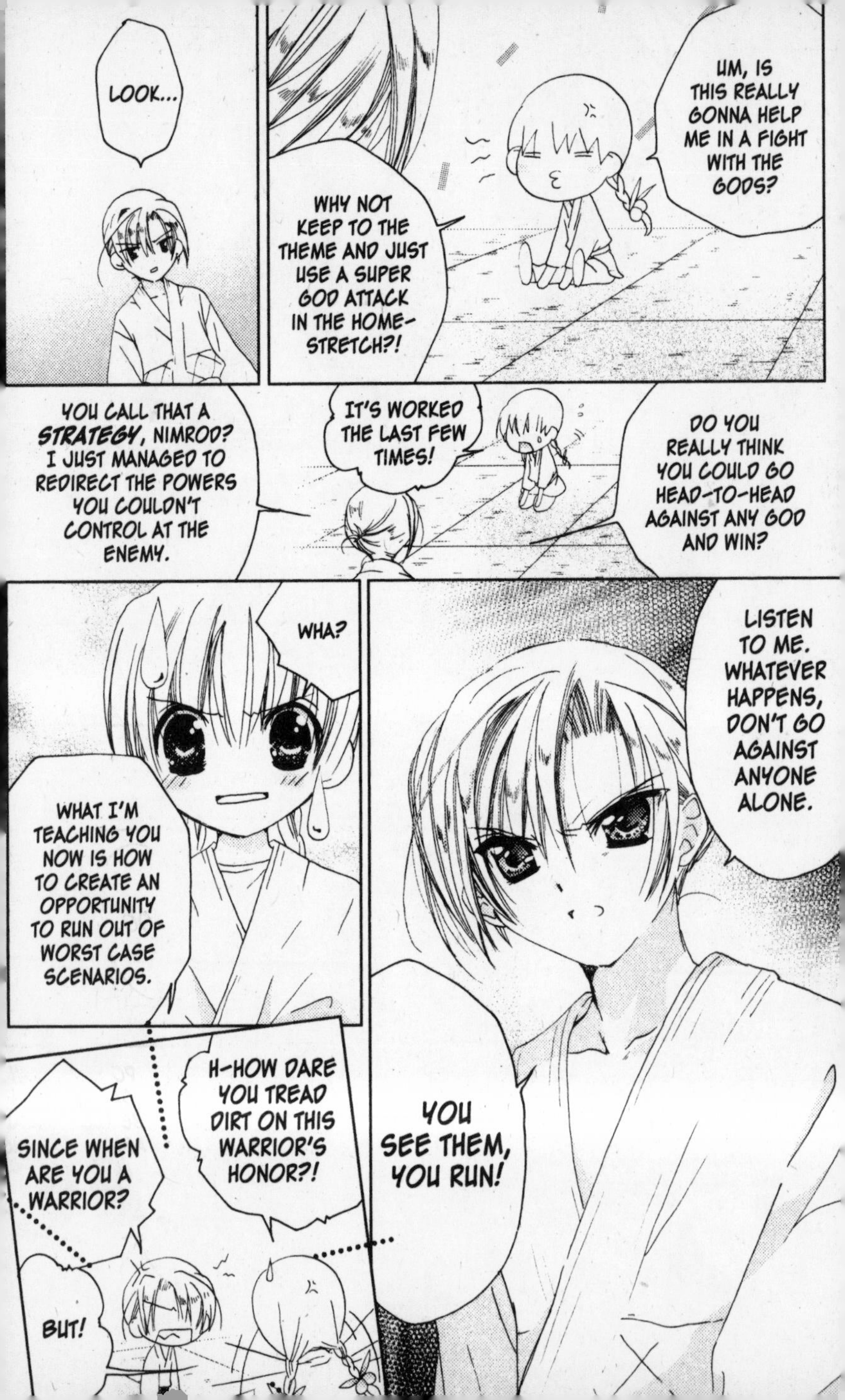
UM, IS THIS REALLY GONNA HELP ME IN A FIGHT WITH THE GODS?
WHY NOT KEEP TO THE THEME AND JUST USE A SUPER GOD ATTACK IN THE HOME-STRETCH?!
LOOK...
DO YOU REALLY THINK YOU COULD GO HEAD-TO-HEAD AGAINST ANY GOD AND WIN?
IT'S WORKED THE LAST FEW TIMES!
YOU CALL THAT A *STRATEGY*, NIMROD? I JUST MANAGED TO REDIRECT THE POWERS YOU COULDN'T CONTROL AT THE ENEMY.
LISTEN TO ME. WHATEVER HAPPENS, DON'T GO AGAINST ANYONE ALONE.
YOU SEE THEM, YOU RUN!
WHA?
WHAT I'M TEACHING YOU NOW IS HOW TO CREATE AN OPPORTUNITY TO RUN OUT OF WORST CASE SCENARIOS.
H-HOW DARE YOU TREAD DIRT ON THIS WARRIOR'S HONOR?!
SINCE WHEN ARE YOU A WARRIOR?
BUT!

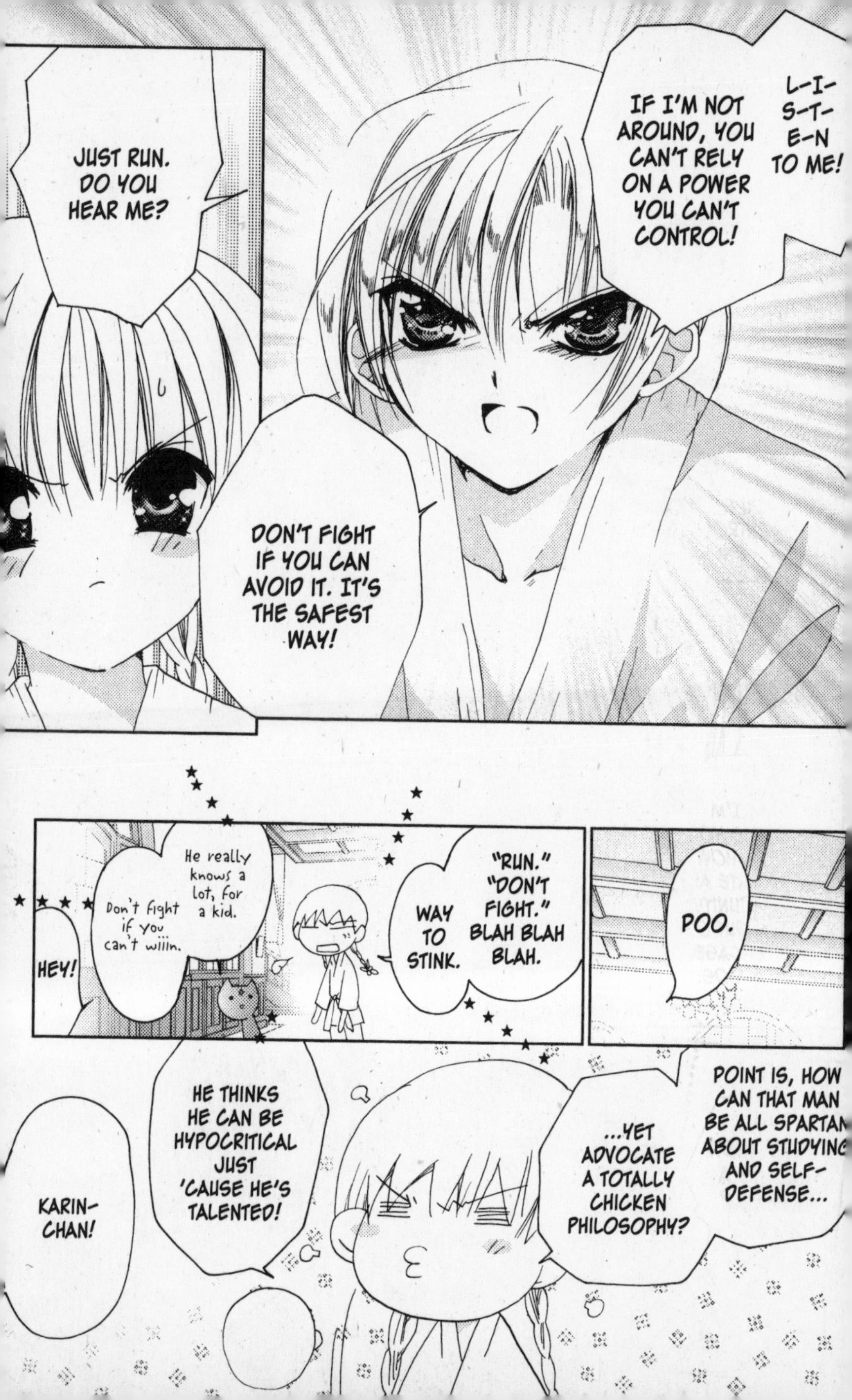
L-I-S-T-E-N TO ME!
IF I'M NOT AROUND, YOU CAN'T RELY ON A POWER YOU CAN'T CONTROL!
JUST RUN. DO YOU HEAR ME?
DON'T FIGHT IF YOU CAN AVOID IT. IT'S THE SAFEST WAY!
POO.
"RUN." "DON'T FIGHT." BLAH BLAH BLAH.
WAY TO STINK.
He really knows a lot, for a kid.
Don't fight if you... can't wiiin.
HEY!
POINT IS, HOW CAN THAT MAN BE ALL SPARTAN ABOUT STUDYING AND SELF-DEFENSE...
...YET ADVOCATE A TOTALLY CHICKEN PHILOSOPHY?
HE THINKS HE CAN BE HYPOCRITICAL JUST 'CAUSE HE'S TALENTED!
KARIN-CHAN!

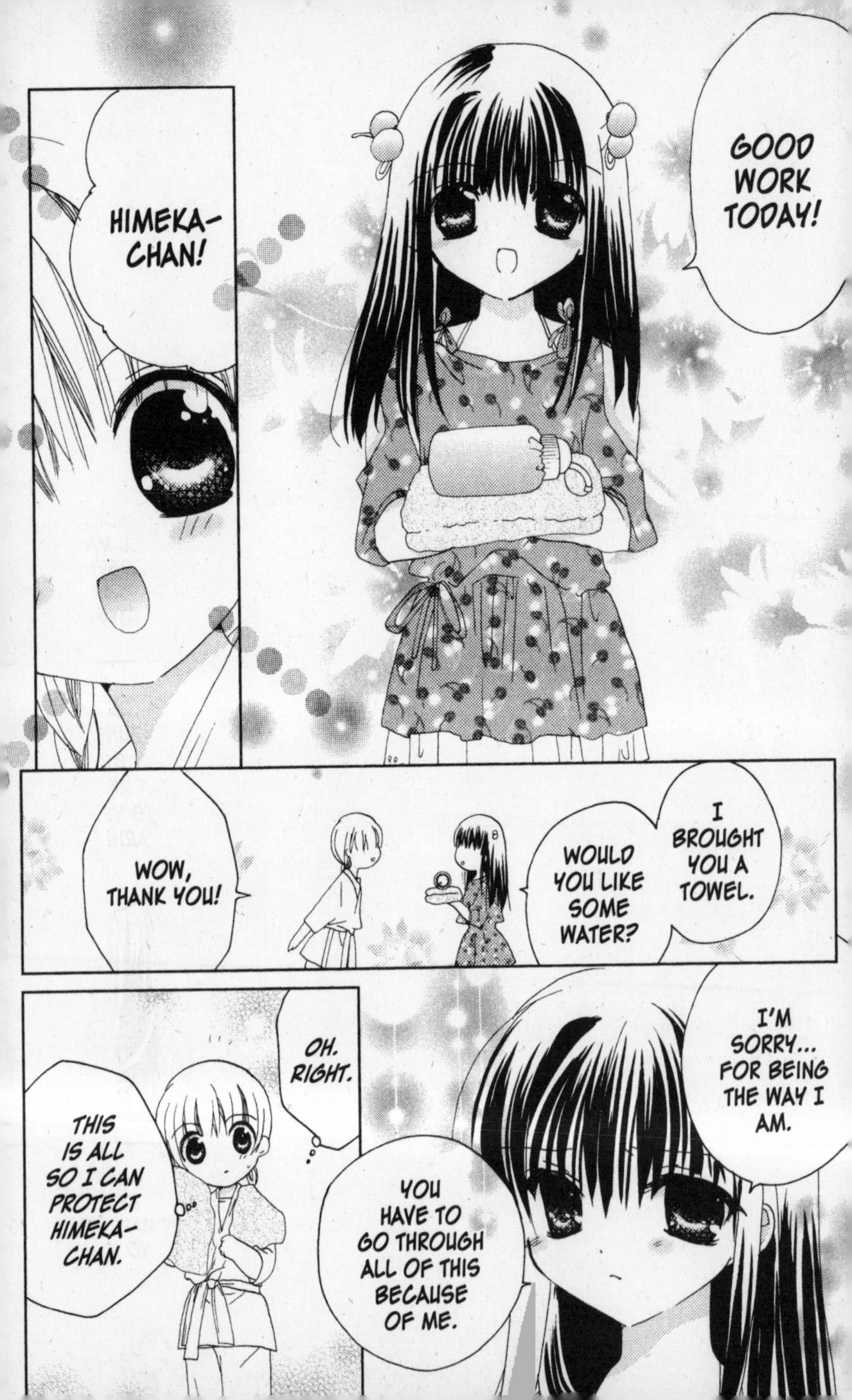
GOOD WORK TODAY!
HIMEKA-CHAN!
I BROUGHT YOU A TOWEL.
WOULD YOU LIKE SOME WATER?
WOW, THANK YOU!
I'M SORRY... FOR BEING THE WAY I AM.
YOU HAVE TO GO THROUGH ALL OF THIS BECAUSE OF ME.
OH. RIGHT.
THIS IS ALL SO I CAN PROTECT HIMEKA-CHAN.

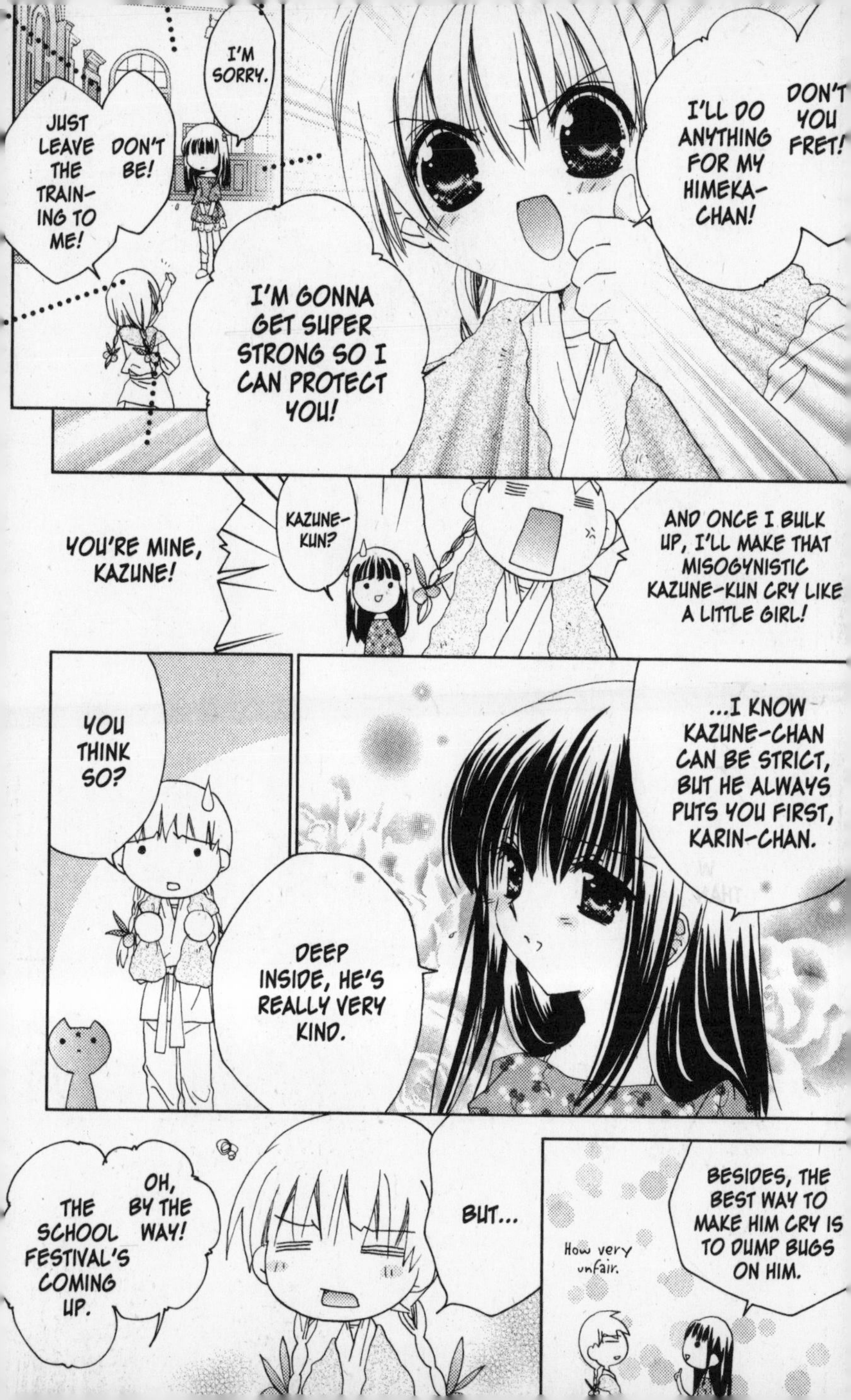
DON'T YOU FRET!
I'LL DO ANYTHING FOR MY HIMEKA-CHAN!
I'M GONNA GET SUPER STRONG SO I CAN PROTECT YOU!
I'M SORRY.
DON'T BE!
JUST LEAVE THE TRAIN-ING TO ME!
AND ONCE I BULK UP, I'LL MAKE THAT MISOGYNISTIC KAZUNE-KUN CRY LIKE A LITTLE GIRL!
KAZUNE-KUN?
YOU'RE MINE, KAZUNE!
...I KNOW KAZUNE-CHAN CAN BE STRICT, BUT HE ALWAYS PUTS YOU FIRST, KARIN-CHAN.
DEEP INSIDE, HE'S REALLY VERY KIND.
YOU THINK SO?
BESIDES, THE BEST WAY TO MAKE HIM CRY IS TO DUMP BUGS ON HIM.
How very unfair.
BUT...
OH, BY THE WAY!
THE SCHOOL FESTIVAL'S COMING UP.

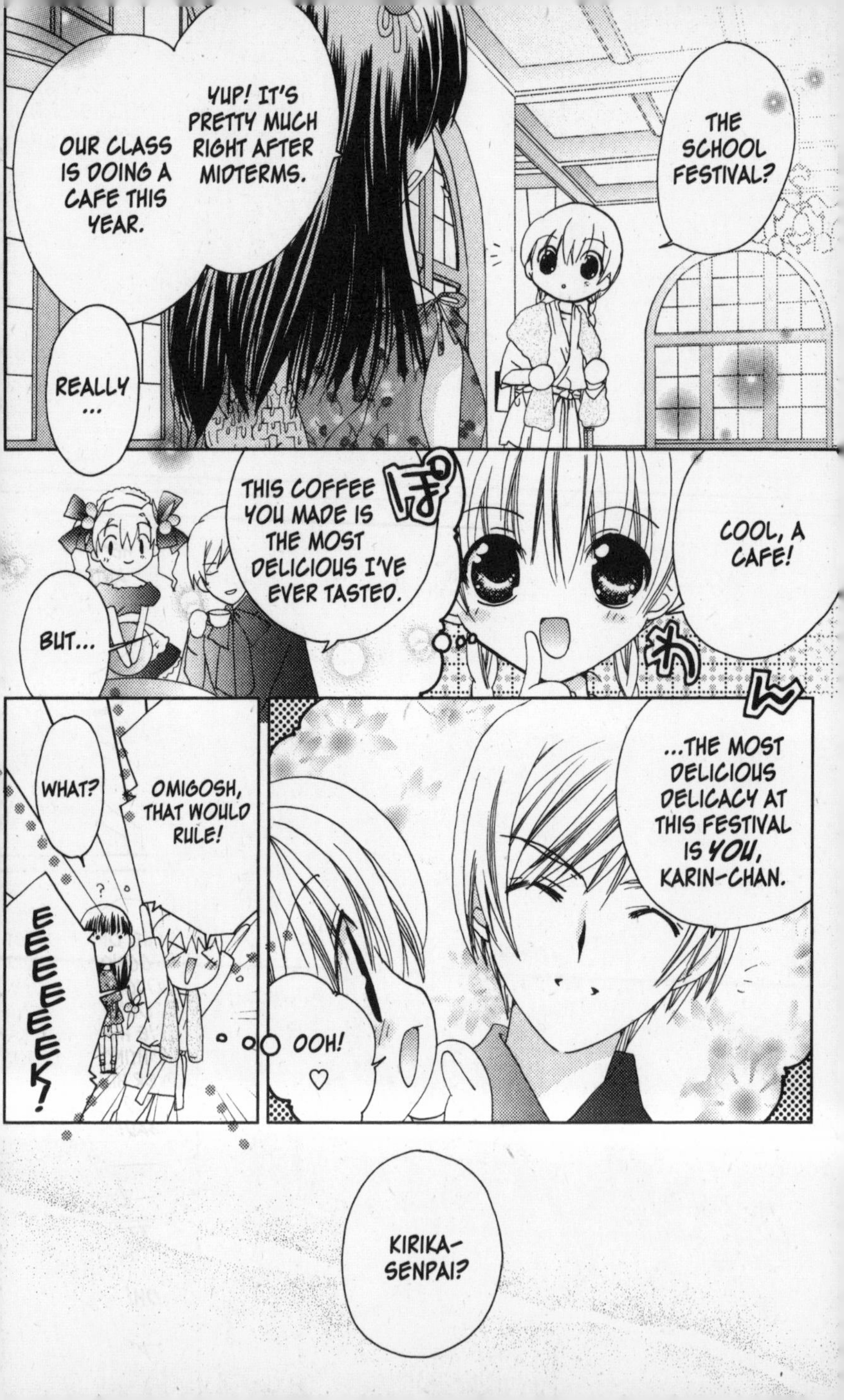
THE SCHOOL FESTIVAL?
YUP! IT'S PRETTY MUCH RIGHT AFTER MIDTERMS.
OUR CLASS IS DOING A CAFE THIS YEAR.
REALLY...
COOL, A CAFE!
ぽ
わ
ん
THIS COFFEE YOU MADE IS THE MOST DELICIOUS I'VE EVER TASTED.
BUT...
...THE MOST DELICIOUS DELICACY AT THIS FESTIVAL IS *YOU*, KARIN-CHAN.
OOH! ♡
OMIGOSH, THAT WOULD RULE!
WHAT?
EEEEEEK!
KIRIKA-SENPAI?

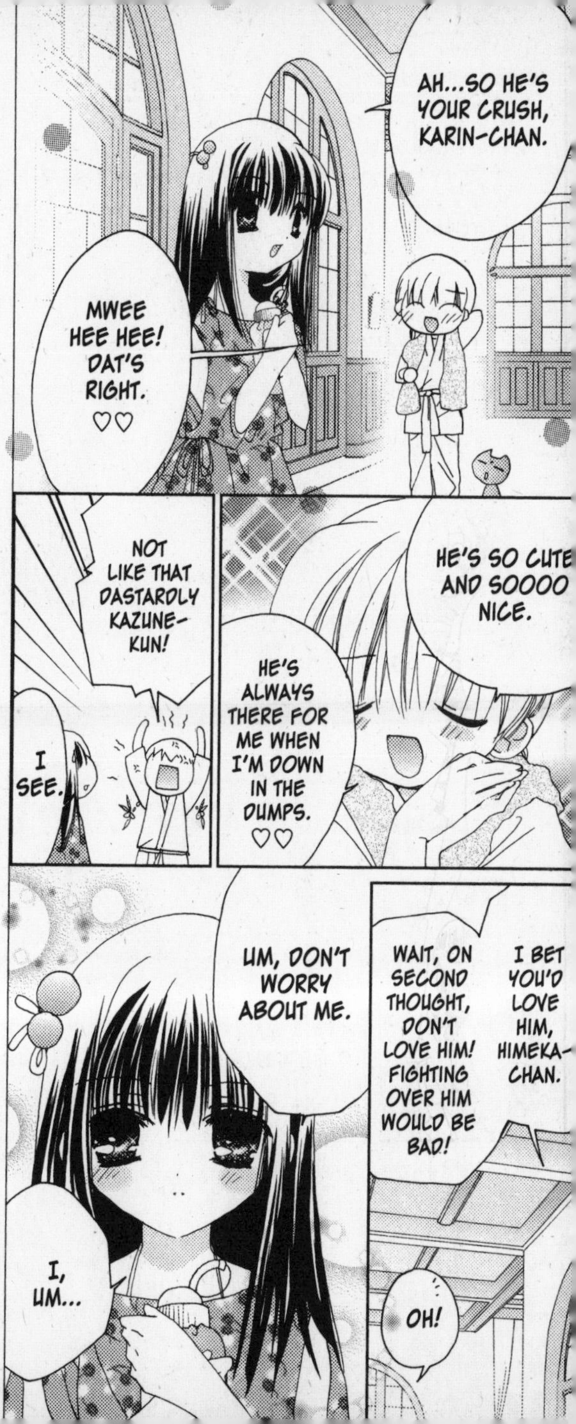
AH...SO HE'S YOUR CRUSH, KARIN-CHAN.
MWEE HEE HEE! DAT'S RIGHT. ♡♡
HE'S SO CUTE AND SOOOO NICE.
HE'S ALWAYS THERE FOR ME WHEN I'M DOWN IN THE DUMPS. ♡♡
NOT LIKE THAT DASTARDLY KAZUNE-KUN!
I SEE.
I BET YOU'D LOVE HIM, HIMEKA-CHAN.
WAIT, ON SECOND THOUGHT, DON'T LOVE HIM! FIGHTING OVER HIM WOULD BE BAD!
OH!
UM, DON'T WORRY ABOUT ME.
I, UM...

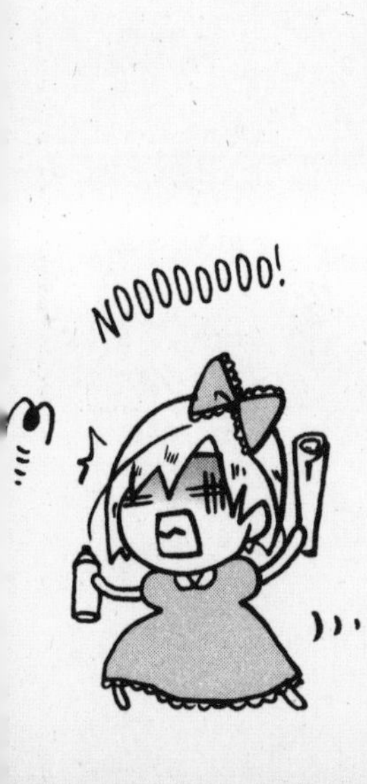
NOOOOOOOO!

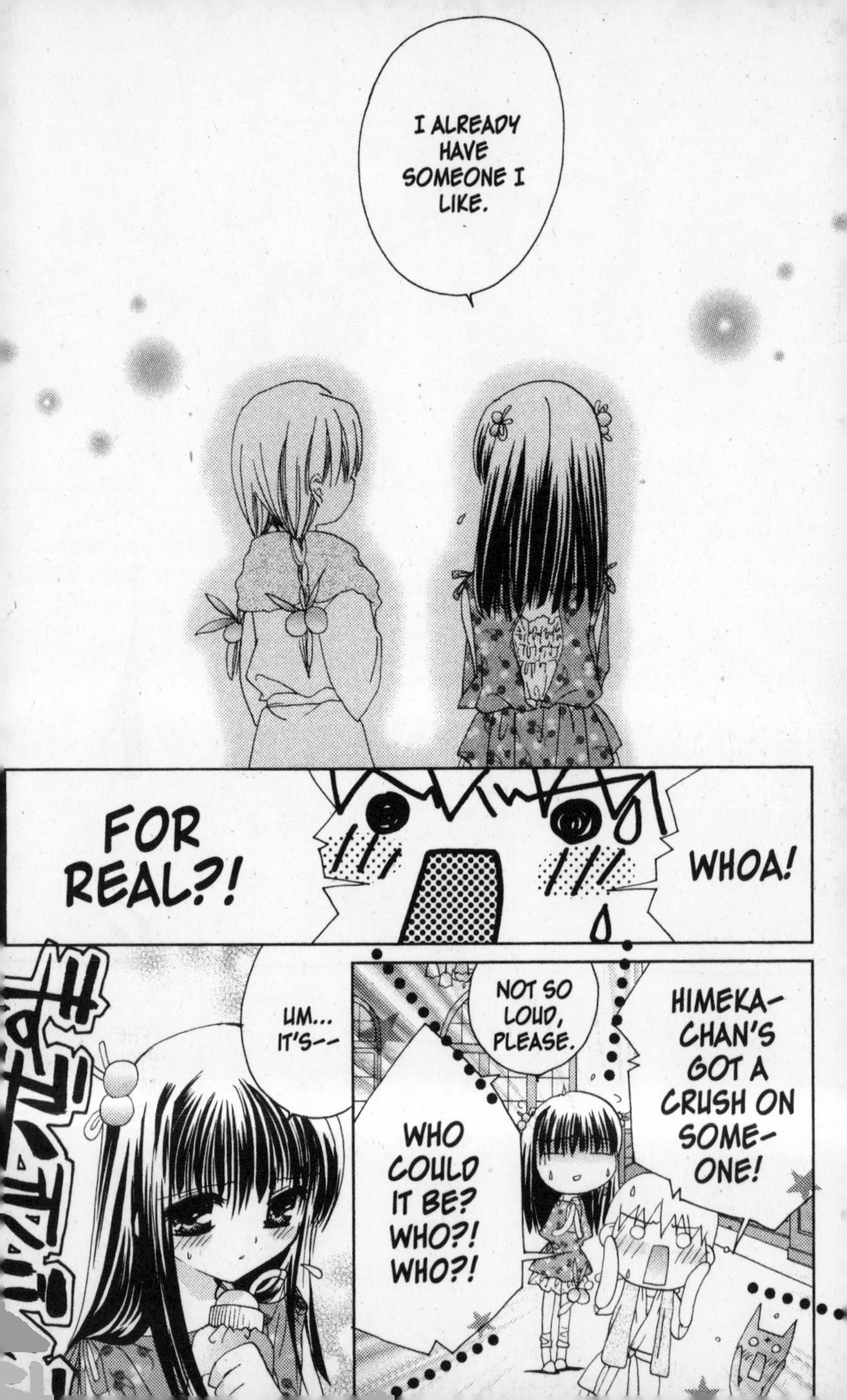
I ALREADY HAVE SOMEONE I LIKE.
WHOA!
FOR REAL?!
HIMEKA-CHAN'S GOT A CRUSH ON SOME-ONE!
NOT SO LOUD, PLEASE.
WHO COULD IT BE? WHO?! WHO?!
UM... IT'S--

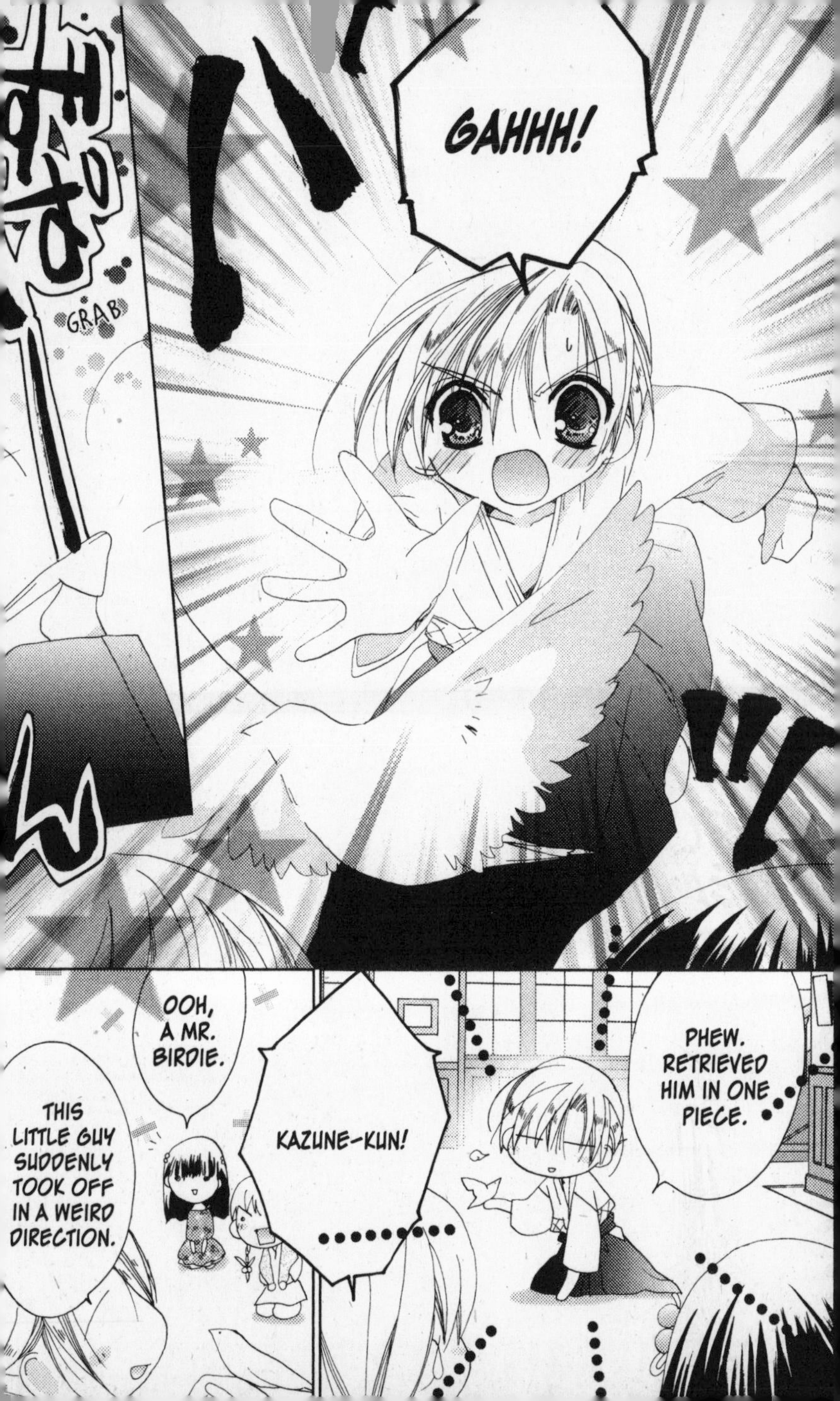
GAHHH!
GRAB
PHEW. RETRIEVED HIM IN ONE PIECE.
KAZUNE-KUN!
OOH, A MR. BIRDIE.
THIS LITTLE GUY SUDDENLY TOOK OFF IN A WEIRD DIRECTION.
....

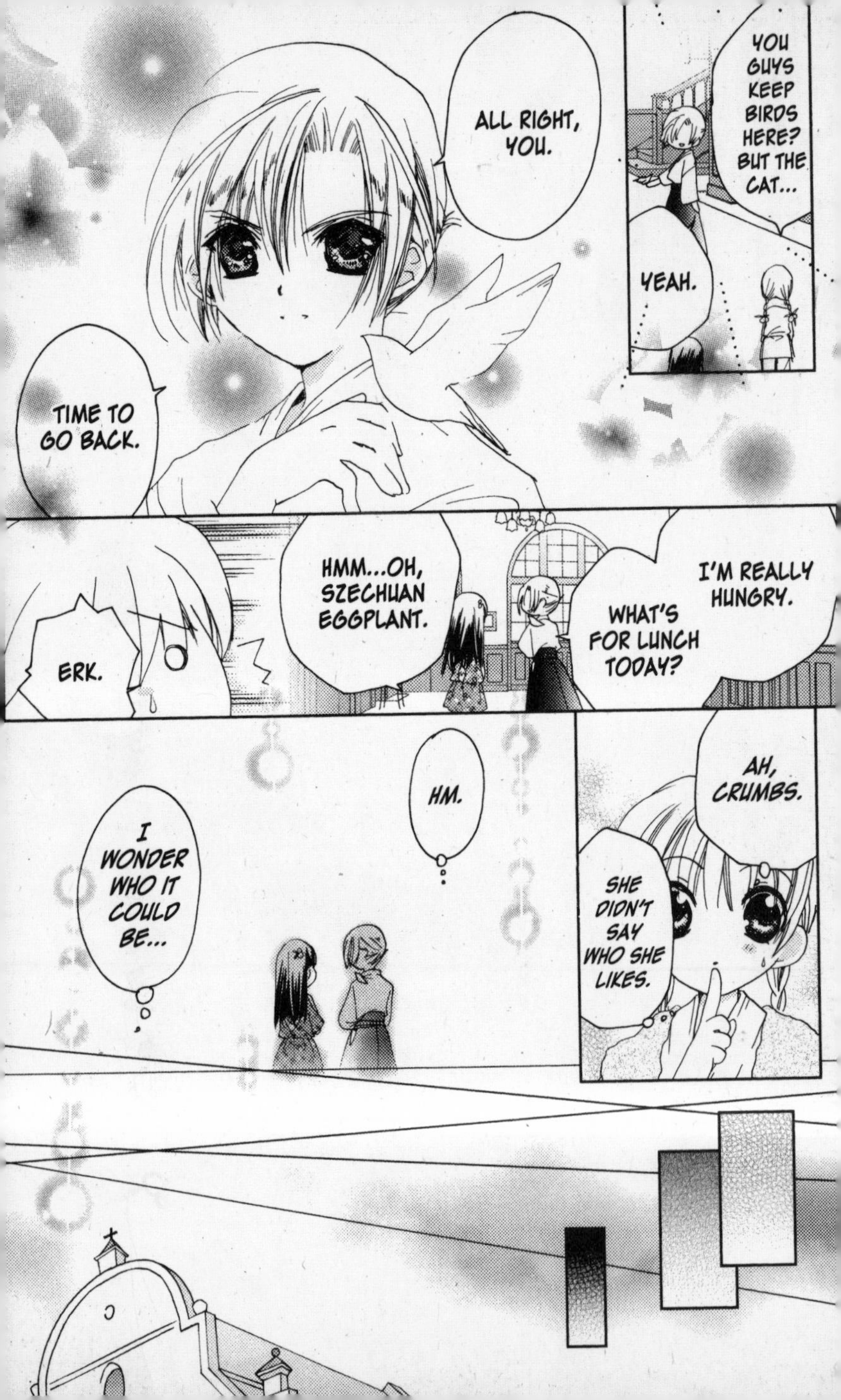
YOU GUYS KEEP BIRDS HERE? BUT THE CAT...
YEAH.
ALL RIGHT, YOU.
TIME TO GO BACK.
I'M REALLY HUNGRY.
WHAT'S FOR LUNCH TODAY?
HMM...OH, SZECHUAN EGGPLANT.
ERK.
AH, CRUMBS.
SHE DIDN'T SAY WHO SHE LIKES.
HM.
I WONDER WHO IT COULD BE...

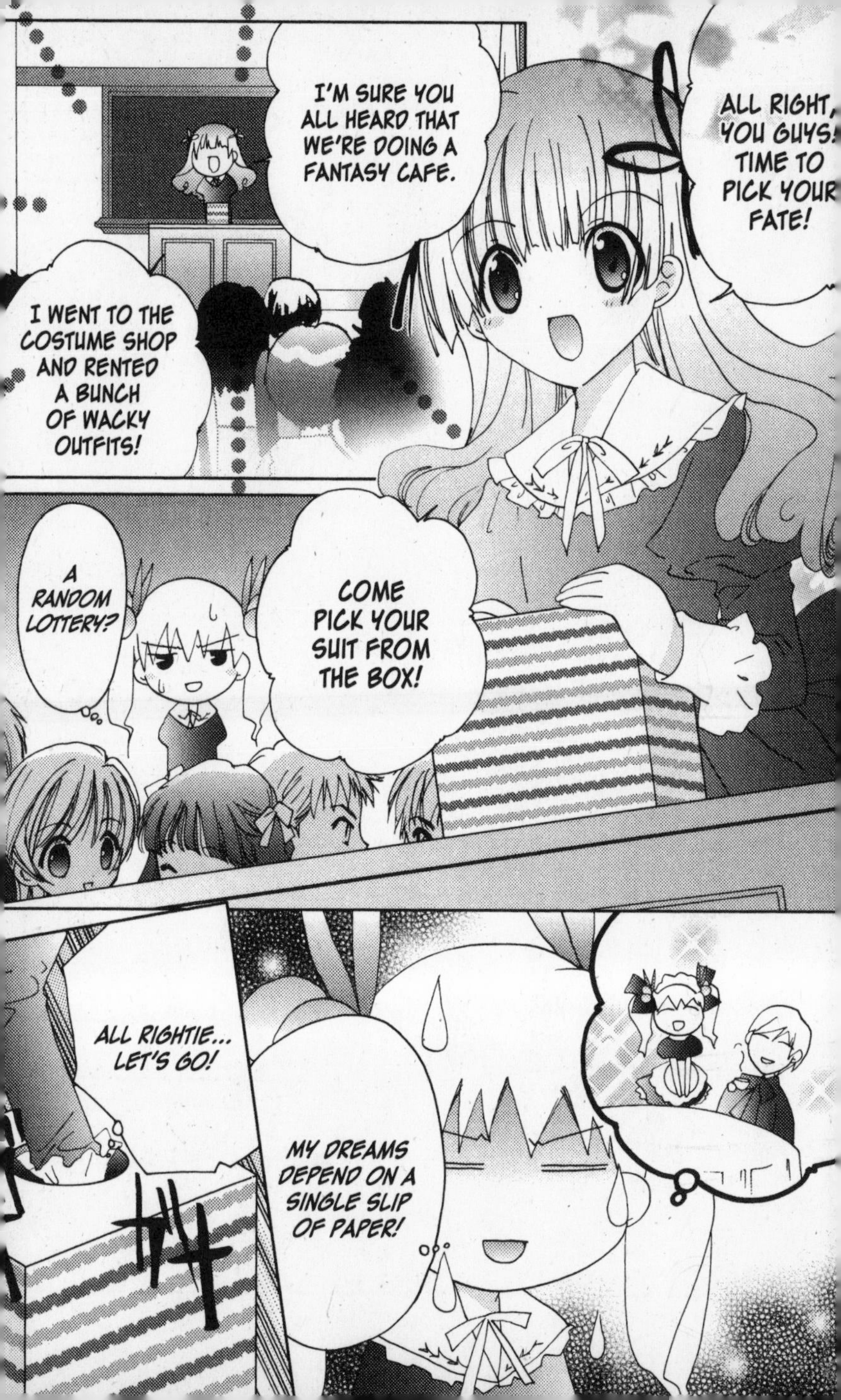
ALL RIGHT, YOU GUYS! TIME TO PICK YOUR FATE!
I'M SURE YOU ALL HEARD THAT WE'RE DOING A FANTASY CAFE.
I WENT TO THE COSTUME SHOP AND RENTED A BUNCH OF WACKY OUTFITS!
COME PICK YOUR SUIT FROM THE BOX!
A RANDOM LOTTERY?
MY DREAMS DEPEND ON A SINGLE SLIP OF PAPER!
ALL RIGHTIE... LET'S GO!

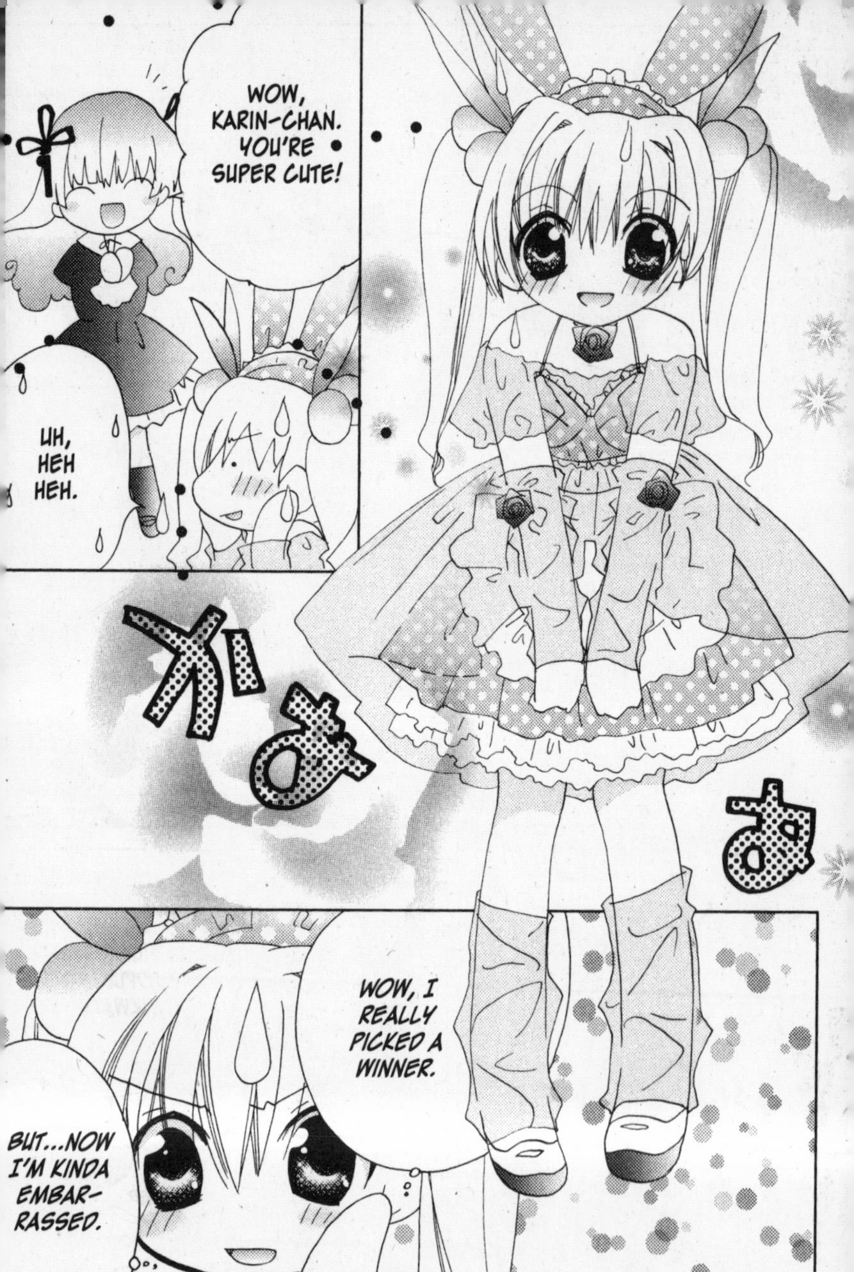
WOW, KARIN-CHAN. YOU'RE SUPER CUTE!
UH, HEH HEH.
WOW, I REALLY PICKED A WINNER.
BUT...NOW I'M KINDA EMBARRASSED.

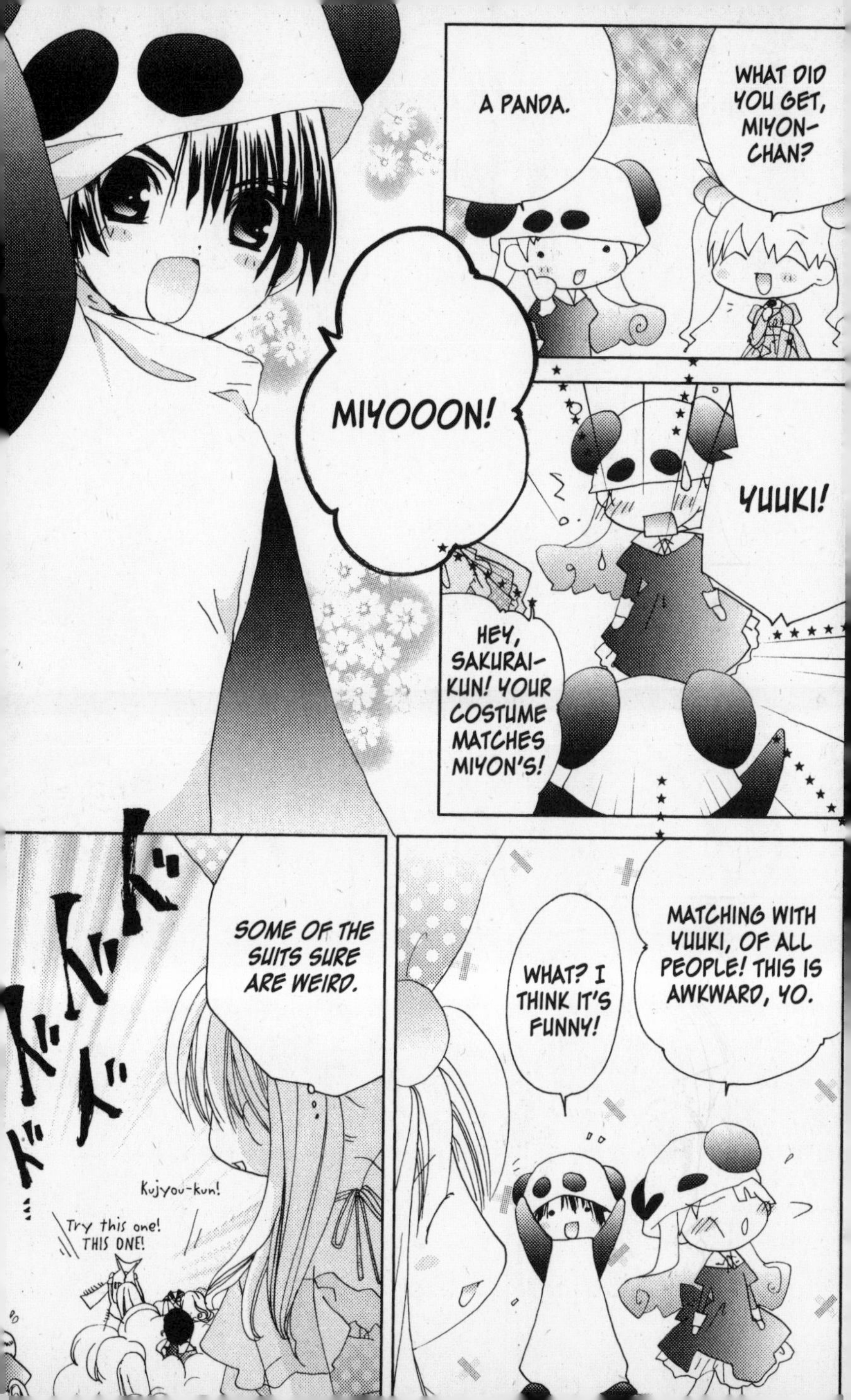
WHAT DID YOU GET, MIYON-CHAN?
A PANDA.
YUUKI!
HEY, SAKURAI-KUN! YOUR COSTUME MATCHES MIYON'S!
MIYOOON!
MATCHING WITH YUUKI, OF ALL PEOPLE! THIS IS AWKWARD, YO.
WHAT? I THINK IT'S FUNNY!
SOME OF THE SUITS SURE ARE WEIRD.
Kujyou-kun!
Try this one! THIS ONE!

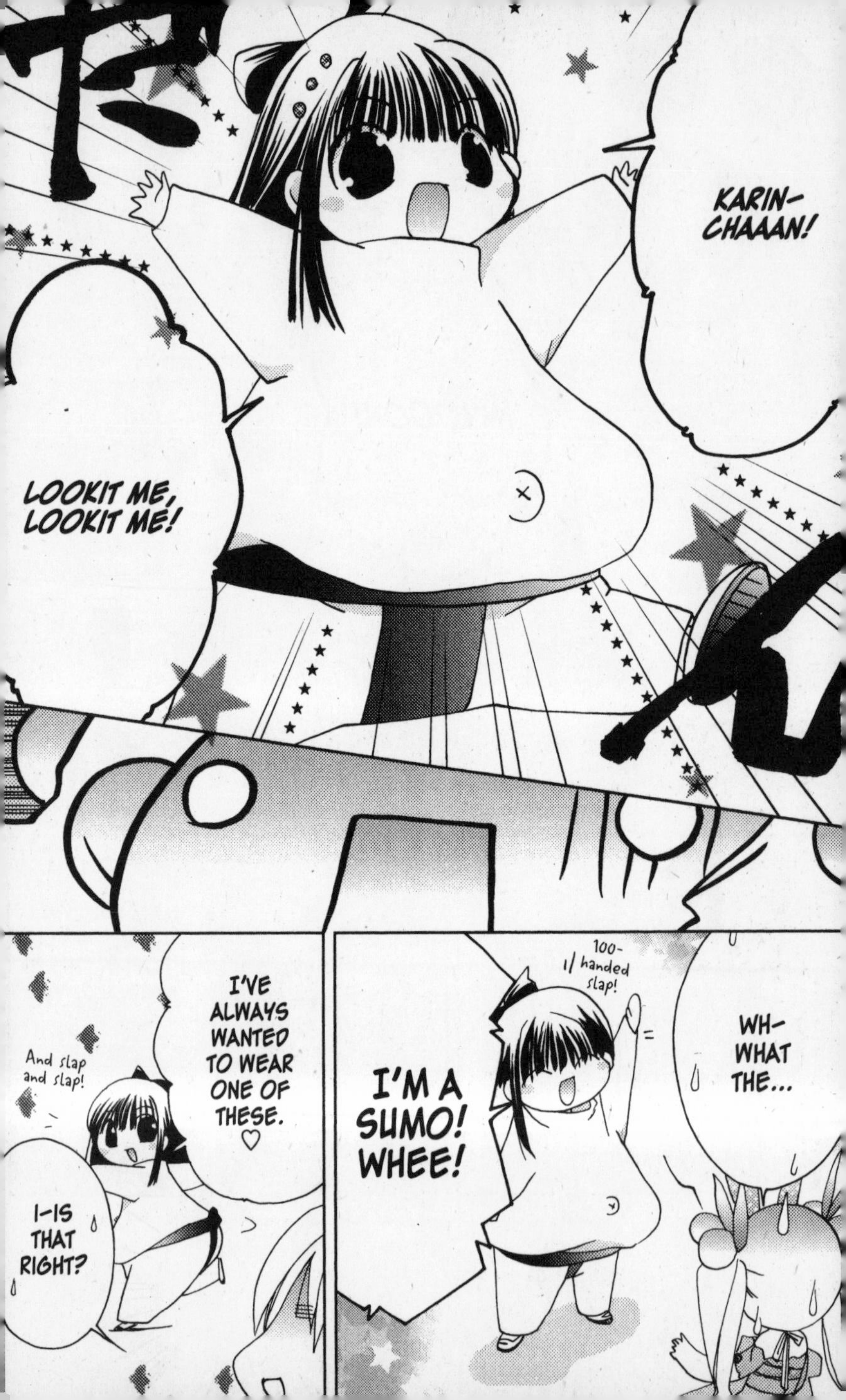
KARIN-CHAAAN!
LOOKIT ME, LOOKIT ME!
WH-WHAT THE...
100-handed slap!
I'M A SUMO! WHEE!
I'VE ALWAYS WANTED TO WEAR ONE OF THESE. ♡
And slap and slap!
I-IS THAT RIGHT?

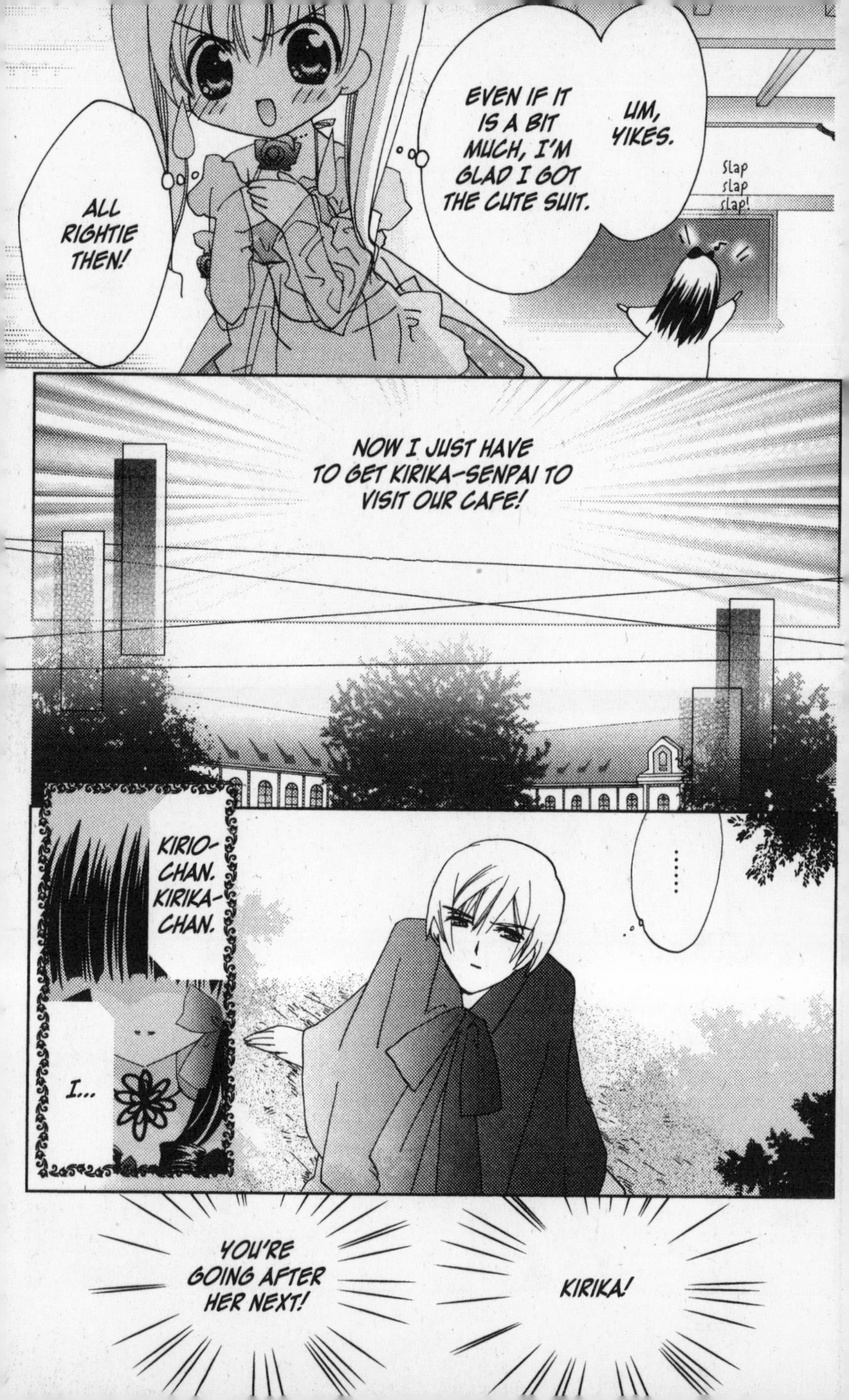
UM, YIKES.
Slap slap slap!
EVEN IF IT IS A BIT MUCH, I'M GLAD I GOT THE CUTE SUIT.
ALL RIGHTIE THEN!
NOW I JUST HAVE TO GET KIRIKA-SENPAI TO VISIT OUR CAFE!
......
KIRIO-CHAN. KIRIKA-CHAN.
I...
KIRIKA!
YOU'RE GOING AFTER HER NEXT!

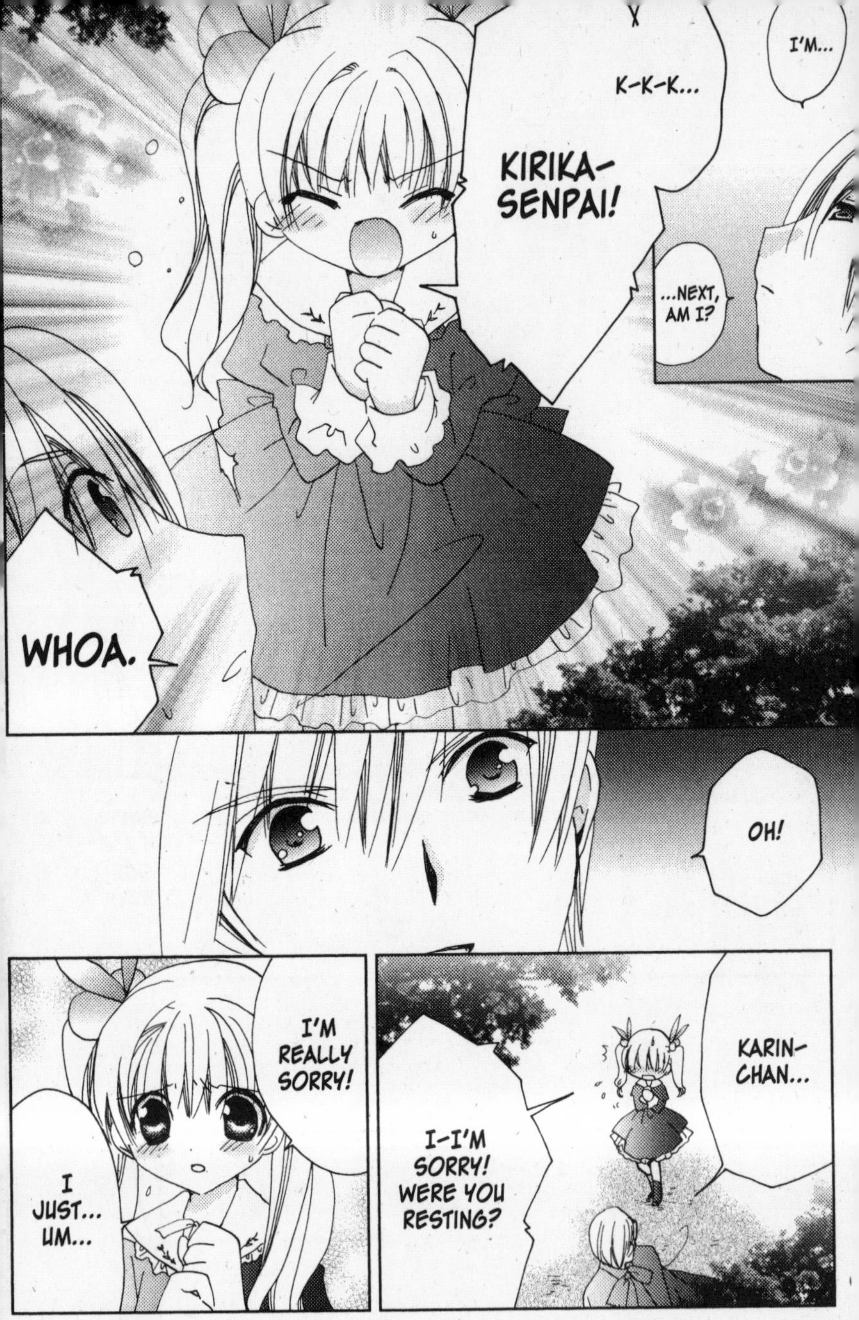
I'M...
K-K-K...
KIRIKA-SENPAI!
...NEXT, AM I?
WHOA.
OH!
KARIN-CHAN...
I-I'M SORRY! WERE YOU RESTING?
I'M REALLY SORRY!
I JUST... UM...

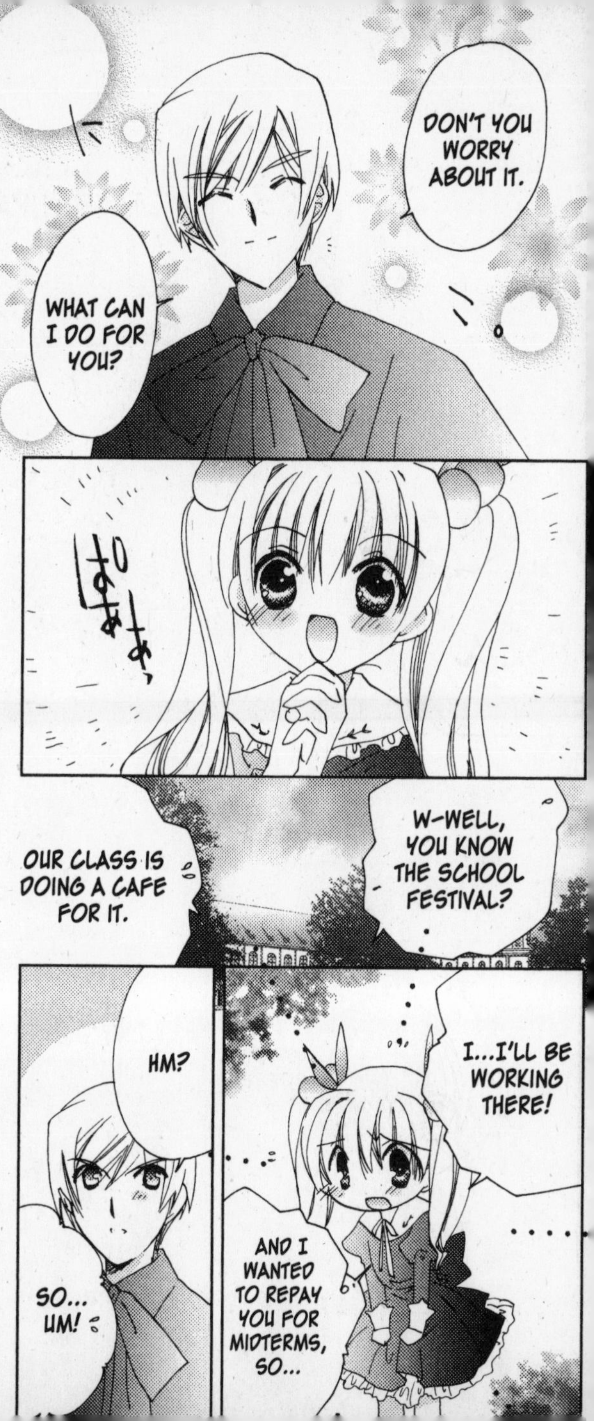
DON'T YOU WORRY ABOUT IT.
WHAT CAN I DO FOR YOU?
W-WELL, YOU KNOW THE SCHOOL FESTIVAL?
OUR CLASS IS DOING A CAFE FOR IT.
I...I'LL BE WORKING THERE!
AND I WANTED TO REPAY YOU FOR MIDTERMS, SO...
HM?
SO... UM!

Hey, Koge-Donbo here! Thanks very much for your perusal of Kamichama Karin Volume 2!

Now, a word about Karin's silly little catchphrase, "I AM GOD!" Some of you may wonder why I didn't have it as "I AM GODDESS!" instead...and yes, it should be "goddess," but that's okay. Why, you ask? Because I think the former fits better. It also seems just a little bit dumber. You get me? Anyhow, you really ought to try saying it sometime. Whenever you're feeling down, just scream out, "I AM GOD!" It's guaranteed to give you a jolt of courage and energy...okay, I'm kidding.

I'll be adding a few new characters and plodding along even stronger in Volume 3, so please also pick that up when it comes out.

2003, November.
Koge-Donbo.

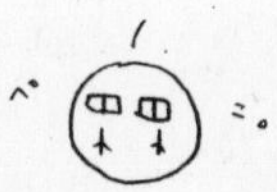

Special ThanX:
Kaie-san and Lee-san.
And all my assistants, and anyone else who's supported me throughout.

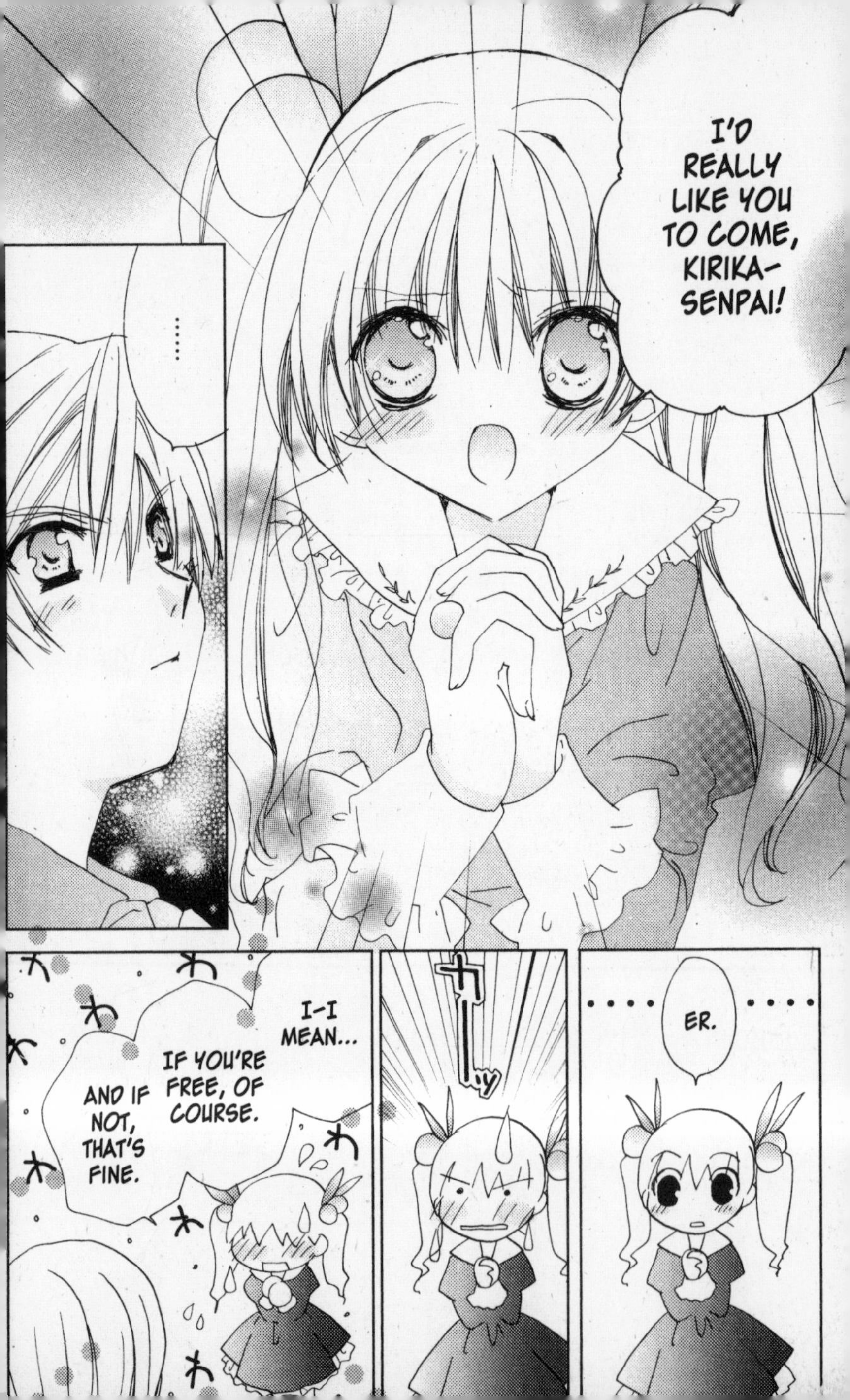
I'D REALLY LIKE YOU TO COME, KIRIKA-SENPAI!
......
.... ER. ....
I-I MEAN...
IF YOU'RE FREE, OF COURSE.
AND IF NOT, THAT'S FINE.

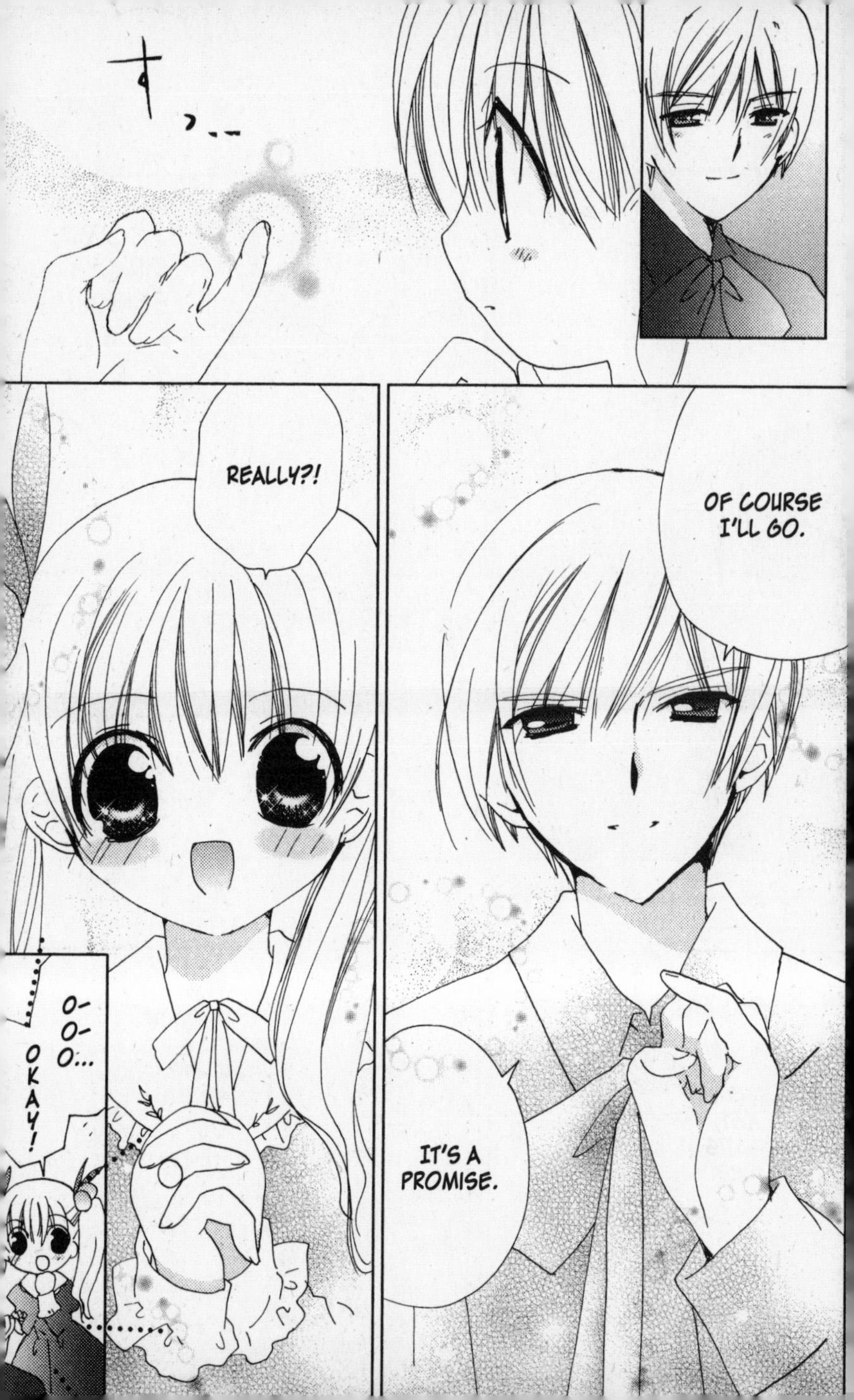
すっ…
OF COURSE I'LL GO.
IT'S A PROMISE.
REALLY?!
O-O-O... OKAY!

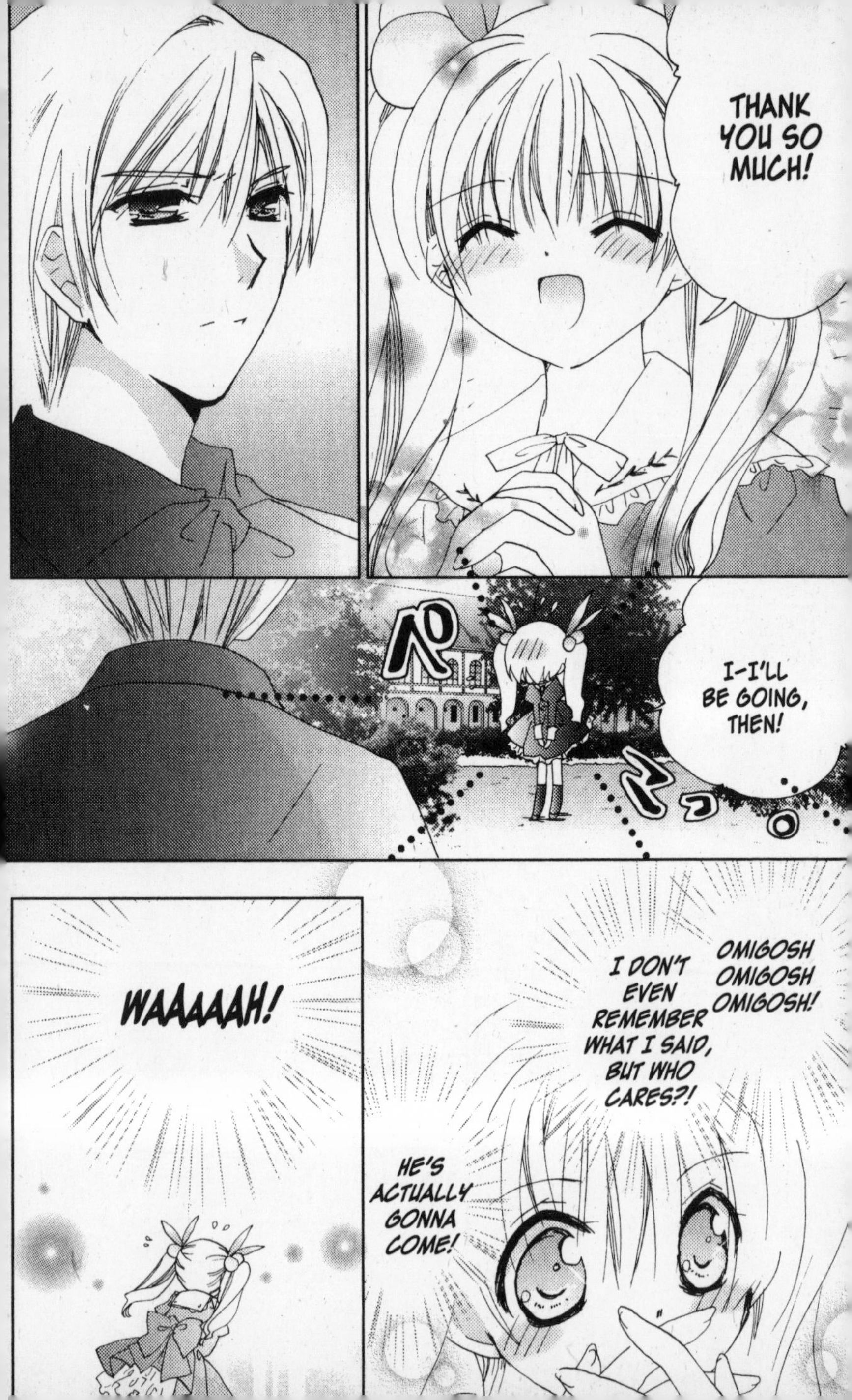
THANK YOU SO MUCH!
I-I'LL BE GOING, THEN!
OMIGOSH OMIGOSH OMIGOSH!
I DON'T EVEN REMEMBER WHAT I SAID, BUT WHO CARES?!
HE'S ACTUALLY GONNA COME!
WAAAAAH!

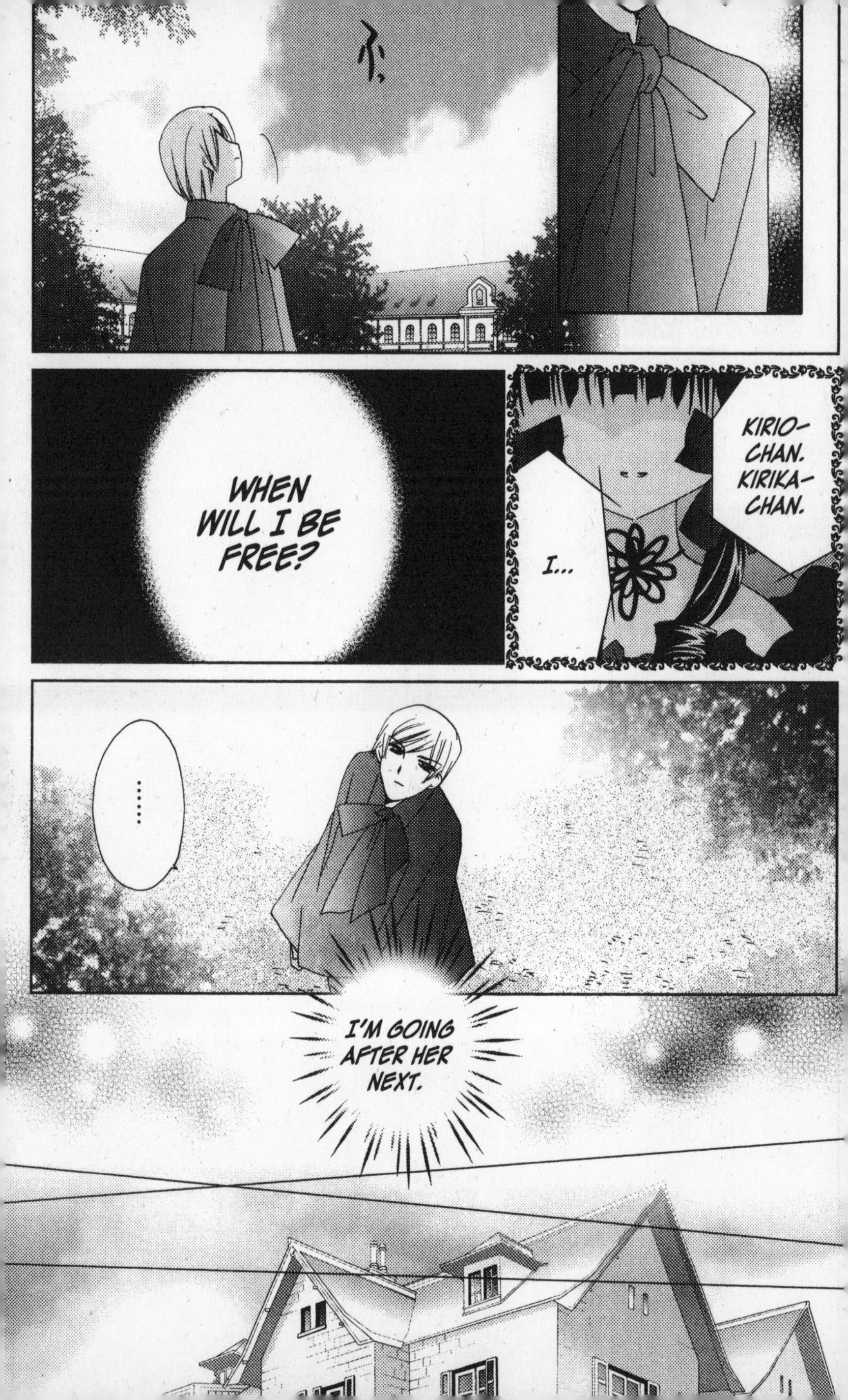
KIRIO-CHAN. KIRIKA-CHAN.
I...
WHEN WILL I BE FREE?
......
I'M GOING AFTER HER NEXT.

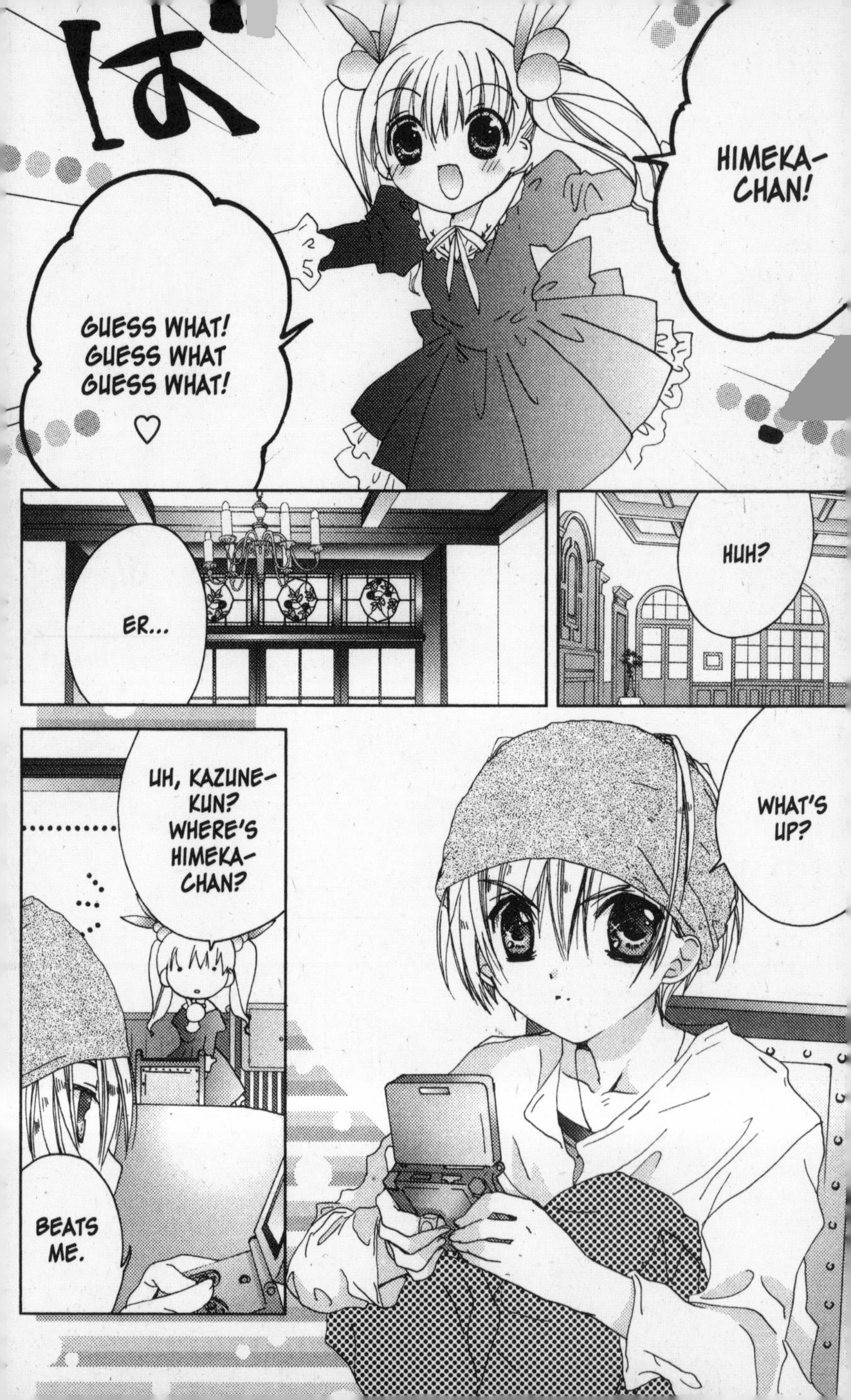
ぱ
HIMEKA-CHAN!
GUESS WHAT! GUESS WHAT GUESS WHAT! ♡
HUH?
ER...
WHAT'S UP?
UH, KAZUNE-KUN? WHERE'S HIMEKA-CHAN?
...
BEATS ME.

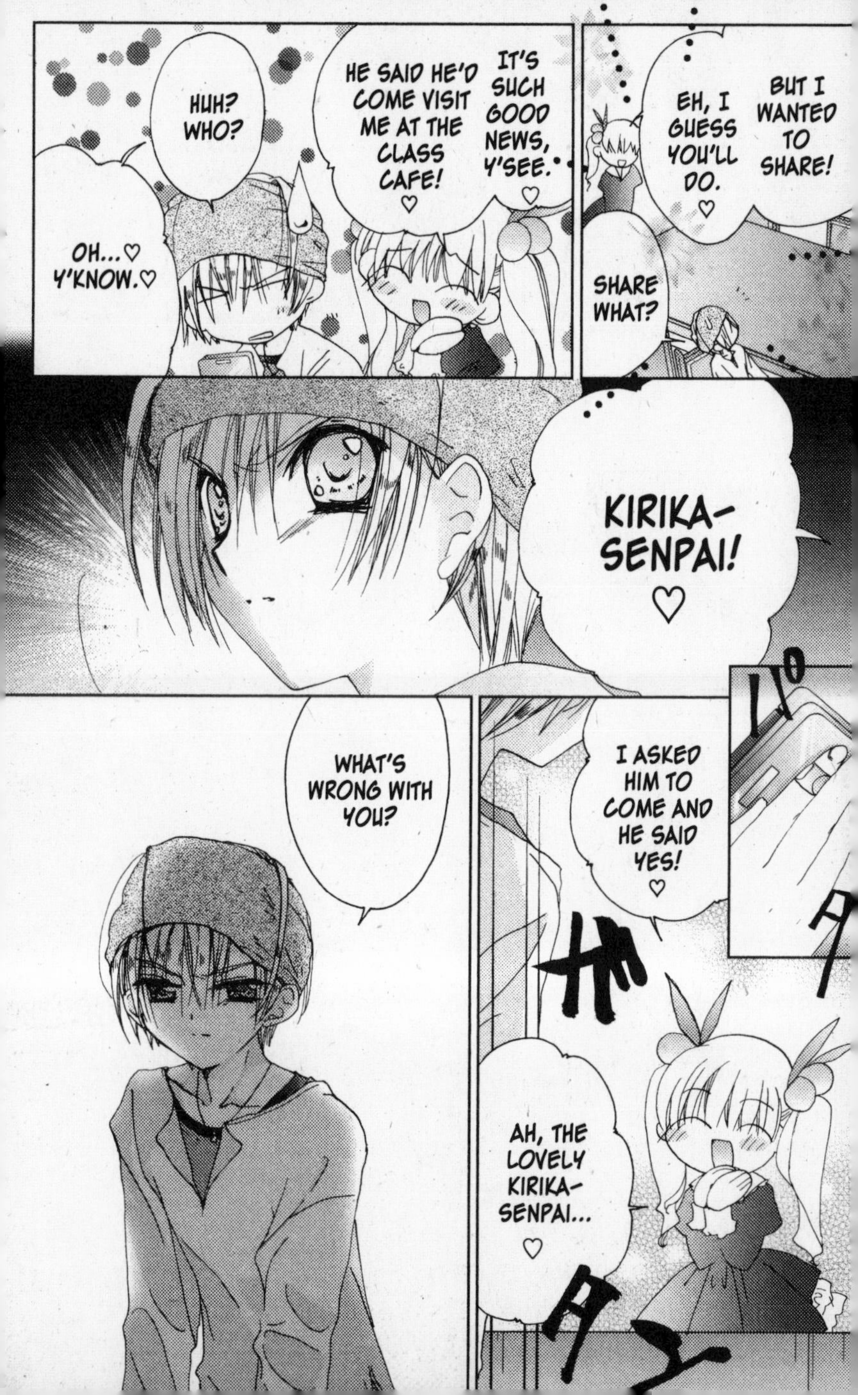
BUT I WANTED TO SHARE!
EH, I GUESS YOU'LL DO. ♡
SHARE WHAT?
IT'S SUCH GOOD NEWS, Y'SEE. ♡
HE SAID HE'D COME VISIT ME AT THE CLASS CAFE! ♡
HUH? WHO?
OH...♡ Y'KNOW.♡
...KIRIKA-SENPAI! ♡
I ASKED HIM TO COME AND HE SAID YES! ♡
AH, THE LOVELY KIRIKA-SENPAI... ♡
WHAT'S WRONG WITH YOU?

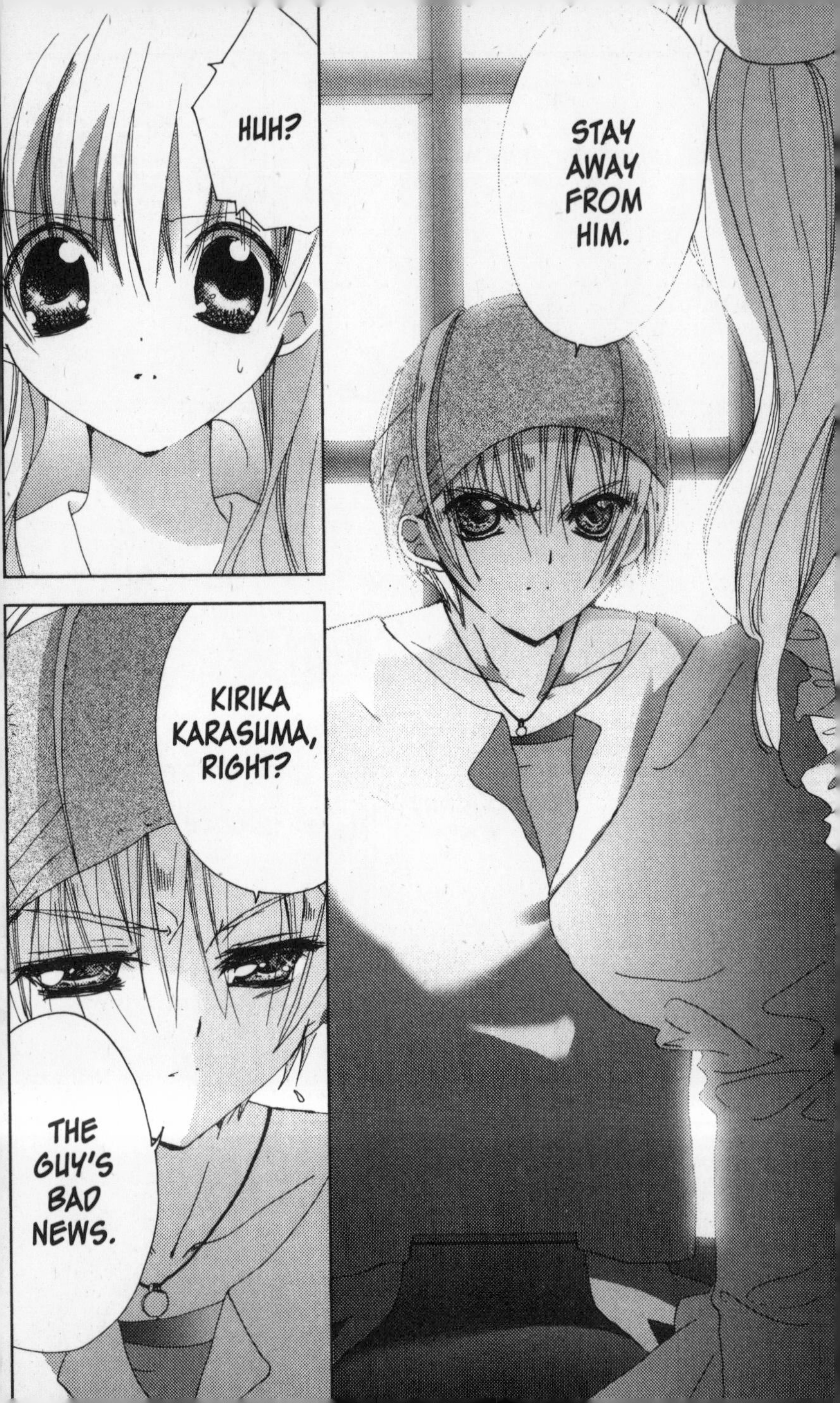
STAY AWAY FROM HIM.
HUH?
KIRIKA KARASUMA, RIGHT?
THE GUY'S BAD NEWS.

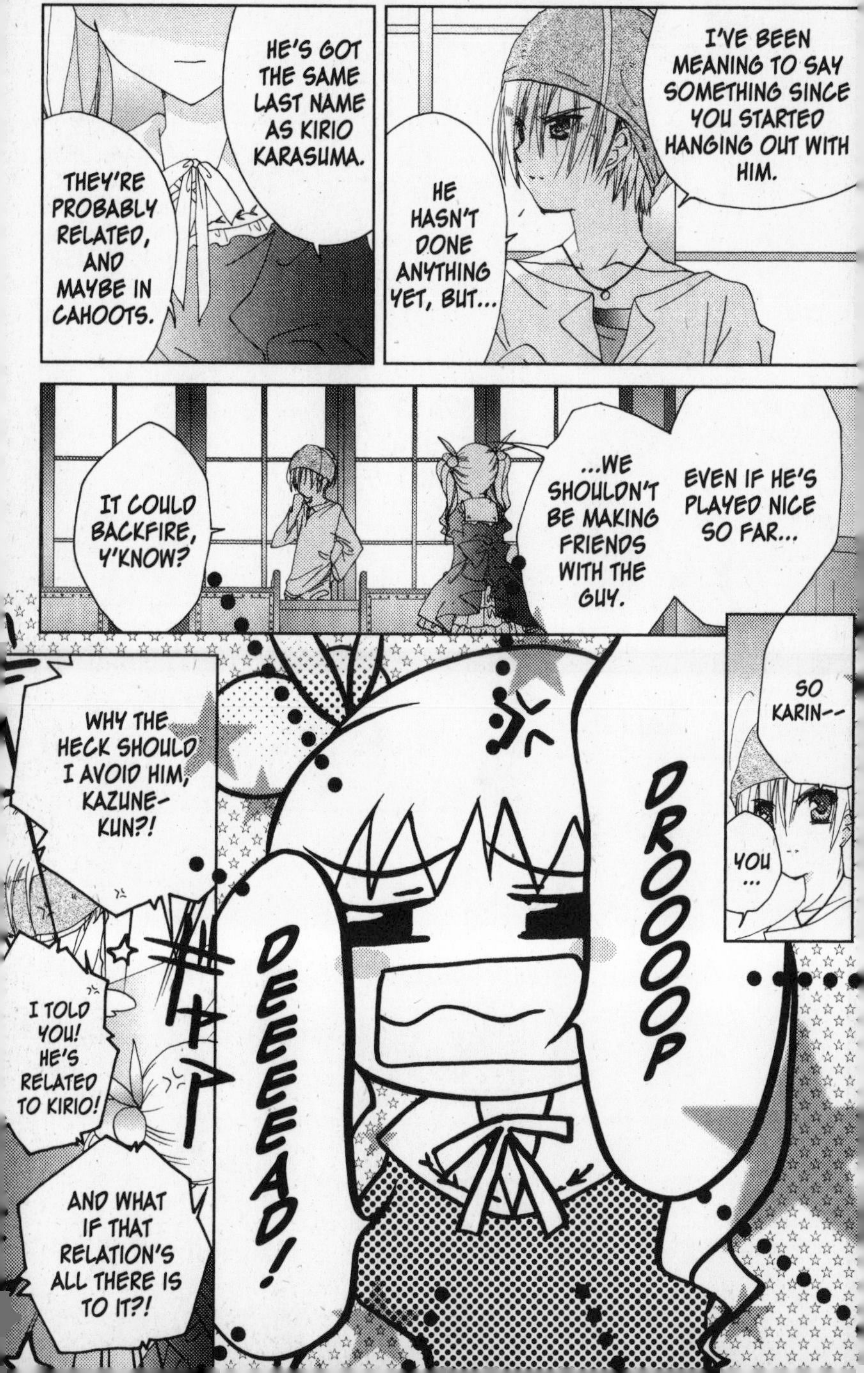
I'VE BEEN MEANING TO SAY SOMETHING SINCE YOU STARTED HANGING OUT WITH HIM.
HE HASN'T DONE ANYTHING YET, BUT...
HE'S GOT THE SAME LAST NAME AS KIRIO KARASUMA.
THEY'RE PROBABLY RELATED, AND MAYBE IN CAHOOTS.
EVEN IF HE'S PLAYED NICE SO FAR...
...WE SHOULDN'T BE MAKING FRIENDS WITH THE GUY.
IT COULD BACKFIRE, Y'KNOW?
SO KARIN--
YOU...
DROOOOOP
DEEEEEAD!
WHY THE HECK SHOULD I AVOID HIM, KAZUNE-KUN?!
I TOLD YOU! HE'S RELATED TO KIRIO!
AND WHAT IF THAT RELATION'S ALL THERE IS TO IT?!

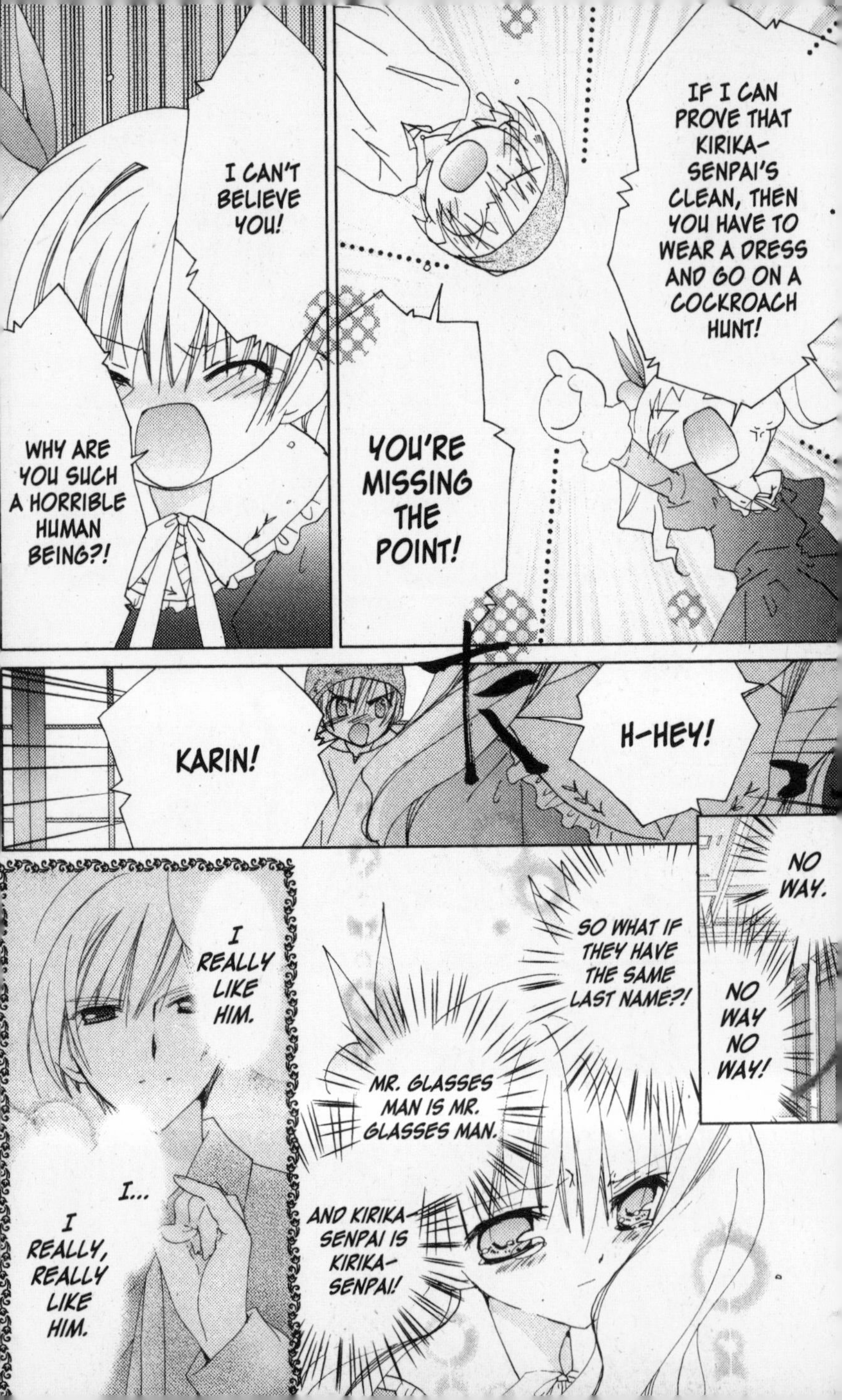
IF I CAN PROVE THAT KIRIKA-SENPAI'S CLEAN, THEN YOU HAVE TO WEAR A DRESS AND GO ON A COCKROACH HUNT!
YOU'RE MISSING THE POINT!
I CAN'T BELIEVE YOU!
WHY ARE YOU SUCH A HORRIBLE HUMAN BEING?!
H-HEY!
KARIN!
NO WAY.
NO WAY NO WAY!
SO WHAT IF THEY HAVE THE SAME LAST NAME?!
MR. GLASSES MAN IS MR. GLASSES MAN.
AND KIRIKA-SENPAI IS KIRIKA-SENPAI!
I REALLY LIKE HIM.
I...
I REALLY, REALLY LIKE HIM.

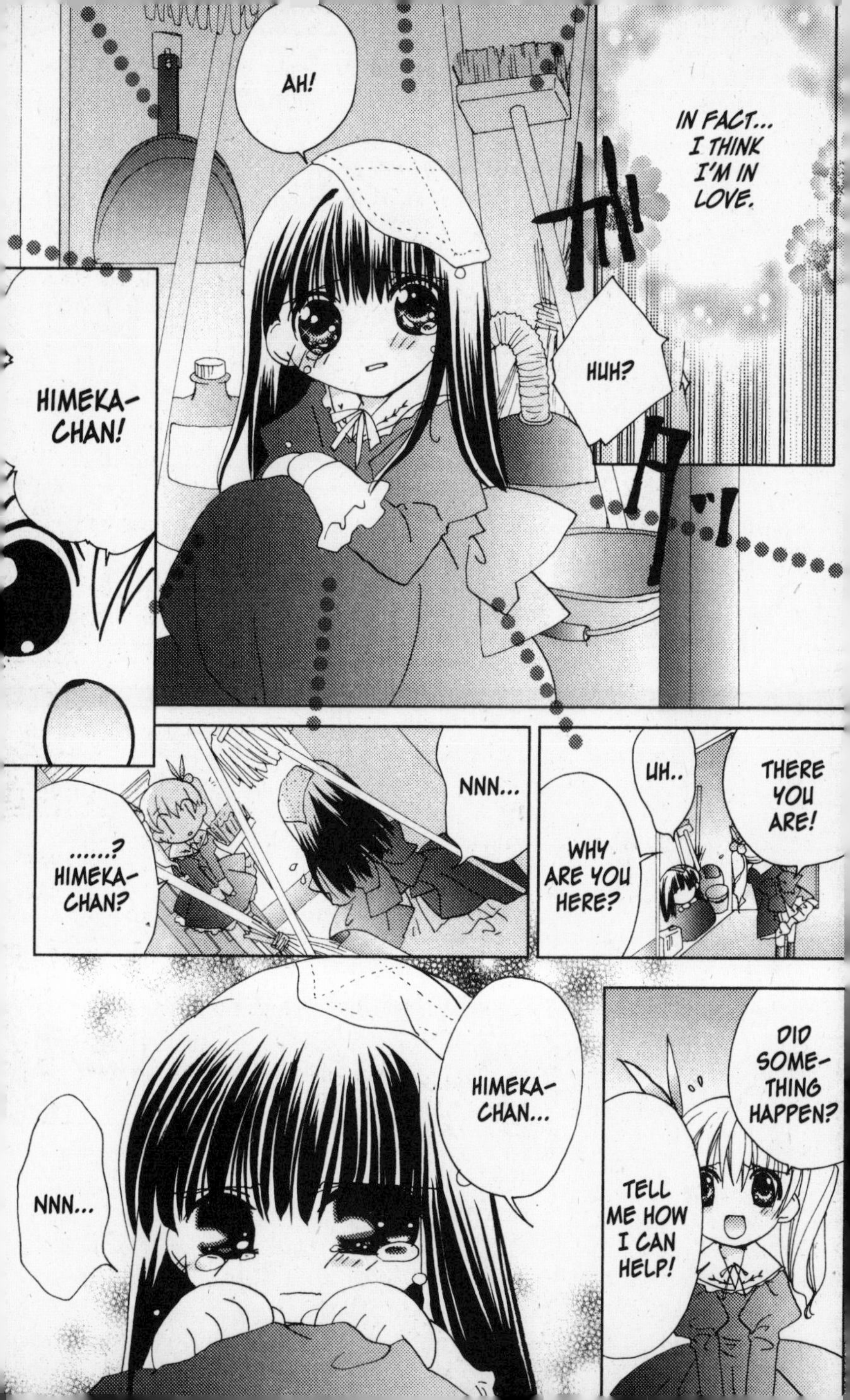
IN FACT... I THINK I'M IN LOVE.
AH!
HUH?
HIMEKA-CHAN!
THERE YOU ARE!
UH..
WHY ARE YOU HERE?
NNN...
......? HIMEKA-CHAN?
DID SOME-THING HAPPEN?
TELL ME HOW I CAN HELP!
HIMEKA-CHAN...
NNN...

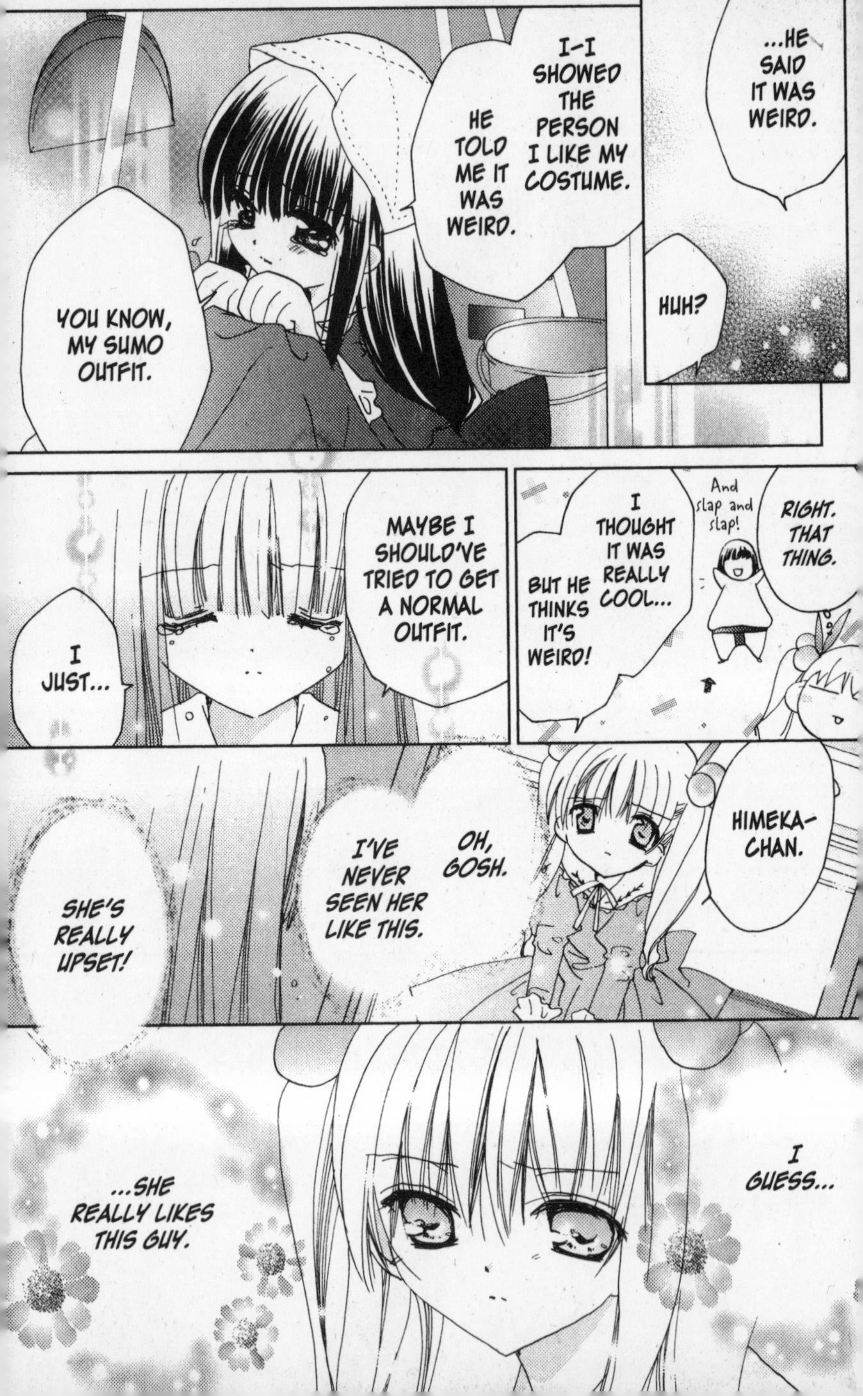
...HE SAID IT WAS WEIRD.
HUH?
I-I SHOWED THE PERSON I LIKE MY COSTUME.
HE TOLD ME IT WAS WEIRD.
YOU KNOW, MY SUMO OUTFIT.
RIGHT. THAT THING.
And slap and slap!
I THOUGHT IT WAS REALLY COOL...
BUT HE THINKS IT'S WEIRD!
MAYBE I SHOULD'VE TRIED TO GET A NORMAL OUTFIT.
I JUST...
HIMEKA-CHAN.
OH, GOSH.
I'VE NEVER SEEN HER LIKE THIS.
SHE'S REALLY UPSET!
I GUESS...
...SHE REALLY LIKES THIS GUY.

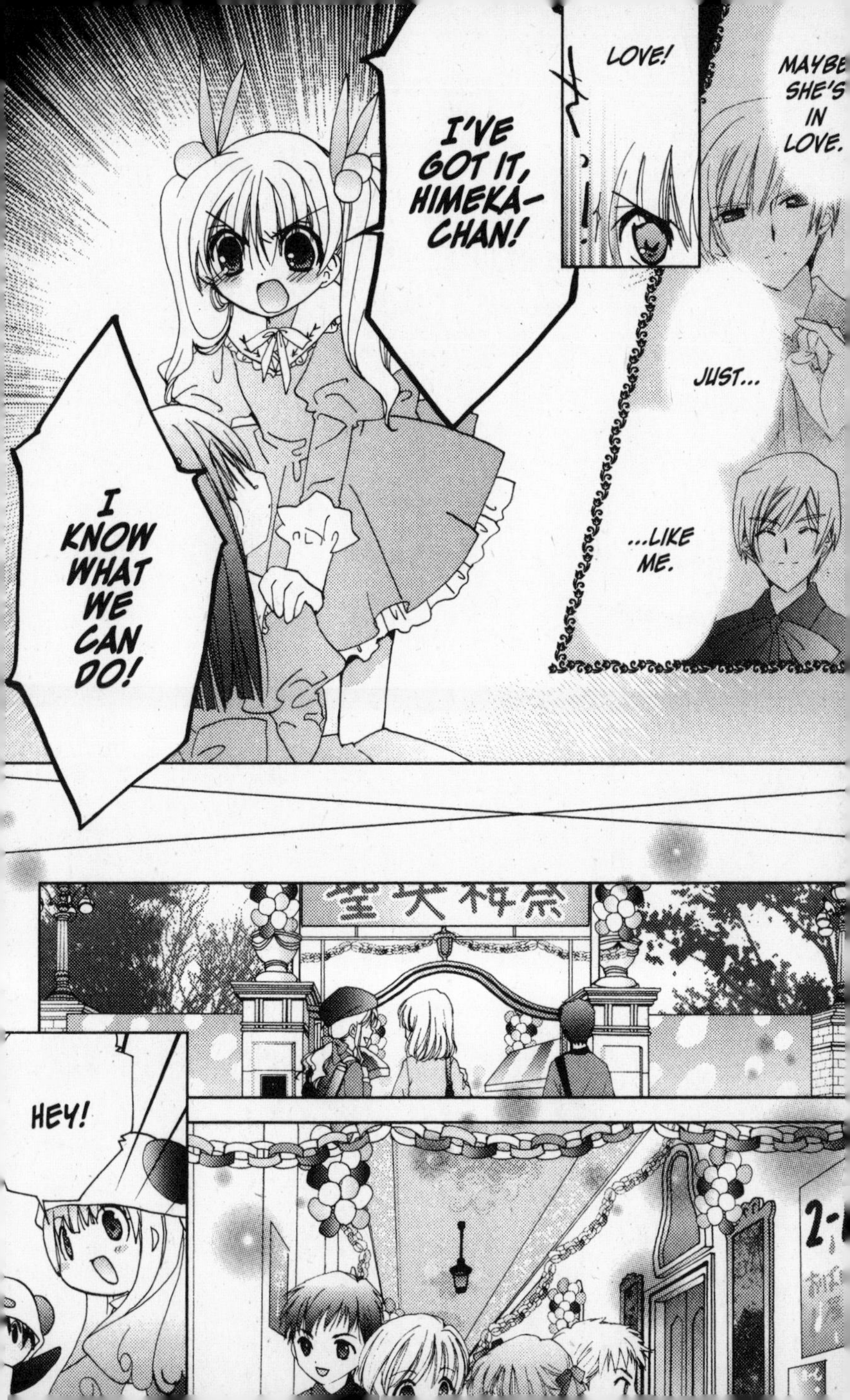
MAYBE SHE'S IN LOVE.
JUST...
...LIKE ME.
LOVE!
I'VE GOT IT, HIMEKA-CHAN!
I KNOW WHAT WE CAN DO!
HEY!

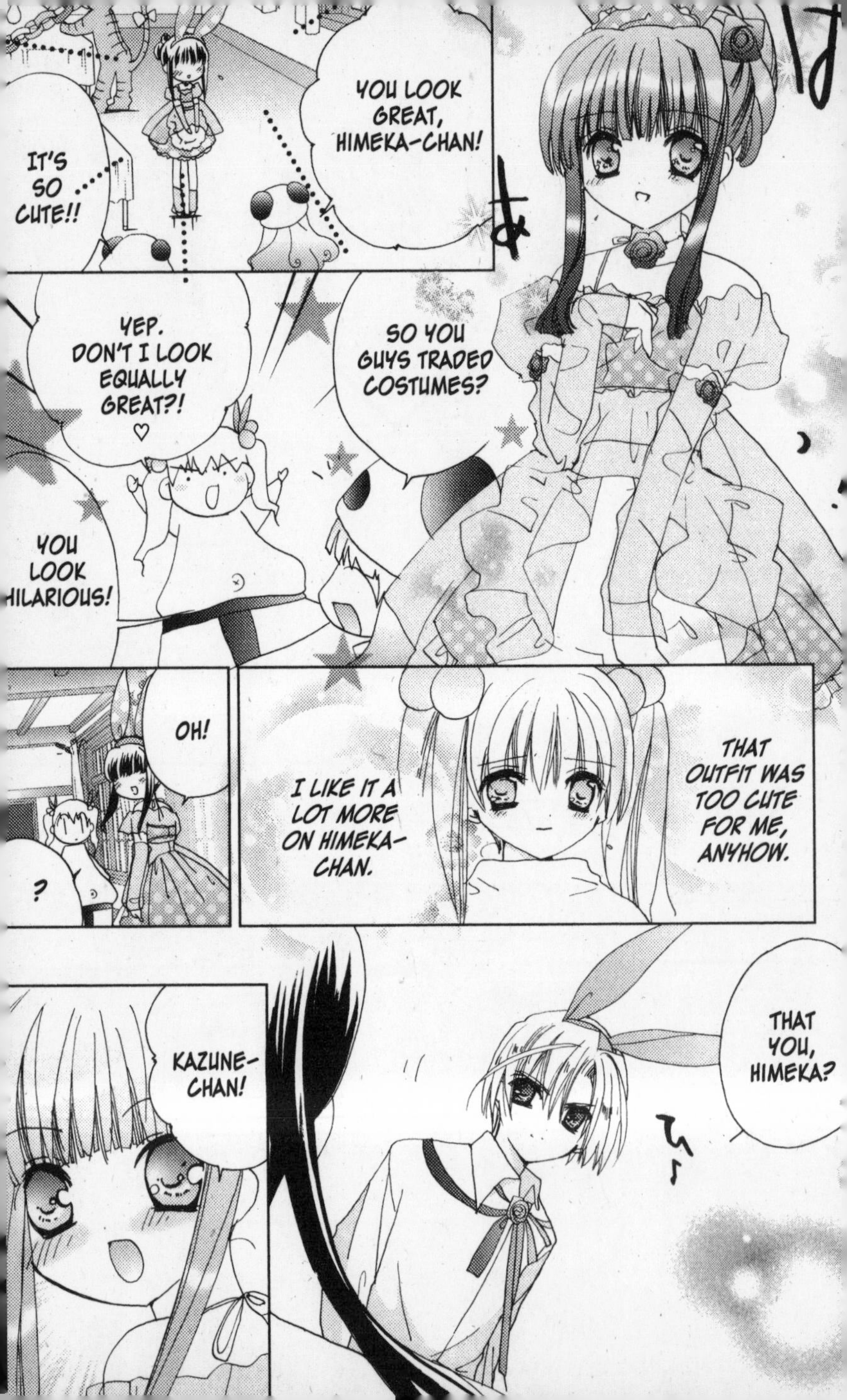
YOU LOOK GREAT, HIMEKA-CHAN!
IT'S SO CUTE!!
SO YOU GUYS TRADED COSTUMES?
YEP. DON'T I LOOK EQUALLY GREAT?! ♡
YOU LOOK HILARIOUS!
THAT OUTFIT WAS TOO CUTE FOR ME, ANYHOW.
I LIKE IT A LOT MORE ON HIMEKA-CHAN.
OH!
?
THAT YOU, HIMEKA?
KAZUNE-CHAN!

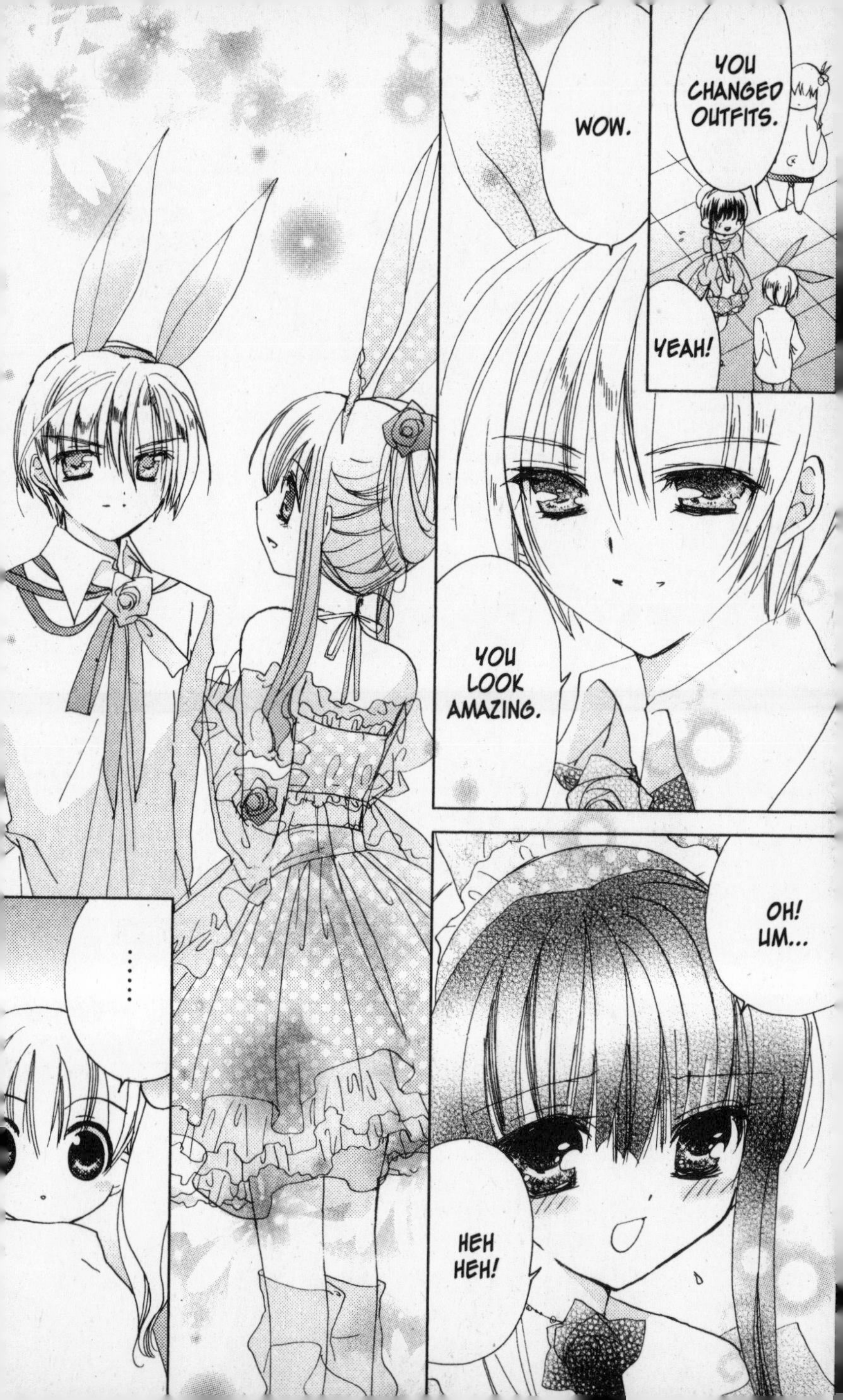
YOU CHANGED OUTFITS.
YEAH!
WOW.
YOU LOOK AMAZING.
OH! UM...
HEH HEH!
......

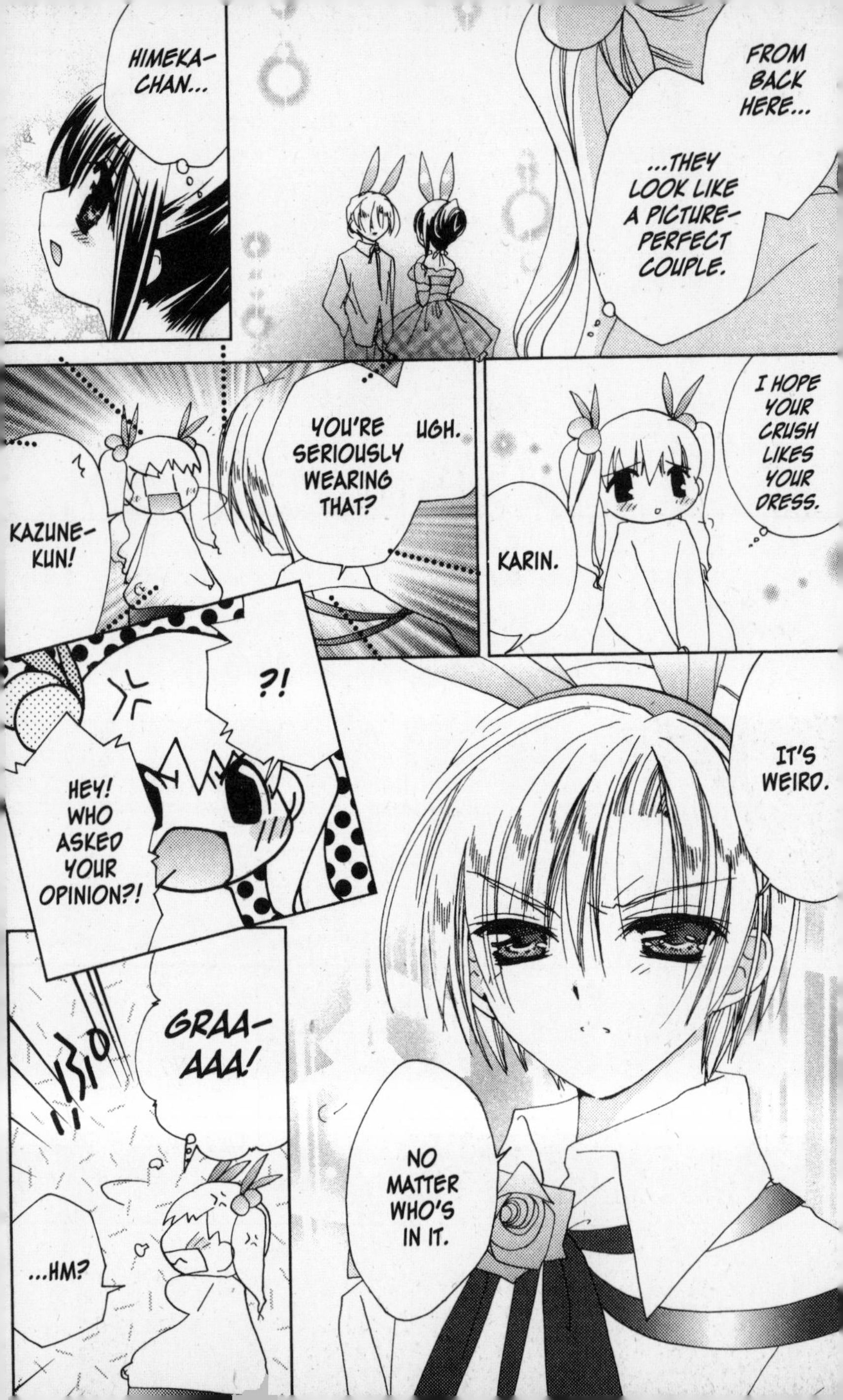
FROM BACK HERE...
...THEY LOOK LIKE A PICTURE-PERFECT COUPLE.
HIMEKA-CHAN...
I HOPE YOUR CRUSH LIKES YOUR DRESS.
KARIN.
UGH.
YOU'RE SERIOUSLY WEARING THAT?
KAZUNE-KUN!
IT'S WEIRD.
NO MATTER WHO'S IN IT.
?!
HEY! WHO ASKED YOUR OPINION?!
GRAA-AAA!
...HM?

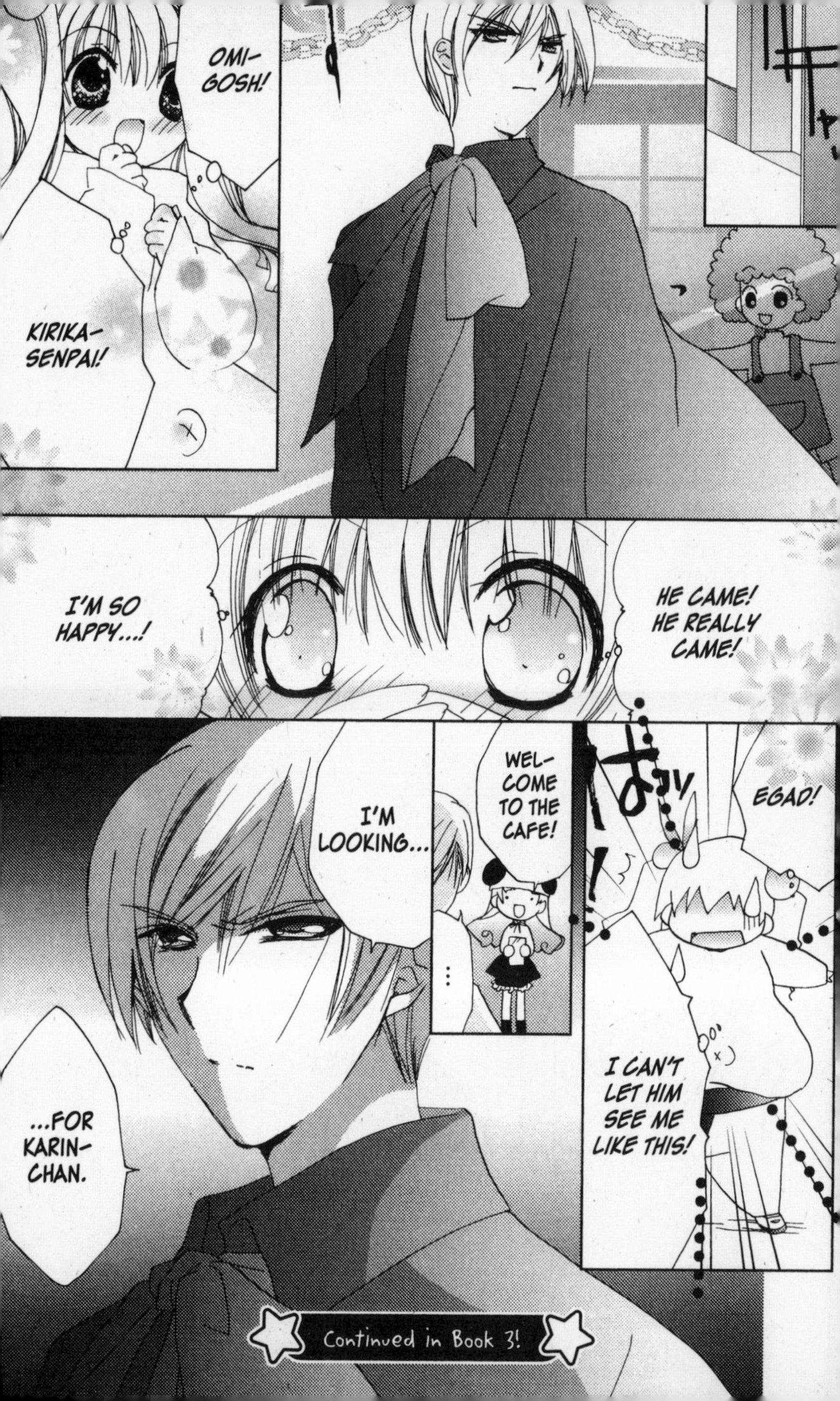
OMI-GOSH!
KIRIKA-SENPAI!
HE CAME! HE REALLY CAME!
I'M SO HAPPY...!
EGAD!
I CAN'T LET HIM SEE ME LIKE THIS!
WEL-COME TO THE CAFE!
...
I'M LOOKING...
...FOR KARIN-CHAN.
Continued in Book 3!

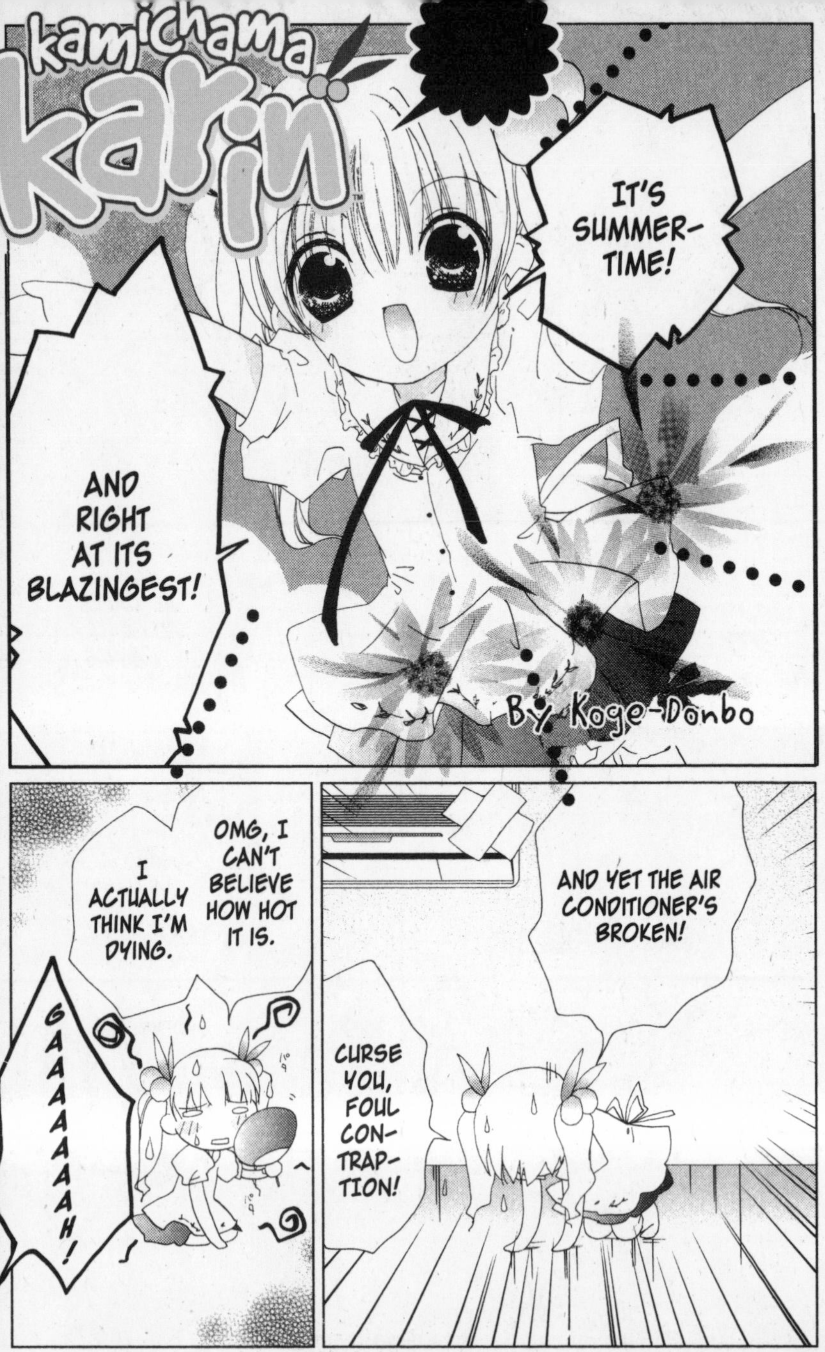
kamichama karin™
IT'S SUMMER-TIME!
AND RIGHT AT ITS BLAZINGEST!
By Koge-Donbo
AND YET THE AIR CONDITIONER'S BROKEN!
CURSE YOU, FOUL CON-TRAP-TION!
OMG, I CAN'T BELIEVE HOW HOT IT IS.
I ACTUALLY THINK I'M DYING.
GAAAAAAAAH!

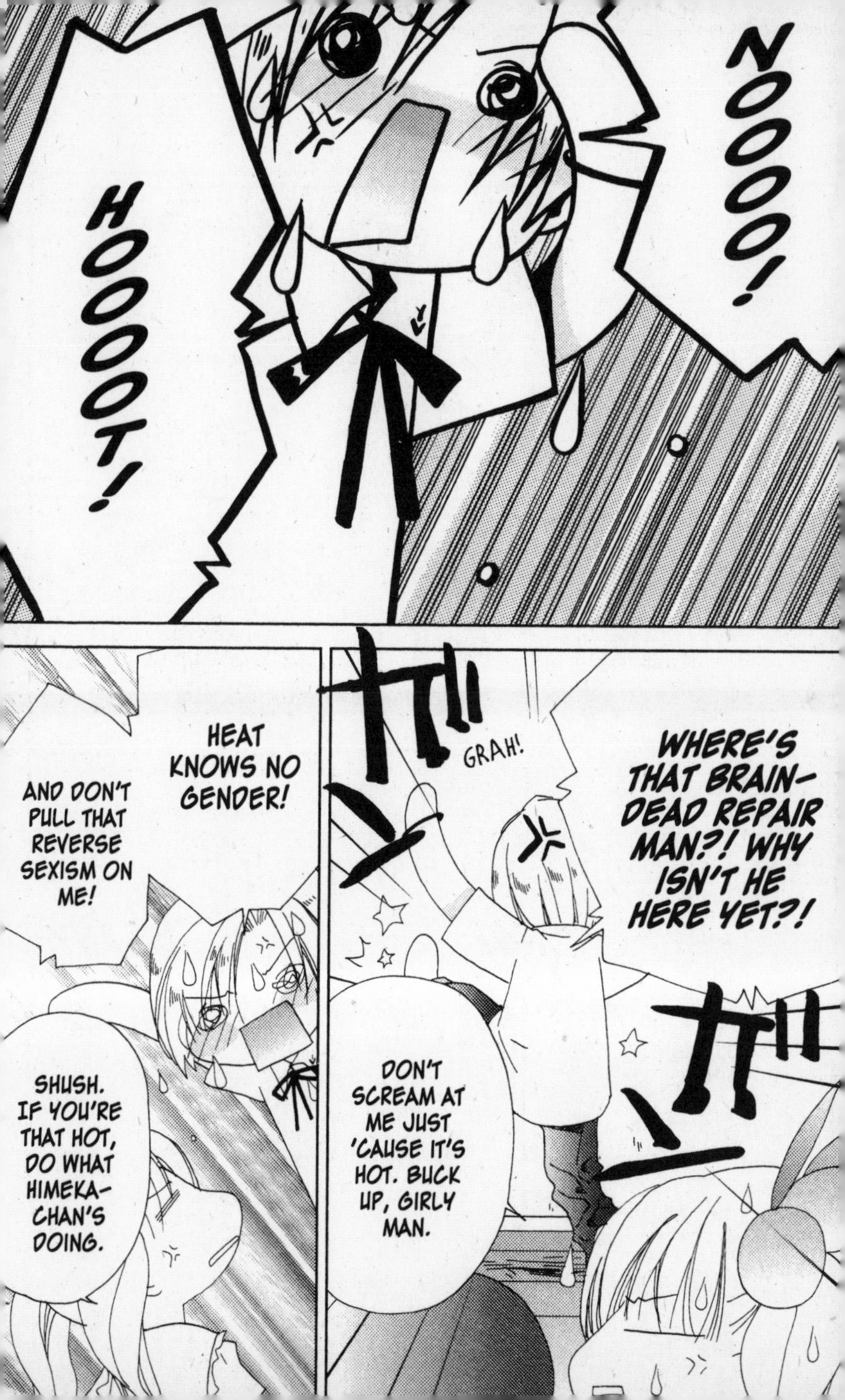
NOOOOO!
HOOOOOT!
GRAH!
WHERE'S THAT BRAIN-DEAD REPAIR MAN?! WHY ISN'T HE HERE YET?!
DON'T SCREAM AT ME JUST 'CAUSE IT'S HOT. BUCK UP, GIRLY MAN.
HEAT KNOWS NO GENDER!
AND DON'T PULL THAT REVERSE SEXISM ON ME!
SHUSH. IF YOU'RE THAT HOT, DO WHAT HIMEKA-CHAN'S DOING.

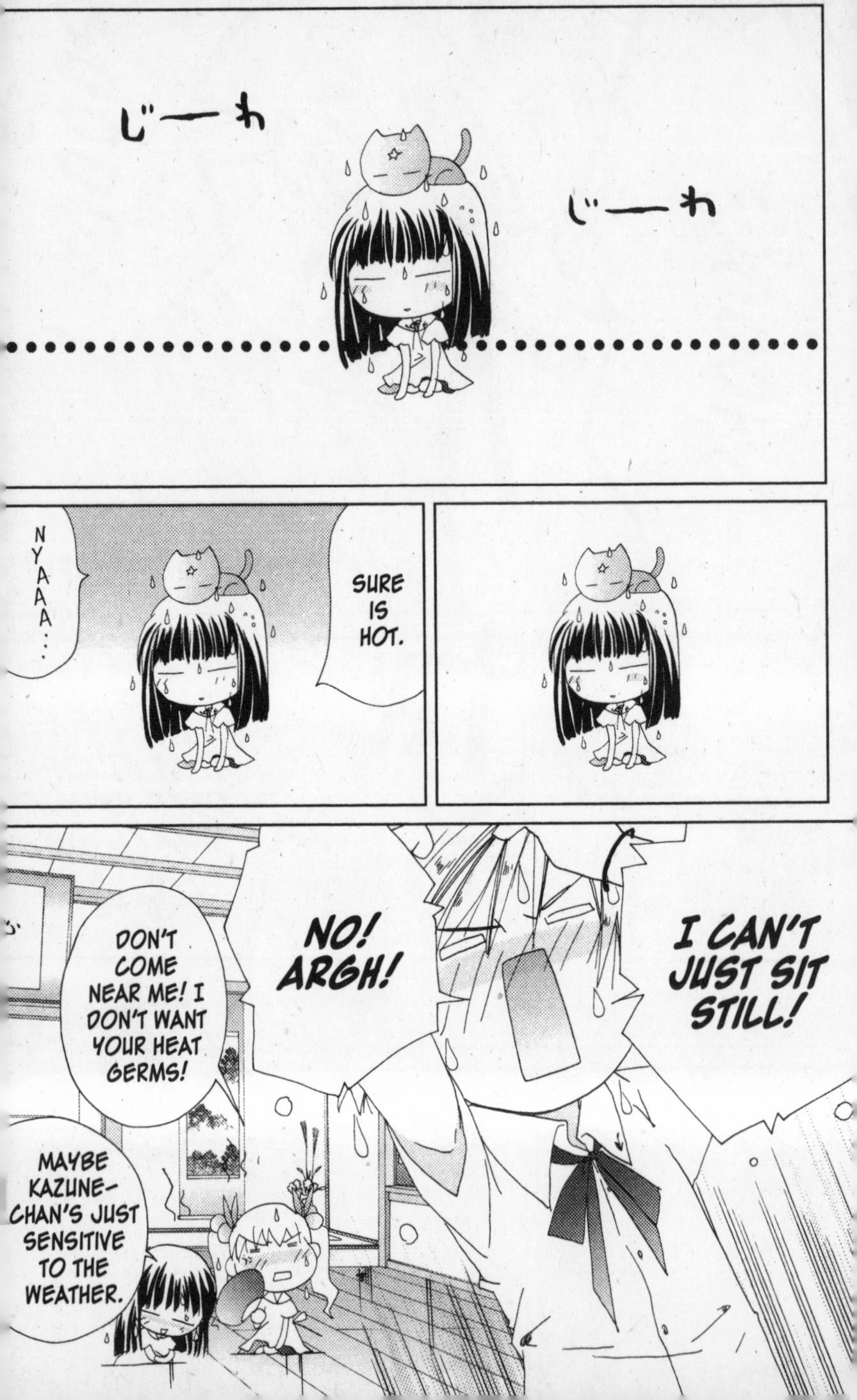
じーわ
じーわ
SURE IS HOT.
NYAAA...
I CAN'T JUST SIT STILL!
NO! ARGH!
DON'T COME NEAR ME! I DON'T WANT YOUR HEAT GERMS!
MAYBE KAZUNE-CHAN'S JUST SENSITIVE TO THE WEATHER.

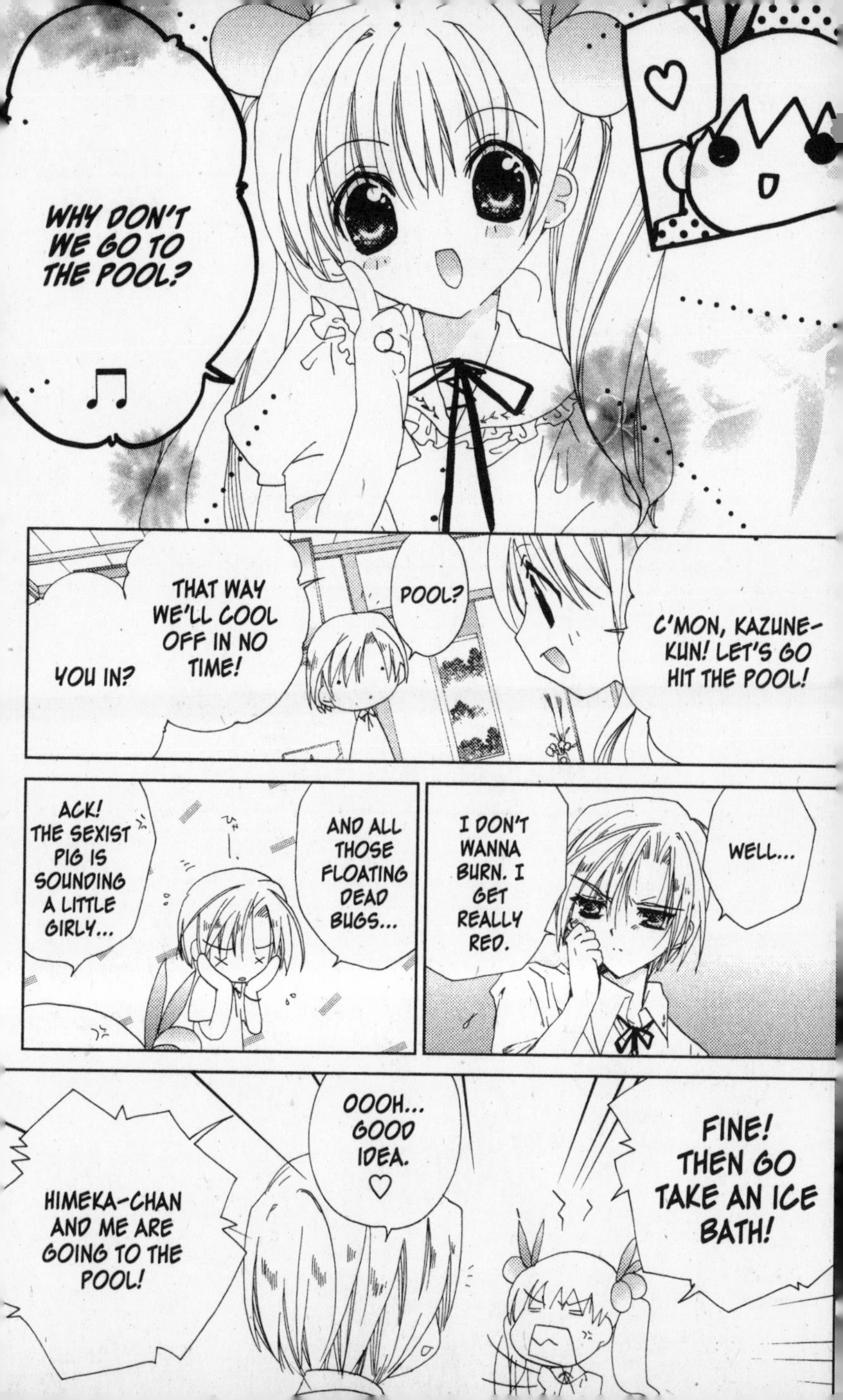
WHY DON'T WE GO TO THE POOL? ♫
C'MON, KAZUNE-KUN! LET'S GO HIT THE POOL!
POOL?
THAT WAY WE'LL COOL OFF IN NO TIME!
YOU IN?
WELL...
I DON'T WANNA BURN. I GET REALLY RED.
AND ALL THOSE FLOATING DEAD BUGS...
ACK! THE SEXIST PIG IS SOUNDING A LITTLE GIRLY...
FINE! THEN GO TAKE AN ICE BATH!
OOOH... GOOD IDEA. ♡
HIMEKA-CHAN AND ME ARE GOING TO THE POOL!

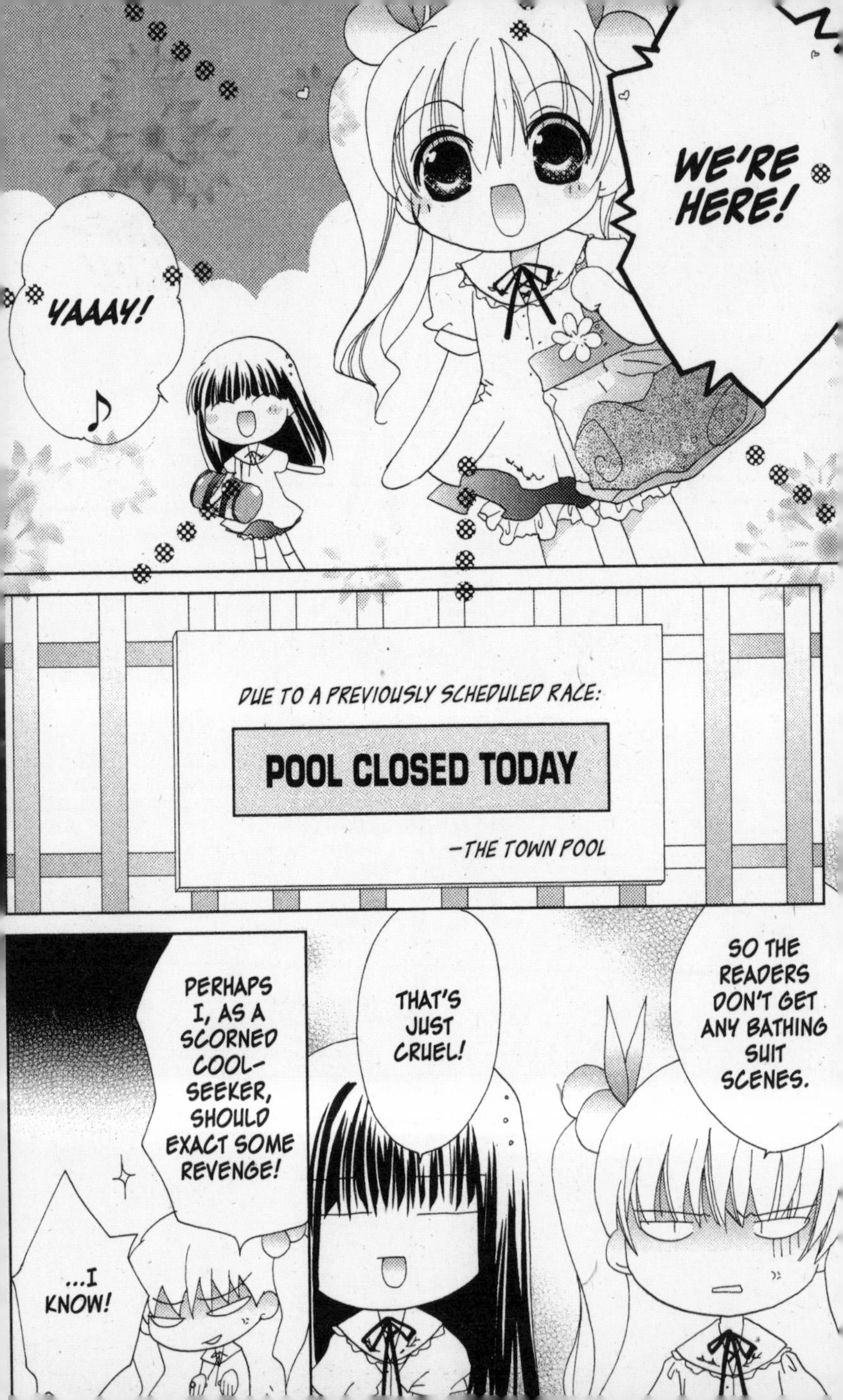
WE'RE HERE!
YAAAY! ♪
DUE TO A PREVIOUSLY SCHEDULED RACE:
POOL CLOSED TODAY
—THE TOWN POOL
SO THE READERS DON'T GET ANY BATHING SUIT SCENES.
THAT'S JUST CRUEL!
PERHAPS I, AS A SCORNED COOL-SEEKER, SHOULD EXACT SOME REVENGE!
...I KNOW!

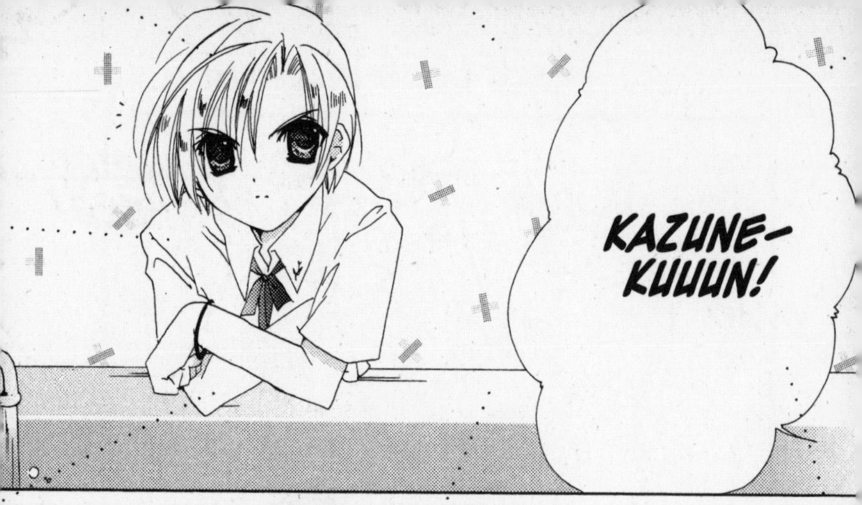
KAZUNE-KUUUN!

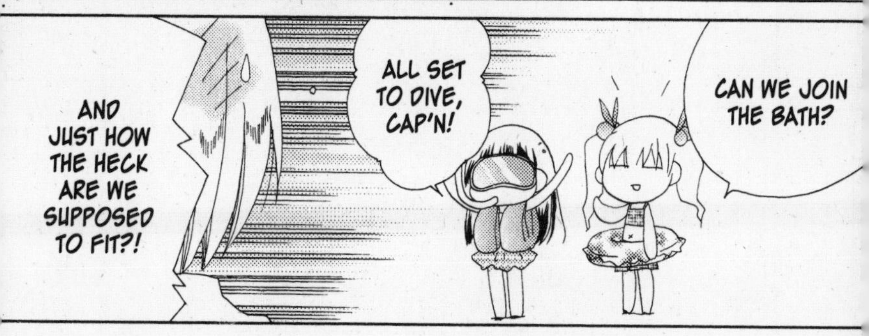
CAN WE JOIN THE BATH?
ALL SET TO DIVE, CAP'N!
AND JUST HOW THE HECK ARE WE SUPPOSED TO FIT?!

Continued in Book 3!

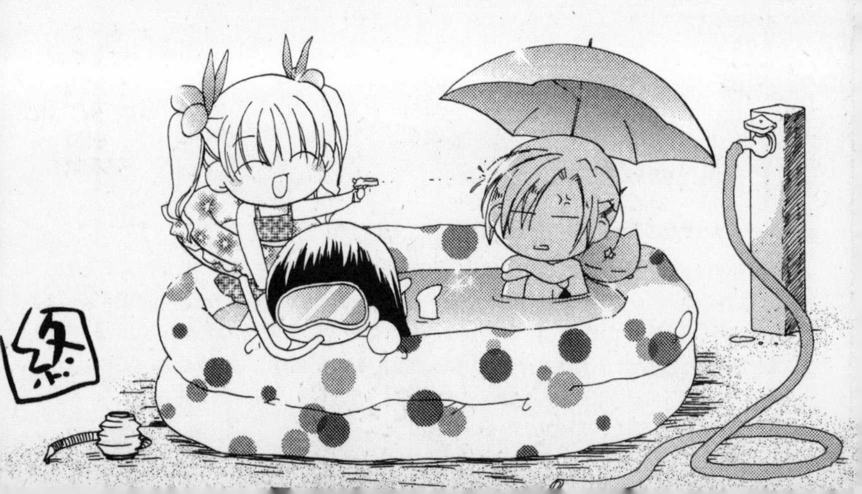

Next time in...

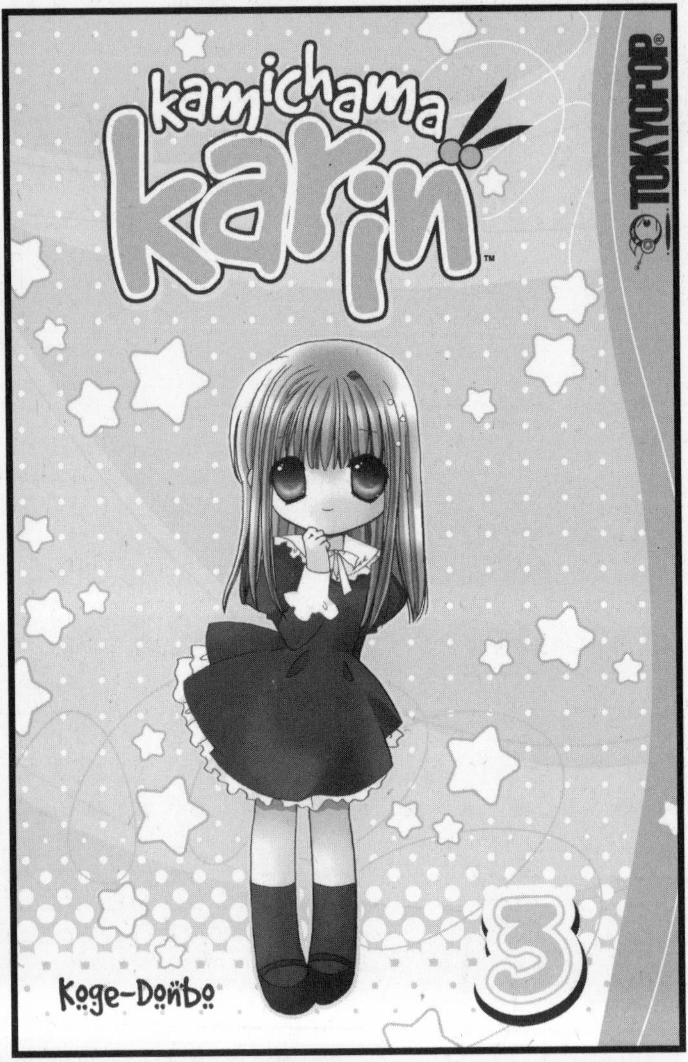
TOKYOPOP
kamichama karin
3
Koge-Donbo

After prancing around in a sumo suit all day, Karin dances the night away with Kirika--much against Kazune's wishes! But Kirika's got less-than-romantic motives...will Kazune blow his cover? And what will happen when the group goes to the hot springs?!

Calling all fan artists!

Crazy for Kazune? Head over heels for Himeka? Mad about Miyon? Now's your chance to show it! Draw your favorite character from Kamichama Karin, get your parent's signature if you're under 18, and send your masterpiece to:

Kamichama Karin Fan Art
ATTN: Carol Fox, Editor
TOKYOPOP
5900 Wilshire Blvd.,
Ste. 2000
Los Angeles, CA 90036

You may just see your work in the next volume of Kamichama Karin!

Oh--and while you're at it, please let us know what you think of the book.

Thanks for reading!

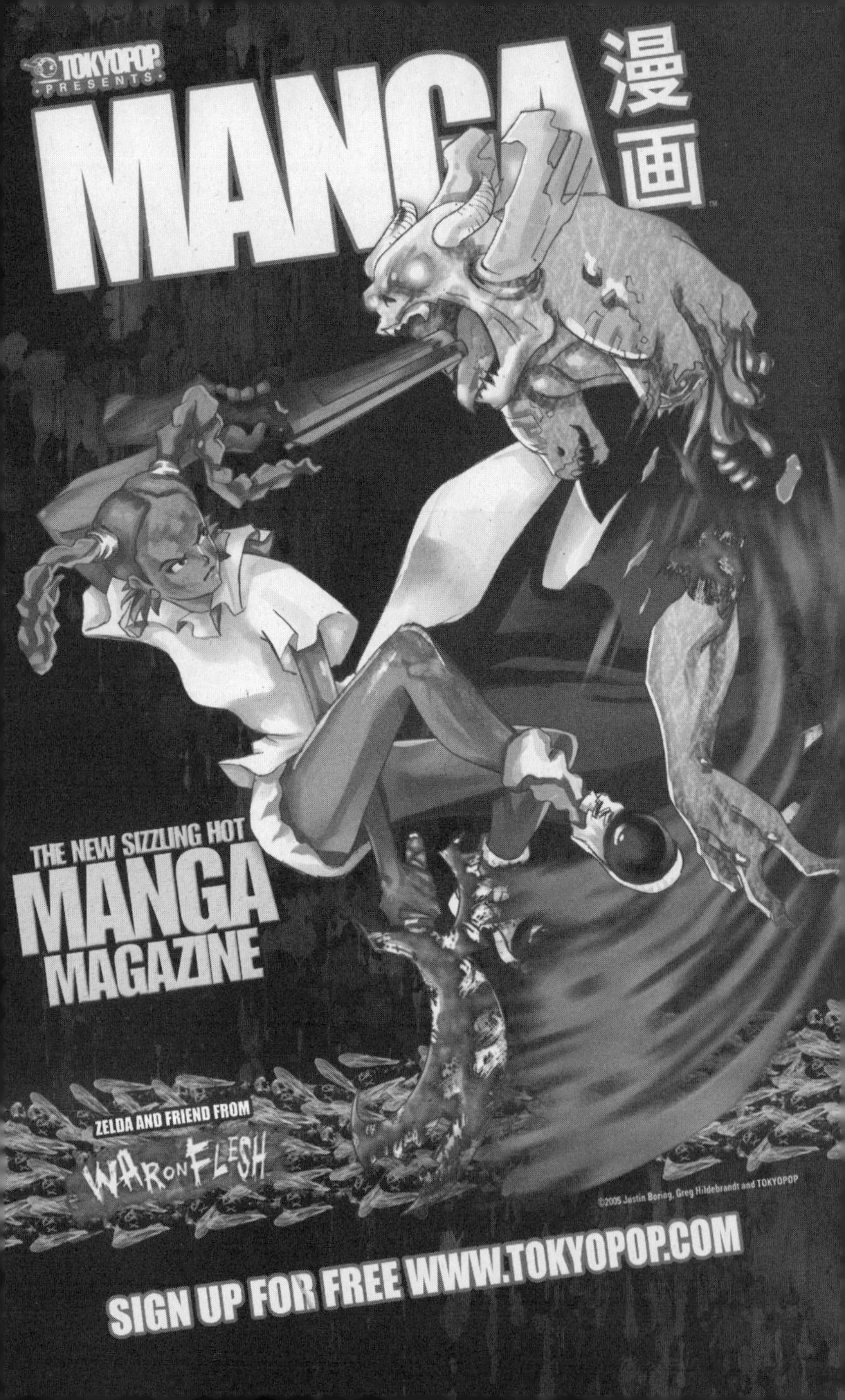
TOKYOPOP PRESENTS
MANGA 漫画™
THE NEW SIZZLING HOT
MANGA
MAGAZINE
ZELDA AND FRIEND FROM
WAR ON FLESH
©2005 Justin Boring, Greg Hildebrandt and TOKYOPOP
SIGN UP FOR FREE WWW.TOKYOPOP.COM

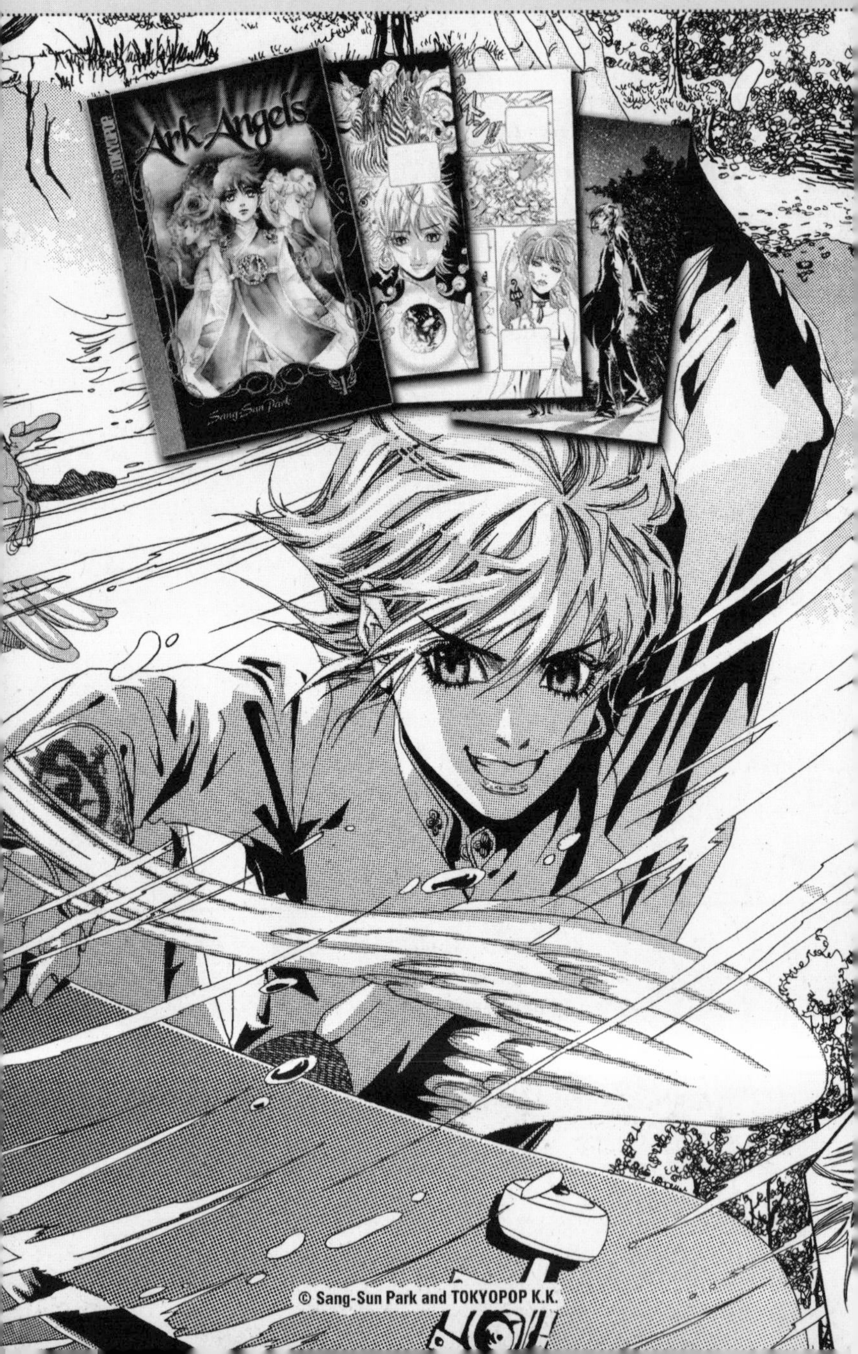
Ark Angels
Sang-Sun Park